Instruction to Deliver

Fighting to Transform Britain's Public Services

For Karen, Naomi, Anja and Alys
'Even on the deepest ocean, you will be the light*'

*Dolores Keane, 'You'll Never Be the Sun'

Instruction to Deliver

Fighting to Transform Britain's Public Services

Michael Barber

METHUEN

First published in Great Britain 2007
Revised paperback edition published 2008 by
Methuen Publishing Ltd
8 Artillery Row
London
S W 1 P 1 R Z

10 9 8 7 6 5 4 3

A CIP catalogue record for this book is available from the British Library.

ISBN 978-0-413-77664-8

Typeset in Sabon by SX Composing DTP, Rayleigh, Essex
Printed in the UK by CPI William Clowes Beccles NR34 7TL

Contents

A note on sources

Much of the information in this book is based on private notes made by
the author at or near the time of the events described. Where these are
quoted directly, it is clear in the text. Where newspapers or news
magazines are quoted, the specific publication and date are given in the
text or in an endnote. All other published sources are referenced in the
normal way in the text and listed in the bibliography, which includes a
wide range of sources (not all of them quoted directly) on the issues
covered in the book.

Foreword

This book is a rare example of 'buy one' and get not just 'one free', but two. First, Michael Barber's insider account of the public service delivery strand of the second Blair premiership will stand as a prime historical source for as long as people are interested in the Blair governments. Second, on top of this, the reader is given a fascinating treatment of how the centre of government (a problem which, one way or another, has vexed all Prime Ministers since 1945) might be better organised in future without finally dynamiting collective Cabinet government and building an excessively prime ministerial version with the fragments.

The additional bonus that runs throughout *Instruction to Deliver* is an absorbingly candid human story written by a very self-aware individual who does not delude himself with a self-induced 'Messiah complex'. For Michael Barber is neither starry eyed about himself nor – for all the friendship and admiration he feels for him – about his former boss, Tony Blair. This is how memoirs should be but political ones at least all too rarely are.

Michael Barber's formation as a historian at university, as a schoolteacher in Hertfordshire and Africa and as an author of a fine study of the making of the 1944 Education Act is a definite plus. So are his gifts for recalling moment and mood as well as simply for getting on with people. He had five constituencies to square simultaneously while running the Prime Minister's Delivery Unit between 2001 and 2005: Tony Blair, Gordon Brown, several Cabinet ministers, the senior civil service, and the entourages surrounding the most commanding Prime Minister and the most commanding Chancellor of modern times. There is plenty of evidence that he pulled it off – most of the time! Given the bumping and grinding of government, both human and procedural, since 1997, this verges on the miraculous.

As a subject, delivery can be complicated and sloggy. For the uninitiated it can seem both boring and nerdy. But not in this book. There is a danger that the drum-and-trumpet aspects of the Blair years (especially when the drum-roll was war and the consequences of war) will overwhelm the histories of 1997–2007 that are to come. (And, given his instincts and his background, Michael Barber was perhaps fortunate in not being involved on the road to war in Iraq). But again not here. The publication of *Instruction to Deliver* means there is a real chance that this crucial element in the New Labour story will gain and retain the place it deserves in the historical sum.

One of the perils that await ex-Prime Ministers is the flow of diaries and memoirs from the pens of former colleagues that come back, like a burp, to bring discomfort to their retirements. Not this one. *Instruction to Deliver* is not a soft treatment of Tony Blair. But it's one which he and we can relish in the years to come.

Peter Hennessy, FBA
Attlee Professor of Contemporary British History
Queen Mary, University of London
February 2007

Preface to the second edition

The second edition is being published less than a year after the first, so in editing the original text, relatively few changes have been made. The biggest relevant development of all since publication of the first edition – the change of Prime Minister – required a few, relatively minor, changes but none to the substance. A small number of minor errors which had been drawn to my attention have been corrected. Other changes result from the publication of a number of new books relevant to the period discussed. The most important of these is Alastair Campbell's diary, to which I now make references, largely in the footnotes; nothing there required me to change the narrative or any of my judgements. Anthony Seldon's *Blair Unbound* similarly provides valuable background, but did not lead me to change the story I had told or the case I had made. Less widely noticed, but nonetheless significant, was Jon Davis's book *Prime Ministers and Whitehall 1960–74*, which is a fascinating account of how, in an earlier era, Macmillan, Douglas-Home, Wilson and Heath wrestled with the issues Blair faced in the period covered by *Instruction to Deliver*.

A number of reviews and, more importantly, private dialogues or notes led me to refine my thinking on some of the analysis in the first edition. Where this is so, I have addressed them in the wholly new postscript, 'Second Thoughts'. I am grateful to all those who read the first edition and commented.

The debate that followed publication undoubtedly helped to sharpen my thinking and I've sought to explain my vision in the postscript on what needs to happen in the future. I am especially grateful to those members of the family who had to watch me live through (and hear me go on about!) the Delivery Unit experience and then had to relive it through my eyes by reading the book. My father and my brother David said they found it interesting to know what I'd been up to these past few years. My sisters said they enjoyed it. Karen, my wife, claims, no doubt with good reason, that there's no need for her to read the text from cover to cover since she's heard it all before (several times!). My daughters Naomi and Anja still don't like graphs, but enjoyed other parts of the book. Meanwhile, my youngest daughter, Alys, really does like graphs, as well as the book; I'm grateful for her interest in what is the bureaucratic equivalent of an extreme sport and I hope she doesn't find it too much of a burden through life! The dedication to all of them remains as heartfelt now as it was then.

February 2008

Preface to the first edition

This is a book about the drive to deliver public service reform in Tony Blair's second term (2001 to 2005) and its impact. For those four years, as head of Blair's new Delivery Unit, I was at his side, an active participant in this process, and can therefore hardly claim to be objective, but I have sought to be sober and balanced throughout. The views expressed here are entirely personal and certainly not those of any of my employers past or present.

I have attempted to weave together four strands into a single story. In part this is a political memoir – a personal account of four years in No. 10 (including its effect on me and my family); in part it is the history of Blair's drive to reform the public services and the impact of that drive on the country; in part it is an analysis of the relationship between the Prime Minister's Office and the rest of government and how this might profitably be developed in the future. Above all, though, it is an account of getting things done in government; the story not so much of the 'What?' of public service reform, but of the 'How?' The central task of the Prime Minister's Delivery Unit was to answer the question 'How?', not just for the Prime Minister, but also for the Cabinet ministers and departments responsible for the implementation of vast and ambitious reforms. In the writing of history and politics, 'How?' is a relatively neglected question. As my history teacher used to say, textbooks write of some medieval king or other that 'he gathered an army and hastened north' without pausing to consider just how difficult that was to do. In the modern world, the 'How?' question remains just as difficult to answer but, as the pages that follow will show, we learnt a great deal between 2001 and 2005 about the answer. This not only helped the Prime Minister to deliver more than would otherwise have been the case; it also became of great interest elsewhere, because governments across the world are wrestling with this same 'How?' question.

The book is in three sections, like a sandwich with a serious filling. The central section – which encompasses Chapters 2 to 8 – is the story of delivery under Blair, warts and all. This can be read, if the reader chooses, without reference to the other two brief sections. Section 1 explains the unlikely series of career accidents which resulted in my being asked to set up and lead the Delivery Unit. Section 3 examines what the lessons of the entire experience are for a future Prime Minister set in the wider context of the academic debates about the power of the Prime Minister and the changing nature of the state. Finally, there is an appendix – the Delivery Manual – which, through speeches, letters and summaries of documents, provides insight into the main techniques applied by the Delivery Unit.

*

While this is my story, it is also the story of many others; there are thus numerous people who deserve to be thanked.

First and foremost is the Prime Minister himself. If he had not placed his trust in me, there would be no story for me to tell. He was a pleasure to work with and is in my view both a remarkable person and a remarkable leader. Others will assess his overall legacy and will be influenced by the international scene, not least the consequences of the war in Iraq, as well as domestic policy. Here you will find a portrait of the man at work and an assessment of his legacy in relation to the public services and the changing nature of society. It is a positive picture – which I believe is one that history in time will paint – but I have been unsparing in criticism where I believe it appropriate. As Boswell said of his *Life of Johnson*, 'in every picture there should be shade as well as light.' Churchill made a similar point: 'To do justice to a great man, discriminating criticism is always necessary.' Either way, I thank Tony Blair for the extraordinary opportunity of working with him and hope to have done justice to him in the following pages.

Then there are the ministers, both in the Cabinet and out of it, with whom I had the pleasure of working. I have in the past been accused sometimes of being starry-eyed about politicians. I do not believe this to be the case, although in many conversations with both civil servants and people in the public services I have constantly sought to counter the weary cynicism with which politicians, as a class, are regarded. First, I believe it is an absolutely essential bedrock of democracy that we respect those who are elected to serve us. It is not easy to campaign for election, and still harder to make decisions on behalf of the public. Moreover, my experience of politicians of all major parties does not support the view, propagated in parts of the media, that most politicians are self-serving, power mad and only interested in doing whatever it takes to get re-elected. This is not to say that there are not some bad apples, nor that in even some of the best politicians there are no flaws – they are human beings after all. It is to say that, in my view, politicians such as Gillian Shephard or Alistair Darling – to pick just two of those mentioned in the pages that follow – are in politics because they want to make the world a better place, in line with the values they hold. We can disagree with them and hold them to account for their mistakes and failures, but the current vogue of cynicism about politicians is wholly destructive. Either way, I thank all those who gave me time and attention. The only one I want to single out is David Blunkett. No doubt he, like the rest of us, has made mistakes but, for all those, I think his achievements in government were substantial and the experience of working with him from 1997 to 2004 was genuinely inspirational.

Of similar significance to the politicians during the time described in this book were a number of important colleagues in No. 10 and the Cabinet Office. Jeremy Heywood, Andrew Adonis and Peter Hyman became close friends with whom I often discussed many of the themes dealt with in this book. Anji Hunter, Sally Morgan, Jonathan Powell, Liz Lloyd, Alastair Campbell, David Hill, Godric Smith, Tom Kelly, Geoff Mulgan, Pat McFadden, Matthew Taylor, John Birt, Ivan Rogers and, in particular policy areas, Simon Stevens and then Julian Le Grand (health), Justin Russell (crime etc.) and Gareth Davies (social security) were great colleagues, as were the many other staff with whom I interacted routinely. As a result of the talents and commitment of the people there, it was always a pleasure to work in No. 10.

In the Treasury, Gordon Brown, Ed Balls, Gus O'Donnell (while he was permanent secretary there) and, last but far from least, Nick Macpherson, were consistently collaborative and supportive of the Delivery Unit's efforts.

Then there are the many civil servants with whom I worked during my time at the Delivery Unit. We didn't always make their lives easy – that was not our mission – and we were often, as I am in these pages, sharply critical, but we were always given time, treated with respect and surprisingly often welcomed, even though we did not come bearing gifts. Three successive Cabinet Secretaries – Richard Wilson, Andrew Turnbull and Gus O'Donnell – were consistently supportive of my efforts, even when it might have been easier not to be, as were two successive permanent secretaries in Education, Michael Bichard and David Normington.

Meanwhile, I cannot thank my staff in the Delivery Unit too much. They were absolutely fantastic: a pleasure and an inspiration to work with, and responsible collectively for the impact of the Delivery Unit described in these pages. A number of them are mentioned by name in the book, but these should be seen as representative of everyone who ever worked there; all are due my gratitude. We all knew as we lived through the experience that it was quite out of the ordinary and that afterwards we'd never be quite the same again, but I doubt anyone who worked there has ever regretted it in retrospect.

Four people from the Delivery Unit deserve special mention: the people who at different times organised my private office and my diary – Kate Myronidis, Lindsey Olliver, Nurten Yusuf and Karen Wells. Under sometimes intense pressure, they tolerated my obsessions and kept my feet firmly on the ground.

Some close friends outside of government helped me understand what I was doing and why. David Pitt-Watson, mentioned several times in the text, is a rigorous and analytical thinker, driven by the values that we've shared through thirty years of friendship. Alan Evans has been a mentor to me for over twenty years now. Tim Williams, with his sweeping sense of history and passionate belief in the importance of collective public action in support of a more equal society, constantly challenged and questioned me in ways that were immensely helpful. Robin Alfred constantly brought me back to the ethical basis of my work, often through questions. David Puttnam in our all-too-fleeting meetings never failed to offer remarkable insights into people and organisations while simultaneously accentuating the positive. Peter Hennessy, with his vast store of knowledge of contemporary history and government, questioned my judgements and connected thoughts and actions to their precedents in the past.

Peter was one of several people who read and commented constructively on drafts of all or part of the book. These include Gus

O'Donnell, Peter Riddell, David Pitt-Watson, Tony Danker and Georgina Cooke. I am especially grateful to Simon Rea, who read the complete draft from the perspective of someone who worked in the Delivery Unit, and offered numerous helpful suggestions. Alan Gordon Walker and Jonathan Wadman of Methuen's have been sympathetic and insightful throughout, and Bruce Hunter, my agent, was a consistent source of hard-headed practical advice.

Two people played a major role in the production of the text and deserve special mention. Tanya Kreisky, with whom I worked on several books in the 1990s, was nevertheless delighted to return to the fray for this one. She prepared the script, brought the consistency in small things on which books depend, and made more corrections and refinements than I care to remember. She did so with unfailing good humour and in spite of giving birth to her first child, Owen, while the book was in its final throes. Georgina Cooke, who has run my office since I left the Delivery Unit – my guide to life on the outside, as it were – has been an incredible support throughout the past eighteen months, organising the necessary meetings and refusing to let me despair when I thought I would never complete the task – a great colleague and a good friend.

Last but by no means least, I must mention my wife, Karen, and my three daughters, Naomi, Anja and Alys. They too appear occasionally in these pages. Through all the ups and downs that any family experiences – and in the years described here we had plenty of both – let me just say that the love and solidarity among us as a family are the rocks on which, for me at any rate, all else rests. Hence the dedication of this book to them.

Needless to say, any errors of fact or judgement that remain are my responsibility and mine alone.

April 2007

'A mandate for reform . . . an instruction to deliver'

Tony Blair, on the meaning of the general election he had
just won by a landslide, 8 June 2001

Section 1

Learning to deliver

'Philosophers have only interpreted the world in various ways; the point is to change it.'

Karl Marx, *Theses on Feuerbach*

1

What on earth am I doing here?

In mid-2003, two years into my job as the Prime Minister's chief adviser on delivery, I arrived marginally late for a meeting in the Cabinet Room in No. 10. I had been delayed checking out a couple of points in the Prime Minister's private office. It was a Health stocktake and, unusually, Tony Blair had pulled out, given the pressures on the international scene.

As I stepped into the famous room where Cabinets have met since 1856, I saw the Health team – led by their permanent secretary – ranged down the far side of the table. On the near side was the usual collection of No. 10, Delivery Unit and Treasury officials. In the absence of the Prime Minister, I knew it would be my job to chair the meeting. What I hadn't anticipated was the emotional impact of seeing that the others had left only one chair vacant: the Prime Minister's, in front of the fireplace. It hit me – 'like a freight train' as Bob Dylan would put it – that I was expected for the first time to sit in *that* chair.

In the half-dozen paces it took me to cross the room and take my place, I remember very clearly thinking, 'What on earth am I doing here?'

Winning, losing and Quakerism

What on earth indeed? Looking back, my upbringing might have had something to do with it. I grew up obsessed with sport, supporting – with an absurd degree of passion – Liverpool (where I was born) at football and Lancashire at cricket. My mother remembered finding me in tears after Liverpool had lost a routine league game at West Ham some time in the 1960s. By contrast, I remember us both shouting with joy as we watched Clive Lloyd score a wonderful century for Lancashire in a cup final at Lord's shortly afterwards. The other side of this obsession was that I loved winning and hated losing when I played games. I once broke a window in frustration after I lost a supposedly friendly game of table tennis at school. Cricket, which I loved, was a mixed blessing because – as the late Brian Johnston would have famously said – I was always getting out in the middle of a great innings. Being a bad loser has little to commend it (and I know sometimes I must have infuriated my brothers and sisters) but stubborn refusal to accept defeat – in spite of the facts – turned out to have its value when faced with securing the implementation of government targets, some of which bordered on the heroic.*

There is another aspect of my upbringing which I draw on deeply and often in my working life. Our family, going back many generations, have been Quakers. We all dutifully attended 'Meeting' in my youth and learned to sit in silence. Then I attended a Quaker school, Bootham in York, where I developed my love of history from a succession of great teachers (but continued to be a bad loser). More importantly perhaps, I imbibed both at home, especially from my mother, and at school a strong sense of Quaker values: I was on the planet to make a difference, to make the world a better place. My father's principles, which resulted in him spending much of the war as a pacifist driving medical supplies across China and later led him to the chairmanship of Oxfam, were an inspiration to me. I was influenced by other important aspects of Quakerism – the value of silence or treating everyone as equally worthy of respect regardless of their status, for example – as well as that profound commitment to non-violent means of changing the world. This is a potentially powerful combination, indeed much more powerful than many Quakers themselves realise.

In fact, at its most active, it is irresistible, particularly when combined with common sense and the occasional lapse from purity. My father tells the wartime story of a colleague in the (pacifist) Friends' Ambulance Unit in China who had been brought up in an extremely violent family in the East End and, as a reaction against it, became a Quaker. On one occasion on an emergency mission, he and his mate were held up pointlessly for an inordinately long time by a petty Chinese bureaucrat. Finally, aware of the importance and urgency of his mission, his patience snapped and he laid the official out with a

---

*Others feel the same but few own up to it. One who does is the Arsenal manager, Arsène Wenger: 'You should not be in this job unless it really hurts you to lose a match . . . I always feel terrible.' (Interview in the *Times*, 15 September 2007.)

practised right hook and drove on. 'I didn't oughta have done that,' he commented laconically to his mate. Perhaps it's a stretch to call this Quakerism in action, but patience isn't always a virtue. Certainly there were times in a lengthy negotiation with a civil servant about improving delivery that this story came to mind and a right hook – had I been capable of one – seemed sorely tempting. A. J. P. Taylor, the historian whose work I idolised as a youth, also attended Bootham School and, as usual, exaggerated slightly in summing up the legacy of his education there: 'Quakers are often irritating: always looking for common ground and reluctant to admit that it is sometimes necessary to fight; metaphorically or literally. Still, they are about the best thing the human race has produced.'[1] Broadly, I agree.

I left school with this paradoxical combination of hating losing and adhering strongly to Quaker values. Also, leaving school in 1973, I caught the end of 1960s radicalism and took the view that, with a combination of long hair and left-wing politics, I could change the world. When I saw my (excellent) history teacher Peter Braggins a few years later, he said, 'Your year were the last of the idealists.'

Politics

At Oxford – where I started in October 1974 – I acted in plays, continued to win (mostly) at table tennis, occasionally played football and cricket, spent the evenings talking and drinking, and (eventually) got around to studying history, especially American history, which in my third year became thoroughly absorbing. Most of all, I became politically active, not so much in party politics, but in college politics. Early in my second year I was elected president of the Queen's College Student Union (known as the JCR)* with my very good friend David Pitt-Watson as vice-president and treasurer. Naturally enough, this being the mid-1970s, we organised a rent strike, no doubt to very little effect. We might have had more impact with our referendum on whether Queen's College should become mixed. Needless to say, an overwhelming majority of an electorate made up of 18–22-year-old men

---

*My manifesto, which someone sent me after reading the hardback edition of this book, was boringly moderate. 'The strike action . . . was a last resort. In the long term, better and more effective relations with senior college must be sought [etc.].'

voted in favour of admitting women. Even most of the staff were
sympathetic but, as my tutor explained, they had no problem with the
thought of female students; it was the prospect of female dons that
terrified them.

By far our biggest achievement – largely David's, I must say – was one
that makes me think we were New Labour far ahead of our time. We
inherited a huge deficit (which no doubt was par for the course) and a
year later left a huge surplus (which wasn't). If Gordon Brown had
invented his fiscal rules by then, we would no doubt have applied them;
in fact, turning the finances around depended on the traditional
remedies of spending less and earning more. We held another
referendum, on which newspapers people liked best, and found we
could reduce the order by dropping the *Morning Star* and the *Daily
Express*, both of which were despised. We also decided not to pay our
dues to the university union and then turned our attention to the income
side. There was no room for another pinball machine or bar billiards
table, but there was a gap in our services – no cigarette machine, which
would have great potential as an income stream. In those days, smoking
– especially Gauloises – was still seen as a sign of left-wing decadence,
with images of Sartre and de Beauvoir in the Café Flore, rather than as
an anti-social act. Even so, the medical students and the non-smokers
were a powerful lobby. David made a succinct and brilliant speech at
the crucial showdown: 'Everyone knows', he cried, 'that the three best
things in life are a drink before and a cigarette after – we've got a beer
cellar and a Durex machine. Now we need to complete the trinity.' The
opposition was routed and our coffers filled with ill-gotten gains.*

From student activism to the Labour Party was a small step in the late
1970s. My history degree had left me admiring some labour heroes from
the past, especially James Keir Hardie and Aneurin Bevan, but I had
other heroes in history too – including John Bright, the nineteenth-
century Liberal and Quaker, Theodore Roosevelt, the progressive US
President at the turn of the twentieth century, and Rosa Luxemburg, the
German socialist. I always had a soft spot for Benjamin Disraeli too. In
short, I saw active politics as a way to change the world. I remember
watching with admiration as Denis Healey made his famous speech at

*The December 2006 issue of the *Queen's College Record* informs me that the students
have recently campaigned successfully for a ban on smoking in all public rooms in the
college, including the beer cellar. Thirty years is a long time in student politics.

Labour's 1976 party conference defending his decision to go cap in hand to the International Monetary Fund and the cuts that ensued. In 1979, while doing my teacher training in Oxford, I campaigned forlornly for Labour in the election campaign but was swept away like everyone else by the Thatcherite tide coming the other way. The man in the chip shop in St Clements had summed it up for me the week before: 'The weather will get better if the Tories win,' he said.* At least Liverpool won the League Championship. In 1983, the election result was even worse.

How was it that everyone you met hated Margaret Thatcher but she still won by a landslide? Becoming a genuine activist from 1985 onwards, as opposed to a mere footsoldier in election campaigns, soon taught me the answer. The Labour Party in my borough of Hackney was chock full of mad people – mad but very persistent.† That year, Neil Kinnock took the step that began the process of turning around his beloved party – though it took another twelve years to win an election – by denouncing the Militant Tendency and beginning to drive its members out. In Hackney, this clarified the situation entirely. Of course, everyone still hated Margaret Thatcher, but the real enemy had now become apparent – it was Kinnock. The Hackney South General Committee debated a motion condemning Kinnock's 'witch hunt'. The chair said, 'I assume it is condemned unanimously?' Not quite – three of us hesitantly raised our hands opposing the motion, a traitorous act of bourgeois weakness in the eyes of the fifty or so who shared the view of 'Comrade' Chair.

Shortly afterwards, the same august body debated how to involve more local women in the party. Perhaps now common sense would prevail and the comrades would come to see how far their 'issues' were from the ordinary people of Hackney. Housing, education, health or unemployment, for example, were all matters of huge anxiety across the borough. The General Committee had other ideas, though: it decided

---

* This comment is powerful evidence of Jim Callaghan's famous remark on the 1979 election. 'There are times . . . when there is a sea change in politics. It then does not matter what you say or do . . . I suspect there is now such a sea change – and it is for Mrs Thatcher.' Eighteen years later John Major must have felt similarly.

† My cousin Diana commented on reading this that, while she agreed that they might have been 'mad', they 'presumably thought they were being logical at the time'. She makes a good point, but remember that they called me and our small band of Kinnock fans 'the sensible caucus', which suggests deep down that they knew they were mad – or at least not sensible.

that the way to attract more local women into the party was to hold a meeting on imperialism.

It was tempting to flee this madness, but the obsessive in me became more deeply involved. In 1986, I stood for election to Hackney Council in one of the borough's few marginal wards, my own. Kevin Hoyes and Mark McCallum had honed our ward party into an election-winning machine by defining our ward in opposition to the rest of the local Labour Party and by ruthlessly calling party members until they agreed to tramp the streets. (We knew all the excuses: 'I can't canvass on Sunday morning – childcare responsibilities, I'm afraid,' said one reluctant member hopefully, until we pointed out that both his children were in their twenties!) To everyone's surprise, including my own, I won.

Almost immediately, I faced the first of many dilemmas between my competing obsessions. The newly elected Labour group – which in spite of its madness had swept the board, winning more than fifty of the sixty seats in the borough – decided to meet at 3.00 on the Saturday afternoon. I was marked out by the prospective chief whip as a rebel from day one because I told him I had another engagement at that time. 'What is it?' he asked. 'I shall be watching the television; Liverpool are playing Everton in the Cup Final,' I replied. Unbelievably decadent. Liverpool won 3–1 with two goals from Ian Rush, and I enjoyed every minute of it. I was less happy to discover that at the meeting a good friend (and one of the few sensible people in the Labour group) had missed election as chair of the Housing Committee by one vote.

I turned up assiduously to the evening meetings and, especially for the first couple of years, paid close attention to my ward and in particular to its council housing. My weekly surgeries were filled with people who had housing complaints, most of which I was unable to get the bureaucracy to resolve. As I visited more and more homes, though, I came to realise that the problem was not that people complained too much, but that they didn't complain enough. Faced with an impervious bureaucracy and a mad Labour Party, people had given up. Incredibly, though, they kept electing Labour and, when faced with alternatives to council manage-ment, preferred to cling to the certainty of incompetence rather than reach for the uncertainty of change. This is what powerlessness does to people.

Meanwhile, in the council meetings themselves, I watched the madness around me and tried to vote sensibly. In fact, there was a minority of us in the Labour group whom the others described disparagingly as 'the sensible caucus', which left me wondering what they thought they were. For some reason in the distant past, Hackney had been twinned with the beautiful German university town of Göttingen, where I had spent a year as a student. When the resolution came to the council meeting that we should end this relationship and twin ourselves with somewhere in Nicaragua (where no Hackney resident would ever go), I refused to support it and – with the help of the opposition, some absences and a few votes from councillors who didn't know whether they were coming or going – the resolution was lost. The town of Göttingen – rather surprisingly perhaps – was pleased the link was maintained. Looking back, I find it bizarre that I chose to spend my evenings doing this kind of thing.

In 1987 I added to my political activity by becoming the parliamentary candidate for the Labour Party in Henley-on-Thames. By now, the party, with Kinnock driving it, was becoming much more sensible in most of the country, but even so, overturning Michael Heseltine's gargantuan majority seemed unlikely. I threw myself into the campaign with real enthusiasm though, staying with my parents, who lived in the constituency, when I was there. 'That's at least two votes,' I thought. Mobilising the tiny local party wasn't easy. Though the membership was committed, it wasn't used to activism. Years of defeat had sapped its ambition. The party joke ran: 'What should a Labour candidate for the council do if they win?' Answer: 'Ask for a recount.' During the campaign, I was asked in a public meeting when Labour had last won Henley. Grasping at straws, I said, 'I'm not sure, but I do know it was occupied by Parliamentary forces during the Civil War.' When I introduced myself as the Labour candidate to a passer-by in Thame High Street, he said, 'I hope you drown in your own vomit.' Towards the end of the campaign, I gave up calling out Labour slogans from the loudhailer on the roof of my campaign van and instead began to update people on the score in the Test Match. They seemed to prefer this.

Incredibly, I remember convincing myself that I could win in the last few days. It wasn't just that I hated losing; I had discovered that in the Labour landslide of 1945, the Tories won Hackney North, so I knew miracles did occasionally occur. Of course, the required political earthquake did not take place, and in fact there was just a marginal swing to Labour across the country. Thatcher had won another landslide. Being more sensible than four years earlier was not enough. I comforted myself with the knowledge that Henley had seen the biggest swing to Labour (3 per cent) in the south-east. As we had done in our ward in Hackney the year before, we achieved this purely by persuading Labour voters – many of them to be found in Berinsfield, an inner-city housing estate curiously located in the Oxfordshire countryside – to go out and vote. Also, I had sent most of the active party members to support the Labour campaign in Oxford East, where Andrew Smith won. I had learnt a lot, though: about what Middle England thought, about dealing with hecklers and public speaking and about the fact that most of the Labour Party was not as mad as it was in Hackney.

There, though, the madness continued, and not just in the Labour Party. On one occasion a Liberal fired two shots from a gun in the council chamber and was (rightly) locked up; on another a group of squatters wrestled the chair of Housing to the ground while he was speaking – but the tide was beginning to turn. The chair of Housing was being wrestled to the ground because he was, at last, taking on the squatters. Tough Tory laws requiring councillors to set a balanced budget generated fiery speeches of opposition, but few people wanted to risk personal penury, however mad they were. Meanwhile, the council leader, Andrew Puddephatt, was maturing into a genuine star. With real determination, he took on both corruption and inefficiency. When the left resisted – egged on by the public sector unions, whose members were the main beneficiaries of the grotesque mismanagement all around – he turned their sub-Marxist rhetoric on them brilliantly: 'Inefficiency is theft from working-class people,' he cried. Here at last was a Labour leader speaking up for the consumer, not the producer.

In 1988, the government carried the Education Reform Act, which – as it turned out – completely reshaped my subsequent career. At the time, though, the aspect that had the greatest impact on me was the section which broke up the Inner London Education Authority and gave the boroughs – including Hackney – responsibility for education. I ran as the 'sensible caucus' candidate to be Hackney's chair of Education. I won, partly as the outsider and partly because, now that the madness had subsided somewhat, my fellow councillors decided that electing someone who, as a result of his work, knew about education might have its advantages, if not in the party, where I was still seen as incorrigibly right wing, then at least out in the education system itself, where anxiety was understandably high.

The brilliant Janet Dobson (the only council employee at the time who had an education role) and I worked unbelievably hard to produce 'the plan' which the new law required us to submit to the Department for Education early in 1989. I visited dozens of schools across the borough and listened. I visited community groups and discovered what parents from all ethnic backgrounds really wanted (as opposed to what teachers said parents wanted). It was striking with what vehemence they stated over and over again that they wanted high standards of literacy and numeracy, good discipline and to be treated with respect. Meanwhile, we also consulted a sample of children; one sad little girl responding to a question about what she hoped for from the new education system wrote, 'I want to stay awake in the afternoons.'

I invested time in building our relations with neighbouring boroughs and, above all, with central government. I felt our negotiations as a group of boroughs with Kenneth Baker, the Secretary of State for Education, were going reasonably well until the chair of Education from Lambeth turned up in a ludicrous bright pink shirt. By contrast, Puddephatt and I had decided to look the part. He may have had only one tie, but at least it was a genuine Armani. I also took the opportunity to build relationships with sensible Labour education leaders elsewhere in the country and at this time first became acquainted with several ministers of the future, including Stephen Byers, Hilary Benn and, indeed, Jack Straw, who led at the time for the opposition on education. Labour's policy at this stage was beginning to move – admittedly from a long way back – in the direction that became New Labour. Straw supported a national curriculum, embraced some devolution of resources to schools and promoted voluntary-aided status not just for Anglicans and Catholics, but for Muslims, Orthodox Jews and other religions too. On this, he and I had similar views, in part in response to the places we represented. Prior to Blair, this view had minimal support elsewhere in the party. When the spectacular new building of Yesodey Hatorah School for Girls in Hackney was opened by Tony Blair in October 2006, one of the numerous new voluntary-aided schools established during the Blair years, it was the culmination of a campaign by Hackney's Orthodox Jewish community which I had been actively supporting for eighteen years.

Creating a credible, ambitious plan for Hackney's schools, in consultation with the community, was tremendously invigorating, but gaining the necessary votes for it among Hackney's Labour councillors was a desperate chore which gave me sleepless nights. On a single day I received letters of congratulation on the plan from a leading Conservative Party supporter, Sir Michael Coleman, who chaired a school governing body in Hackney, and from the local branch of the Communist Party, but the fact that I had enthusiastic support across the spectrum counted for little in the local party, which was heavily influenced by the left-wing local branch of the National Union of Teachers and obsessed with a tokenistic attitude to equality. There was no debate about the shockingly bad standards of achievement among, for example, black boys in Hackney schools, but there was a massive row over whether or not the word 'anti-heterosexist' should appear in the published version of the plan. I learnt then more than ever that getting the words precisely right makes all the difference. In place of the mindless criticism of anti-this and anti-that, we included a sentence that said we would 'develop policies which presented positive and accurate images of minority sections of the community'. Amazingly, everyone was happy. Sanity had broken out. 'You must have done a lot of work,' said one of my fellow councillors. I learnt that too: in politics you don't win votes without paying personal attention to the people who cast them and the cost in time is immense.

Having steered the plan through the council and barely seen my young family for months, we began setting up the authority, appointing people (including Gus John, one of the country's first black chief education officers), preparing a budget and even taking decisions about school closures. That summer, Neil Fletcher, the leader of the Inner London Education Authority, and David Mallen, the outgoing chief education officer, published a list of the worst schools in inner London, including Hackney Downs School in our patch, which in a few months we would inherit from them. It caused outrage in the borough. I promised to go and lobby them on the subject, but privately agreed with them completely. Until then, the betrayal of pupils represented by schools such as Hackney Downs had been kept a secret. Now Fletcher and Mallen had blown it into the open. A courageous chair of Education would have recommended closure there and then, but I did not think I could deliver the votes, and ran away. Fletcher and Mallen had sown the seeds of what would become hallmarks of New Labour education policy – transparency and a robust approach to school failure, both themes I would come back to soon enough. Meanwhile, the problem of Hackney Downs lay in wait to haunt me again a few years later.

In September 1989, I took a job incompatible with remaining chair of education in Hackney and reluctantly had to step down. In January 1990, Karen, my wife, set off to Bologna for a semester there, leaving me with the three girls and two cats. Overwhelmed by a new job and overrun by the girls, I left the council at the end of my four-year term, having learnt some hard lessons. As Andrew Puddephatt used to say, 'If you can do it in Hackney, you can do it anywhere.'

Work: becoming an educator

While I was learning politics in the hard school during my evenings in the 1980s, I spent the daytime for much of the decade in real schools. In fact, ultimately I became so heavily involved in education only as a result of two accidents. When I finished university, I could think of nothing better to do than to become a teacher. I had spent some months working in a school for children in need of special care. My sense of idealism had been sharpened, and I had also decided I liked working with young people. Also I knew I loved history, so becoming a history teacher made sense.

In September 1979, I took up my first post at Watford Grammar School for Boys. To my friends on the left, I explained that it was 'becoming comprehensive' as part of Hertfordshire's reorganisation. This was true, but the change was slow and the head, Keith Turner, insisted on maintaining the grammar school ethos. In part, the educational views I came to hold so strongly a decade or more later were shaped here: yes, equity really did matter, but it would be achieved not by lowering expectations or abandoning traditional good teaching, but by demanding them everywhere. Moreover, I became convinced that everyone should be inducted into the narrative of British history during their school days.

My only claim to fame came through my commitment to cricket. I ran the school's second XI and took it as seriously as someone who hated losing would be expected to do. In the first game I was in charge, our fast bowler bowled a (rare) good ball early on: it caught the edge of the bat and flew to the wicket keeper. Our whole team, including me, appealed for the catch. Then I realised I was the umpire and gave it out. (Later I was accused by some in the media of doing the same thing with government statistics.)

On Saturday 1 May 1982, a day when I would otherwise have been umpiring a second XI match, I married Karen. The sun shone and we had a long weekend in Bath before I returned to history teaching on the Tuesday morning. Karen and I had in fact met more than a decade earlier and – in a genuine case of love at first sight – decided at age thirteen that one day we would marry each other. We then took our different paths through the ensuing decade, Karen choosing to leave school (in fact several schools) early, have two children in her late teens, marry someone else, divorce him and then write to me. Not a day had gone past in all that time when I hadn't thought about her – she says the same about me – so when I received her letter out of the blue in 1981 it wasn't hard to know what to do.

I went from being a single person with a flat in north London to being a husband, father and victim of overcrowding as Karen, of course, brought her daughters, Naomi (then age seven) and Anja (age five), with her. A year later, I was able to adopt them and they became my daughters too. I left my job in Watford and we set off to Africa in 1983. We lived on the southern edge of Harare, surrounded by fruit trees. At first, the girls attended the local primary school which, in spite of the coming of independence to Zimbabwe three years earlier, was still in its colonial phase. When the teacher left the room, the largest boy in the class was left in charge, armed with a rope. On national tree-planting day, our girls were appalled to find that the boys planted the trees while the girls watched. Then, on parents' evening, the head told the assembled crowd that the reason he encouraged sport was so that his pupils might some day 'become rich like John McEnroe'. After that we taught the girls at home. The times tables were on posters on the wall, and the girls first discovered my obsession with graphs. They have never let me forget that they spent an entire morning sitting in a tree in the garden counting the different modes of transport on view in Kilwinning Road and were then, of course, made to draw a graph. As a consequence, during family rows when they were teenagers, they were always able to crush my attempts to be reasonable by saying scathingly, 'He's going to make us draw a graph now!'

We kept up with the news from home by listening to the World Service, one of Britain's finest cultural institutions. This was the era of the miners' strike. The picture conveyed by the World Service was unmistakeable. There was a rampant and unforgiving Conservative government; there was an influential, thoughtful but somewhat distraught opposition party called the Church of England, which was led by the Bishop of Durham and which published a seminal report called *Faith in the City*; and there were some other fringe parties: the SDP, the Liberals and Labour (before Neil Kinnock's crucial speech).

I joined a car pool with two local teachers so we saved fuel on the 17-mile journey out to Chitungwiza, a huge, sprawling township of 300,000 people which, at independence, had not boasted a single secondary school. My colleagues in the car pool were not only my mentors at school, they also helped push our seventeen-year-old Ford Anglia down the hill to get it started in the early mornings. Such was the demand for education that there was a morning shift from 7.00 to 12.00 and an afternoon shift from 12.00 to 5.00. On balance, in spite of the early start and the problems with the Anglia in the early morning chill, I preferred the morning shift because in the heat of the afternoon, even the keenest students sometimes considered sleep more important than history.

I taught African and European history to eight classes of about forty-five pupils each. (This might explain my later scepticism about the government's class size policy.) This was a hopeful time in Zimbabwe's history, and most of the students were desperate to learn. They sang the national anthem, 'Ishe Komborera Africa', with such passion (and in perfect four-part harmony) that it brought tears to my eyes – until the government made it compulsory to sing it every day, at which point enthusiasm waned.

The extent of teacher shortage, though, was desperate, and anyone who had passed O-level history the year before was considered a credible candidate for teaching. The staff broke into three groups – the highly traditional black teachers who had trained in the colonial era and believed in corporal punishment ('You must never be kind to the pupils,' one of them told me), the expatriates like me, and then this wave of inexperienced new teachers trying to make up the numbers. In part because they were so keen to learn, the students sometimes gave the new wave of teachers a hard time. I remember seeing from my classroom across the dusty, sun-parched courtyard a young teacher staggering backwards out of his classroom followed by some chairs which had clearly been hurled at him.

Naïvely, I believed I was making a contribution to building a model African democracy on the ashes of colonialism and apartheid. My pupils believed that was what lay ahead for them too. Karen was never convinced. She would tell me in the evenings over endless cups of tea that there was a meanness about the Mugabe regime which would become destructive. I rejected this sceptical analysis, buoyed by the enthusiasm of the pupils and the common decency of my fellow teachers. I ignored the signs of incipient dictatorship all around – the limited debate in the media and Parliament, the oppression in Matabeleland and the occasional evidence of clumsy authoritarianism. One trivial example: an Australian colleague of mine rang his mother and, responding to her questions, explained that she needn't worry about the Mugabe government. Shortly after the call finished, his phone rang. The caller – obviously official – said he had been listening to the conversation that had just finished and wanted to congratulate my friend for making such a robust defence of the government! Later, the full, appalling consequences of this tendency unfolded. All Karen's fears were proved to be justified several times over. My pupils, now in their thirties, those who have survived Mugabe and the AIDS epidemic, must feel utterly betrayed.

In spite of the vagaries of our Ford Anglia, we travelled far and wide, including somehow – with the brake fluid requiring top-ups at frequent intervals – making it to and from the breathtaking shores of Lake Malawi. Our youngest daughter, Alys, was born in Harare shortly after this epic trip. This was my first experience, incidentally, of a private health system. Karen was unimpressed by the cockroaches in the maternity ward, but – being at the time the one who paid the bills on a lowish income – what I objected to most was the doctor sending me a bill for delivering our baby, even though he hadn't been there. Karen and the midwife, aided by some flapping from me, did all the work. The doctor showed up twenty minutes later, smiled at everyone and left. (He reminded me of the Harley Street left-foot specialist in one of Spike Milligan's stories: 'Sir Ralph paused but went on charging.') My complaint about the bill was overridden, though, because Zimbabwean law allowed the doctor to charge if he got there within half an hour of the birth.

When Alys was aged seven months and had developed her passion for mangoes, we returned home to Hackney. It was the spring of 1985. I would have taken a job anywhere at that moment. The fact that I had become a teacher at all had been the first career accident; now another turned me into an education policy wonk. I accepted a job in the Education Department of the National Union of Teachers. Our role was to advise the union's executive and members on the implications for them of government education policy. Other departments dealt with the bread-and-butter union issues of pay, conditions, pensions and legal advice. It was a grim time for teacher unions. Government attempts to rein in public expenditure led to a wave of teacher strikes, but in the immediate aftermath of the crushing of the miners, Margaret Thatcher had no intention of giving in to the teachers. Meanwhile, public opinion was inflamed by lurid tales of left-wing education authorities over-dosing on political correctness while failing to secure the three Rs. My experience in Hackney soon revealed that there was more than a grain of truth in these stories.

In this climate, the government found it relatively straightforward to push through its Education Reform Act (1988) and shortly afterwards to abolish teachers' negotiating rights and replace the outmoded and ineffectual Burnham Committee with a review body which ever since has set teachers' pay and conditions. The NUT wept bitter tears and campaigned pointlessly for years for the restoration of negotiating rights, but it had only itself to blame. It had dominated the teachers' side of Burnham, but failed to reach agreement for successive years, thus undermining any case for a negotiating forum. Moreover, the other teacher unions, who found the NUT's attitude at Burnham overbearing, welcomed its replacement.

The era ushered in by the 1944 Education Act was being overthrown before our eyes, and while it was inevitably depressing for the old guard in the NUT to see the certainties of their world fall apart, for a young policy official it was invigorating, particularly as the Education Department, unlike the union as a whole, was led by a visionary educator, Alan Evans, whose commitment to the potential of public education and sobering analysis of the times were an inspiration to me. Along with some forward-thinking executive members, we began the process of coming to terms with the new world that was emerging. Maybe a national curriculum would bring benefits; perhaps devolving funding to schools and reducing local authority bureaucracy would improve teaching; and surely dedicated funding for teachers' professional development would help secure the introduction of GCSE. Alan created a department which was a hotbed of educational thinking and then in 1989 he left to pursue his passions outside the trammels of a union going through a leadership and funding crisis.

The poisoned chalice of Evans's job passed to me. This was the moment I had to give up being chair of the Education Committee in Hackney and seek to become an educational leader. The *Times Educational Supplement* wrote a generous profile of me, but speculated on whether I would be tough enough for the hard-bitten world of teacher union politics. After four years as a Hackney councillor, I had no such doubts. Much more importantly, I worried about how the educational vision which, under Evans's tutelage, I had begun to develop might ultimately be put into practice.

For four years from September 1989, I worked with a highly committed team of staff in the NUT's Education and Equal Opportunities Department to interpret the extraordinary educational changes going on around us. Just four years earlier when I had begun at the NUT, we had been able to respond to each and every government circular on its merits. Now this was impossible – there weren't enough hours in the day. To make sense of what was happening, it became necessary to step back from the detail and understand the strategy.

The government's overall approach soon became apparent, if not in the publications of the Department of Education, then in the speeches of ministers and the pamphlets from the government's favourite think-tanks, such as the Centre for Policy Studies. In essence, through the national curriculum and national testing, the government had decided to set standards and then to check whether they were being achieved; through devolving power and money to schools they were giving headteachers the responsibility for meeting those standards. Meanwhile, the influence of local education authorities – those bêtes noires of Thatcherites – was steadily reduced. Increasingly, schools were encouraged to 'opt out' of them altogether and receive funding direct from Whitehall. The school, in effect, had become the point of accountability. Later in 1992, the theme of transparency was added – school results would be published and a new agency, Ofsted, incorporating the old Inspectorate, was established to inspect all schools once every four years instead of on an occasional basis.

The principles behind the reform were bold and sensible. The problems were all in the implementation. Ministers came and went with bewildering regularity; the national curriculum, created by committees of subject experts, became so overloaded that even Margaret Thatcher rebelled against it. While funding was devolved, it was also scarce, so the benefits of the new approach were at first limited. Worse still, no extra effort was made to assist pupils or schools in disadvantaged circumstances. In addition, there were obvious sequencing errors: for example, devolving power to headteachers changed the nature of the role, but training for them in how to exercise this power was thought of only after the event.

From a personal point of view, watching this drama unfold provided an extraordinary set of lessons on how to (and how not to) implement large-scale education reform, lessons on which I based my later efforts in government. I also came to understand how organisations such as the NUT respond to dramatic changes in their circumstances. The first reaction inside the union, as in many organisations facing a threat, was one of disbelief – they won't really do this, will they? As the old certainties are questioned and begin to crumble, people in this state are tempted to close their eyes and wait for it all to go away – 'It'll blow over,' they say, to choose a different metaphor.

The second reaction now became apparent – accommodation: we'll resist what we can and learn to live with what we can't. While the left in the union clung to the first response and sought to wind the clock back, the majority began to adapt. Since the unions no longer negotiated pay deals, education policy became the central issue. As the government's implementation errors compounded one another, the NUT found that it made sense to work more closely with the other teacher unions. The divisions that had dogged the teaching profession for generations had been largely over pay and conditions, but on education reform there was more room to collaborate. We began to agree joint statements among the six unions on subjects such as how teachers should be appraised and how classroom teachers might respond to the national curriculum. Often responsibility for drafting and negotiating them fell to me, which was when I discovered for the first time the benefits in negotiations of my Quaker upbringing.*

---

*Actually I sometimes went beyond what Quakers would approve of to secure unanimous agreement and still feel a marginal sense of guilt as a result. Once four out of the six unions had agreed a text, I used to ring each of the remaining two and tell them that their union was the only one not yet signed up . . . this usually did the trick.

But accommodation of changed circumstances is not enough. Once it becomes clear there is no going back and that there might be benefits from the new situation, or even unexpected opportunities, a third stage of response is required: strategic repositioning. At just this time, I happened to read a book by two American academics, Charles Taylor Kerchner and Douglas Mitchell, called *The Changing Idea of a Teachers' Union*. It might not have been a bestseller, but to me it was a revelation. Supposing, I began to think, that instead of resisting accountability for results, the NUT became genuinely strategic and embraced it. Supposing, instead of arguing – as unions had for years – that if only governments would spend more and pay teachers more, then perhaps the system would improve, we turned this argument on its head? The argument would then become: we the teachers of this country will embrace accountability and we'll show you how much we are improving the system, then you'll realise how much it is worth investing in us and in public education. It was a bold, perhaps excessively idealistic, way of thinking, and it was certainly strategic.

Who knew what might have happened had the government of the day been competent, but they weren't. After the 1992 election, John Major made the mistake of appointing John Patten as Secretary of State for Education,* and the implementation of a complex and challenging reform descended into chaos. Instead of carefully piloting and then refining the proposed English tests for fourteen-year-olds, Patten proposed a headlong rush to implement them in May 1993, claiming no tests in history had ever been better prepared. The word 'boycott' began to be whispered. In December 1992, the NUT executive supported a resolution which I had drafted, arguing for a consultative ballot of English teachers on boycotting the tests. Over 90 per cent voted in favour. Far from promoting the embrace of accountability, I now found myself playing a leading role in bringing it – at least temporarily – crashing down. The NUT's main rival, the National Association of Schoolmasters and Union of Women Teachers, voted in March 1993 to boycott all national tests on workload grounds. The government remained intransigent, but ineffectually so. The packages of tests were

---

* Whenever I think of that time, I remember the line from that famous 1940s song: 'Oh how the ghost of you clings | These foolish things | Remind me of you'.

left unopened in school offices that May, and the government's strategy was left in tatters. Finally, Patten at last made an excellent decision. He appointed Sir Ron Dearing to review the entire national curriculum and the associated tests, which, in consultation with teachers and others, he did. I found myself acting often as the spokesperson for all six unions in discussions with the Dearing review.

Dearing, open and pragmatic throughout, simplified the curriculum, cut the associated bureaucracy and recognised teachers' professionalism. He argued that teachers should be trusted, but in return they should accept accountability – 'the greater the trust, the greater the accountability must be,' he said.[2] With workload reduced, sanity restored and an intellectual underpinning for a new relationship between teachers and government established, most teachers and unions were satisfied, if not delighted. All the unions called off their boycott for the 1994 tests, except the NUT. This was a matter of immense frustration to me. Suddenly, the new strategic vision which had attracted me before I'd even heard of Dearing was opening up, but the union I worked for chose to turn back when it could have led the way forward. Meanwhile, inside the union, wrangles over staff reductions and other issues had soured my relations with the general secretary, Doug McAvoy.

At the end of November 1993, I left the NUT and became a professor of education at Keele University, and a few weeks later – I think in the *Times* – I wrote an article getting my frustrations off my chest. Exaggerating only a little, I wrote that the NUT had to choose between accountability and oblivion. Either way, I was liberated, and the excellent vice-chancellor at Keele, Brian Fender, encouraged me to get out and about. I poured out articles for newspapers promoting accountability, urging acceptance of the principles of the Conservative government's reform but arguing for greater coherence, greater emphasis on equity and, not least, the funding to match the ambition. I spoke at hundreds of headteacher conferences, from Poole in Dorset to Ambleside in Cumbria, arguing my case. In the boot of my red Vauxhall Astra I had five or six standard speeches. When I arrived at a venue, I'd scribble out a new front sheet and then deliver whichever one caught the moment. Eventually my car was stolen along with the speeches – what did the thief do with them? – but by then they were committed to memory.

It was while I was preparing to deliver one of these speeches – in Sheffield this time – that I heard that John Smith, leader of the opposition, had died. A few weeks later I was rung up at home by a young man called James Purnell, who was working for Tony Blair and said he was writing a speech about education which Blair would deliver as part of his campaign for the leadership. Since Purnell knew nothing about education, he wondered whether I would help. We met – inevitably over a coffee in Islington – and together wrote a speech. It was one of those turning points in life.

Blair, Blunkett and New Labour education policy

Within days of winning the leadership of the Labour Party, Tony Blair began to overturn its schools policy. Contradicting Ann Taylor, the education spokesperson he had inherited from John Smith, he announced on 26 July 1994 that he supported league tables. This was the first clear signal from Blair that in reforming the public services, education included, he would place himself firmly on the side of the consumer rather than the producer. A Labour leader supporting league tables as a positive good was a new departure.

In October the same year, Blair prepared the ground for a complete revolution in Labour's education policy by appointing David Blunkett as his education spokesperson. Meanwhile, David Miliband became head of policy for Blair. I had known Miliband for a couple of years by then because in 1992, with Tim Brighouse (then a charismatic professor, later an equally charismatic leader of Birmingham's Education Service), I had jointly written a pamphlet on teachers for the Institute for Public Policy Research.* Now he organised a seminar for his new boss in the Shadow Cabinet Room at Westminster, inviting Blunkett and his chief policy and press aide, Conor Ryan, whose quiet, unselfish authority rapidly made him indispensable. Brighouse and I were the outside experts present, and I was invited to prepare the paper.

This meeting at the end of January 1995 was the first occasion on which I met my future boss, Tony Blair. Two impressions struck me at

---

* A very young Miliband had been through our draft with a copious red pen. Brighouse commented: 'Do you know the most annoying thing of all is that he was right almost every time?'

the time as most important. One was just how open the agenda was. There were none of the shibboleths that had so often stood in the way of radical rethinking in Labour's recent past. The fact that the Conservatives supported an idea did not make it automatically suspect; the idea would be judged on its merits. The second was that Blair really was committed to making education his top priority, which had not been the case under his predecessor. Looking back, I feel I was rather bold. I told Blair that numerous leaders had said they would be the 'Education Prime Minister' or 'Education President', including John Major and George Bush Senior, but few if any had really sustained it once in office.

It was also in the paper for this meeting that two phrases of real significance for later policy were first used. 'Intervention should be in inverse proportion to success' was the first. The Conservatives had, with limited success, been encouraging schools to opt out of local authority control and a key test for New Labour was whether it would reverse this policy. Needless to say, both unions and local authorities demanded nothing less. 'Intervention in inverse proportion to success' implied something different – how much freedom a school should have should depend not on the whim of a moment, but on its performance.

The second phrase – 'Standards matter more than structures' – also became influential. Research showed that the biggest influence of the system on pupil performance was the quality of teaching. Governments could play about with the structure of the system as much as they liked, but if they failed to influence classroom teaching, the performance of the system would remain unchanged. This became a mantra for the first Blair term, justifying the focus on the 'literacy hour' for example, but also the refusal to abolish the remaining grammar schools. Towards the end of his first term, Blair, seeking to make his reforms self-sustaining, began to argue that 'standards not structures' had been a mistake. In the second term, structures became his focus. By then, I was working for him and owned up to originating the 'standards not structures' phrase. I have no doubt it was right for the first term, because it was the key to improving results in the first few years, which in turn gave people confidence.

After this meeting, I found myself regularly in touch with Miliband and Ryan, and occasionally with Blunkett, as speeches and policy documents were drafted and the policy revolution advanced. In May

1995, I delivered the Greenwich Lecture, which at the time was a prominent event in the education calendar. A few months earlier, David Pitt-Watson – my friend from university days – had said provocatively, 'Why do we have to have any failing schools?' I began to recite the usual litany of excuses offered by the education establishment of which I was a part. On reflection, I realised the obvious truth that any failure at all was disastrous for the pupils concerned and that accepting it was regressive. By contrast, a progressive should surely be determined to root it out, not least because schools that failed were overwhelmingly serving the very pupils whose life chances depended most on receiving a good public education. I decided to devote my Greenwich Lecture to this theme.

By early 1995, regular school inspections had begun, and they showed that between 1 and 2 per cent of schools were failing, and a further 5 to 10 per cent were struggling. In preparation for my lecture, I did a very simple piece of arithmetic – at this rate, by the time every school had been inspected (which would take four years), between 250 and 500 schools would have failed, and another 1,250 to 2,500 would have been identified as struggling. No one else had done this sum before (or at least not in public) and it was a lot of schools. In addition, I worked through to logical conclusions what it would take to solve the problem of all of these schools, hence the title of the lecture, 'Imagining an End to Failure'. The far end of this argument was that where a school was too intractably damaged to be turned around within a year, and could not be closed, something more radical would be required.

In these circumstances, I strongly endorsed an idea which Blunkett had floated during the Easter teacher union conferences a few weeks earlier. The school should receive a 'fresh start', including new governors, new leadership, new resources to attract new and excellent staff, and the complete refurbishment of the site. The idea, which we had developed together in the run-up to Easter, had caused huge controversy, with Blunkett famously being jostled and pushed by the lunatic fringe of activists at the NUT conference. The television pictures of this shameful moment did more to promote New Labour's education policy than any other event prior to 1997.

Now, in the Greenwich Lecture, I was providing the theoretical underpinning for what, after 1997, became government policy. Indeed, the seed of the city academy idea is clearly visible. In the marbled

grandeur of Greenwich Town Hall, the idea was less than enthusiastically received by some. There was even some mild heckling, but I
relished this because the lecture was intended to be an assault on a
complacent culture.

> For too long, it has been a powerful strand of the culture of this country
> that failure in education is inevitable and, like the poor, it will always be
> with us . . . We, as educators, might be expected to be in the vanguard of
> a campaign to challenge this poverty-stricken culture. In fact, all too often
> we reinforce it . . . The traditional response to those who raise the question
> of failure is to suggest we should discuss the success of the many, not the
> failure of the few . . . [whereas a] serious debate about failure is in fact a
> precondition of success.[3]

The lecture generated extensive debate, both because of the numbers
and because of the ideas. What interested me most was that both
opposition and government accepted the general thrust.

A couple of months later, as if to test my willingness to put my time
where my mouth was, Gillian Shephard, then Secretary of State for
Education, invited me to be one of six members of the blandly named
North East London Education Association. Our task was to consider on
her behalf what to do about Hackney Downs School and make
recommendations to her as soon as we could. The chairman of our 'hit
squad' (as the press inevitably dubbed the group) was a calm businessman called Richard Painter, but as both the most prominent
educationist and only local resident on the group, I felt myself to be
firmly in the firing line.

During the autumn of 1995, having examined every aspect of the
school, especially the education it offered the 200 or so boys who were
meant to attend, we reached the conclusion that the school should be
closed as soon as possible, and alternative school places found for the
boys in nearby schools. For those with GCSEs in prospect the next
summer, we suggested extra individual tuition, which the government
should fund. While of course there was a risk in this course of action –
such disruption could hardly be considered ideal – it was one of those
cases I found so common later in government, where the risk of acting
was far less than the risk of doing nothing. After all, the boys were
learning hardly anything. In the previous year's GCSE results, the best

grades had been in Turkish, a subject in which the pupils received no teaching at all. In a maths class for 16-year-olds, a significant number of pupils struggled to divide 168 by 12; in another class several were unable to say how many pence there were in £1.85. These appalling standards had become wrapped in a culture of excuses and low expectations. Above all, the high poverty of many of the students' families was blamed for their poor performance.

The closure, needless to say, caused huge public controversy, in which I played a prominent part. I defended the decision repeatedly in print and on public platforms, and have never regretted it. It was surely good for the boys, whose interests were paramount; I checked their GCSE results in each of the next three years. It was also good for the education system: a line in the sand had been drawn; catastrophic, ongoing failure was morally unacceptable.

Shephard had shown great courage in taking this step, and Blunkett, with whom I kept in touch throughout, took a principled and supportive position when a lesser politician might have exploited the controversy for short-term political gain. Indeed, the stand we took on Hackney Downs became a foundation for New Labour's education policy once Blair won power. Ten years later, the magnificent, high-achieving Mossbourne Community Academy, standing on what was the site of Hackney Downs, is perhaps the most powerful symbol of Blair's legacy in education.

In late 1995, I moved from Keele University to the Institute of Education at London University. As I was making that transition I found myself invited to what seemed to be a remarkable meeting, chaired by Peter Mandelson and involving other New Labour luminaries including David Miliband. Eighteen months before the first New Labour election victory I was asked to prepare a paper on what the party's agenda might be for the *second* term; I argued for 'a radical shift of power and direction from producer to consumer'. Inevitably as my career developed our own children's schools became a public issue. Once we were back from Africa, Naomi and Anja attended our local primary school, where the education was cheerful but did not include learning the times tables or the capitals even of European countries. They then attended an inner London comprehensive school, where their education varied from the good (Naomi's English) to the awful (Anja's maths). Both Naomi and Anja were subjected to a 'progressive' maths programme called SMILE Maths. Each pupil followed their own path, which allowed them to sink to their own lowest level. A good teacher could make it work but others struggled with it. Anja did not get lucky. She told me one evening that her maths teacher had said he was 'too busy' to answer questions from pupils, which I assumed was her somewhat implausible excuse for not being able to do her homework – but when I asked the teacher in question he confirmed that it was true: fitting in answering questions between marking and filing was too much for him. My complaint to the head was politely received but made no difference. The whole school suffered from a take-it-or-leave-it culture. Later, when Anja attended a different (state) school for the sixth form, I was devastated when she said to me, 'Unlike my last school, here they actually care how well I do.'

When Alys was due to go to secondary school, Karen took a stand. There was no way another of her daughters was going anywhere so thoroughly mediocre – Alys would go private. I agreed we'd visit several schools, state and private, and then choose and I wouldn't let my involvement in Labour's policy-making prevent us doing what we thought was best for our daughter. The visits reinforced Karen's view. Once the private choice was made I rang Blunkett and offered to stop advising him but he said, 'You're not a politician . . . as long as you'll work with me to make state schools so good anyone would choose them, I can live with this.' Then I rang a journalist, figuring I'd rather prompt the story than appear to hide it. In the aftermath of Tony Blair's choice of the grant-maintained Oratory and Harriet Harman's of a selective state school, our choice was big news for a few days. Alys, age eleven, commented only, 'I hope they spell my name correctly.' I met some hostility in the university but letters of support outnumbered others by two or three to one and the journalists let it fade, I think because I had been open about it. Most importantly, Alys enjoyed school.

About the same time David Pitt-Watson asked me another of those innocent questions: how come, he asked, we are unable to teach every child – or at least almost every child – to read and write well? I began to think systematically about this question. We knew by then that literacy at primary school level was a key indicator of performance in all subjects at age sixteen, and indeed that literacy at age seven was strongly correlated with a person's earnings age thirty-seven. If education was to bring greater equality of opportunity, improving literacy performance was surely absolutely central. As Pitt-Watson pointed out, the founders of the Labour Party at the start of the twentieth century surely expected that the achievement of universal public education would bring greater equity and therefore greater opportunity for working people. Wouldn't they be terribly disappointed with the actual result almost a century later? An education system which did little more than reproduce the social inequalities of one generation in the next and in which, as a report published in 1996 from the National Foundation for Educational Research showed, standards of literacy that year were about the same as they had been in 1948.[4] Shocking. 'Education, education, education', Blair's famous declaration, had to mean more than this.

With Conor Ryan and Sophie Linden in his office, I opened up this theme with Blunkett. He responded with alacrity. With his roots in working-class Sheffield, he understood this challenge viscerally. All around him he saw that children were being betrayed by an education system characterised by low expectations and a refusal to accept any definition of what was best practice in teaching. He asked me to chair a literacy task force* which would report to him before the election, widely expected in May 1997, and make recommendations for ensuring that every child learnt to read and write well. As a group, we soon realised that this would require a massive programme of retraining for primary headteachers and teachers as well as a change in the wider culture. We also decided we wanted a target. Given that in 1996 just 57 per cent achieved the necessary standard, what would be a good milestone on the way to universal high standards? As part of a group working for the opposition, we had little data to go on, but plumped for an ambitious 80 per cent by 2002.

At the heart of the strategy, though, there needed to be a proven best practice in teaching literacy: no point in a massive retraining programme if there was no defined content for it. Here we were helped again by Gillian Shephard, who, also worried about literacy standards,

---

*The task force included the bestselling author Ken Follett, who in a generous review of the first edition of this book pointed out that as a result of the efforts of members of the task force, including himself, 'doubters were reassured, implacable opponents were taken into account. By the time we came to put our ideas into practice, there was powerful momentum for reform.' I readily acknowledge this and am glad to have the chance of this second edition to put the point on the record.

had the same year set up the National Literacy Project and appointed one of Her Majesty's inspectors, John Stannard, to run it. This project was planned to operate in just 300 (out of 19,000) primary schools, so had no chance of transforming the performance of the entire system, but John – one of the education system's unsung heroes – meticulously drew up, with his colleagues, a framework for teaching which set out, term by term for pupils aged five to eleven, what they should be taught when and, above all, how. Thus was the Literacy Hour born with a strong dose of phonics at its core. My first meeting with John in late 1996 was a turning point for the literacy strategy – he had the detailed content, we had the ambitious strategy. All we had to do – in Franklin Roosevelt's famous phrase – was knit them together. Blunkett lent his strong support at the launch of our report in February 1997, with Blair standing (metaphorically) firmly behind him. Meanwhile, though, Shephard had a couple of months left as secretary of state; with an election coming up, I wanted the Department for Education to be briefed in advance. With Blunkett's permission, I took the permanent secretary, Michael Bichard, through our proposals. I also explained them to the controversial chief inspector of schools, Chris Woodhead.

I knew Woodhead pretty well by then, having met with him regularly throughout the 1990s. There were many who wanted an incoming Labour government to remove him as soon as possible, given the harshness of his attacks on poor teaching, poor teacher training and poor local education authorities. In fact, for these very reasons, it was important for him to stay. After all, on the issues of school failure and standards of literacy, the New Labour critique was not that the government had been wrong to focus on them, but that it had not done enough to tackle them. Woodhead became a strong ally of the New Labour government at first, both on dealing with school failure and – after a cautious initial reaction – on literacy.*

Policy development on school failure and literacy was therefore well advanced by the time of the May 1997 general election, while on the many other major issues, David Miliband and Conor Ryan, through the speeches they prepared for Blair and Blunkett and the policy documents

* Blunkett comments in his diary: 'Chris Woodhead had many qualities which he did his best to hide, but collegiality and modesty were not among them.' (David Blunkett, *The Blunkett Tapes: My Life in the Bear Pit* (London: Bloomsbury, 2006, p. 32) This is a pithy summary of what lay ahead.

they drafted, had established a radical and comprehensive New Labour education policy. These included reducing class sizes for infant schools, devolving more funding and responsibility to all schools – not just grant-maintained schools – and proposals to expand the number of specialist secondary schools. In addition, areas where there were concentrations of disadvantage would become education action zones.

As the election approached, both Miliband and Blunkett discussed with me what I might do if Labour won the election. I was tempted, of course, by working in No. 10 – that front door, that address, and an ambitious new Prime Minister to work for – but in the end I was tempted more by Blunkett's idea of setting up a Standards and Effectiveness Unit in the Department for Education, which would be the engine room of driving the new government's school reforms. David's analysis, reinforced by Bichard, was that the Department for Education as then constituted could never deliver what the new government would require; the new unit which I would lead would therefore seek to change the culture of the department as well as implement the school reforms.

Given my lack of significant management experience, the prospect of succeeding in this mission seemed to be at the far end of credible, but it was impossible to turn down the chance to reshape England's underperforming school system, and I had a perverse view from the outset that we would not fail. The day I started, I had to negotiate my pay and boldly asserted that I wanted it directly linked to the performance of eleven-year-olds in literacy tests. This, I was told, was impossible, but was another sign, in new circumstances, that I still hated the prospect of losing.

Reforming schools

Looking back across the messy reality of eleven years of Labour government, it is easy to forget the euphoria of 1 May 1997. For me personally there was a complication: it wasn't just election day, it was our wedding anniversary, which we always take seriously. Moreover, Karen was sceptical about my association with the incoming government. By contrast, this was a day I had been waiting for, the first shift of the political tectonic plates since Margaret Thatcher's victory eighteen years earlier, and the chance to play a major role in the policy area –

education, education, education – that Tony Blair had declared his top priority. I wanted to be at the now-famous party at the Royal Festival Hall to mark this historic moment. Karen was not remotely impressed by my compromise that I would stay home until midnight, after which it would no longer be our wedding anniversary, and then go to the Festival Hall. Looking back I must admit that this was a bit like those court cases which are won and lost on a technicality. Nor was she bought off by the amber necklace I presented to her before midnight.* Even so, I went, stayed up all night, met old friends (David Pitt-Watson), future colleagues (David Miliband) and celebrities (some of whom, David Puttnam for example, became friends), then walked across Waterloo Bridge and home in the dawn to make sure I was there to get Alys up for breakfast and off to school. Karen's temporary frostiness was not thawed much by the fact that the next evening I had dinner at Shepherd's in Westminster with David Blunkett, Michael Bichard and Blunkett's new private secretary, Alun Evans (not to be confused with Alan Evans), and then, over the Bank Holiday weekend, attended a series of meetings at which we sought to communicate the new policy agenda to the department's top officials.

The first few weeks were utterly chaotic, but incredibly productive. Throughout, there was an air of unreality and above all a confidence among the incoming team (which, in relation to schools, included Stephen Byers and Estelle Morris as well as Blunkett, Ryan and me), that for a while defied gravity.

On my first full day in the office – Tuesday 5 May – I made sure my first meeting was about the National Literacy Strategy. A handful of incredulous-looking officials were summoned into my office and we discussed what was required. I was clear in my own mind that our strategy would only work if it was consistently given top priority. With David Pitt-Watson, I had costed it on the back of an envelope – very accurately as it turned out – and I stated at that meeting how much I wanted for it: a mere £40 million ('Tens of millions are relatively easy to find,' one senior official told me at that time, 'hundreds a little harder.') A few days later, we announced the 80 per cent literacy target and the establishment of a numeracy task force which eventually made proposals for numeracy which mirrored those we already had for

---

* Though I'm glad to say she still wears it.

literacy. Meanwhile, Blunkett, with Tony Blair's support, was – unknown to me – overriding an attempt by Robin Butler, Head of the Civil Service, to block my appointment.[5]

Both the confidence and chaos were in evidence on the Thursday of that first week. I bumped into Ryan in the foyer of the department and he asked me if I was ready for that morning's meeting with the PM at No. 10. 'What meeting?' I asked. Shortly afterwards, I found myself for the first time in the Cabinet Room, gulping for air as Blair asked whether we were sure the 80 per cent target would be met and everyone went silent and looked at me. If there was a single moment when I realised the extent of my personal accountability, that was it. It was strongly reinforced later when Blunkett said his 'head was on the block' in relation to the target, and I later received one of what I would come to call Blunkettograms, stating cheerfully, 'If I go down, you're coming with me.'

Also in those first few days, driven powerfully by Byers, with Blunkett's backing, the idea of publishing a list of the worst schools in the country was advanced. Before the first month was out, this had been done. 'Naming and shaming', as its critics came to call it, was decisive both practically and symbolically. In practical terms, it was the first step in implementing the policy developed by Blunkett, drawing on the Greenwich Lecture and the Hackney Downs experience. We made it clear that, however difficult it turned out to be and whatever mistakes were made along the way, the government would not rest until school failure was consigned to history. As Blunkett points out in his diaries, the central message was that children's achievement was the government's top priority – if that upset some people, so be it.[6]

The symbolic value of the announcement was the shock it gave to the system. Officials in the department tried desperately to block it; out in the system itself it conveyed the message that New Labour would be as hard as nails and a degree of disillusionment that never fully evaporated set in. Since I often had to advocate this policy at teachers' conferences, I had to feel confident of my case: 'Zero tolerance of failure is the reverse side of the same coin as success for all; you cannot have one without the other,' I argued.

We were also writing a White Paper, which we were determined to publish before the summer break. In a rolling series of meetings, usually chaired by the clear-eyed Byers and involving Miliband, now head of policy at No. 10, we hammered out the policy while, with able support from a young official called Rob Read, I tried to hammer out the words. Successive drafts had to be read onto tape on Friday afternoon and dispatched to the implacable Blunkett for him to listen to over the weekend. On Monday, his comments, often highly critical, would be returned to me and Read and we would start the next edit through. On 3 July, the White Paper was published to widespread acclaim although with an undertow of criticism that this would all mean too much change in too short a time. If the accusation was an excess of ambition, we pleaded guilty; after all, the education system we inherited patently suffered from a lack of it. 'So there we have it – the first White Paper of the new government, the largest consultation paper in many years on education, and the first major one for any Labour government – and we did it in nine weeks,* which, even though I say it myself, is remarkable,' commented Blunkett in his diary.[7] All the preparatory policy work that Miliband, Ryan and others had done prior to the election was now formally enshrined in government policy, and a year later would become statute in the School Standards and Framework Act.

Through all this I found myself learning how to manage not just officials, but also the system as a whole. After working in universities, my first impressions of departmental officials were positive – unlike academics, when asked to do something, they generally did it. Nor was there any sign of a politicised civil service blocking an incoming Labour government's agenda. Soon, though, the problems began to emerge. While the civil service was not party political, it was heavily influenced by the various lobby groups who competed for influence in the department, which thus tended to see issues from the producer angle. This in turn led to a tendency to see problems rather than opportunities, and to favour incrementalism rather than discontinuous change. Moreover, the lack of ambition which characterised the education service as a whole inevitably affected the department too.

The result was that while the department expected to produce policies and regulations, its civil servants did not really expect to succeed in transforming the service. Injecting the belief that visible change was possible thus became a central task for me and one I sought to carry out

---

*To my knowledge, no incoming government before or since has matched this record for a White Paper on any subject.

through every single daily interaction with civil servants. Bichard, a brooding presence as permanent secretary, was consistently supportive. Once we had produced the big leaps in literacy and numeracy test results in 1999 and 2000, people – even the doubting Thomases – began to believe, but until then all I had on my side was moral force. Whenever I did have doubts – during numerous sleepless nights – I kept them to myself. As the months passed, more and more officials would quietly drop into my office to drink the elixir of ambition.

But the key to making a difference lies in effective implementation. Prior to government, I had read numerous management handbooks, some of which I really enjoyed. From them, and from watching the struggles of successive Tory governments to implement radical change in education, I had learnt all I knew about making things happen. In the absence of any significant experience, I fell back on this body of knowledge and discovered, somewhat to my surprise, that it worked. Also, we began to appoint people into the Standards and Effectiveness Unit who had really worked out in the system. People such as Ralph Tabberer and Paul Hanbury became hugely influential because they really knew what it was like, out in schools and local authorities, to be on the receiving end of poorly constructed government policy. The central point was that if we were going to be as ambitious as we intended and if, as Blunkett wanted, we were going to drive things rapidly from the centre, we had to do so excellently.

An opportunity to exemplify this new attention to getting the detail right presented itself in the autumn of 1997. We organised a conference in London for the directors of education of each local education authority, at which we planned to set out their role in driving the National Literacy Strategy and suggest to them what their targets for 2002 should be if we were to meet our national target. The officials reported to me with delight a couple of weeks before the event that two-thirds of local authorities would attend – far more, they said, than usual. I said I wanted 100 per cent attendance and that they should ring up every local authority that hadn't replied and explain that we expected them to be there. A week or so later, I got them to do another ring round and soon just one local authority had not accepted the invitation. I rang the director there and asked him if he was aware he was the only one not down to come. Sure enough he came too. This kind of thoroughness, a sense of common purpose, was exactly what was needed to make a difference.

The following summer, every primary school headteacher and one or two other teachers from each school attended one of more than 300 two-day conferences at which the National Literacy Strategy and the excellent materials, including precise instructions on how to teach a literacy hour – including the phonics – were explained. In September 1998, teachers started teaching literacy hours. The schools facing the greatest challenge received extra support. Soon afterwards, the positive feedback began to pour in. Teachers might not have liked being told how to teach by government, but they loved the fact that their children learnt more and faster. Meanwhile, the National Year of Reading put the whole strategy on the map. Increasing numbers of parents read to their children at bedtime. Three times in little more than a year, schools got substantial grants to spend on books – enough to buy more than twenty million.

There was a sense of momentum. With the numeracy strategy rolling out almost in parallel, it became evident that in just over two years the face of primary education had been changed forever. In the summer of 1999 there was the first big jump in the results, followed by another a year later. In 2001, an international comparison showed that England's performance in reading among ten-year-olds had improved significantly relative to other countries (including Scotland, which had no strategy). Now we were third in the world. Above all, primary school teachers could see the difference in their classrooms, as could many secondary school teachers, who found that their intakes after 1999 were noticeably better at English and maths.* Teachers of foreign languages in particular noticed the difference because now – at last – children were being taught grammar in primary schools. Parents, needless to say, were also positive.

A few academics continued to whinge on the sidelines, trying to prove that nothing had changed, frustrated that their dire predictions of

---

* In 2007 the same international comparison showed that England had slipped back relatively; it was still above the EU average, above Scotland and above France but it was now behind five Canadian provinces and thirteen other countries. This reinforced the evidence that in that initial phase standards had risen but that after 2001 the follow-through was not all that it might have been (see p. 268).

† Even the most sceptical academics accept that English and maths improved. The debate is how much.

failure had been proved wrong.[†] The more generous reaction came from directors of education in local authorities, who had begun by complaining that the national strategy reduced their discretion (as indeed it did) but came to see that when it worked they could claim credit locally. We published their results in league table form and rapid climbers such as Tower Hamlets and Blackburn were rightly able to savour their success. Bob Clark, director of education for Wigan at the time, summed up their views in speaking to Blunkett and me in 1999: 'A year ago we thought you were mad and it wouldn't work. Now we think it will work, but we still think you're mad.' I think this is a fair summary of what was achieved.

Of course, not everything was plain sailing, and we made mistakes. Certainly I did. We took on too much, not all of it central to changing the system. We failed to design some programmes properly: education action zones was the classic case. I blundered badly on the day the announcement was made. With ministerial support, I had included the details of how EAZs would work in a speech I made in Bradford. I briefed journalists afterwards, and before the day was out the front page of the *Evening Standard* read 'Private firms to run bad schools' (6 January 1998). The next day, several newspapers led with the story. There was uproar in the system, especially among local authorities, who thought they were about to be replaced.[*] John Prescott, taken by surprise, rang Blunkett and asked him to fire the 'mad professor'.[8]

Of course the storm died down, but once the expectations of a policy are skewed by the media – as a result in this case of my blunder – it is hard to straighten them out. Stephen Byers's private secretary told me several years later that his comment on the affair was 'that's what happens when you let a boffin make an announcement'. Fair cop, I thought, particularly as my next major speech – on the apparently unnewsworthy subject of 'The Ethics of Education Reform' – resulted in a front-page story in the *Guardian*, incredibly (and misleadingly) headlined 'Schools adviser urges moral code to replace God' (23 March 1998), and a phone call from the Archbishop of Canterbury's office. Fortunately Blunkett was more amused than ruffled but for a while

---

[*] I personally have never had a problem with private firms taking over and turning round poorly performing state schools – as happens in Philadelphia, for example – as long as they deliver results for pupils. The problem was that this was not government policy (and still isn't).

after that Conor Ryan and the ministers were understandably reluctant to let me out. The lesson for me was powerful, though: while it might be the case sometimes that governments are more interested in managing the media than delivering real change, the truth is that unless you manage the media well, it becomes very difficult to deliver change at all. Loaded with negative associations though the word has become, 'spin' really does matter; the danger comes when it is divorced from substance.

Crucially, we learnt from the mistakes with education action zones and followed up with a more radical, and ultimately more successful, policy called Excellence in Cities, which was designed both to solve the real problems teachers face in tough inner cities – such as behaviour and attendance – and to make schools in these locations more attractive to those parents who would otherwise abandon them, through encouraging specialist schools, programmes for the gifted and talented, and city academies. The policy was implemented first in six large urban areas, including London, and then spread. Andrew Adonis, a rising star of journalism who joined the No. 10 team in 1998 to lead on education policy, and I worked hard to make sure it combined Blair's emphasis on aspirant parents with Blunkett's on equity, and the results were good. A more intensive version was later developed for inner London – the London Challenge – which had even more impressive results.

From 2000 on, the most difficult policy of all came to dominate our time and energy in the Standards and Effectiveness Unit – intervening in bad local education authorities. Using the powers we had taken in 1998 which enabled central government to force a local education authority to contract out its services where inspectors had found them to be failing, we encouraged Chris Woodhead to embark on an accelerated programme of inspections of local education authorities. As his inspectors identified problems, we in the SEU sought solutions and forced the contracting-out of services in several local authorities. Most, but not all, of these interventions worked. Estelle Morris provided outstanding political leadership throughout, willing to take on Labour, Liberal Democrat or Conservative authorities, as long as the evidence for intervention was there.

In the last year of the parliament, we were almost overwhelmed by a teacher shortage crisis. Though it was much exaggerated by the media, it was very real for schools in disadvantaged locations and in London.

Blunkett's instinct as ever was to micro-manage, which in a crisis usually turns out to be right. If the media are going to hold the minister to account for a single, far-flung school on a four-day week, he reasoned, the department ought to be on the case first. The crisis also provided the rationale for one of the most successful of all our reforms in that period – in the Budget in March 2000, bursaries were offered to attract students into teacher-training, with higher bursaries for those going into shortage subjects such as maths and science. Ralph Tabberer, newly appointed as chief executive of the Teacher Training Agency, completely overhauled it and turned it into a thoroughly modern marketing and regulatory organisation which won awards for its brilliant advertising and treated any inquiry as an opportunity to build a lasting relationship with the caller. The government had already set clear standards for teacher training. The TTA rewarded those universities that performed well while penalising those who didn't; in rare cases, whole schools of education were closed (intervention in inverse proportion to success all over again). By 2005, the UK's teacher-training system was admired across the world.

By the end of 2000, the Standards and Effectiveness Unit had grown too large. Its impact by then, especially on school failure and primary school literacy and numeracy, was unquestioned, so the understandable tendency was to shift other policy areas into its domain – 11–14-year-old standards, Excellence in Cities, specialist schools and so on – and I was always flattered and happy to take something new on, especially since in the civil service the number of people you manage is (wrongly) seen as a measure of virility. But this was my mistake; and the widening span of responsibility meant I was no longer on top of the detail. The core agenda – literacy and numeracy – received less of my attention than it should have done. Here were the seeds of the plateau in primary school results in 2001 for which I must bear significant responsibility. (On the basis of this experience, at the Delivery Unit I resisted the temptation to take on ever-wider responsibility. In achieving big change, focus is vital.)

Furthermore, the election – widely anticipated for the summer of 2001 – was fast approaching. There was never any danger of Labour losing, but Labour had never won 'an historic second term' and ministers across government became cautious. In the Department for Education, the heady, risk-taking days of 1997 to 2000 were behind us.

Since progress in primary school performance was one of the few unadulterated successes in reforming the public services, the government's message became 'we've done primary schools; now for the secondary schools'. This was the underlying message of the Green Paper we published in February 2001 in the run-up to the election. 'I did not enjoy trying to put together the Education Green Paper,' Blunkett says in his diary.[9] I know how he felt: in the end, with Jon Coles, an excellent official, I stayed up all night making the amendments that Blunkett and others, including Adonis, continued to make, right up to the last minute. Often we had to square circles and make judgements because the text was due at the printers the following morning.

The most challenging aspect of preparing the draft was to square Blair's desire to state clearly that for secondary education we were now moving to 'a post-comprehensive era' with Blunkett's caution that this would lead to a huge, unnecessary row with teachers and the Labour Party in the run-up to a general election. I was summoned over to No. 10 several times to try to draft our way through this, but none of it mattered in the end, because on the day of the launch, Alastair Campbell said the Green Paper marked the end of 'the bog-standard comprehensive' and the row erupted anyway. Looking back, I think it turned out to be true that February 2001 did mark the end of 'the bog-standard comprehensive', and almost everyone is pleased about it. I certainly am. Still, it is a bizarre but well-established rule of Labour Party politics that you cannot pre-empt the inevitable without upsetting the apple cart, and this is what Campbell had done.

Then the election campaign took over. Increasingly, my thoughts were devoted to the design and potential of a Delivery Unit, as the next chapter recounts. The four years in education had been extraordinary. There had been plenty of errors, to be sure, but we had changed the educational landscape irrevocably for the better. Blair wrote a letter to all the staff of the Standards and Effectiveness Unit: 'Your contribution to delivering our objectives as a government has been outstanding . . . you have been true pioneers.'[10]

No doubt this view of our track record was the chief reason why, with the 2001 election campaign out of the way, Tony Blair asked me to set up and run his Delivery Unit.

*

That, then, is what on earth I was doing walking across the Cabinet Room with the dizzying prospect of taking my place in the Prime Minister's chair. I sat down, hoping no one would notice I was trembling.

Section 2

Pursuing delivery

'Between the idea
And the reality
Between the motion
And the act
Falls the Shadow.'

T. S. Eliot, 'The Hollow Men'

2

The mission

> The country has given us a fresh chance but they are deeply
> concerned about the condition of Britain and public services,
> disillusioned with politics and insistent we deliver. It is all that
> matters.
>
> Private note to colleagues from
Alastair Campbell, 25 July 2001

Origins

On 8 June 2001, a few hours after he had won the landslide election
victory that gave him a second term, Tony Blair told the British people
that he interpreted the election result as a 'mandate for reform . . . an
instruction to deliver'. The *Daily Mirror*, one of Britain's best-selling
tabloids, summed up the feeling of the country in its front-page banner
headline: 'GET BACK TO WORK'.

A few days later I received a call from the Prime Minister's principal
private secretary, Jeremy Heywood, to tell me the PM had confirmed
that he wanted me to establish and lead a Delivery Unit, responsible for
ensuring the delivery of the Prime Minister's public service priorities.

'On the conditions we agreed?' I asked sharply.

'What conditions?' Heywood replied, stiffening and perhaps expecting an impossible salary demand.

'An office in No. 10 and answering direct to Blair,' I said.

He relaxed. This was no problem.

The following week, I was ushered in to see the Prime Minister
himself to confirm the proposal. He didn't put it this way, but I felt at
that moment that the 'instruction to deliver' he believed the electorate
had given him was now being transferred to me. I had one question for
him above all: would he give the Delivery Unit and its agenda sustained
personal commitment? I gave him the example of Sir Derek Rayner's

reviews of departments in the 1980s, in which Margaret Thatcher had always taken a close personal interest. Blair readily agreed. Immediately afterwards I was shown to the small, slightly shabby office a few yards away from Blair's that would be mine. Having read that, in the White House, status was in direct proportion to the proximity of your office to the President's, I had no complaints.*

A day or two later, my appointment was made public: 'School standards chief to beef up Whitehall,' said the *Times* (22 June 2001). Meanwhile, David Blunkett, the new Home Secretary, with whom I had worked so closely for the previous four years in the Department for Education, wrote thoughtfully to offer 'heart-felt congratulations . . . I look forward to working with you . . . Try not to give us too hard a time.' The challenge seemed immense, but I never hesitated to seize the opportunity. Reform of Britain's creaking and under-performing public services was something I believed in passionately. Significantly improving them could make a real difference to millions of people.

I felt that the moment was a tipping point in British politics: either we would prove that investing taxpayers' hard-earned money in the public services demonstrably resulted in a better society, as I hoped, or we would find ourselves, whether we liked it or not, heading towards a situation where the wealthy opted out of common provision and the public services increasingly became a shabby last resort for those who could not afford anything better. Moreover, the school reforms Blunkett and I had been responsible for implementing in the previous parliament were seen both by Blair and by the public as the government's most conspicuous delivery success. Though at the time I thought no job could possibly match the one I'd had in Education, I relished the opportunity to refine and then apply the lessons learnt from education reform to other areas of public service.

I was in any case hoist by my own petard. For the previous year or more, I had been telling Blair's key advisers, such as David Miliband, that they didn't ask me the right questions. When they spoke to me about education policy, it was usually to press me for new and bolder ideas. No harm in that, of course, but I used to say to them, 'Why don't

---

*I discovered over time that this was not true in No. 10, and a year or so later happily gave up this little office.

you also ask me whether we have implemented existing policy effectively and whether it is making a real difference on the ground?' My questioning struck a chord inside No. 10 because the Prime Minister and his closest advisers were themselves frustrated by the lack of progress on public service reform. Blair and his team had arrived in power with a tremendous track record of political campaigning but minimal experience of delivering large-scale change. Apart from a political party, Blair had no experience of running large organisations, unlike any other Prime Minister since the war. They assumed that the techniques which had brought their stunning electoral triumph of May 1997 would serve them well in government too, and for much of the first year that appeared to be true. Meanwhile, they were learning about the nature of the civil service machine. Naturally enough after eighteen years of Conservative rule, the new Labour team expected to find a Thatcherite bias against them. Indeed, historically, the Labour Party had assumed that senior civil servants were part of the establishment and therefore not to be trusted. In fact this suspicion proved unfounded – which was a pleasant surprise. What we had found in the Department for Education was mirrored across Whitehall: on the whole civil servants welcomed a government with real authority and direction, not least because both these had been lacking in the last year or two of the spent Major government. So, where direction was clarified – as in Education under Blunkett or the Treasury under Gordon Brown – the civil servants were highly motivated. Where political leadership was lacking – as in Social Security – motivation was, of course, less evident.

In the Education Department in the first term we also benefited from the restless excellence of the permanent secretary, Michael Bichard, at the time a rare mandarin who had delivered operational results outside Whitehall, both in local government and at the Benefits Agency. Too much of Whitehall lacked such leadership, and had little grasp of what successful delivery required in practice. The discovery that this was so was a less pleasant surprise for Blair and his colleagues. Indeed, the failure to grasp the need for radical reform of the civil service in the first term was a mistake which Blair himself came to realise had cost him dearly. The White Paper *Modernising Government* published in 2000 was platitudinous and lacked real bite.

Alongside this weakness, attempts to achieve political grip through the Cabinet Office were also of doubtful effectiveness. Ministers there in the first term, such as Peter Mandelson and Charlie Falconer, undoubtedly had influence through their relationships with the Prime Minister and strengthened co-ordination, but the idea of the Cabinet Office as the 'enforcer' of the Prime Minister's will across government failed. In the summer of 1998, in Blair's first major reshuffle, Jack Cunningham was appointed to the Cabinet Office with an explicit mission to be the 'enforcer', but had minimal impact. Mo Mowlam, coming to the Cabinet Office with a similar mission after her exertions in Northern Ireland, was no more effective.

With an unreformed civil service, and a lack of capacity to enforce his political will, no wonder Blair felt the frustration he expressed in his famous 'scars on my back' speech of July 1999. In spite of the overwhelming mandate the election had given him, and his – at that point – almost complete mastery of the political scene, he had discovered not just the weakness of the levers he controlled, but also the lengths to which leaders of the public service workforce will go to defend the status quo, even, perversely, when the status quo is manifestly inadequate. Hence his remarks to the Venture Capital Association:

> You try getting change in the public sector and the public services. I bear the scars on my back after two years in government and heaven knows what it will be like after a bit longer. People in the public sector [are] more rooted in the concept that 'if it has always been done this way, it must always be done this way' than any group of people I have come across.[1]

The remarks caused controversy at the time and, among public service union leaders, outrage. How dare a Prime Minister be so critical of the workforce they claimed to represent? Received wisdom became that the Prime Minister had made 'a gaffe'. Perhaps, seen objectively, it was, but my own reaction at the time – when I was deeply engaged in driving through the government's literacy and numeracy programmes and its tough approach to tackling school failure – ran counter to most people's views. First of all, I thought the Prime Minister had hit the nail on the head. At the frontline of his public service reforms, that was exactly how it felt to me at the time. Secondly – and this is crucial to the origins of the Delivery Unit – it was evidence of the Prime Minister learning the hard lessons about the messy, complex and always controversial task of really getting something done. 'Spin' was not the answer.

The winter of 1999–2000, with its flu epidemic and massive controversy over the state of the Health Service, reinforced these lessons. The combination of radical reform and serious investment which has underpinned Blair's approach to health ever since was the result. In Alan Milburn, appointed Secretary of State for Health just months before the crisis broke, Blair found an ally who had the intellectual rigour and political toughness to take the ambitious agenda forward and break the producer stranglehold. As Peter Riddell has written, 'a clear "narrative" or strategy did emerge after 2000, a recognisably social democratic one: the belief that active government backed by rising public spending was necessary to address Britain's problems and to improve public services.'[2]

Once this strategy (which emerged in the NHS ten-year plan published in 2000) was applied more generally to the public services in the spending review of the same year, the need for both effective enforcement of the Prime Minister's programme and a competent civil service became more starkly apparent than ever. In short, by 2000 it was clear to Blair that in relation to the public services – the reform of which has always been central to his mission – he had to deliver or die. Riddell went on to say: 'It was in this period that Blair's advisers, particularly David Miliband in the Policy Unit, were persuaded that the government needed to concentrate more on the practicalities of delivering on their targets, rather than an endless stream of new initiatives.'[3] My own experience confirms Riddell's claim, as Miliband began to send officials from other departments to come and see me in the Education Department, where I offered them the policy equivalent of psychoanalysis.

Out of this experience came discussion about the creation of something like a Delivery Unit. A few weeks before the election, following a conversation I had with Miliband, Jeremy Heywood invited me to write them a paper about how a Delivery Unit might work. This paper became the text for conversations first with Heywood himself, and then with Jonathan Powell, Blair's chief of staff, and Sir Richard Wilson, the Cabinet Secretary. Now I had formally been asked to establish the Delivery Unit, this paper became the design brief. It included two intellectual breakthroughs which, with hindsight, can only be called blinding flashes of the obvious.

First, rather than design a Delivery Unit which checked up on the implementation of all domestic policy, the paper suggested a rigorous and relentless focus on a relatively small number of the Prime Minister's key priorities. This tighter focus brought vital benefits. It required the Prime Minister and government to identify – and stick to – a set of priorities, something which had not happened either in Blair's first term or in many previous governments. It also meant the Delivery Unit could be small and flexible and avoid becoming a big bureaucracy overseeing an even bigger bureaucracy, which would risk Kafka-esque absurdity.

Second, the paper proposed tying the Prime Minister's time to these priorities by organising a series of stocktake meetings on a two- to three-month cycle. Here, the relevant ministers would be required to account for the progress they had made on the chosen priorities. The Prime Minister's time is the most precious resource in Whitehall, and the stocktakes, an idea which the Prime Minister welcomed when he asked me to set up the unit, made sure that the delivery agenda secured significant chunks of that resource. For the ministers involved, while they obviously implied a threat, the stocktakes also provided an opportunity to explain, discuss, resolve, engage and/or enlist the Prime Minister in their agenda. Cabinet ministers have regular access to the PM, of course, but most junior ministers outside the Cabinet relished the opportunity to bring their work before him – promotion might depend on it. Here, in short, was a sketch of how the 'enforcer' role – though without the name – might be carried out effectively.

Priorities

So when I accepted – with alacrity – the invitation to set up the Delivery Unit and take on the 'enforcer' role, I had both an opportunity and a design brief. There was no disguising the fact that, at the same time, it involved a huge risk. At the most basic level, there was no Delivery Unit to inherit, so the people would have to be found, the methodologies invented, the processes designed and the relationships established. The design brief, after all, was sketchy. It was one thing to suggest priorities, but quite another to decide what they should be. And yet everyone, not least the Prime Minister himself, was in a hurry. At one of my first meetings with him in my new role, he agreed he wanted reform to be 'more radical, more urgent and more comprehensive', but at that time I had no staff and only the vaguest idea what to do!

We established the priorities in a series of meetings in late June and early July 2001. The first of these took place in brilliant sunshine on the terrace outside the Cabinet Room. As ever, tea arrived on a silver tray. In addition to Blair and myself, about half a dozen of Blair's policy team were there. We were already agreed that the departments to focus on were Health, Education, Transport and the Home Office, and no others. What Blair made clear in this meeting, however, was that he also wanted to narrow the focus within each departmental area: 'I want the Delivery Unit focused on issues of real salience . . . for example, in transport, I only want Michael to sort out the railways.' In fact, at that stage the Prime Minister's determination to narrow the focus – reinforced strongly by Alastair Campbell – was such that I was worried our scope would be too limited, but over time this rigorous prioritisation was completely vindicated. The list of delivery priorities, after all, is hardly a walk in the park (see Table 2.1).

Armed with the agenda that emerged from this and other conversations with the No. 10 entourage, I talked the whole picture through with Lord (Gus) Macdonald, the minister for the Cabinet Office who had been given responsibility for day-to-day oversight of the Delivery Unit. He combined a background in business with a long career in Labour circles, and proved to be a sterling ally of the unit in ensuring it had freedom to operate and the necessary relationships with key figures such as John Prescott, the Deputy Prime Minister. We ended up with a list that changed to a degree over the four years of the parliament, but the core of which was a selection from the government's existing targets (see Table 2.1; see also Delivery Manual, Document 10 for the progress made by 2005 on the targets listed).

For each of these aspects there were a series of criteria or sub-targets which, if met, would represent success. On hospital waiting times, for example, a maximum wait of six months was set for non-emergency surgery, as well as a maximum four-hour wait for people to be seen, treated and either admitted to hospital if necessary or discharged by

Accident and Emergency departments. Most of these specific targets were taken from either the 2001 manifesto or the government targets published the previous year at the time of the spending review. Their importance lay in the fact that they translated airy aspirations into specific measurable commitments.*

Table 2.1: Delivery priorities

Department	Delivery Unit priorities
Health	Heart disease mortality
	Cancer mortality
	Waiting lists
	Waiting times
	Accident & Emergency
Education	Literacy and numeracy at 11
	Maths and English at 14
	5+ A*–C GCSEs
	Truancy
Home Office	Overall crime and breakdowns by type
	Likelihood of being a victim
	Offenders brought to justice
Transport	Road congestion
	Rail punctuality

I then opened up negotiations with the relevant Cabinet ministers, their departments and the Treasury. I also had to create space for the Delivery Unit within the Cabinet Office, where, to put it bluntly, there were rivals such as the newly established Office of Public Service Reform, which potentially had an overlapping agenda. Macdonald proved to be a powerful ally here too, both acting as 'traffic cop', to use his phrase, and keeping intruders out of the Delivery Unit's way.

The process of establishing this myriad of relationships was perhaps

---

*In the first year there were one or two goals such as higher education reform where it turned out we were unable to make much impact because the policy wasn't settled. We dropped these in 2002. We reviewed what was in and out of the Delivery Unit portfolio annually with the Prime Minister.

the greatest risk of all. The first threat was what might be called the 'meetings quagmire'. 'Delivery' had become the buzzword of the moment, so everyone wanted the head of the Delivery Unit at their meetings and everyone wanted to contribute to the delivery agenda, creating the phenomenon my friend Michael Fullan calls 'the helping hand strikes again'. After I'd been in the job a week, I told the PM that I could easily spend my entire life liaising with people in meetings, rather than actually getting anything done. I asked him for his backing in ignoring much of this official machinery so I could focus my attention on the departments whose actions would make or break delivery. 'That's absolutely right,' he commented, 'you must.' After a few months I began to realise which meetings I had to be at either to defend my corner or to make sure I was visible – and which meetings were simply bureaucratic process.

I also picked out which people mattered most in No. 10 and elsewhere. In short, I began to manage the Delivery Unit brand and work out for each of the key relationships what the 'deal' was. For each of these relationships – to put it in *Monty Python* terms – I wanted to be able to answer the question: 'What will the Delivery Unit ever do for us?' Eventually, when the Delivery Unit model had become internationally renowned, our discussions with other governments or organisations such as the World Bank tended to focus on the techniques we had developed and applied. These were, and remain, extremely important, but it is worth pointing out up front that unless we had worked out early on how we would make each of our key relationships a 'win-win' – to use current jargon – we would never have been given the chance to develop the techniques at all.* We could so easily have been sunk without trace or relegated to a bureaucratic backwater with a suite of offices, a budget, a myriad of meetings to attend and papers to write, but no influence whatsoever. This is, after all, the normal fate of new units within Whitehall, once they have ceased to be flavour of the month.

---

* The grandest and most profound statement of this insight was Franklin Roosevelt's shortly before his untimely death: 'Today we are faced with the pre-eminent fact that, if civilisation is to survive, we must cultivate the science of human relationships.' (Quoted in Jon Meacham, *Franklin and Winston: An Intimate Portrait of an Epic Friendship* (New York: Random House, 2003), p. 367.)

Key relationships

The Prime Minister

The first and most central relationship was, of course, with the Prime Minister himself. The win-win here was straightforward. I needed him to give me access, sustained focus, consistent backing and the influence that unlocks Whitehall. In return, I would make sure I only demanded access when I really needed it, would never waste his time and, above all, would remain relentlessly focused on delivering his key priorities all day, every day, whatever demands his office made of him from time to time. For a Prime Minister who, for good or ill, was to devote so much time to foreign policy from 2001 onwards, my commitments to him were vitally important. Moreover, given the Prime Minister's lack of departmental experience and his lack of knowledge of (and sometimes interest in) what delivery takes, he had little choice but to trust the operational details to me in order to reap the gains.

Prime Ministerial backing certainly opens all the doors and ensures all the phones are answered when you call. It was not an accident that we made a point – at the insistence initially of Kate Myronidis in my office – of always describing ourselves as the 'Prime Minister's Delivery Unit'. But, as with all truly precious resources, you have to use prime ministerial influence carefully, wisely and sparingly. In the end, once the door is open or the phone answered, it's what you say and how you say it that counts. As I used to tell my staff, 'the PMDU brand will get you through the door; after that, you're on your own'.* If you overplay your hand, you sound arrogant; if you make unreasonable demands, you weaken yourself for the next time; if you claim to speak for the Prime Minister on an issue but don't really, you risk ridicule; and if you are rude, aggressive or ill informed, you bring the Prime Minister himself into disrepute. Worse still, if you persistently do any or all of these things, in the rumour mill that is government the world over, the word soon gets back to the man himself. And if he loses confidence in you or your unit, the game is up. A central theme throughout this book is prime ministerial power and how to make the most of it; the key, I believe, is

*Prime Minister Clement Attlee's advice to Jim Callaghan on his appointment as a minister is the classic text on this subject: 'If you are going to negotiate with someone tomorrow, don't insult him today.' (Quoted in Peter Hennessy, *The Prime Minister: The Office and Its Holders since 1945* (London: Allen Lane, 2000), p. 150.)

to act on his behalf with humility, persistence, insight and a mastery of the facts.* One of the aspects of the Delivery Unit of which I'm proudest is that just before I left, the Prime Minister told me he had never received a single complaint about it. This was because we saw the Prime Minister's influence as our greatest asset, and rather than spending it, we invested it.

No. 10

The second set of key relationships was with the Prime Minister's people – the ones who see him day in, day out: people such as Sally Morgan, who advised on political management; Alastair Campbell and (later) David Hill, who dealt with the insatiable demands of the media; Jeremy Heywood and (later) Ivan Rogers, who ran his office; Jonathan Powell, his chief of staff; Peter Hyman, his speechwriter and confidant; and Katie Kay, the Prime Minister's diary secretary. These people were very talented, intensely loyal and quick to judge. When a Prime Minister reflects aloud or has a question to which he requires an instant response, inevitably he asks the trusted person closest to him – and during the time I was in No. 10 the chances were it would have been one of the charmed handful just mentioned. So I asked myself the question, 'If the PM asked any of them what they thought about the Delivery Unit and its work, what would they say?' I then sought to influence the way they would answer. Worse than 'It upsets people', I thought, would be 'We don't even notice it' or 'Michael who?'. I therefore made it my business to speak to each of them regularly, to copy them in on my notes to the PM and to attend meetings where several of them would be, even if slightly off my agenda. Though my staff were on the other side of Whitehall in those early days, I always spent some time each day in my little No. 10 office. Throughout my time as head of the Delivery Unit, I spent much of my day tramping around Whitehall and, even if it was sometimes a slightly longer way round, I used to pass through No. 10 on the off-chance of running into one of these characters. And since they were

---

*It has to be admitted that if you work for the Prime Minister – to paraphrase Theodore Roosevelt – even if you speak softly, you do carry a big stick. When Peter Hyman, Tony Blair's former speechwriter, left No. 10, he gave me Razor Smith's book *A Few Kind Words and a Loaded Gun*, whose title was based on a quote by Al Capone, 'Sometimes you can get more with a few kind words and a loaded gun than you can with just a few kind words.' I often wondered what Hyman was trying to tell me.

inevitably in a hurry, I would try to have one piece of positive news about Delivery Unit impact on the tip of my tongue so I could say it in a moment and then we'd both go about our business. Sometimes I was lucky enough to run into the Prime Minister himself. Hyman, in particular, became a good friend. He was full of ideas, intensely optimistic, and very passionate about the New Labour cause. Also, he had always just read something interesting – history, current affairs, a speech or even a business/leadership book – and asked questions that never failed to make me think.

Just as important for the Delivery Unit as these central figures in the Prime Minister's life was the Policy Directorate, made up of political appointees working on the aspects of policy where the Delivery Unit was also involved. For example, Simon Stevens and later Julian Le Grand (who led for the PM on health) or Andrew Adonis (on education) were extremely talented and hugely influential. I had to ensure at all times that the Delivery Unit understood where policy was going and was aligned. Our credibility would soon have been undermined if we had been conveying one message to departmental colleagues while they received another from the Policy Directorate. Soon after I had been appointed, David Miliband, newly elected to Parliament and not yet a minister, told me a cautionary tale about the Clinton administration, which he knew well: in Washington under Clinton, he said, when you called someone and announced you were 'from the White House', the reply invariably came back, 'Which part?' This was a fate I was determined to avoid. As a result, I urged my staff to stay close to their counterparts in the Policy Directorate, to keep them informed and to see them as powerful allies. The central point was this: delivery and policy are integrally related and neither can be fully successful unless both are firmly rooted, formally and informally, in the power structure of the organisation.

At the beginning, I invested a great deal of personal time in these relationships. In 2001 it was still the case that the deadline for the Prime Minister's weekend box was Friday evening (later it was sensibly brought forward to midday), so I discovered that if I wandered around the upper floors of No. 10 at about 6.00 p.m. on a Friday I could catch up with all the Policy Directorate people furiously writing notes to the PM for that weekend. Normally I didn't have a specific agenda – I just wanted to be sure we were all in touch and if there was no need to discuss policy, the weekend's Premiership fixtures were a good substitute. In any case, it helped me keep in the loop.

As I said to my staff in a reflective note towards the end of my time in the Delivery Unit, around a Prime Minister, or indeed anyone really powerful, there is a vortex, and the nearer you get to the centre of the vortex,

> the less space and time there is. The moment you step away, the space is filled, so no one notices you've gone . . . This is not a bad thing. It's how it has to be . . . In short, you have to have a strategy for being noticed or you will get marginalised. There is nothing in between.

This is only a slight exaggeration. Once the Delivery Unit came through the early months, and its brand became valued, life in the vortex got easier, but in the early days of the scramble for influence, I often found myself whirling around No. 10, quashing a rumour, apologising quickly for a blunder, volunteering a proposal or simply making sure I was being noticed . . . and never being defensive, whingey or long-winded, characteristics which guarantee no one wants to see you at all. It helped of course that I liked the people who worked for Blair, and even when the press was reporting a 'bunker mentality' in No. 10, the reality was a strong, positive team working for a common purpose. In his marvellous book on four years as Clinton's Labour Secretary, Robert Reich describes how, on some occasions, he resorted to hanging around in the White House car park to pick up the snippets of gossip that would keep him in the loop.[4] By unobtrusively but persistently passing through the vortex, I avoided his fate, but I know how he felt.

The Treasury

The third crucial relationship was with the Treasury. In the previous parliament, the Treasury, led by its powerful Chancellor, Gordon Brown, had been hugely successful in giving control of interest rates to the Bank of England, sustaining economic growth in spite of various challenges to the global economy, paying off some of Britain's debts and steadily, from 1999 onwards, beginning to release substantial investment for the country's ailing public services. Moreover, it had introduced a new framework for public expenditure which was a major step forward. Instead of the annual expenditure round, which had dominated Whitehall for as long as anyone could remember (and which is still the norm in most countries), the Treasury had introduced a spending review process that allocated funds for three years and renegotiated these allocations every two years. Crucially, from the point of view of the Delivery Unit, it had also introduced the concept of Public Service Agreement (PSA) targets – the published outcomes, department by department, which the government was committed to delivering in return for the public money it was spending. Given the political risks of not meeting targets (interpreted in some quarters as not fulfilling a promise), this was a bold and risk-laden innovation.

When the Delivery Unit was established, the Treasury, with 200 years of history and a strong recent track record, was naturally suspicious of this new kid on the block who might threaten its hard-won, functioning framework in two important ways. First, departments might see the Delivery Unit as an alternative means of lobbying for extra public money – they might argue, for example, that a given prime ministerial priority could not be achieved with the funds the Treasury had allocated to them. Then, the fear not irrationally ran, the Delivery Unit would lobby the PM and the PM would lobby the Chancellor. If this came to pass, the new discipline established over public expenditure would dissolve. I quickly quashed the Treasury's fears greatly to their satisfaction: we simply built into the DNA of the Delivery Unit the assumption, however unreasonable it might have sometimes appeared, that the allocated funds were always sufficient. If a department disagreed, we sent them to the Treasury.

The second fear was that the prime ministerial priorities we were in the process of agreeing with departments would cut across, distract from or even conflict with their PSA targets. Had that occurred, the government's goals, instead of becoming clearer, would have become more confused. To assuage this fear, we in the new Delivery Unit spent several long meetings with Treasury officials and Ed Balls (the brilliant chief economic adviser who was Brown's right-hand man and later became an MP and minister), ensuring that the Prime Minister's new priorities and the PSA targets published in 2000 were brought into alignment. Indeed, the PSA targets became the basis of our work. The only additions we proposed were either contained in departmental ten-year strategies published after the 2000 PSA targets or in manifesto pledges from the election campaign that had just finished, and, of course, the Treasury was as committed to those as it was to the PSA targets.

The Treasury is always tough to negotiate with – a necessary part of the culture of a treasury anywhere in the world – but we hammered out, for each of the departments the Delivery Unit was to work with, an agreed delivery contract, which set out both the prime ministerial priorities to which the department was committing and the measurable outcomes which would show whether or not they were on track to achieve them. These were then cleared by the Prime Minister, whose general approach was to reduce the number of priorities and simplify the targets; and by the Chancellor, who accepted them once his justifiable concerns had been addressed.

From that moment on, the Treasury became a firm ally of the Delivery Unit. Nick Macpherson, then in charge of public expenditure, later the permanent secretary of the Treasury, was unwavering in his commitment to it. His quirky humour turned out to be combined with a flair for management and the necessary hard edge to get things done. The working relationship we established between us was not only mutually beneficial, it also assisted government departments because a common process (and language) for public expenditure, targets and delivery emerged. The centre of government was doing something it was not famed for – singing from a single song sheet. In 2002, when refined PSA targets were negotiated as part of the spending review that year, the alignment achieved in 2001 was completed.

From the Treasury's point of view, the deal was a huge gain. It had developed an advanced new framework, admired elsewhere in the world, which linked public expenditure to published outcomes. The Delivery Unit would now design a system to ensure that departments really did turn the money into outcomes rather than, as happened with much of the money allocated in the 1998 spending review, have it simply disappearing into a departmental black hole and, too late, the Prime Minister and Chancellor discovering that not enough had actually happened. For this reason too, once we were established, the Treasury asked us to help train its staff who were monitoring progress on those PSA targets which were not among the Prime Minister's priorities, but still represented outcomes for which large sums of money had been allocated.

For the Delivery Unit the deal was pure gain too. With the Treasury as an ally, we seemed to speak not just for the Prime Minister, but also for the Chancellor. This appearance was strengthened in early 2003 when the Delivery Unit staff moved from its shabby, temporary accommodation (above a café called Churchills and next door to the Red Lion pub) into the newly refurbished Treasury building, where we occupied the suite of offices directly under the Chancellor's, over-looking St James's Park. From a brand management point of view, being the Prime Minister's people operating from these particular offices could not have been bettered. Working so closely and informally alongside the officials responsible for public expenditure was a major benefit too, while the opportunity to run into Brown in the Treasury canteen provided further 'chance' opportunities for me to 'manage the brand'. Gus O'Donnell, then permanent secretary of the Treasury (and later Cabinet Secretary) was a strong supporter of our relationship with the Treasury and took every opportunity to strengthen it.

In addition, it was a positive blessing to be able to make it clear to departments that we wouldn't discuss money with them. Once we had been firm on this for a few weeks, departmental representatives didn't even try. As a departmental official, when you visit the Treasury (as I had often done for the DfEE), your mindset, whatever the ostensible purpose of the meeting, is to convince them that you need or could use more money – so you tailor your contribution to that end. Treasury officials know this, of course, so they factor it into their thinking and practise saying 'no' in their spare time. (Just as Inuit people have many ways of saying 'snow', so Treasury people have many ways of saying 'no'.) The result is that in a meeting with the Treasury, there are often two conversations going on at once: the explicit and less important one relating to the formal agenda, and the implicit and more important one in which the departmental representatives are seeking to convince the Treasury that they really do deserve more money. By contrast, departmental officials in discussion with the Delivery Unit, knowing that money was an impermissible subject, expected and got an honest conversation about performance. Somehow the fact that we in the Delivery Unit were in constant dialogue with Treasury colleagues in the same building made no difference to this. It was a matter of perception.

Cabinet ministers

The fourth relationship on which a great deal depended was with the Cabinet ministers of the departments on the Delivery Unit agenda. The suspicions they might have had of this new agent of the Prime Minister are obvious – and unless allayed could have proved fatal. For a Cabinet minister, a direct relationship with the Prime Minister is central; they certainly wouldn't welcome anyone, least of all a bunch of technocrats, getting in the way. Also Cabinet ministers rightly think their job is to run a department; what are they going to think if they find a Delivery Unit, on behalf of the PM, marching through their department issuing instructions? And most sensitively of all, Cabinet ministers depend for their tenure on the PM's confidence in them – a Delivery Unit checking up on their performance and reporting secretly back to the PM sounds like the stuff of nightmares. Perceptions of this threat were perhaps heightened by the well-documented fact that, in his first term, Blair had done little to develop the Cabinet as a collective entity and had dealt bilaterally with each Cabinet minister.

With Gus Macdonald's help, I had to tackle these fears at the outset and put in their place a mutually beneficial working relationship. It helped that at the beginning I knew each of the four key ministers reasonably well. David Blunkett (the new Home Secretary), Estelle Morris (the new Education Secretary) and Stephen Byers (the new Transport and Local Government Secretary) had all been at the Department for Education for some or all of the previous parliament, and we'd been through tough times and good times together. Alan Milburn, at Health, and I had discussed reform strategy occasionally in the previous parliament. So in each case there was a foundation to build on. I also worked hard to build effective relationships with the relevant special advisers. For example, in the case of Milburn, the Cabinet minister whom I knew the least, I was fortunate that his special adviser, Paul Corrigan, was someone I had worked with in the early 1990s and knew well. There were times when a quick conversation with Corrigan could save many hours of meetings and official briefings. So knowing people helped, but the key to this relationship, as with others, was to create the win-win deal.

The proposition I put to Cabinet ministers was, in effect: 'You and the Prime Minister are agreed about the priorities for your department during the course of this parliament, and the entire government knows its success depends on them; the task of the Delivery Unit is to help you get your bureaucracy to deliver these priorities . . . Furthermore, while I do want access when required, I will never waste your precious time . . . I'll share with you what I share with the Prime Minister . . . and above all, if as a result of our collaboration a problem is solved or a success delivered, we, the Delivery Unit, don't want any credit.' Essentially this deal, received with varying degrees of scepticism but largely positively at the outset, stuck through the parliament and all the inevitable ministerial resignations and reshuffles. The quality of my relationships with the various Cabinet ministers I dealt with naturally varied, but only between cordial at worst and excellent at best. One can be sure that characters such as David Blunkett or Charles Clarke (not to mention John Prescott or Gordon Brown) would have given us short shrift if we upset them, but they never did. Of course, their knowledge that the Prime Minister strongly supported the Delivery Unit might have deterred them from comment for a while. On the other hand, I knew that the reverse was always a possibility too, and that the Prime Minister's confidence in us would have fallen away if we had kept landing him in uncomfortable conversations with his senior Cabinet colleagues. The effect of this might not have destroyed us, but would certainly have marginalised us.

The biggest threat of all to this set of relationships, I was well aware, was leaks. Nothing is more likely to upset a minister than being caught on the hop by the media. By definition, the material the Delivery Unit generated for the Prime Minister was extremely sensitive since it commented unsparingly on departmental performance; it sought to provide explanations for underperformance and suggestions for solving problems. In effect it was performing for the Prime Minister the internal performance management function of a large company. Many of the conclusions we reached were dynamite. So, from the outset, I was determined to avoid 'becoming the story' or even to do off-the-record briefings for journalists, except on the rare occasions when the No. 10 press office recommended it. This way, the ministers' relationship with the media – always delicate – would not be upset by the Delivery Unit. When the two leaks in four years did occur, they powerfully reinforced my gut caution.

The mandarin class

The final relationship vital to our success was with the 'mandarinate' –

especially the Cabinet Secretary and the four permanent secretaries who ran the departments we were to work with. To most civil servants in Whitehall, permanent secretaries, and even more so the Cabinet Secretary, who is also head of the civil service, are distant figures who have attained dizzying heights in the hierarchy and whose quiet influence is legendary. The extraordinary worldwide success of TV's *Yes, Minister* has given them an almost mythical status in the public eye. Among their many subtle skills is the ability, with the merest twitch of their collective muscle, to see off central units set up by Prime Ministers to improve departmental performance. One way to do so, for example (which some departments tried with us for a while), is simply not to share information. The result can then be a long bureaucratic war of attrition, in which the energies of the tiny unit are sapped while the departmental monolith is barely affected. From a permanent secretary's point of view, central units, such as the Delivery Unit, are irritants that come and go; the enduring issues for them are their relationships with whoever is secretary of state, and the defence of their department's interests over the long term.

I began with the Cabinet Secretary himself, Sir Richard Wilson. He had been tremendously supportive of the idea of a Delivery Unit since before the election; he respected my track record in the Department for Education and knew that I had built good working relationships with civil servants. He had also seen me in action in some of David Blunkett's meetings with Blair on education policy. If I could build on this foundation and secure his full support, I thought I would have a chance of building good relations with his colleagues, the permanent secretaries. I knew I would at some point upset one, perhaps all, of them, and that they would then go privately to Wilson to complain. When that happened, I wanted him to be as robust as possible in my defence and also to give me an inkling of the content of the conversation. So I kept Wilson fully informed, copied him in on (almost) all my notes to the Prime Minister and gave him credit not only for the Delivery Unit's achievements, but also for its very existence. I had had a conversation with him before the election in which (prompted by Jeremy Heywood, I think) he asked me to offer him some private advice on his idea of a Delivery Unit and how it might work. I promised him a paper within a few days, without revealing either my conversations with No. 10 or the fact that I already had in my briefcase beside my chair my draft paper on exactly these lines which I had already discussed with the Prime Minister's people. At the time, I thought this was a slightly devious but worthwhile device to get him on board. Later, it occurred to me that perhaps it was he who had manipulated me as a pawn in his game, rather than the other way around.

Either way, it worked. Ideas often fail in Whitehall – and many other places – because of the nefarious impact of the 'not invented here' syndrome. Looking back, part of the success of the Delivery Unit might perhaps be attributed to the much less well-known positive equivalent, the 'invented by everyone who matters' syndrome. Tony Blair and Wilson, along with Heywood, David Miliband, Jonathan Powell and others (I include myself) all thought they were the inspiration behind the Delivery Unit and no doubt they all – admittedly some more circuitously than others – really were.

Once in post, I had regular meetings with Wilson. I made as few demands as possible on him, I shared with him some inside information from No. 10 which oiled the wheels, and I found his support, encouragement and goodwill genuinely helpful. In my first week, for example, he told me: 'This is your moment of power . . . we should nail our colours to the mast and go for it.' I made a point of asking for his advice and listening carefully to it, but I also made a point of not asking his permission, because I wanted as much freedom of manoeuvre as I could lay my hands on, and to be accountable directly to Blair and, as far as possible, no one else. Once we began to roll, the relationship was exactly as I wanted it – one of 'benign neglect' most of the time, but actively supportive where I needed it to be. In return I was more than happy for him to take credit for our success. The truth is that, for most of history, the Cabinet Secretary's time has been swallowed up by a perverse combination of routine and crisis, so if you successfully get on with your job and don't bother them, they won't bother you.

Given the nature of my commitment to the Prime Minister and the deal with Cabinet ministers, it was clear to me that, even with Wilson in support, I had to find a way to defy historical precedent and build a productive, enduring relationship with the permanent secretaries and their top teams too. Since previous units had almost always been seen off, the logical way to achieve this goal, I decided, was to work out roughly what units had done in the past and do the opposite. I had some direct experience because in my time at the DfEE the Regulatory Impact

Unit had intervened to try to get me to reduce the bureaucracy in the school reforms. Reducing bureaucracy was indeed necessary, but what the RIU actually did was send people who knew nothing about education policy (the kind of people Nigel Lawson might have dismissed as 'teenage scribblers') and had consulted a couple of union representatives, to ask me to take the pressure off teachers! No chance. Conceptually, they were unable to distinguish between pressure and bureaucracy. In the end I discovered I could save myself a lot of trouble by not answering their calls.

David Normington, newly appointed permanent secretary at the Department for Education and a close colleague for three years in my time there, told me on the day I was appointed head of the Delivery Unit that I could find the new unit 'shunned by the Treasury, separated from Blair by the Policy Unit and institutionally resisted by the departments. It would be buried.' The evidence supported him. So, with the permanent secretaries, I exploited the element of surprise. Most units start as flavour of the month, get steadily bigger and become permanent – and at the same time their influence fades and they become marginal. To defy this trajectory I decided we would stay small, stay influential and seek to abolish ourselves after three or four years – and I said so to the permanent secretaries. In fact I was ushered to an awayday of the permanent secretaries on my first day in post and it was in a spontaneous answer to a question there that I set a cap on our size which I stuck to throughout the next four years. After stumbling through my presentation, somewhat daunted by the audience, I was asked rather imperiously by one of them: 'To the nearest hundred,' – contemptuous smile – 'how many staff are you planning to have?'

I took my chance. 'To the nearest hundred,' I replied, 'none.'

From then on I was committed to a maximum of forty-nine, but in fact kept it at around thirty-five to forty. This was a happy number.* We could all fit in one room so everyone could easily keep well informed; I could personally involve myself in the appointment of every single member of staff so I could build a consistent, can-do culture and

* The Central Policy Review Staff under Ted Heath had up to eighteen professional people plus administrative and clerical support; in other words it was a similar size and by all accounts had a similar atmosphere: 'The most enjoyable and exciting two years of my life,' said William Plowden, one of its key members (see Jon Davis, *Prime Ministers and Whitehall 1960–74* (London: Hambledon Continuum, 2007), p. 120).

maintain quality; our budget was limited and flexibility relatively easy to achieve. Of course it wasn't all sweetness and light – we worked under tremendous pressure, especially in the first year – but the quality of our people became renowned across Whitehall. Once the reputation was established, good people wanted to work for us so we could constantly build and enhance the quality. This was, in turn, crucial to the relationship with permanent secretaries. They quickly realised that meetings with the Delivery Unit, while they might be challenging, were nearly always worthwhile.

The second key insight was again based on my experience in education reform. Units in the past had considered their relationships with departments on a linear spectrum with 'hard' at one end and 'soft' at the other. If you're hard you upset people, they thought, so on the whole they were soft. I thought this was a misunderstanding – senior people don't mind being challenged in a tough way as long as the challenge is based on evidence, made by people who know what they're talking about and expressed with due humility. In fact, this kind of conversation is worth giving up time for, whereas a 'soft' conversation with someone ignorant is a waste of time. Put simply, a small number of excellent people is infinitely better than a large number of ordinary people. Being small had other advantages too. It meant our budget was smaller than almost all other units and, since I did not want the Delivery Unit to grow, I did not ask for more money each year. Indeed I strove to underspend and return money wherever I could. I made my budget case on the ratio of the amount spent on the Delivery Unit versus the amount spent on the huge public services we sought to influence; it turned out to be in the order of 1:50,000.

Most crucially, though, we sought to build a unit that did not impose a bureaucratic burden. It would have been disastrous – but not at all unusual at the time – to create a Delivery Unit that got in the way of delivery. So we came up with the idea of a contract with permanent secretaries. At early meetings with each of them, I put the following page of A4 in front of them.

OUR WORKING APPROACH SEEKS TO AVOID
- micro-management
- generating bureaucracy or unnecessary work
- getting in the way

- policy wheezes
- being driven by headlines
- short-termism
- opinion without evidence
- changing the goalposts

OUR APPROACH EMPHASISES
- keeping the PM well informed about his key priorities
- consistent pursuit of those priorities
- data and evidence
- plain speaking
- early identification of problems
- imaginative problem-solving
- application of best practice
- recognising differences as well as similarities between departments
- urgency
- building capacity
- leaving responsibility and credit where they belong
- the expectation of success

I then explained to them that we would live by the second list and that if they came across anything in the first list they should call me and I would stop whatever it was that moment. The first list made them smile because all of those behaviours were familiar to them . . . but not one of them ever felt it necessary to call because we (almost always) lived by our values. There are obvious small ways of doing this. For example, busy people hate meetings that overrun and love meetings that finish early, so I urged Delivery Unit staff to book, say, forty-five minutes but finish in thirty. In my one-to-one meetings with the PM I was usually allocated thirty minutes but I'd finish my business in twenty and only stay if he wanted to extend the conversation. We spent hours in the Delivery Unit preparing ourselves to be effective in short meetings. Add up small things like this and you create a culture of action-orientation, people in a hurry to get things done, a Delivery Unit that contributes to delivery.

*

I have emphasised the building of these key relationships because it was so central to our impact. At the core of the approach is what I think of as resonance; not a new concept, but perhaps a new term for a very old concept. The basic idea is that if you exceed expectations often enough and if you sometimes surprise and delight people, they start to mention it to each other, word gets back to the Prime Minister and you create a climate of success. As I put it in the leaving note to my staff:

> I've often conceptualised my job as managing the frontiers – making sure that in No. 10, the Treasury, the Cabinet Office and generally among the political classes we are trusted so that everyone in the unit can get on with their job. As trust in and respect for the brand increases, each member of staff is quite literally able to add more value because departments are more receptive . . . [After I've left] you will need to invest in the brand all the time . . . Being associated with 'can-do', 'success' and 'quality' will all be crucial.

Creating the climate provides the opportunity for staff to do their job well, and if they exploit this opportunity, the climate improves further . . . and so on. A harmonious progression – resonance.

*

The frenetic work of establishing the Delivery Unit's existence and credibility culminated in the last week of July, just before the summer recess began and the politicians – exhausted after an election campaign and the whirl of activity that followed it – left London for the Dordogne or Tuscany.

First there was an awayday for Blair's top team at Chequers to clarify the agenda for the second term. Reform of the public services was vigorously discussed. Blair himself emphasised the importance of real choice for patients or parents. He was dismissive of any advice that fell short of his own radicalism. When someone suggested 'preference' might be an easier sell to the unions and the party, he replied simply: 'Choice is choice.' Later he added, presciently as it turned out: 'It's going to be hell for a large part of the time we're doing this . . . [but] I don't see any point in being Prime Minister unless we take risks.' Looking at me across the table, he stressed the importance of making rapid progress. If I had needed reminding of the centrality of delivery to Blair, it could not have been put more clearly.*

Meanwhile, Jeremy Heywood and I had prepared a four-page job description for the Delivery Unit which would become its formal, Cabinet-approved mission statement. We patiently negotiated the detail with the Treasury and the relevant officials and ministers. The Treasury pressed hard and successfully to ensure that the description was consistent with the spending review process and their already-established targets. Cabinet ministers, in their turn, wanted to be clear what their lines of accountability would be.

In the previous parliament, a Cabinet committee chaired by Gordon Brown had been established to oversee public expenditure (PSX). In so far as Cabinet ministers were held accountable for delivering results on their targets, it had been in this forum. Treasury officials produced rather formulaic briefings with questions which were allocated out among Cabinet ministers on the committee, who then quizzed whichever minister and permanent secretary were before them that day. Even if their opening question was good, it rarely flustered the Cabinet minister, who was invariably much better informed than the committee members, with the exceptions of Brown and Andrew Smith (Chief Secretary to the Treasury at the time the Delivery Unit was established). Furthermore, because the committee members were normally hastily skimming the Treasury brief, rather than thinking for themselves, effective follow-up questions were rare. Brown concluded each meeting by summing up vigorously, thus ensuring that the issues which most concerned him were firmly on the record. Thus PSX achieved its main objective: helping the Chancellor keep the necessary grip on public expenditure.

When the Delivery Unit was set up, Cabinet ministers such as Alan Milburn worried that they would now be held to account on the one hand by Blair at the newly proposed stocktakes and on the other by Brown at PSX, certainly wasting their time and possibly pulling them in different directions. The four-page text had to resolve this issue to everyone's satisfaction.

Three steps resolved it in practice. First, it was agreed that Smith

---

*Around the same time, I got a similar message about how important my new job was . . . from my daughter Alys. I happened to call her while she was delayed on a train from Bristol. I said I thought the railways were awful. 'Dad,' she interrupted, 'it's your fault now . . . don't blame anyone else.'

would attend Blair's stocktakes. Second, the collaborative working arrangements between the Treasury and the Delivery Unit reassured everyone. Third, the four-page description of the Delivery Unit was put formally to PSX for approval in that last week of July. This was a big moment for me – if the paper went through, the Delivery Unit would have the support not just of Blair, but of the Cabinet as a whole. The risk I'd taken in leaving my beloved education reforms behind would look a little better calculated. If not . . .

The meeting took place in Committee Room A, a room whose bland name obscures its overwhelming historical significance. It was here that the original eighteenth-century Cabinet met; the table they sat at is still there, as is the throne – set back a little – where George II sat to listen to his ministers' deliberations. Gus Macdonald proposed the four-page paper in a steady monotone; no one said a word, and the Chancellor, nodding slightly, moved the meeting on to the next agenda item. So without a bang and rather less than a whimper, the Delivery Unit was born. By cheerful coincidence, the next item on the agenda was a report from two outside experts on the reasons for the lack of progress on delivery in the previous parliament . . . no planning, lack of clear leadership, poor quality data of the wrong kind, and a muddled chain of command. The case for a Delivery Unit had never been better put, as the committee could not help noticing.

Milburn called me later that day. Despite PSX approval, he remained sceptical as to whether the proposals would work in practice. He favoured the Delivery Unit agenda, but did not want conflicting accountabilities. As it turned out, his fears were not realised. The Treasury and the Delivery Unit really did 'work closely together' – one of Whitehall's favourite phrases, more usually honoured in the breach – and PSX tended to focus on the central questions of public expenditure rather than on progress towards the targets the Delivery Unit was monitoring. As so often happens in politics, the fiercest controversy had been about an issue that ultimately turned out to be beside the point.

That week also saw a Delivery Unit seminar, chaired by Macdonald, led by me, and involving ministers of state from the four key departments. It took place in the magnificent Pillared Room upstairs in No. 10, and was opened by Blair himself, who stressed how much importance he personally attached to the Delivery Unit and its agenda. The content of my presentation was sound and provoked good discussion, but the value of the occasion was all in the symbolism. The Delivery Unit had been anointed by the PM in the presence of its key stakeholders. So often symbolism crucially underpins influence. I noted at the time:

> As [Blair] got up to go – he was off to Cumbria on foot-and-mouth business – he just touched my shoulder as a friendly gesture to say goodbye. I doubt this was thought through from his point of view, but to me, in front of that audience, the gesture was of incalculable benefit.

So as I, like most of the rest of Whitehall, retired for the summer holidays – three weeks in Hackney in my case – the unit had a mission, a set of relationships and the beginnings of a reputation.

Now we just had to decide what to do.

3

'Deliverology'

> Michael's going to talk about how the Delivery Unit works –
> I call it 'deliverology'.
>
> Nick Macpherson, Treasury official, to his staff

The nature of the task

Terrible word, 'deliverology', but once Nick Macpherson had coined it, it stuck as a piece of Whitehall shorthand for all the methods we in the Delivery Unit developed in order to get our job done. If I ever hesitated about the need for deliverology, a trivial incident from the very beginning always came back to me. It was decided to locate the fledgling Delivery Unit staff in 53 Parliament Street, just opposite the end of Downing Street. Squeezed between the Department of Health and the infamous Red Lion pub, where spin doctors passed on their coded snippets to grateful journalists ('casting false pearls before genuine swine', as someone once defined teaching in prep schools, but just as appropriate here). The building itself was dirty and shabby. Once-white net curtains had turned decidedly grey, and our rooms were at the top of a forbidding wooden staircase which might have appealed to Alfred Hitchcock. Its only saving grace was that it had been the site of Isambard Kingdom Brunel's London office, so there was at least one legacy of truly impressive delivery for the place to pass down to us.

We were happy in any case to be able to get started and, as a first step, Kate Myronidis from my office thoughtfully placed an order with Cabinet Office supplies for a set of six new cups, saucers and teaspoons so that even if we couldn't offer guests cleanliness or modernity, at least they could have a respectable cup of coffee. Then she waited. Six weeks and many more polite but insistent phone calls later, a huge cardboard container was finally delivered. 'They've arrived!' thought Kate, tearing open the box like a child on Christmas Day. She began emptying out the swathes of soft packaging inserted to protect the crockery . . . and kept on emptying it out . . . and kept on . . . and there at the bottom of this huge container were six teaspoons and just one solitary saucer. We tried to imagine the person, somewhere in the bowels of the government bureaucracy, who had laid hands on this huge container, found six teaspoons and one saucer, placed them lovingly in the bottom of it, carefully stuffed the container with all that soft packaging, sealed the box safely, addressed it correctly (including the postcode) and then, having arranged its despatch, had presumably sat back and thought, 'Good. Job done!'

Absurd and irrelevant, of course, but hugely emblematic of the challenge of civil service transformation that lay ahead. And I remembered too what the outside experts had found when they looked at the failure to deliver one of the government's major commitments in the first term: 'There was no plan.'

While the relationships we had established in July were a precondition of success, they were no more than that. We had not even begun to answer the huge central question facing us: namely, how could forty people (or just a handful, as it still was in those first few weeks) possibly make a difference to the delivery of outcomes to millions of citizens? Or, to broaden the question slightly and make it relevant the world over, how does a government, even one with all the apparent powers of a Prime Minister such as ours, ensure that the vast bureaucracies that are government departments and the even vaster public services (in England we are talking here about perhaps five million employees, or nearly a quarter of the workforce) actually deliver measurable improvements in performance within a three- to four-year period? Put more succinctly, how do you exercise prime ministerial power in practice?

The question was tough enough long before modern bureaucracies and public services were invented in the nineteenth century. In the 1640s, the hapless Charles I lamented (shortly before they cut off his head): 'There's more to the doing than bidding it be done.' He was neither the first nor the last to realise a profound insight only when it was too late. Commenting on the attempts, more than 300 years later, of Conservative governments to reform the welfare state, Nicholas Timmins made a similar point: 'Much of the story of education, health and social services during the 1980s is of a search by Ministers for levers which, when pulled, produced measurable results.'[1]

My favourite lament, though, is that of a recent Russian Prime Minister, Viktor Chernomyrdin, who, like so many politicians, had a mercurial career which began with high hopes and ended in deep frustration. 'We tried to do better,' he shrugged forlornly, 'but everything turned out as usual.'

And of course it's not just the politicians who find themselves becoming wearily cynical. The public servants often became affected too because they so often experience – at the sharp end – reforms which, announced with a fanfare, sink without trace. They too have often been promised a tea service and received a solitary saucer. After a while, the hype of another announcement generates no more than a marginally raised eyebrow and a purse of the lips. 'Reforms are like London buses,' one public servant told me in the 1990s: 'it doesn't really matter if you miss one because there'll be another one along in a minute.'

There are so many barriers to successful reform that one wonders sometimes how anyone ever achieves anything at all. It is not just the cynicism resulting from the track record that gets in the way. There is the tendency to have pleasant little projects which tinker at the edges of a service but do not change the core business. There is the ever-present risk of watering down a proposal to gain consensus, with the result all too often that a roaring lion becomes a squeaking mouse. There is the risk that before a reform has really made a difference, the agenda shifts, attention is diverted elsewhere and the service slips back to its pre-existing state. Most of all, there is the danger of under-estimating the extraordinary deadweight force of institutional inertia. No wonder most reforms fail, and I haven't yet mentioned the two barriers – bad ideas and gross incompetence – which are so obvious they would hardly need stating but for their historical pedigree. Remember the poll tax?

In this context, the challenge for a government badgered by a Prime Minister with 'a mandate for reform' is to design an effective reform programme, prepare a strategy to take it forward, and seek to motivate a huge, sceptical workforce to implement it. Government is full of people who will generate policy, but often it is by no means clear that the sum total of the policies they generate will add up to anything approaching either a design or a strategy. In fact, a more likely outcome than either of these is a series of initiatives. I knew this from sobering personal experience in the first Blair term. I would ban the word 'initiative' in government if I could.

The task of overseeing the development of design, strategy and policy on behalf of the Prime Minister fell largely outside the remit of the Delivery Unit. Among the plethora of units Tony Blair had established, he had a powerful Policy Directorate to deal with the short and medium term, and an increasingly effective Strategy Unit to deal with the long term. Between them these two parts of the Blair operation answered the questions 'Why?' and 'What?'. The Delivery Unit came into its own with the question 'How?'. Having built our relationships and agreed the priorities, we began to ask these 'How?' questions: 'How will you deliver that?' 'How, at any given moment, will you know whether or not you are delivering that?' 'How, if progress is not what you hoped, will you solve the problem?' 'How can we help you?' But the very first question was one we had to answer for ourselves: 'How will we do our job?'

There are thousands of people in government bureaucracies whose job it is to complicate matters (lawyers spring to mind – 'It all depends,' they begin). I don't necessarily criticise this – government is, after all, a complicated thing. However, to get anything done, a countervailing force is required; people who will simplify, keep bringing people back to the fundamentals:

- What are you trying to do?
- How are you trying to do it?
- How do you know you are succeeding?
- If you're not succeeding, how will you change things?
- How can we help you?

These five simple questions became the essence of the Delivery Unit. The secret lay in asking them calmly and persistently. And to do that, we had to develop techniques or methods that would result in convincing, reliable, evidence-based answers to our five questions. It was the collection of these techniques that Nick Macpherson christened 'deliverology'.

Having once been a professor, I naturally started my holiday that summer of 2001 by reading some books that might help me work out what to do. There was Derek Bok's magisterial but ultimately depressing analysis of the failure of American federal policy over a generation, *The Trouble with Government*; there was Bill Bratton's dramatic, inspiring story of how he successfully drove down crime in New York, *The Turnaround*;* and John Kotter's clear, concise account of what it takes to transform a large business, *Leading Change*. Finally, there was Richard Olivier's *Inspirational Leadership*, a brilliant transformation of Shakespeare's *Henry V* into a leadership manual.

Out of all this reading, two phrases – one inspirational, the other analytical – struck me as central to our mission in the years ahead. In the first, Olivier quotes from Theodore Roosevelt to draw out a moral from Henry V's leadership:

> The credit belongs to the man who is actually in the arena; whose face is marred by dust and sweat and blood and comes up short again and again, because there is no effort without error and shortcoming, but who does actually strive to do the deeds; who knows the great enthusiasms, the great devotions; who spends himself in a worthy cause; who at best knows in the end the triumph of high achievement and who at the worst, if he fails, at least fails while daring greatly, so that his place shall never be with those cold and timid souls who know neither victory nor defeat.[2]

This stirring insight from my favourite former US President, I thought, should inform my personal approach to the challenge (see pp. 76–7). I wasn't sure how to do my new job, but if I failed it would not be for want of trying.

The second was a key political insight: 'The neglect of implementation issues is more than a simple intellectual mistake: it may be a rational response to the fact that our political system confers more rewards for the shrewd deployment of symbols and generalised arguments than it does for detailed realistic analysis and forecasting.'[3] This comment on the US political system was, I thought, peculiarly apposite as a critique of Blair's first term. The Delivery Unit would have to change the incentives in the political system and bring 'realistic

---

*Rudolph Giuliani tells a similar tale of how this was done in his book *Leadership* (New York: Hyperion, 2002). For whatever reason, neither he nor Bratton seems willing to share the credit for this transformation with the other, even though it was quite clearly a joint achievement.

analysis and forecasting' to bear. I tried to connect this whirl of ideas to my own experience over the four years in Education. Meanwhile, catching up on my sleep over the holiday eased the process of distillation.

Planning for delivery

When I arrived back at work with the politicians still in recess, though I still had only the vaguest notions of what to do, I also felt a naïve but powerful surge of optimism. At the office, I found the two crucial ingredients which set us in the right direction – a small, enthusiastic team of staff and an urgent need to act.

The previous parliament had taught me just how short a time four years is to bring about significant change. As I put it to the Cabinet once, misquoting Harold Wilson, 'A week may be a long time in politics, but four years is a very short time.' Reading John Kotter's book reinforced my view. He argues that the first of eight steps to delivering effective change is to establish a sense of urgency.

To instil this pace and energy, we embarked on two major pieces of work. One was to pull together from departments a list of 'quick wins' that would demonstrate to the public that something was happening. This exercise proved to be an uphill struggle, provoking predictable groans in Whitehall. One permanent secretary, for example, complained that any focus on quick wins would distract from the central task of implementation. This is a classic case of one of Whitehall's favourite pastimes – debating a false dichotomy. I replied cheerfully to this whinge, pointing out that quick wins could indeed be a distraction if the wrong ones were chosen. If, on the other hand, the right ones were chosen, they were essential to creating momentum. Again I was able to quote Kotter in support, who demonstrates the importance of 'generating short term wins' as part of an overall programme. I finished up with an aphorism which I think of as the modern politician's dilemma: you have to have a long-term strategy but unless it delivers short-term results no one will believe you. In the end, the quick wins were pulled together into a paper (prepared with calm determination by Clara Swinson, a new recruit who became a star) for Blair to see when he returned from holiday.

The second, and ultimately more important, piece of work for that August was a letter to permanent secretaries requesting delivery plans for each of the priorities to which their secretary of state was now committed. This letter set out the task and the timetable as we in the Delivery Unit saw it and set the pattern for our entire relationship with departments. I thought very carefully about the tone I wanted to strike, prompted not least by a letter I had already received from a permanent secretary complaining that we were already seeking to 'micro-manage' his staff. Acknowledging his own whingey tone, he concluded his letter by saying, 'We will do our best.' I saw this complaint for what it was – a Whitehall reflex. I wanted my first major letter to defy their expectations, strike a different tone. We worked on it collaboratively in the Delivery Unit and then I consulted trusted friends around Whitehall, not necessarily those in senior positions, but those who wanted change and would tell me the truth, such as Chris Wormald, at that time Estelle Morris's excellent principal private secretary. It took days before I was happy with the letter. I wrote:

> ### The overall approach
> Having had the chance to reflect on the approach, and discuss it with some key departmental colleagues, I am clear that we are – all of us – seeking to design a new, more effective approach to the delivery of the government's key public service objectives. I am also clear that none of us yet has a perfect blueprint!
>
> There is a fear, I know, that the Prime Minister's Delivery Unit will seek, especially through the planning phase, to 'micro-manage', creating a bureaucratic process which hampers departments' efforts to deliver. That would be counter-productive and is not the intention. On the contrary, we want to develop a process with you that results in delivery project plans which . . . are based on best practice in the public and private sectors, and where appropriate, overseas . . .
>
> The nine key issues [required to deliver a target] we have identified are:
>
> #### Accountability and leadership
> Who is accountable both at ministerial and at official level? Who will ultimately be responsible for delivering the priority, including on the frontline?

Project management
On a day-to-day basis how will the work be managed and by whom (including at the divisional level)? What is the chain of decision making? Who are the key people along the chain? Do they have the right skills to deliver what is being asked of them?

Levers for change
What levers for change are available (e.g. data, inspection, audit or benchmarking within a service or across sectors)? How will 'people investment' be handled (e.g. training and professional development)? How will change agents be recognised? What are the carrots and sticks for rewarding success and dealing with failure?

Feedback and communication
How will feedback be sought on a day-to-day basis, both from staff and from consumers? How will this feedback be used to refine policy development and implementation? How will key messages about the change programme be communicated to staff? . . .

Timetable for implementation
What is the timetable? What are the key milestones?

Risks and constraints
What risks and constraints might throw the work off course? How will they be managed?

Interdepartmental collaboration
How will other departments and interdepartmental mechanisms (e.g. official groups or Cabinet committees) be involved? Are there particular handling issues?

Resources
What resources, both manpower and financial, are available?

Benchmarking
What benchmarks should be set in place within a service or with other services and sectors, or equivalents overseas?

I also set deadlines of mid-September for us to receive first drafts of plans and the end of October for final drafts. This certainly created a sense of urgency, and while in reality the deadlines slipped a little, the effect was electric.

I attached to the letter Kotter's list of the eight most common errors, partly to convey (perhaps spurious) academic credibility to our request. His list makes good reading, and over the next few years we saw examples of all eight.

> *The Eight Most Common Errors in Change Programmes*
> * Allowing too much complacency.
> * Failing to create a sufficiently powerful guiding coalition.
> * Underestimating the power of vision.
> * Undercommunicating the vision by a factor of 10 (or 100 or even 1000).
> * Permitting obstacles to block the new vision.
> * Failing to create short-term wins.
> * Declaring victory too soon.
> * Neglecting to anchor changes firmly in the corporate culture.[4]

After I had sent this letter, I suddenly remembered, while cycling home, that I really ought to have cleared it with one or more of Richard Wilson, Gus Macdonald and the Prime Minister. In time, all three came to trust my judgement on these issues and to leave me to get on with it, but at that early stage, I had potentially blundered. So I prepared a brief note to Blair, copied to the other two, explaining the purpose of the letter and attaching a copy, and waited (somewhat anxiously) for a reply. Although he was on holiday, Blair's reply came within a day or two: 'Fine,' it said, and in addition he suggested that he should meet departmental ministers and top officials after the recess to make it clear that 'I'm right behind this'. This was exactly the endorsement I was looking for, but he also asked me to review the text and remove any lines which, if the letter leaked, might be problematic. Since I had already sent it, there was nothing I could do about this but hope. Incidentally, I wondered what kind of holiday the Prime Minister was having if he had turned round my paper, which was hardly a burning priority, in less than forty-eight hours at a time when the Northern Ireland peace process – once again – was under pressure, and British troops had just been deployed in Macedonia.

Even though the Delivery Unit staff were housed in Parliament Street, I always sent my own letters out on Downing Street letterhead. It was not just that I kept thinking I had the opportunity to use the most famous address in the country, it was also, again, a question of brand management. I always wanted to convey the impression – the illusion sometimes – that everything we did emanated directly from the Prime Minister. Once the letter had gone, we had, in effect, made decisions about many of the central concepts of deliverology, the science (or pseudo-science) of marshalling prime ministerial power to deliver significant measurable improvements in the public services.

Deliverology defined*

Setting goals

There has been a continuous debate inside government, and indeed in public, about the merits or otherwise of targets.[†] The debate has sown more confusion than enlightenment. Contrary to much political commentary, targets were not invented by the Treasury as part of the 1998 spending review – they go back much further. In 1909, for example, the Liberal government had a target of building six new dreadnoughts. The opposition thought this was insufficient and proposed a more ambitious target: 'We want eight and we won't wait.'

After the Second World War, when building houses in bombed-out cities was the priority, the Labour government strove to build 200,000 houses a year in highly constrained economic circumstances, prompting Sir John Wrigley, the civil servant responsible, to complain to his minister, Aneurin Bevan: 'If we build more than 200,000 houses I'll be sacked by the Chancellor, and if I build less I'll be sacked by you.'[5] When the Tories won power in 1951, it was in part because they had set

---

*For the technical detail of most of the concepts of deliverology, see the Delivery Manual.

[†]You know an issue has become fully embedded in the culture (as opposed to just a matter for the political classes) when it starts turning up in crime novels. In John Harvey's *Darkness and Light* (London: William Heinemann, 2006) one of the characters says: 'This fucking government has become so obsessed with targets, it's all they fucking see.'

an even more ambitious target of building 300,000 houses a year. Harold Macmillan, the minister in charge, commented: 'The fierce and almost frantic pursuit of the housing target filled my mind.'[6] I know exactly how he felt.

Even under New Labour, the first target came before the 1998 spending review. As described in Chapter 1, the target of 80 per cent of eleven-year-olds achieving level 4 in their English tests by 2002 had been proposed by Labour in opposition, and was announced in May 1997 within days of their taking power.

The debate also conveys the impression that, if a government wanted to, it could do without targets. While it is true that a government could dispense with published numerical targets, and many do, it is also true that any government with energy and aspiration has to be able to explain what it is planning to do and how people will know when it has succeeded. To put it in the management jargon we were sometimes guilty of in the Delivery Unit, in each key area government has to be able to answer the question: 'What would success look like?' Once that question has been answered properly, you have a target in all but name. By stating the target or goal publicly, you create pressure on the system to deliver it and a timetable which drives the urgency. The literacy target mentioned above was, as we've seen, missed in the end, but undoubtedly galvanised the education service. Targets, in one form or another, are therefore both necessary and beneficial.

The problems with them are of various kinds. Obviously enough, if the target is set badly it will cause problems. Similarly, if there are too many targets – and it is generally acknowledged that between 1998 and 2002 there were – it can cause confusion. Then there is the risk of either perverse or unintended (or both) consequences. Here the debate is confused. If one purpose of a target is to enhance the priority of the focus area, it follows inescapably that some other areas will not be prioritised and may suffer relatively. This is why governments find it so hard to prioritise, as Blair had in his first term. He learnt his lesson, as demonstrated by his determination to be selective in identifying the Delivery Unit's agenda. Margaret Thatcher showed this sense of priority right from the start. As Nicholas Ridley put it: 'She was adamant she would not start down this sort of road (reforming the welfare state) at the beginning. There was enough to do sorting out industry, the economy, taxation and the trade unions. "The supply side must come first," she said.'[7]

Unintended consequences are another sort of risk. I found that whenever a new target or goal is set, those who defend the status quo instantly explain all the unintended consequences that will ensue. With the focus on literacy and numeracy, such people predicted that the science results would go down. (They didn't – they went up because children who can read, write and do mathematics better also do better in science.) When we focused on reducing street crime in 2002, senior police predicted that, as street crime fell, burglary and car crime would inevitably rise. (They didn't – they continued to fall, because good policing is good policing.) So in the Delivery Unit, our reaction to all these dire predictions was not to accept them at face value since they so often proved to be urban myths, but always to agree we would check. Then, if the fear proved unfounded, the urban myth would be exploded; and if it proved justified, a political choice could be made about whether it was a price worth paying.

Perhaps the most challenging question about targets is the political one – just how ambitious should they be? Setting an ambitious target helps to ensure improvement. However, if substantial improvement is achieved, but the target missed, the government will surely be accused of failing, as indeed happened with the literacy target in 2002. No matter that by then England was third in the world in reading standards, David Blunkett's brave pledge that his 'head was on the block' for this target came home to roost and contributed to the fall of Estelle Morris in 2002. The political risk can therefore be both sharp and personal. There is also a wider political risk that, as a number of targets are missed, a cumulative impression of failure is established in the public mind.

Cabinet ministers swayed back and forth on this question, sometimes wanting to increase the pressure (like Blair's out-of-the-blue pledge to halve the number of asylum applications in 2003) and sometimes wanting to set achievable targets or no measurable targets at all. I doubt they will ever receive the credit they deserve, but in comparison to the many politicians in other countries with whom I have discussed this question, Blair's ministers showed considerable courage in setting goals for which they could be held to account both by the public and by the media. Just to give one comparison, the targets in *Growing Victoria Together*, the document on which the premier of that Australian state,

Steve Bracks, based a successful career, were cautious and gentle. Bracks took the view that it was better to underpromise and overdeliver, a phrase often used in No. 10 during my time there. As a strategy, this appears to involve less risk, but there is a hidden risk involved in accepting incremental rather than transformational change.

Blair himself sometimes appeared politically ambivalent about targets. He worried they would generate unnecessary bureaucracy. He always favoured fewer rather than more targets, and rightly worried that the system would take them too literally and hit the target but miss the point. On the maximum four-hour wait in Accident & Emergency departments, for example, as we approached the achievement of it, he urged me not to press religiously for delivery of it on every site. He knew that the NHS had already dramatically improved its A&E service and did not want the professionals driven to distraction or the achievement lost in a spasm of hair-splitting. For him, it was a question of common sense. In the end, he was always firm on the subject. Just when you thought he was wavering, he would say definitively: 'No business in its right mind would operate without a few targets or key priorities.'

To summarise, whether or not to publish PSA targets as the Blair government did is a matter of choice. Any credible government, though, must have clear objectives and must have a means of knowing at any given moment whether it is on track – or not – to achieving its objectives. Making those objectives public, as the PSA targets are, requires greater political courage but is also both more transparent and makes it more likely that progress will be made.

The Map of Delivery

It was partly to help resolve the political dilemma over the degree of ambition that, in the autumn of 2002, I developed for the Cabinet the 'Map of Delivery' (see p. 83). This 'map' was designed to help Cabinet ministers think about the array of targets or goals they were responsible for. The vertical axis deals with how radical they want to be. This is the traditional debate in Whitehall, with ministers generally favouring bold reform (one of Blair's favourite phrases) and officials generally urging caution because they remember how often in the past the desire to be bold ended up in maximum conflict and minimum delivery. In response to a minister's desire to be bold, officials have a series of possible sceptical responses: 'Can we afford it?' 'Do you want to take the risk?'

Figure 3.1: The Map of Delivery

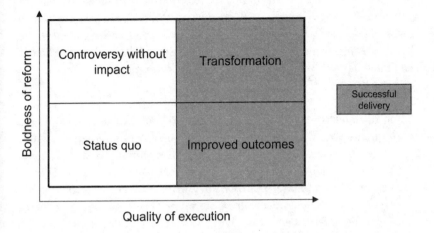

'We tried it before and it failed.' 'Perhaps we should have a pilot study?' 'Should we do some more research?' 'What about phasing it in more slowly?' Or, before the Scottish Parliament was established, 'Why not try it north of the border first?' The problem with this conservative reflex is that it results in a defence of the status quo, which, in an era of rising public expectations, is a recipe for managed decline.

The equation changes when the horizontal axis, the quality of execution becomes the focus. A not very radical but plausible idea, implemented well, will make a difference and deliver improved outcomes – an example would be the commitment to reduce waiting times for elective surgery to a maximum of six months by 2005. More dramatically still, a bold reform, well executed, will deliver transformation – to take a parallel example, the introduction of patient choice of time and place for their operation is transformational. A Cabinet minister and his or her department need to map their portfolio of goals onto this grid and see where they fall. If they are on the left hand side, they need, over time, to shift them across. Incidentally, a controversy without impact might be worthwhile as a step on the way to transformation – a row can help create definition, as the communication people put it – but clearly it is to be avoided as an end-state. If the whole portfolio is destined to end up in the 'Transformation' box, then the programme is probably far too risky. If it is all headed for the 'Improved Outcomes' box, then it probably lacks ambition. As far as targets are concerned, therefore, a single department should aim to have one or two that are truly ambitious ('stretch targets' in the jargon) and a few that are more cautious. With this portfolio approach, the risk is managed. This is why when Nick Macpherson and I appeared before the Public Administration Select Committee we argued that if the government met all its targets, that would represent a lack of ambition.

Plans

Some of deliverology is so obvious that you might think it would go without saying. If a government has an objective or target, it should go without saying that someone somewhere should have a plan for achieving it – a delivery plan in other words. However, this had not been the case in Blair's first term, as we knew from the report of the outside experts to the Public Expenditure Committee. Their words kept coming back to me: 'There was no plan.' So when I wrote that letter to permanent secretaries in August 2001 asking to see their plans, there was an element of bluff involved. They could not possibly say they did not have plans, even where that was the case, so they had no choice but to ensure plans got written by the deadline.

This took us to the next level of challenge. Large swathes of Whitehall were not geared up to write the plans. Whitehall could write policy papers, White Papers, Green Papers, legislation, regulations and answers to parliamentary questions – with varying degrees of quality – but it did not write plans. So, when asked for a plan, Whitehall's traditional response is to write some thoughtful prose, and if it really wants to impress the recipient, to enclose the prose in a glossy cover. In short – to quote a colleague – Whitehall writes 'essays decorated with the occasional number', the hope being that the recipients will be so impressed by the prose that, after reading it, they will leave you alone. This, of course, was not what we wanted. We wanted real, messy, practical, operational plans with folds and creases, scribbled notes in the margins and coffee stains. This, incidentally, was why we decided firmly not to offer a template for a plan which departments could just fill in. That would have made their job too easy, too perfunctory, whereas we wanted them to engage with the harsh reality of getting something done. Helpfully, we could argue that by not offering a template we were responding to their plea that we should not micro-manage them.

The characteristics of the plans we wanted were set out in the letter quoted above. There was nothing original about what we wanted. We were simply asking for standard practice in the management of programmes and projects, a discipline that emerged from engineering in the second half of the twentieth century and became second nature across most of business. Applying programme and project management does not guarantee success, but it does ensure, if applied rigorously, that crucial details will not be missed, and emerging problems will be identified earlier.

Between 2001 and 2003, much of the talk in Whitehall revolved around the need for improved programme and project management, and the Office of Government Commerce along with the Office of Public Service Reform promoted this discipline, not just in relation to the Delivery Unit's agenda but more generally. Their work had significant impact, but it came too late for us in 2001. The plans that were returned to us from departments on or shortly after the deadline varied from the barely adequate to the absolutely dreadful, as we will see later in the chapter. Looking back, I think we could have been more helpful than we were. We should have spelled out with greater clarity a concept at the heart of deliverology, but we couldn't in August 2001 because we were still learning and had not clarified it for ourselves.

The delivery chain

This crucial concept was the delivery chain. Again, it is no more than a blinding flash of the obvious, but none the less important for all that. The best way to think about it is to imagine what is implicit when a minister makes a promise. Supposing that a minister promises, as David Blunkett did, to improve standards of reading and writing among eleven-year-olds. Implicit in this commitment is that, in one way or another, the minister can influence what happens inside the head of an eleven-year-old in, for example, Widnes. The delivery chain makes that connection explicit; so in this case, what is the connection between the child in Widnes and the minister in Westminster? What happens inside that eleven-year-old's head is influenced chiefly by her teacher – the first link in the chain; the teacher is influenced by the school's literacy co-ordinator, who in turn is influenced by the headteacher – the second and third links in the chain. The headteacher is influenced by the governors and the local authority, who are influenced by the regional director of the National Literacy Strategy, who answers to the national director of the strategy. He in turn answers to the head of the Standards and

Effectiveness Unit in the Department for Education, who answers to the secretary of state. And thus we have established the delivery chain.

In practice, many delivery chains are more complex than this.* Even in this example, the child's reading is also influenced by the parents, so there is a shorter chain, also worth thinking about, where the parent can be influenced to read more to the child at home, perhaps through television advertising, for example. Similarly, headteachers are strongly influenced by Ofsted inspectors, so here is another potential chain. The key is – jargon again – to do the 'delivery chain analysis'. Note that it does not depend on a line management relationship, this being only one among many possible means of exerting influence along the chain. Once the chain is identified, those responsible for delivery can then think through how best to exert influence at each link and, when the plan is being put into practice, it is possible to check whether each link in the chain is effective. Where there is a weak link it can be strengthened.

This is just one extended example to illustrate the central and important insight – which is no more than common sense – that there must be some kind of delivery chain if there is to be delivery. If it cannot be specified, nothing will happen, which was precisely the case in parts of Whitehall before 2001. We found that, in a number of cases, the responsible officials had decided in their own minds that because they did not have direct line management responsibility, they had no influence at all. In a phrase I came to hate, they would say: 'We only have rubber levers.' Some officials wallowed in this powerlessness because it enabled them to abdicate responsibility – if results were not delivered, at least it was not their fault. In the Department for Transport, for example, they told us that, since the railways were privatised, there was nothing they could do to improve reliability, even though the bulk of the investment in the railways came from government, making it in effect the biggest single shareholder. In the Home Office, we were told that chief constables were independent and therefore officials had no influence. The problem was psychological as much as anything – instead of setting out to decide what they could do and how they might do it, they decided what they couldn't do and how they might explain away the inevitable failure which would result. In

*See Delivery Manual, Document 2 for an example of a delivery chain set out in the NAO/Audit Commission Report *Delivering Efficiently: Strengthening the Links in Public Service Delivery Chains.*

short, our effort to promote improved delivery was as much cultural as technical.

Interestingly, as time went by, once officials had clarified the delivery chain and started to exert influence along it, they found that their jobs were much more worthwhile. Many civil servants, after all, had embarked on their careers motivated by the thought of making a difference, only to become ground down by the inertia of the machine of which they had become a part.* Often we found we had reignited their motivation; they were once again making a difference.

Data and trajectories

Whitehall often feels a long way from the frontline. Unless civil servants make an effort, they can easily become detached, spending a lifetime in departmental meetings and distant from the services for whose outcomes they find themselves responsible. Worse still, they often have no idea what impact the policies they are in charge of have on the ground. From the late 1980s onwards, there had been a fashion for evaluating every policy that moved. This was intended as a response to the failure to identify impact, but in fact resulted more often than not in long, turgid academic evaluations which were published long after the event and written by researchers more interested in scoring points in the Research Assessment Exercise than in shaping the future of government policy. Indeed, as a professor myself, I often used to say – partly to provoke my colleagues, I must admit – that there's only one thing worse as an academic than having your work ignored, and that's having it taken seriously.

Evaluations, therefore, did not solve the problem. Contrast this with a business driving through a major change: it would collect data at every stage in the process, including sales figures. Moreover, it would seek to ensure such data was available in as short a time as possible so that emerging problems could be identified and corrected rapidly. In some parts of the public sector, a similar approach had been adopted and applied successfully. For example, it was the collection and use of what the jargon calls 'real-time data' that had underpinned the success of

---

*In my most despairing moments on the subject of the civil service, I used to quote Kurt Vonnegut's judgement on the inhabitants of Midland City in his classic *Breakfast of Champions*: 'Their imaginations were flywheels on the ramshackle machinery of the awful truth.'

celebrated police chief Bill Bratton in dramatically reducing crime in New York after a generation of remorseless increases. He used the weekly data from precincts to challenge his precinct commanders to learn from the best and improve their impact fast. He became famous for his so-called 'broken windows' theory – the idea that if you tackle small crimes quickly you will also do better with major crime – but the effective use of data was a much more important factor in his success.

In the Department for Education, I had led a drive to develop one of the best national data systems for schools in the world. By 2001, each school was able to compare its own performance on tests and exams not just to the system as a whole but to schools with a similar intake, and to use this benchmarking data to set targets for future performance. To my surprise, when, in the autumn of 2000, we asked thousands of headteachers which government policies they liked best, target-setting proved one of the most popular. Moreover, because the national system was based on individual pupil data, it was possible to calculate the progress (or value added) that each school was responsible for. At the Delivery Unit, we were keen to see powerful data systems such as those in the New York City police or the Department for Education in place across the board. In fact, when we surveyed the Whitehall scene in 2001, the quality of data varied greatly. There was extensive real-time data on train performance. Indeed, had we wanted to, we could have seen it daily (proof, incidentally of the obvious point that good data, while essential, is only a start – you then have to use it!). Similarly, the NHS generally had reasonable-quality monthly data on key waiting times, but did not integrate the data into an effective system for managing performance.

By contrast, on crime, while there was a survey which showed national crime trends over time on the basis of a sample (the British Crime Survey), no data at all was collected from individual police forces before 2002. It was therefore impossible to see which ones were doing well and which were not. The same applied generally across the criminal justice system – probation, prisons and courts. Worst of all was road congestion, which was measured by a bizarre process of paying thirteen people to drive various routes at different times of day and then aggregating the data they provided once every two years. (Actually, on the day I was told this, the officials concerned apologised for the fact that there were only twelve people driving the routes as one of them had

had an accident the day before.) No wonder no one had a grip on it! Three years later, as a result of pressure from us, the Department for Transport had daily data on every A-road and motorway in the country, and through traffic managers in each key congested area – the so-called Birmingham Box (M6, M42, M5) being the first – started to manage congestion actively and provide vastly improved information to motorists, with benefits all round. The civil servants responsible for road congestion ceased to be resigned and became empowered. Working with them, for example, we were able to quantify and then tackle the chief causes of delay. Gathering data, it turns out, is not only powerful; it's fascinating too. In some cases, it took two or even three years to overcome resistance to improving data systems and for the data to begin to flow, but without fail, once the change had occurred, everyone agreed it was vastly for the better. In fact, I would argue that – unsung though it is – this was one of the Delivery Unit's most significant achievements.

Even before we established these data systems, we had introduced an important new term into the Whitehall lexicon – 'trajectory'.* Like so much of deliverology, the concept is simple but its influence profound. As part of the planning process, we asked the relevant officials to connect, with a single line on a graph, the point indicating current performance to the point where the target suggested it should be in three, four or five years' time (depending on the timetable for achieving the target). This request was intended to ensure that, in the planning process, officials thought about the relationship between the actions they proposed and the outcomes the targets required them to achieve. To put it more simply and more powerfully, it required them to base their proposals on evidence. The request for trajectories was easy to make. But to answer it in any sophisticated way was far from easy. The evidence in the social sciences is not always conclusive, and it's hard to predict how much impact one particular action – say a literacy hour introduced across primary schools – will have among the many other influences impacting on reading standards at the time. For many people, the sheer complexity of finding an answer is enough to deter them from even making the attempt. The Delivery Unit thought otherwise – it is

*Document 9 in the Delivery Manual includes an extract from the presentation on delivery given to the media in July 2004. The graphs there give an idea of what these trajectories looked like.

better, we argued, to make the best informed guess you can and then to see what in fact happens. You can then review the assumptions behind the guess in the light of the real data as it comes in and refine the analysis. In other words, the combination of the trajectory and the actual data enables constant learning. Thus, for example, waiting times data can be analysed against trajectory. Supposing aggregate performance is off track, there may still be some hospitals where it is on track. Then the question arises, what are they doing that the others are not? Or it may be on track with, say, ear, nose and throat operations and severely off track in orthopaedics. Again, the question arises, what explains the variation?

If the data comes in fast enough for the system to be able to respond in time, and if those using the data have the right 'can-do' mindset, then problems can be solved before they become crises or outright failures. To judge from the press commentary on government, it would be easy to think that, for each of the vast array of problems facing modern societies, there are obvious right and wrong solutions – and, the argument goes, if only those obtuse politicians would select the right ones, all would be well. In fact, major public service and/or social problems are usually much more complex than that. The solutions lie not in one simple remedy, but in the sustained implementation of a combination of actions. In these circumstances, the qualities required most by those responsible for policy are a positive attitude and, above all, the capacity to learn rapidly. In fact, in the implementation of complex programmes designed to achieve rapid, large-scale performance improvement, 'making it up as you go along' – learning, in other words – is essential because it is not possible to know everything you need to know at the outset. There is a jargon to describe this, enshrined in the work of Harvard professor Ron Heifetz, who argues that 'complex adaptive problems' require 'adaptive' leadership.[8] President Eisenhower made a similar point in simpler language: 'The plan is nothing; the planning is everything.'

Of course, when the Delivery Unit first requested trajectories, these implications were, for most of Whitehall, some distance away. The more immediate fear of many officials was that they were being required to predict future performance, which raised two problems: first, that the prediction might leak and the press would call the trajectory a 'promise' or a 'target', a very real fear, except that fortunately it never happened; second, the department would be held to account if their prediction turned out to be wrong. Responding to this was an important challenge for the Delivery Unit. After all, we wanted to be hard edged, but we also wanted to exploit the potential of trajectories to generate learning. Thus our response when this fear was expressed was to say that predictions about the future were often wrong. The key, when they turned out to be wrong, was to learn the lessons. Which assumptions turned out to be flawed? What changed that we hadn't anticipated? I used to quote the great conductor Benjamin Zander, who taught his musicians not to swear when they made a ghastly error, but to say to themselves, 'How fascinating!'

So, over time, trajectories became part of the Whitehall routine, a central plank of deliverology. This, of course, did not mean that all the trajectories produced were highly refined and thought through. Some were – such as the excellent one on railway reliability that finally arrived appropriately late (in 2004) – but others were really crude. My esteemed colleague Tony O'Connor – the Delivery Unit's high priest of trajectories – used to joke that the request for a trajectory sent Whitehall searching for its most sophisticated analytical tool, the ruler. Even that, however, was a step forward.

Stocktakes

Central to any process for managing performance is a meeting in which those responsible for delivery are held to account. As we have seen in the previous chapter, the idea of stocktakes where the Prime Minister held the relevant secretaries of state to account had been part of the blueprint for the Delivery Unit. Some semblance of the stocktake idea had emerged in the first term. The Education team – Blunkett, Byers (then Morris), Bichard and Barber – had attended regular meetings every couple of months with Blair and his advisers throughout the first term. Chris Woodhead, the chief inspector of schools, had been invited to about half of these, and he and I prepared a joint paper in advance (not always an easy task*), surveying progress and looking at emerging issues. According to Anthony Seldon's biography, from the autumn of 1999, 'Blair spent more time having bilateral meetings with the Secretaries of State for

---

*He and I often had robust debates on the content of these papers. One such vigorous exchange ended memorably when Woodhead sent a fax conceding my points, and culminating in the immortal phrase 'OK Sweetie'.

Education, Health, Social Security and Transport . . . along with the Home Office'.[9] These meetings may have been prototypes of the stock-takes we organised in the second term, but in practice I suspect many of them were about policy or strategy rather than performance, the crucial defining ingredient of a stocktake. However, at least one, which became legendary around Whitehall, did look at performance. It involved a presentation by Home Office officials in which they purported to show that crime rose during an economic downturn because of higher unemployment and also rose in a period of economic growth because there were more goods to nick! Such fatalism did not go down terribly well with the Prime Minister, as one might imagine, but was surprisingly widespread. For example, Roy Jenkins, himself a former Home Secretary, warned David Blunkett at some point during Labour's first term that if he aspired to be Home Secretary he should avoid any commitments on reducing crime because he had no levers to control it. Not surprisingly, Blunkett did not swallow this counsel of despair.

To succeed, the Delivery Unit-organised stocktakes had to have certain key ingredients. The first was this focus on performance; the second was regularly focusing on the same handful of priorities; the third was the regular attendance of the Prime Minister himself and the relevant secretary of state; and the fourth was ensuring that the data presented to the meeting was shared and accepted by everyone present. Each of these characteristics seems relatively straightforward, but the combination was revolutionary.

Right from the outset, I saw one of my most important functions as securing sufficient time for stocktakes in the Prime Minister's diary. I knew I was asking for a huge amount: four meetings of an hour in length every two months with, if possible, a pre-meeting in advance. This might not seem huge, but consider that in the first few months of the Delivery Unit's existence, Blair had meetings planned with seven European heads of state, two meetings of the European Council, a summit with the French, a visit from the Chinese Prime Minister and many other demands for his time for foreign policy issues. Consider too that he had to sort out the legislative agenda for the new parliament, deal with all the day-to-day pressures including the endless demands of the 24-hour media and get out and about both as Prime Minister and as party leader. At the vortex, time in the PM's diary is the clearest indicator there is of influence, and Blair's willingness to dedicate so much time to stocktakes – even when from within No. 10 there were countervailing pressures – is a measure of his commitment to delivery. Later on, we lengthened the gap between meetings so they were more like once a quarter, and of course sometimes they did get cancelled or rearranged, but by the second half of the parliament the routine was firmly established.

Blair was less willing to concede time for pre-meetings, reasoning, I imagine, that if he had read the papers he did not need further advice. It was even difficult to get two minutes with him in which to reinforce the two or three top-line messages. If you were lucky, you might find yourself walking into the Cabinet Room with him, pressing a point, but even then it wasn't clear whether you had hit home. I always felt that this lack of preparation was a mistake on his part, especially on those occasions when he hadn't after all had time to read the papers. He usually performed well, and the brief presentation at the start of the meeting ensured he had a grasp of the key facts, but with a five-minute pre-meeting he could have done even better.

In preparation for stocktake meetings, there was a great deal of diplomatic coming and going between the Delivery Unit, working with the Policy Directorate, and the relevant department. We had to ensure that the performance data was agreed, that the department provided a paper offering its rationale for the state of affairs and, very practically, a list of the people it was proposed should attend. Whenever a Prime Minister is involved in a meeting, the cast of those who want to attend increases exponentially, so anyone who represents the Prime Minister in preparing for a meeting has to be very tough in demanding that it stays small. I often saw a proposed informal meeting with the PM turn out to have an attendance of twenty or thirty as more and more ministers, plus their advisers, plus their officials, decided they just had to be there. Yet to have an honest dialogue about performance, a degree of confidentiality is required. Normally at a stocktake, the Prime Minister's side included him, me, the relevant Policy Directorate adviser, Gus Macdonald (until he retired from ministerial office in 2003) and sometimes the Cabinet Secretary. The department would have the secretary of state, a permanent secretary, a junior minister, a political adviser and maybe an official or two. Andrew Smith (and later Paul Boateng), often accompanied by an official, represented the Treasury. That is already ten to fifteen people.

Once we had the planning done, we sent a briefing, including the agenda, the cast list and the department's paper, along with the data, to the Prime Minister, usually on a Friday for a stocktake the following Tuesday. The briefing, prepared jointly with the Policy Directorate, provided the PM confidentially with our views of the department's performance and the issues on which he should challenge the department.

In the meetings themselves, the Prime Minister was at his most effective, naturally enough, if he had had time to read the briefing. We normally began the meetings, especially in that early phase, with a five-minute presentation from me that showed graphs of the key data and raised the various challenges. We became experts in the Delivery Unit not just at analysing the data, but at presenting it so that a busy Prime Minister, at a glance, could understand the key message. For the meeting to be effective, I had to be confident that departmental representatives would accept the validity of the data and thus avoid an unseemly wrangle about whether the key messages were true. In that early phase, to prepare for a stocktake almost the whole staff of the Delivery Unit would gather the evening before in my tawdry office overlooking the Cenotaph* and debate and refine the presentation which we projected onto an electronic whiteboard. In these informal gatherings, more than anywhere, the collective learning so important to our impact began. After the stocktakes, normally having successfully ensured the important issues had been raised (if not by the Prime Minister, then by me, chipping in as appropriate), we agreed a minute with the Policy Directorate, circulated it to those who attended, and then followed up with the department to make sure the requisite action was taken.

Of course, since 1856 Prime Ministers had routinely met their Cabinet colleagues in the Cabinet Room in 10 Downing Street. What was different in stocktakes was the content of the conversation. Traditionally, the main subjects had been the media, policy, public opinion, legislation and gossip about colleagues. These subjects will always be the stuff of politics, but we added to the mix a formal conversation about performance based on evidence. I remember the

---

*A first-floor office with large windows opening on to a balcony proved an excellent place from which the Delivery Unit staff could view the Queen Mother's funeral – I was out of town that day.

sense of achievement I felt when Blair said to Alan Milburn, having seen my presentation about waiting times: 'That looks like a plateau to me, Alan. What are you going to do about it?' I also remember dashing back to Tony O'Connor in the Delivery Unit to report to him the first time Blair uttered the word 'trajectory' in a stocktake. A major business would not have found this surprising at all, but these were the early signs not just of a much more focused conversation about delivery, but also of the emergence of a new language in government.

Later in our existence we often encouraged the department to produce the presentation rather than us. There were those on my staff who thought this would help transfer 'ownership'. Also it was how the process would normally happen in business. Personally, I was sceptical, not just because I liked doing the five-minute presentations. When we did them, the presentations were sharp, clear and brief – they set out clear messages for the next steps and ministers and officials had to either accept them or debate them in front of the PM. Sometimes departmental presentations were dreadfully lacking in focus, full of lists and PowerPoint bullets, and above all long-winded. I was repeatedly struck by the inability of so many key officials to present anything in five minutes. When people did ramble on too long, Blair would sometimes interrupt, which was a relief, but the result was often an unstructured meeting. I would be sitting at Blair's side trying to get the meeting back on track, rather than concentrating on the substance.

The meetings did not always go well. In early November 2001, for example, I made a note to myself that the Education stocktake had not gone well. The department had prepared a paper that was 'muddled', it had been defensive about sharing up-to-date data on school perform- ance, and in the meeting Estelle Morris and David Normington, the permanent secretary, were unconvincing about whether key strategies were being implemented effectively. To make matters worse, the Prime Minister had 'barely read' the briefing and began the meeting 'tired and unfocused'.

In the real world, sometimes meetings will turn out this way. On other occasions, the Education Department was much more convincing. From the point of view of the Delivery Unit's impact, it was important to learn the lessons of what had gone wrong, so a couple of days later I reviewed both the preparations and the meeting with Normington himself. He said he and Morris knew the meeting had not gone well and wanted to learn the lessons too. He said the pressure we were applying was beginning to work: simply by asking persistently 'What's happening?' and 'How do you know?' we were making a difference. His ambition – which he knew he had not yet fulfilled – was that the department should be so far ahead of the Delivery Unit that it would prove we were unnecessary. This kind of follow-up conversation ensured that even a relatively poor stocktake was much better than none at all.

That same month, there was an example of a stocktake that went really well. David Blunkett was confident and on top of everything and John Gieve, his permanent secretary, was disarmingly honest in describing the immense challenges they faced. Both welcomed the challenge the Delivery Unit was providing. The only interruption was when youthful crying was heard outside the Cabinet Room door. It was not a frustrated civil servant barred from the Prime Minister's meeting: Blair the father excused himself momentarily and, having checked up on his son, returned to the discussion of crime reduction.

So, having had the first stocktakes in July 2001 to start the process, by November they had become a firmly established feature of deliverology.

The league table

Not everyone in the public services likes league tables, but I love them. I have spent much of the last decade advocating them, usually in front of sceptical or even hostile audiences of headteachers. They make the evidence about performance public, they focus minds on the priorities they encompass, and they make sure, in whatever system they are applied, that something is done about the individual units at the bottom of the league table – whether they are schools, hospitals, police forces or local authorities. This is why I never accepted the idea put forward by many in education that, once we had a measure of value added or progress, this should replace the raw data. I have always advocated the publication of both indicators. The value-added figures show what contribution individual schools are making, which is important; the raw figures reveal where the biggest challenges are in achieving universal high standards and focus the system on those challenges, which is even more important. By laying bare the problems, league tables drive action. The fact that school failure has been much reduced (though there is still a lot more to do) and that the gap between the lowest-performing schools and the average has been narrowed owes a great deal to league tables. In fact, there is no more powerful driver of equity.

When I was appointed to head the Delivery Unit, naturally enough I brought this strongly held view with me. The idea of developing one for the internal performance management of Blair's key priorities, however, did not come from me. It was proposed by a brilliant young DfEE civil servant, Chris Wormald, in a conversation in Starbucks on 15 June 2001, a few days before my formal appointment. Wormald had been working for me on tackling school failure for over a year, during which time he calculated we had each spent in excess of £1,000 in Starbucks feeding our coffee addiction.* I was asking him for advice, and he listed a set of levers that he had seen work in education. First he mentioned money, which was a resource I did not want, except for the minimum, in the Delivery Unit. Then he mentioned league tables and it was as if a light had been switched on. The next time I met Richard Wilson, I suggested to him that a league table of performance on delivering Blair's priorities would be a good idea and, to my surprise, he endorsed it enthusiastically.

However, having the general idea of a league table was a far cry from deciding what it would be a league table of. How were we going to compare, in league table form, rail delays with school test results or crime reduction? This was one of the first major conversations inside the Delivery Unit. I was insistent we would have a league table. Others were cautious, rightly pointing out that whenever league tables were introduced, controversy raged in their wake, and therefore our reputation would be on the line. In any case, we wrestled with the question of what to measure.

Towards the end of the previous parliament, on the basis of the relative success of education in delivery terms, I had been invited to present to a Cabinet Office audience in Admiralty Arch on what the ingredients of successful delivery were. This presentation helped inform our discussion of the league table, because it occurred to us that what we really wanted to compare across Blair's priorities was not so much current performance, as the likelihood that any given target would be delivered. In other words, we wanted a prospective measure – what was likely to happen in the

---

*Of our own money, I hasten to add.

future, rather than what was actually happening now.

A team led by Tony O'Connor, but involving all the pioneers who joined the Delivery Unit at the beginning, began to work out what it was that enabled one to predict that, at some point in the future, a given target would be delivered. After much reflection and debate, and under time pressure from me – I wanted the first league table to be produced in October, just four months after our creation – we came to the conclusion that there were four elements which, when combined, made up what we called the 'likelihood of delivery'. The first element was a judgement about how difficult the goal was to achieve, which we called the 'degree of challenge'. By definition, almost everything we were working on – from improving railway reliability in the months after the Hatfield crash to reducing health waiting times – was difficult, but some things were more difficult than others, especially where (as in education) some very ambitious targets had been set. The only way to judge the degree of challenge was through discussion among ourselves, especially as for this first league table we were determined not to discuss it outside the unit in case the very idea caused controversy, in which case we might have been warned off. Eventually we were able to decide which challenges were 'very high', which were 'high', which were 'medium' and which were 'low'.

The second element concerned the quality of each department's planning. Did they have a credible plan? Did they have arrangements for overseeing the implementation of their plan? Would they know soon enough if insufficient progress was being made or if something was going horribly wrong? Again, through discussion among ourselves of the plans that departments submitted to us in late September, we were able to judge which plans were better than others. We gave them a traffic light rating – green for good, amber for doubtful and red for bad. Later we learnt the lesson of social science research that, if there is a three-point scale, people tend to choose the middle option as the easiest way out, so we split amber into amber-green and amber-red, which forced people to decide one way or another.

The third element we called the 'capacity to drive progress'. Supposing a department had a good plan and arrangements to manage performance, but it had overburdened officials, distracted politicians, a lack of the necessary investment or poisonous relations with key stake-holders such as unions or businesses. Particularly on issues such as drugs, where one department, in this case the Home Office, was responsible, but successful delivery depended on the active contribution of other departments, in this case, Health, Education and Customs & Excise, a good plan could easily founder on poor interdepartmental collaboration. In 2001, precisely this flaw bedevilled work not just on drugs, but also on most aspects of criminal justice and asylum and immigration. One of the unsung achievements of David Blunkett as Home Secretary and later Charlie Falconer as Lord Chancellor, with assistance from the Delivery Unit, was to shift these relationships from conflict to collaboration. Either way, on this question of capacity to drive progress, we also reached a traffic light judgement.

The fourth and final element of likelihood of delivery related to the timetable. If a strategy is still being worked out and requires legislation to pass, and yet the clock is already ticking, then clearly there is greater risk of a failure than if the policy is already in early or late implementation. So we arrived at a four-point scale again – 'policy development' (for example writing a White Paper, consulting on the policy), 'early implementation', 'embedding change' and – the nirvana – 'irreversible progress'.

Figure 3.2: Template for judging likelihood of delivery

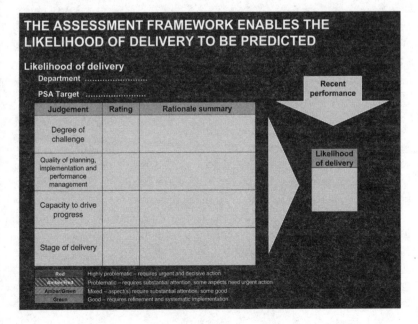

By reaching judgements on all four key elements and then looking at current performance as a reality check, we were able among ourselves to reach an overall judgement on likelihood of delivery, for which again the traffic light scheme was applied. The result was that we could fill in the template illustrated in Figure 3.2.

It needs to be emphasised, of course, that this was not pure science; it was a question of a small number of people making the best judgements they could with the limited information they had. The test, though, was not whether the league table judgements were perfect – which they could never have been – but whether, when they saw the light of day in the Prime Minister's or Chancellor's office, or even more tellingly in the various departments, they were accepted as being broadly right. More importantly still, the methodology underpinning the league table would in time need to stand up to intense scrutiny.

Faster than I had dared to hope, the league table methodology became not only accepted, but widely used throughout the Treasury and across government departments. It is easy to underestimate how innovative this process was: it not only allowed apparently unlike things (railway performance and health waiting times, for example) to be valuably compared, it also enabled us to predict with a reasonable degree of confidence what would deliver in future and, more importantly, what wouldn't, unless action was taken. Of course, we collectively got steadily better at making the necessary judgements. Later it became a routine part of the process for departments to assess the 'likelihood of delivery' of their own priorities as a first step towards a discussion with us. In time, we produced a 'how-to' guide called the Assessment Framework (see Delivery Manual, Document 3) to support this process. At the beginning, though, we intentionally avoided the involvement of departments and were only too aware that we were sometimes skating on thin ice. There were sensible colleagues in the Delivery Unit making a rational case for not having a league table in October 2001. If we were going to make judgements, why have a rank order? Why not just have three or four groups varying from good to poor, or have star-ratings as were later developed for hospitals?

It was a good case, but I wanted us to make an impact. It is so easy to sink without trace in the vast government machine, and all the evidence showed, I thought, that there is no better way to generate controversy than to produce a league table. Moreover, I wanted to shock Whitehall, particularly the permanent secretaries, some of whom had been making knowing predictions of our inevitable demise. I had backing from Richard Wilson for the idea and I was confident that the Prime Minister would warm to it, as long as the information it revealed was sound and could be defended from irate ministers or senior officials. Thus the league table became the centrepiece of deliverology and, as we shall see later in this chapter, had precisely the explosive consequences we anticipated.

The delivery report

The Prime Minister, and indeed ministers and permanent secretaries, needed more than a league table. They also needed a report which explained the judgements in the league table and offered advice on what to do next. The advice was needed on three levels: What were the lessons from the Delivery Unit for Whitehall as a whole? What were the messages for each department? And what were the specific messages in relation to each target? We therefore produced, in addition to the league table, a report for each department that covered each of these themes. I copied the reports to the Prime Minister, and then wrote a specific, confidential note to him, copied only to Gus Macdonald, Richard Wilson and the No. 10 inner circle, explaining my views on the overall state of delivery.

These delivery reports generated a huge amount of work in the Unit, and were refined and greatly improved over time. I thought of them as the engine room of delivery. As with the league table, the first time we did them, we wrote them in the Delivery Unit without consulting and then, when we were as happy as we could be with the limited evidence we had at that time, and after endless editing – not least by me – we sent them to departments and simultaneously to the Prime Minister. This ensured that the process of delivery reporting was established without Whitehall's forces of conservatism being able to water down, over-complicate or postpone the reports, all tactics that had been successfully deployed in the past to undermine a variety of departmental review processes. I knew very well we were staking our reputation on the league table and these reports, but the bottom line was that by giving him unvarnished information about performance on his key priorities they enhanced the power of the Prime Minister.

9/11

As September 2001 unfolded, it became clear that departments were taking the process of planning for delivery – as set out in the letter I had sent them in mid-August – very seriously. We ran some sessions on planning with them, and regularly debated their progress with the people we called the key contacts, senior officials from each department given the task of building a relationship with us. We also asked each department to present to us during September on the progress it was making with planning for delivery. By then we had appointed a number of people – Delivery Unit associates – from outside Whitehall with experience of delivery in both business and the public sector, and they joined us for these departmental presentations. We had careful pre-meetings to determine our line of questioning and then at the end of the meeting I summed up, offering what I thought the key messages were. If we had needed confirmation that departments were far from ready to deliver, these meetings provided it. They gave us evidence for our traffic light judgements on both planning and the capacity to drive progress. The associates were shocked by the confusion about delivery among obviously intelligent people. Some hoped to hide their confusion behind modern management jargon, others defensively suggested that they were on top of everything in spite of appearances. Occasionally a PowerPoint slide designed to explain the situation to us was so convoluted it was obvious the situation was hopeless – the one explaining the governance of the privatised rail service was a classic case in point.

On 11 September 2001, we had a meeting of the departmental key contacts to report on how the previous week's stocktakes had gone and to prepare departments for the stocktakes over the following days. There had been an awayday at Chequers the previous week, at which Blair had reaffirmed his determination to drive through not just delivery of results, but serious structural reforms in health, schools and universities. There had been a sense that the Delivery Unit had made a good start, but the real work of driving delivery had barely begun. At the key contacts meeting I wanted to emphasise once again the Prime Minister's personal commitment to our programme.

Passing through No. 10 on the way to this meeting, I dropped in to see Jeremy Heywood. 'Have you seen this?' he asked, pointing at the television screen. I saw the pictures of the first plane crashing into the

World Trade Center. I assumed it was a terrible freak accident, and set off for the meeting. During the meeting, reports came through that the Twin Towers had collapsed. By then, Blair was on his way back from the TUC conference, never having delivered the controversial speech on the role of the private sector in public service reform, to which several of us had contributed since the Chequers meeting. By the end of the day, it was clear to me that the day would not just change the world, but more parochially transform the Prime Minister's priorities and role. That evening, naturally enough, the entire Downing Street machine had refocused on the global crisis. I knew the best way I could contribute was to do my job as well as I could while others dealt with the incalculable consequences of what had happened. On Friday 14 September the entire Delivery Unit assembled on Parliament Street near the Cenotaph. The traffic stopped the moment Big Ben struck eleven and, along with the whole country, we stood in silent remembrance of those who had died.

Looking back, the most remarkable fact, from my point of view, about the extraordinary period from 11 September to the fall of the Taliban a few months later is how much time Blair continued to give to the delivery of public services in spite of the demands of the global agenda. On 27 September, for example, at a No. 10 staff meeting, Jonathan Powell strongly affirmed that delivery remained a central priority for the Prime Minister. I knew that in his first term the Prime Minister had, with some justification, felt that when he was distracted by crises, progress on delivery seized up. In response to Powell's encouraging remarks, I set out where we were on delivery – departments were genuinely focused on it, but their plans were poor – and then emphasised my key message: 'The whole point of having a Delivery Unit is that whatever the PM is doing and however distracted he may be, he can be sure we are always on the case.'

That same week, I was summoned to a meeting with the PM up in the Downing Street flat. I found Heywood and Andrew Adonis running through the domestic policy agenda, and they wanted my perspective. Though I was completely unprepared, I discovered that I had most of the Delivery Unit programme in my head, and could answer the PM's questions and press home the decisive messages. I was critical of the state of delivery across Whitehall and pulled no punches. Blair looked exhausted, but paid careful attention. He must have been alarmed by the lack of preparedness for delivery, but in his fifth year as Prime Minister, hardly surprised. I offered him the same commitment I gave to the staff meeting, and added: 'If you wake up in the night worrying about delivery, just remember, "Delivery Never Sleeps".' When I left No. 10 in the summer of 2005, Blair commented that the knowledge that his delivery agenda was always being pursued, whatever he was doing, was the single most important benefit the Delivery Unit had brought.

The state of delivery

Just over a week later (9 October), I sent Blair the first delivery report, complete with the first league table. Looking back on that report, it was very hard-hitting. The report told the Prime Minister that we had examined draft delivery plans from departments and required them to present their thinking to panels of experts from inside and outside government. 'The process cannot be considered perfect,' I said, '[but] it has certainly provided us in No. 10 with a much better picture of Whitehall's capacity to deliver key priorities than has ever been available in the past. I have reasonable confidence that the judgements in this report are broadly right.' The conclusion, asserted before going into detail, was:

> Overall, I believe the government's key priorities can be delivered 'on time, on standard' but only if:
> - the lessons of successful delivery, wherever it occurs, are learnt and applied;
> - urgent, decisive action is taken to tackle the problems this first phase of our work has identified; . . .
> - there is a sustained focus on their effective implementation from now until 2004–5.

I then gave the Prime Minister an overview of delivery, starting with the positives (I was desperate to find some positives but the truth was that I had been alarmed by the state of affairs). The positives were:
- There was a strong commitment to delivery from both key politicians and permanent secretaries – 'In all key departments delivery is undoubtedly top of the agenda'.

- There was greater clarity than in the past about what the priorities were.
- There was a refreshing openness to adopting practice which had worked elsewhere.
- There were a few examples of success from which Whitehall could learn.

That was the best I could do. Then came the daunting truth:
- The delivery culture was not developed or embedded; the positive shift had only just begun.
- Planning for delivery was 'in many cases weak'. I added: 'There is a lack of clarity about the critical steps to take, about which levers are available and how they can be pulled in the right sequence . . . In some policy areas, there is even a lack of understanding of the end-to-end process, never mind what is required to improve it.'
- The officials responsible for delivery did not have in place the means to find out rapidly and frequently what impact policies were having at ground level, and they were therefore unable to assess progress regularly and refine implementation where necessary.
- There was a lack of urgency. Here I reinforced the message to the PM with evidence from his first term. 'It is worth noting that in relation to most of the key delivery successes of the last Parliament, much of the policy work had been done before the 1997 election, yet delivery still took until 2000 or 2001. Yet in relation to many of the current priorities, either policy is still being developed . . . or the necessary capacity to deliver is not yet in place.'
- There was little recognition that the trend towards devolving responsibility to the frontline (to schools or primary care trusts, for example) required a corresponding strengthening of the quality of leadership.
- Cross-departmental working was very poor or even non-existent.
- Perhaps most depressing of all, in parts of Whitehall there was little confidence that we would ever get beyond crisis management or incremental change.

My report then went on to explain how the league table worked before revealing the state of play. On just two of the PM's top twenty or so priorities, the likelihood of delivery was rated 'green'; all the rest had 'either significant concerns (amber) or severe challenges (red)'.

Whenever I sent a note to the PM, particularly one full of bad news, I was always at pains to say what we planned to do next. I was conscious that all Prime Ministers always have a myriad of problems on their plates, and the least they should expect is that their advisers actively seek solutions. I remembered the famous remark Margaret Thatcher made about (Lord) David Young: 'the others bring me problems, he brings me solutions' – and I wanted to be remembered by Blair in the same way.

So the report concluded by setting out the next steps. 'My over-whelming priority is to do all I can to persuade departments to act decisively and robustly.' I was greatly assisted in this endeavour by the commitment Blair had made in August to visit departments, meet their ministerial and official teams and reinforce the delivery message. These meetings were now in the diary and due to take place in the next few weeks. They were 'a vital opportunity'. In the meantime, departments were being asked, in effect, to do their homework again; we required revised plans by the end of October, just two or three weeks later. We also asked them to identify the 'single named official' who was personally responsible for the delivery of each priority. 'This should be the person who spends most of his/her time on the priority and has sleepless nights, worrying about hitting the targets.' (Later I was told by one political adviser that no one should take delivery so seriously as to have sleepless nights. I disagreed then, and still do.) The idea was not just that these people could be held to account but that in addition we would organise a series of masterclasses in delivery for this select group. There would, in other words, be support as well as pressure. We also asked departments to show us how they were organising themselves to deliver, and finally in relation to each of the specific priorities offered specific practical comments and suggestions to help them improve their plans next time.

Before I finalised these first delivery reports and circulated them, I had briefed Blair, Gus Macdonald and Richard Wilson, because I firmly expected to cause some noise in Whitehall. I gave Blair the headlines over the phone. 'That sounds pretty bad,' he replied. I told him I thought he might receive some complaints and I needed to be sure he supported my approach; 'I certainly agree with that,' he said.

Macdonald was supportive too. In some ways, I thought Wilson might be the greater challenge. After all, the civil service would bear the brunt of my critique in this report, and he had been head of it for three years. To his credit, he did not flinch when I told him in outline what I intended to say. On the contrary, he commented that there was 'a whiff of success about the Delivery Unit' and confirmed that he would back me up if he received complaints. Curiously, he said that our conversation had cheered him up. With my bases covered, I now proceeded to act.

Once the report was done, I rushed over to No. 10 to ensure it made it into the Prime Minister's red box before he left on an overseas visit. I also gave a copy to Alastair Campbell, who was travelling with him. He glanced at the report, frowned and swore. I responded by saying I was determined 'to keep things shifting on the domestic front'. 'Absolutely,' came the reply.

With the report securely in the PM's box and therefore no longer susceptible to further alteration, I called each of the permanent secretaries concerned, to warn them what their departmental delivery report would be like. Most of the conversations, despite their daunting content, went well, but one permanent secretary came to the conversation very angry indeed. He had just heard from Wilson at a gathering of permanent secretaries that the reports were due to go out. His basic objection was that I had sent the report to Blair before I had discussed it with him. The conversation became even more tense when I informed him of the league table and how we'd constructed it. 'Bloody hell,' he said. 'You've even traffic-lighted it.' I returned to his main point; I said it was my job to inform the Prime Minister of the state of delivery. I also made a more telling point. Ever since there have been Prime Ministers, they have asked their closest advisers to comment on the performance of key ministers and officials, and in reply the advisers had given their opinion. This was a closed process. What the Delivery Unit had developed was different. Yes, we had sent the report to the Prime Minister without consulting; importantly, though, our comments were evidence based and we were sending them to the permanent secretaries too, so our judgements on them were open. If they could provide evidence that our judgements were wrong, we would have to change them; if our judgements were right, surely the Prime Minister had a right to know. The case was unarguable.

The permanent secretary said he would now consider whether his department would continue to be open with us. I said that was a matter for him, and that I would reflect on his comments. In fact, partly as a result of this conversation, we shifted our approach for future reports, encouraging departments as a first step to assess themselves using our traffic light framework. Then the department's permanent secretary and I would debate any differences between us on the phone. I always maintained the right to decide in the event we could not agree, because the delivery reports were my reports, but mostly we agreed, and when we didn't, we agreed to differ. Even so, I never regretted acting without consulting on the first occasion. Had the reports been open to alteration, I am sure I would have been subjected to intense pressure to soften them and would then, knowing me, have buckled.

The following day, I discovered that the Prime Minister had now read the report too. I was at a dinner in the City when one of the waiters came over to me and said I needed to ring the Prime Minister's office. Disturbed, I rang the switchboard and was put through to the duty clerk in No. 10, who said the PM was worried about the delivery reports and wanted to know to whom they had been sent. I told her they had gone to permanent secretaries but no one else. She didn't know what the PM's concerns were, which left me feeling tense. Was the most important week in the Delivery Unit's fleeting history about to unravel? Had I acted without authority? After all, I had not even attempted to clear the written content of my reports with the PM, Macdonald or Wilson.

Later, Jeremy Heywood explained that the PM's anxieties were not to do with the content, but with the risk of a leak. I relaxed a little. The following morning, I was visiting Islington police station – I liked to spend time at the frontline when I could – when the Prime Minister himself caught up with me on my mobile: 'I wanted to talk to you about the Delivery Report . . . it's excellent . . . but I think it should go to permanent secretaries and secretaries of state only,' he said. I replied that the officials responsible needed to see the comments on the relevant sections, but that I would ring permanent secretaries and require that any copies should be numbered. Thereafter with delivery reports we always numbered them before they were circulated, and never sent them by email, to reduce the risk of leaks. At the time, I was a little disappointed that Blair's chief concern had been about presentation, not substance, but this was also an important part of my education in working for a Prime Minister. With the opportunity to write notes on

10 Downing Street letterhead comes the responsibility of realising the risk of a leak, and understanding that the impact, if there is a leak, will be much greater. The tension between this clear risk and the need to circulate our material to those who need to know ran right through my four years with the Delivery Unit. Some of my staff thought I was excessively cautious on the issue – but when the occasional leak did occur I felt my position, established during this conversation with the Prime Minister, was vindicated.

More importantly, I was delighted that we had successfully made a huge stride forward. The hard-hitting delivery reports had gone out and, while the process had been fiercely debated, the content had been accepted. In a note to myself at the end of 'a tremendous week', I wrote that our emerging strong reputation

> was put to the test . . . when the Delivery Report went to Blair and to each department. It's too early to say what the consequences will have been for our reputation and for mine, but for sure it will have changed irreversibly.
>
> Above all, I think, people know we're there and we're staying there . . . [they] might have thought we'd become another marginal unit at the centre. I don't think they'll be thinking that now. Nor will they be thinking we're cuddly and collegiate.

Deliverology was firmly on the map. Through developing and applying it we had enhanced the Prime Minister's power to get things done.

*

There is one codicil to this episode which I have still not explained to myself. When I left for the dinner in the City at which I got that message to call No. 10, I forgot my mobile. Only Kate Myronidis knew my destination and she had gone home by the time No. 10 called me. The following morning, she confirmed that no one had spoken to her about my whereabouts, so how on earth had the famous switchboard tracked me down? The mystery reaffirms my view that the No. 10 switchboard is in fact the most effective arm of Britain's secret state.

4

Routines

All that I can hope to make you understand is only events: not what has happened. And people to whom nothing has ever happened cannot understand the unimportance of events.

T. S. Eliot, *The Family Reunion*

The long, grinding haul

I once travelled the stretch of the Trans-Siberian railway from Irkutsk, place of exile for dissidents under the Tsars, to Krasnoyarsk, a vast city lying on the massive river Yenisei, which flows north into the Arctic Ocean. This journey, which, as a glance at a map will confirm, is only a small fraction of the immense distance from Vladivostok to Moscow, nevertheless took eighteen hours. After the train left Irkutsk, the scenery barely changed – forlorn trees, rolling hills, patches of snow left over from the winter, endlessly. Occasionally, the train stopped at some godforsaken, small and invariably bleak town. I remember one such place called Zima (Russian for 'winter'), where the buildings were crumbling and a ruined alcoholic staggered around the station platform.

I loved this journey – perhaps I am that kind of person – not because of the places on the way, but because of the steady roll of the train wheels along the track, because of the rhythm the train rattled out mile after mile after mile, across a thousand miles of frozen waste, because when the train arrived in Zima and every other place along the way, it was exactly on time (I checked), and because all the time, with a steady monotony, the landscape slipped away and slipped away. In short, there was a constant sense of steady progress.

Similarly, I once watched Michael Atherton score 108 against the

West Indies at the Oval.* He ground out every run, scoring four times more than the second highest run scorer that innings, but he did not score fast. My friend Alan Evans, who joined me that day, arrived half an hour late and did not miss a single run. The greatness of that innings lay not in its occasional aggressive shots, but in its relentlessness, its routine, its persistence. It wasn't beautiful, but England won. To switch sporting metaphor, as a football fan, one of the best matches I can remember was England drawing 0-0 against Italy in Rome in 1997, ensuring qualification for the World Cup.

These characteristics of the Trans-Siberian Railway, a Mike Atherton innings and the England defence at its best were qualities I consciously sought to build into the way the Delivery Unit worked. Stubborn persistence, relentless monotony, attention to detail and glorying in routine are vastly underestimated in the literature on government and indeed political history. Inevitably the literature focuses on incidents, events and moments of drama, all of which cry out for explanation. Take Andrew Rawnsley's entertaining account of the first Blair term, *Servants of the People.*[1] It provides numerous insights into how the government worked, but each chapter is built around an incident: the row about social security policy (Chapter 7), the Good Friday Agreement (Chapter 8), tension between Blair and Brown over the euro (Chapter 9) and so on. Each chapter is riveting, no doubt, but the overall effect conveys a misleading account of what government is truly like.

Rawnsley's approach is like judging a family on the basis of its photograph albums: here we find birthdays, wedding anniversaries, Christmases and holidays, but special occasions are not the real test of the quality of relationships in a family, precisely because they are special. All of us know that it's the routine day-to-day interactions that shape a family – the mealtimes, the television-viewing, the missing cap from the toothpaste tube, the getting ready for school, the coming home from work . . . But Rawnsley's account of government misses out the day-to-day. Take a single example: one looks in vain in the index of Rawnsley's book for the national literacy and numeracy strategies

*For the non-British reader, Michael Atherton was captain of the England cricket team in the 1990s, and the Oval is a famous cricket ground in London. Cricket is best defined by Lord Mancroft as 'a game which the English ... have invented in order to give themselves some conception of eternity'. Atherton understood this better than anyone.

which were transforming the performance of primary schools; they were not on his radar because there was no legislation, no row, just steady, persistent implementation. The Department for Education is in fact mentioned just once in the book (on page 147), characteristically in relation to a row with the Treasury.

In the Delivery Unit, a key part of our mission was precisely to develop and prioritise these understated qualities which make so much difference to delivery. The key insight is that well-established routines are as important to the exercise of prime ministerial power and the delivery of results as major decisions on strategy or people; moreover they were precisely what Tony Blair had lacked in his first term.* Sometimes I even found I had to debate this issue with my staff. Inevitably, their attention would be drawn to things that were going wrong and the interventions this required us to make (see Chapter 5), but the danger came when any of us shifted from rightly paying attention to these interventions to wrongly thinking that they were the only way we had an impact. Often at staff meetings I would wrench people's attention back to the routines of deliverology – the stocktakes, tracking the data against trajectory, writing delivery reports, keeping the focus. Just as historians and commentators can easily fall into the trap of focusing on the events, so can those in government. In fact, without the routine, events cannot be fully understood and, more importantly, results will never be delivered. From outside, government always looks chaotic, partly because it often is, and partly because only the events – in effects the breaks in routine – get reported. Part of the mission of the Delivery Unit was to establish, at least internally, the primacy of order over chaos.

This chapter is therefore largely about how we sought to combine the elements of deliverology into a steady, relentless routine. Mario Cuomo, former Governor of New York, once said, 'You campaign in poetry. You govern in prose.' I would push this point even further – it doesn't even have to be good prose as long as it covers the key points. The only political commentator who came close to capturing this was Matthew d'Ancona, writing in the *Sunday Telegraph* on 6 January 2002: 'There is no drama in delivery . . . only a long, grinding haul punctuated by

---

* Perhaps Nelson Mandela had the same insight when he finished his farewell speech to the South African Parliament with the words 'the long walk continues' (26 March 1999).

public frustration with the pace of change.' I leapt on this quote, using it in a meeting with the Prime Minister later that month and repeatedly thereafter because it was a rare third-party endorsement of the mindset I wanted to engender early in the parliament.

The pursuit of coherence

In the autumn of 2001, one of the most demanding and energy-sapping themes dominating my time was what might be called the search for coherence at the centre of government. Coherence was highly desirable, of course, but a vain search for it could so easily eat up precious time. It rapidly became evident to me, at that time, that coherence would not be achieved, only discussed. In fact, talking about it (or its absence) became a substitute for action and an excuse for inaction. Though Blair had agreed at the outset that I should not waste my time in meetings about how the various parts of No. 10 and the Cabinet Office fitted together, he had in part created the problem by setting up so many competing units and functions. Furthermore, I could not afford to avoid these meetings altogether. Some of them would indeed be a pure waste of time, but others might make decisions, and if I were absent, I could find that Delivery Unit interests had been damaged. The problem was knowing which were which.

In any case, there was no appetite for a radical redesign of the centre of government at that stage. The task was to make the most of what we had. Thus, my personal interest throughout these meetings became to establish and maintain the room for manoeuvre that the Delivery Unit needed. I was guilty, in those first few months, of parochialism. By 2002, I felt I had strong enough bonds with both the Prime Minister and Richard Wilson that if I had found myself dealt a rotten hand, I could have pulled these aces from my sleeve. However, I didn't want to have to do so if I could avoid it, partly because by definition it would be an admission of weakness, and partly because Prime Ministers and Cabinet Secretaries have better things to do than sort out squabbles between Cabinet Office units.

Thus, through that autumn, tiresome though it was, I patrolled our frontiers, seeing off any marauding unit or section which seemed to threaten our agenda or inhibit our capacity to act. It wasn't fun. Once I wrote myself a note saying, 'Early each week I wonder whether I've done the right thing in taking this job . . . because sometimes it is dominated by "keeping-in-touch" meetings . . . It's all deeply tedious.' In building a significant working relationship with the permanent secretaries of the four departments, I had heard their (justified) complaints about confusion at the centre and, in the absence of radical redesign, decided the solution lay in keeping other new and existing units out of their way. In this, Gus Macdonald was a steadfast ally. He came over to the Delivery Unit to meet the staff, promoted it in meetings he and I had with the No. 10 Policy Directorate, and in the Monday afternoon meetings he chaired of all the various units, invariably ruled in favour of the Delivery Unit. Wilson too, delighted to see it beginning to have an impact, was steadily supportive. When he asked me what I thought about the changes at the centre, I resorted to Christopher Hill's phrase about the English Civil War: 'a revolution stopped halfway'. I said I thought Blair had more powerful capacity and more brain at the centre than in his first term. For example, the new Strategy Unit, led by Geoff Mulgan and involving John Birt, was a major gain, but arrangements were still chaotic. To finish the job, I suggested, a fully fledged Prime Minister's Department – no apologies required – was necessary (see Chapter 9). To the outside world, a Prime Minister, especially one like Blair or Margaret Thatcher before him, with a large majority, might look all-powerful. By contrast, from inside No. 10 looking outwards, the strong sense is of a small number of people trying to influence a vast, unwieldy and unmanageable bureaucracy.

The two dominant institutions on which I had to rely to defend my corner successfully were firstly No. 10, especially the Policy Directorate, and secondly the Treasury. Though the Delivery Unit was widely seen in both of these revered institutions to have made a good start, I was constantly insecure about both relationships and therefore constantly investing in them. For example, when it was proposed that, on top of our work with the Home Office, Health, Education and Transport on delivery, the Office of Public Service Reform should conduct departmental reviews of them using a long and complicated set of criteria, I whirled round Whitehall – No. 10 and the Treasury especially, but also Macdonald and Wilson – arguing that this would both overload 'my' departments and distract their permanent secretaries from delivery just when, as a result of our efforts, they had focused on it. In the end, I won this encounter by acting more like a rugby forward than a corporate citizen of the Cabinet Office; sometimes the game in a bureaucracy is a rough one. Instead, the OPSR turned its attentions to the Lord Chancellor's Department, the Department of Environment, Food and Rural Affairs (DEFRA) and the Scottish Executive.

By early 2002, the search for coherence had vanished, since palpably nothing could be done during that parliament. Everyone had decided they had better things to do. Meanwhile, the Delivery Unit, strongly allied to No. 10, the Strategy Unit and the Treasury, had firmly established itself. Over dinner in January 2002, Jeremy Heywood remarked that the Delivery Unit had 'massively increased the power of the Prime Minister without damaging any relationships'. The key from then on was to put that power to good effect, and the key to that was the steady routine that was now beginning to emerge.

Happy Christmas, Prime Minister

In December 2001, just a couple of months after the previous ones, we issued our second round of delivery reports. Departments had sub-mitted revised plans following our October feedback. We had had a further round of conversations with them, again involving outside experts where appropriate. In the unit we had discussed the extent of progress with these experts, sought the views on the revised plans of the other key parts of the (incoherent) centre and then assembled as a staff in the airless Westminster Room in 53 Parliament Street and prepared our second league table. As always, these long meetings, which were ultimately hugely productive, passed through a phase of tetchiness. My staff felt badgered and cajoled by me; I felt doubted and questioned by them. There is a name for this: learning. It was important, difficult work and we were still feeling our way.

In the end, though, we got there. We were able to report significant improvement since October. This was important to me, partly because I was desperate to see the development of some sort of momentum from the terribly low base we had reported previously, and partly because I felt that unless there was some progress, our own contribution as a Delivery Unit was open to question. Even so, it was important to be objective, and the debate with the staff ensured this. They argued cogently against reporting improvement unless it was really significant. Clara Swinson, who led for us on Health was, I remember, eloquently sceptical. Looking back, I am very glad they took this line because our objectivity was more important to our reputation in the long term than making improvement in the short term. On 13 December I cleared my diary, cancelled a dinner I was supposed to have been at and stayed late in No. 10 finishing the delivery reports, and especially the overview I prepared for Blair. After a day of scribbling in what I think of as 'mad professor mode', I had a long note I was happy with. This time, in addition to the league table and an overview, I provided him with a five-to-ten line summary of my views on each of the priorities.

The note informed him of his most intractable problems, which included robbery, rail reliability and Health Service waiting times. The last, it said, was both the most important to the public and the most complex. There were prescient comments: 'The two major challenges in this area [crime] are street robbery, where the Home Office still has poor plans, and anti-social behaviour, where policy thinking is still at an early stage. The reality is that unless these two issues are cracked, the gains on the rest of the crime agenda will not be seen as the achievement they are.' Within weeks, in fact, street robbery and anti-social behaviour (in that order) came to dominate the crime and policing agenda.

On the railways, I told the Prime Minister that while 'Gus [Macdonald] thinks I am hopelessly optimistic on this issue', I believed that progress would be possible because Stephen Byers had taken the necessary tough decisions to stop bailing out Railtrack, which was the proverbial bottomless pit, and to set up the financially more sustainable Network Rail. This too turned out eventually to be true, though Byers never received the credit he was due.

On NHS waiting times, I argued that 'a much more sustainable approach' was required and that the pilot offering a choice of provider to patients who had waited up to six months for an operation should go ahead. On illegal drug use, the report said that 'the risks to delivery remain immense; collaboration across departments and services is relatively weak'.

By December 2001, then, we had identified accurately the more intractable challenges that would dominate the parliament. It is striking in retrospect how long it was before government collectively was able to muster the necessary leverage to shift these systems and deliver results. It was eighteen months before anyone could be confident on waiting times, for example, and over two years before the rail results began to shift steadily in the right direction.

My report was less accurate on one or two areas on which I was optimistic at the time, most notably secondary education: 'Planning and preparation for transformation are now much stronger and in places impressive.' Perhaps because, in my previous post, I had worked so closely with the education people, including the secretary of state, Estelle Morris, I was biased.

The report also identified some general lessons. It emphasised the need for consistent focus and avoiding distractions, however tempting: 'Delivery needs to be pursued urgently, consistently and strategically, and policies need to be seen through to implementation; media frenzies and new initiatives can easily deflect us from strategic implementation.' Again it placed emphasis on ensuring that good leadership was in place and the importance of departments 'knowing rapidly how their policies are working at the frontline'. Finally, it emphasised the importance of persuading people that step change was possible. The torpor that resulted from years of underperformance hung like a cloud over the vast bureaucracy and needed to be lifted. I finished the note: 'Delivery on the scale we are attempting . . . requires . . . a tremendous collective act of will. I sense this coming into place too. As you anticipated back in June, we can expect 2002 to be a tough year and we mustn't flinch.' I suppose this was one way of saying, 'Happy Christmas, Prime Minister.'

As the note went to Blair, so permanent secretaries and secretaries of state again received their delivery reports. As in October, I spoke on the phone to each of the four permanent secretaries. I was relieved that none of the October reports had leaked, but I had noticed that someone – a top official, I presumed – had briefed the *Financial Times* diary somewhat bitterly:

> Much gnashing of teeth among the Whitehall mandarins. Michael Barber, Tony Blair's chief efficiency guru, has sent out half-term reports to the heads of Whitehall's departments. Worse still, he has confirmed the government's obsession with league tables by producing an unprecedented ranking of the department's supposed performance. The reaction of many mandarins is unprintable.[2]

In fact, I found permanent secretaries ready to engage with a process they were beginning to respect. There were no major arguments this time, though one or two of them were edgy and argued vigorously that I had been too negative in my judgements. Where we were unable to agree, I stuck firmly to my guns in the league table, but recorded the disagreement in the note to the Prime Minister.

On this occasion, I spoke to each of the four secretaries of state too. Estelle Morris welcomed our advice but remained nervous about the Delivery Unit and indeed about No. 10 as a whole, though she and I were always on friendly terms. (I knew from an inadvertent comment that Education Department officials had been told to talk to me only with permission, but knew this was not on her orders.) In this phone call, Morris was relaxed, as at this stage Education looked like the best department. She herself had sensibly decided to commit Tuesday mornings to quizzing the officials responsible for her delivery priorities. David Blunkett was relaxed too, for the opposite reason: he wanted a challenging delivery report because he thought it would help drive necessary change through the Home Office. He had had a tough week; his emergency legislation on terrorism had been mauled in the Lords. He chuckled when I quoted what Churchill had said to Asquith on 3 January 1911, having just come across it in Roy Jenkins's biography of Churchill: 'We don't want any more dilatory vapourings from the Lords.'[3] On the delivery issues, he said he wished his top officials would be much more rigorous and urged me to keep the pressure on.

Stephen Byers, at the end of a torrid few weeks which had included the Jo Moore affair and the intervention in Railtrack, asked about the detail. I told him that it would need nerves of steel and great determination to bring about improvement. I thought he had done well in appointing Richard Bowker to head the Strategic Rail Authority. Alan Milburn took the view that I had been a little too negative about Health. He wanted to press forward with the introduction of choice, he said. I said I would give time and attention to his pilots of choice for patients and argued that the department lacked strategic capacity. He said I should continue to press that argument. Overall, the basic deal I had struck with the Cabinet ministers had stood the test of these calls – they were beginning to see the Delivery Unit as largely on their side, assisting them in shifting cautious or ineffective bureaucracies.

Most important of all, I had to speak to Blair, whose time was under immense pressure. I defended my slot with him – on the Monday before Christmas – with great vigour. Gus Macdonald and several members of Blair's closest advisers joined me as I went through the key messages with him. An hour later he was due to make a statement to the House on Europe and Afghanistan, and not surprisingly appeared 'distracted and less than attentive', as I noted after the meeting. It was one of those occasions when the symbolism of the meeting taking place at all was important to me, but the value of it was limited. The note of the meeting recorded simply that he was 'very pleased with the progress since the last report'.

By Christmas 2001 I also knew that Gordon Brown was happy with our work. At the end of the previous month, Macdonald had arranged for me to brief the Chancellor. I took the opportunity to explain how the Delivery Unit was approaching its work; in return he quizzed me vigorously on the state of the Health Service, and though I felt out of my depth I did not crumble. Shortly afterwards, I realised I must have made a sound impression, because in relation to the pilots of patient choice, the Chancellor insisted that the Department of Health gain the approval not just of the Treasury, but also the Delivery Unit before they went ahead. This was a major breakthrough – the first formal acknowledgement of our value from Brown.

Gentle pressure, relentlessly applied

An American colleague once told me that the key to delivery was 'gentle pressure, relentlessly applied'. The phrase describes the Delivery Unit routine perfectly. After December 2001, delivery reports became something we did twice a year, in December and July – a routine that continues. They were the centrepiece of our internal accountability system, and we became steadily better at them. Our relationships with departments settled down and their trust in us and our methods increased, which meant the preparation of the delivery reports became a more collaborative venture. They always remained my personal reports, but our staff increasingly drafted the various sections in consultation with the relevant officials. This meant that later reports caused less of a frisson around Whitehall than the first two, even though they became if anything sharper and more challenging over time. They ceased to shock the system and became instead a constructive and steady routine.

A crucial advance came during 2002 when we prepared, for the first time, the assessment framework (see Delivery Manual, Document 3) which set out for departments the questions we asked ourselves when deciding league table judgements. We refined this a couple of times over the years, and each draft was developed in consultation with departmental officials responsible for delivery. Once the assessment framework itself had been circulated, departments themselves could reach traffic light judgements and indeed apply the framework to areas of their responsibility in which the Delivery Unit was not involved. The Treasury also adopted it and began to use it more generally. We were, in short, beginning to professionalise our own – and Whitehall's – thinking about delivery.

Through this process we were, in effect, systematising and making explicit what parts of Whitehall had been doing haphazardly and implicitly for years. For example, for years officials had been willing to write down all the risks they could think of; now we were urging them to manage them actively. On one level, all we had done was introduce a simple unremarkable routine, on another it was a breakthrough – by describing what it took to drive delivery, we made it possible for people to debate it, understand it and, above all, get better at it.

There were similar developments in other aspects of our routine, for example our monthly notes to the Prime Minister on the different areas. In the autumn of 2001, Jeremy Heywood repeatedly urged me to send more brief weekend notes to Blair, particularly ones with key statistics on the major areas, such as crime. In response, I urged my staff to prepare a note on each major department every four weeks, which would mean that Blair would get a note a week from us routinely and any other notes I did would be additional. To my surprise, the staff did not warm to this at first. They argued that we should only send notes when we had something to say. In reply, I said most people in the country would die to have the opportunity to communicate directly with the Prime Minister once a month, that it was important to ensure our visibility at the vortex and that, if they were on top of their jobs, they would always have something to say.

Reluctantly they began to write these notes. Health proved to be the best because, even at that early stage in our existence, the department provided monthly data on key indicators such as waiting times. In the other areas we sometimes laboured to relate interesting stories or insights until, during 2002 and 2003, we secured regular monthly data on most indicators. Then the 'PM notes', as we called them, became routine too (see Delivery Manual, Document 1). My task in editing them on a Friday before they went into the Blair box was to delete management jargon – extraordinary phrases such as 'front-end delivery' were always at risk of proliferating – and to sharpen the messages to the PM; in effect making sure we called a spade a spade. Since I thought Blair had enough to worry about, I also insisted that the notes told him what we planned to do about the problems we described. Often I then asked him to confirm that he was happy with the course of action. The simple, routine act of reporting progress to the PM consistently ensured the gentle pressure we required.

Meanwhile, the stocktakes too were becoming a steady routine. In the early days, establishing the importance of the stocktake routine with departments was not always easy. In March 2002, for example, I scribbled myself a note about Department for Transport officials who claimed 'they were too busy [to prepare a stocktake paper] and – reverting to their traditional bleat – there was not much they could do about rail reliability anyway'. It took a call to a political adviser and the permanent secretary to ensure that 'Whitehall began to jump'. 'It's important', I concluded, 'that the Delivery Unit is taken seriously.' A train journey to Edinburgh in April 2002 when I arrived seventeen hours late (counting an unwanted night in Carlisle) sharpened my attitude too.

Throughout 2002, stocktakes tended to be on Tuesday mornings. For each department they came round every two months or so – later every three months – but for the Prime Minister and me that meant on average a stocktake every fortnight. We ground them out just as the Trans-Siberian trains grind out all those miles. Sometimes they went absolutely according to plan, and Blair was able to congratulate the relevant officials.* On other occasions, the discussion wandered off into more general areas of reform. In one Education stocktake, for example, we debated reform of the secondary curriculum. Blair questioned the way

*He often offered praise warmly, as leaders should, but it can be overdone: take for example Catherine the Great in her congratulatory letter to Potemkin after he had captured Ochakov: 'I take you by the ears and kiss you in my thoughts.'

Estelle Morris planned to assess extracurricular activities, and suggested sceptically that playing the guitar in a band might count. Andrew Adonis, equally sceptical, added, 'Or newt-collecting,' at which point someone chipped in, 'And one became Prime Minister and the other the mayor of London.' Sometimes my staff were elated by the Prime Minister's engagement (which was most common on Health), and sometimes disappointed by his lack of it (most common on Transport), but I kept telling them that we had to take the rough with the smooth. The demands on a Prime Minister can be overwhelming and sometimes his mind will be elsewhere. And anyway, I would remind them, the Prime Minister's attention on a given day wasn't the main point; it was the routine itself that mattered.

Between stocktakes there were sometimes issues which required a more thorough investigation. For these we often set up a departmental presentation. The relevant senior officials would present to a panel comprised of relevant Delivery Unit, Policy Directorate and Treasury people, a few outside experts and people from the frontline of the service in question. We would then quiz and challenge the departmental officials for a couple of hours to put them under pressure. We would book one of the upstairs rooms in Downing Street, which gave the meetings a status and formality we could never have achieved elsewhere. Then, following the meeting, I wrote the top official in the department a three- or four-page, sharply worded letter on what we had concluded, and copied this to the relevant minister and permanent secretary. This would be based on the points I made in summing up the meeting.

These summings-up became legendary in the Delivery Unit, and my staff used to ask me how I could chair a meeting and still come up with sufficient notes to make ten or twelve really telling points at the end of the meeting. The answer is simple – with their unwitting assistance, I prepared the summing-up before the meeting began. Anyone chairing a meeting who is on top of the issues should be able to predict, with an accuracy of 80 per cent or more, what issues will emerge and how to deal with them.

A typical example was a discussion in April 2002 on improving behaviour and discipline in secondary schools – always a priority for parents, teachers and indeed well-behaved pupils – which, at that moment, was an even higher priority because of the epidemic of street crime that peaked early that year. We urged the department to give the issue the priority it deserved and not to rely on the classic Whitehall defence that they were already doing a lot. Whatever it was, it wasn't working. There was plenty of activity but no impact. We urged them to make their approach practical for teachers, to answer their question: 'How will it help me in practice to do my job better?' The subtext here was that sending out wordy guidance or jargon-ridden summaries of education research findings was not the answer. Finally, we urged them to be bold in ensuring parents took their responsibilities seriously, if necessary by recourse to the law – to make parenting orders work, in other words.

So often on issues such as this we ran into a wet liberalism that stood in the way of making a practical difference. Anti-social behaviour orders (ASBOs) were another case in point. On both parenting orders and ASBOs at first, the relevant departments watered them down, overbureaucratised them and hesitated to promote their use. They may not have been perfect instruments of social reform but in fact, in both cases, once these hesitations and barriers were overcome, the positive impact was almost immediate. The Prime Minister, sitting in Downing Street, would be metaphorically tearing his hair out waiting, sometimes for more than a year, for common sense to prevail in the departments. Presentations such as the one I've described, or a prime ministerial variation where he quizzed a dozen or so practitioners in front of the relevant ministers, often helped to unblock the system.

Educating Whitehall

Meanwhile, we had begun a programme to train the senior civil servants who were personally responsible for delivering Blair's top priorities. We introduced them to leading businesspeople and arranged sessions in which they explored each other's challenges as a way of jolting them out of their silos. Blair himself came to one of their events, answered questions and concluded by telling them that while they might worry that failing to deliver would affect their careers, he was certain the risk to his career was greater. Then, in October 2002, we held a conference not just for these twenty or so senior civil servants, but for their teams and around 200 others across Whitehall. This was the first in a series of events designed to spread the delivery culture. I used the occasion to sum up in five words what the Delivery Unit had learnt in its first year of operation, as a conscious challenge to the prevailing culture. The idea was to show that successful delivery often lay not in the big decisions, but in the everyday routine; the endless micro-decisions and interactions with officials, partners and stakeholders. In other words, the barriers to success, more often than not, were in people's heads – none but ourselves can free our minds, as Bob Marley summed it up. The presentation summarised how we in the Delivery Unit saw the prevailing Whitehall culture at the time and what needed to change (see Delivery Manual, Document 4).

The key words – which I repeated time and again from then on – were *ambition, focus, clarity, urgency* and *irreversibility*. The central message was:

> Things have moved on since the then Prime Minister, Lord Salisbury, said at the turn of the previous century, 'All change is for the worse so it's in our interests that as little should happen as possible.' At the turn of the current century, our Prime Minister has an opposite view. He talks about 'step change' and asks, 'How long have we got?' . . . People are impatient for change and sceptical about our capacity to deliver.

We should prove them wrong, I argued, show them that we could deliver and bring rapid, effective change. I remembered a joke from long ago and appropriated it for this audience:

> What have civil servants traditionally chanted on demonstrations?
>   'What do we want?'
>   'Procrastination!'
>   'When do we want it?'
>   'Next week!'

These delivery conferences became part of the annual routine, each one an opportunity to hammer home the same messages in different ways.

Over the next three years, the delivery culture in Whitehall did change in the direction indicated in this speech. Senior civil servants, to their credit, generally recognised the need for change, but found it hard to bring it about – the deadweight of the culture held them back. Even so, looking back, it is disturbing that the shift fell far short of what is needed. All our efforts in the Delivery Unit for four relentless years brought welcome change but not irreversible progress in the civil service culture. Indeed, at the end of Blair's second term, it had only just begun, even in the departments where we were most actively engaged. Bringing about this culture change, it could be argued, is the central challenge facing Gus O'Donnell, the Cabinet Secretary appointed in 2005.

Educating the Cabinet

That same autumn of 2002 was also the first time I had the opportunity to present to the Cabinet, something else which became a routine thereafter. On each occasion the opportunity came round, I became completely obsessed with preparing to use the slot well. As I used to explain to my staff, in the absence of natural talent, good preparation is all there is. Each time, I was offered about ten minutes, the view being, I think, that the Cabinet's attention span was no more than that. Each time I took twelve minutes; I know because by the time I presented I had rehearsed on my own several times. I obsessed over every detail of the presentation: the graphs, the phrases I would use, the pace and timing of the key messages. I tested out these presentations on my staff, who were always critical and constructive, and even my long-suffering wife Karen and our daughters, who were subjected to rants about delivery at the kitchen table. I can remember my daughter Alys on one such occasion correcting my grammar. I once worked out that, for each of these Cabinet presentations, I personally spent more than twenty hours preparing; in addition, there were the days contributed by a number of Delivery Unit staff, especially Tony O'Connor, our irrepressible number cruncher, and Kate Myronidis, who patiently designed the PowerPoint presentations and (almost) never complained at my control-freak tendencies.

Was it worth it? Absolutely – this was the Cabinet, after all; if they could act with common purpose, the chances of bringing about successful change would be immeasurably enhanced, but it was not just the power they collectively wielded that focused my mind, it was the history they represented. They were the heirs of leaders who had changed our nation: Pitt, Wellington, Peel, Gladstone, Disraeli,

Churchill, Attlee, Thatcher . . . how could I not prepare with all the thoroughness I could muster? Yet I have met very senior civil servants who prepared for a presentation to the Cabinet as if it was just another seminar. I once recommended to a colleague, who was due to present to the Cabinet a few days later, that he should clear his diary and focus on it. 'My usual approach', he said in reply, 'is to wing it.' Breathtaking.

That first time I presented, I made the argument about the five key words, as I had for the civil servants, but I wanted to do something more. I wanted to provide a rationale for delivery which showed it was not just a technocratic process, but a crucial aspect of the political agenda of the second term. I wanted to excite them about delivery. I built the rationale around Blair's statement to the Labour Party conference, which had taken place a few weeks earlier, that we were witnessing a shift from the big state of the twentieth century to the enabling state. I contrasted two possible futures, the enabling state as advocated by Blair, and the minimalist state as was emerging in some parts of the United States and in the Far East. It is worth setting out the argument I made, because it explains so much of the Blair government's approach to the public services and why delivery is critical.

If the minimalist-state option came to pass, I argued, the public services of the second half of the twentieth century would become, in the new century, private and paid for through insurance or at the point of use, with the residual public services becoming a mere safety net for those who could not afford anything better. This option is devastating for social cohesion or equity, but has the major political benefit of allowing significantly lower taxes – say a tax burden at 30 per cent of GDP rather than the current figure in this country of 40 per cent. As the incomes of the majority grow, it therefore has significant appeal. It can be seen in operation in, for example, New Orleans, where anyone with wealth buys private education, taxes are low, spending on education is low and the school system, even before the flood, was shockingly bad; a classic example in fact of what Richard Titmuss, years ago, described with ruthless honesty as 'poor services for poor people'.

The enabling state as proposed by Blair requires a wholly different approach to the public services. It requires first a recognition of the fact that modern societies are diverse – in culture, ethnicity, lifestyle and aspiration. Whereas under the Attlee settlement after 1945, universal also meant uniform, in the early twenty-first century only public services which respond to this diversity can be universal. This, in fact, is the key underlying difference between old and New Labour: the one hankers after uniformity ('the neighbourhood comprehensive' for example), the other embraces diversity. In explaining this theme to the Cabinet, I was drawing on ideas I had written about when Blair was in opposition.

Most people over the age of forty have read the Sellar and Yeatman classic *1066 and All That*. For those with short memories or excessive youth, it was a light-hearted romp through a thousand years of British history. Among their many pearls of wisdom, Sellar and Yeatman invented an important classification. Writing about the English Civil War, they defined the Cavaliers as 'wrong but wromantic' and the Roundheads as 'right and repulsive'. The more one thinks about this classification, the more aspects of life it seems to apply to. It helps to explain, in any case, the difference between old Labour and New Labour (and indeed the challenge for the modern Conservative Party as David Cameron seeks to radically reposition it).

Table 3.1: Equality and diversity

	Inequality	Equality
Diversity	Wrong but romantic	Right and romantic
Uniformity	Wrong and repulsive	Right but repulsive

The challenge is summarised in Table 3.1. The traditional political right, it will be seen, are to be found in the top left corner of the table, favouring a combination of inequality and diversity. In Sellar and Yeatman terms, they are wrong about equality but romantic about diversity. The traditional political left are to be found in the bottom right corner; right in that they favour equality, but repulsive in their support for uniformity.

The table has two remaining corners. In the bottom left corner, we find the entirely objectionable combination of inequality and uniformity. No one, surely, would set out to be both wrong and repulsive, at least not on purpose.* The top right corner of the table brings

*It is, of course, true that some politicians achieve this unwelcome combination by accident.

together equality with diversity. Even the phrase has a positive ring to it. The case for choosing this aspiration is not only that it has an obvious appeal. More importantly, the combination of equality and diversity recognises two increasingly important underlying social trends which have made the stale conflicts of the post-war era redundant. On the one hand, we need public services which are of a universally high standard; on the other, those same services need to take account of the extent to which society has become dramatically more diverse in the past thirty years or so.

In addition, if they are to be universal, modern public services have to be so good that the growing numbers of people who can afford the private alternative still choose them. This is a much higher bar of quality than prevailed in the twentieth century. It is of decisive importance because, in the long run, the relatively wealthy will be willing to pay taxes for public services only if they use them. And only if they are willing to pay sufficient tax – around 40 per cent of GDP – can the public services be designed to provide not just steadily rising average standards of performance, but also greater equity. In other words, Blair's central political insight in domestic policy is the recognition that the public services can improve the lot of the disadvantaged only if they also appeal to the middle classes. In Gordon Brown's speeches this is referred to as 'progressive universalism'.

The crunch point from the delivery perspective is this: delivering this vision is a massive challenge. It requires bold reforms which transform mediocre services into excellent services, and the reforms will only work if they are excellently implemented. In short, meeting the delivery challenge is central to achieving the political project.

By contrast, the minimalist-state vision requires nothing of the sort. In fact, it benefits from running down the public services so they lose support; then those who can opt out do, and taxes can be cut. Meanwhile, if governments which seek the enabling-state solution fail to deliver, then those who are able to will opt out incrementally, perhaps over many years, and the minimalist state will arrive by default. In other words, minimalist-state public services can be achieved either as a conscious political strategy or through incompetence. I set out this argument for the Cabinet because I wanted them to realise that their political aspirations depended on successful delivery, and because I believed strongly that only if they individually and collectively took delivery seriously could we succeed.

I finished up by asking them a set of questions about their own contributions to delivery. For example, did their diaries reflect their priorities? I could tell from the nervous laughter that here I had struck a chord. In fact, one of the clearest indicators of the effectiveness of ministers is whether they control their diaries or their diaries control them. Left to their own devices, private offices will fill ministers' diaries with meetings, and ministers will feel busy and indeed really be busy, rushing from pillar to post but achieving nothing. And once in a meeting, I asked them, did they challenge, question and press hard? Did they have independent evidence from sources outside the civil service which enabled them to contest the smooth reassurances of the 'good civil servant'? (In the Delivery Unit, when we described someone as a 'good civil servant' we were conscious of the ambiguity.) My one and only scoop as a journalist – a role I took on only in my spare time as a professor in the mid-1990s – was when I interviewed Kenneth Baker in 1996, on the tenth anniversary of his appointment as Secretary of State for Education. He described to me how Margaret Thatcher was briefed for her meetings with him. She had a note from his department, a note from her own Policy Unit in No. 10 and then sometimes, he said, she would pull a note from her handbag with a flourish, make a telling point and say, 'What do you think about that, Kenneth?' It turned out that some of this briefing came from her hairdresser in Lambeth, who had children in the local primary school and was appalled by what went on there.* The key point is that Thatcher had independent sources of information, in contrast to so many ministers who accept the reassuring accounts of their unruffled civil servants at face value.

As I left the meeting, I sensed that it had had an impact. Referring back to one of the points I had made, one Cabinet minister told me cheerfully, 'We haven't got the right people in the right place with the right support, but at least we know we haven't.'

'That's certainly a start,' I replied.

---

*Since Thatcher, when Prime Minister, had her hair done once and sometimes twice every day, it can be assumed that her hairdresser had more access to her than most members of the Cabinet.

The 2002 spending review and the NHS

Another important routine for the Delivery Unit was established in 2002: our role in spending reviews. The concept of spending reviews had been developed by Gordon Brown in his first year as Chancellor. Rather than continue with the remorseless annual cycle of the spending round, which had been such a dominating feature of previous governments, Brown introduced a three-year spending cycle. It is easy to underestimate how radical Brown's reforms of public expenditure have been. Most governments around the world are still driven by the annual cycle of negotiating spending settlements. This means that – like painting the Forth Bridge – as soon as one round is finished, the bureaucracy starts on the next. I once had the pleasure of visiting the then US Secretary of Education, Richard Riley, on the day President Clinton signed the US government's budget. I travelled with Riley to the White House and sat in the Rose Garden while Clinton delivered his speech. The moment we were back in the car, Riley was on the phone starting the negotiation for the next year's budget. This is the stuff of politics in much of the world, but it makes it very hard to get anything done. Politicians and bureaucrats find themselves locked in an introverted game rather than looking at the effects of their actions in the real world.

The 2002 spending review, Brown's third, allocated funding for the period 2003–6. Its centrepiece was Health. In the autumn of 2001 there had been the inevitable squeals from the NHS about not being able to get through the winter without extra funding. I couldn't help wondering why, every year, winter seemed to come as a surprise to the Health Service. In the pre-Budget statement in November 2001, the Treasury (and No. 10) reluctantly accepted the case made by the Department of Health, and found an extra billion pounds to tide the NHS over the winter, but Brown had already made up his mind that this was not the way to do business; a more sustainable settlement was required. Such an iconic service could not continue to live hand to mouth. He therefore brought forward the Health spending settlement to his Budget in April, and in a spellbinding Budget speech set out the five-year settlement he proposed, which he would fund through a 1 per cent increase in national insurance: 'I believe it is right that when everyone – employees and employers – benefits from the insurance provided by the National

Health Service, everyone who can should make a fair contribution.'[4]

From that moment on, the central challenge of the second term was to ensure that there was powerful evidence that the NHS had significantly improved, especially by massively reducing waiting times. The challenge was about more than the Health Service, however, important though that was. As Robert Peston has pointed out, it was a challenge to one of the givens of British politics since Thatcherism that direct taxes could not be increased without wreaking huge damage to the governing party. 'It was the first proper test of whether voters now had confidence in a British government to spend their money wisely.'[5] Since I knew by then that Brown set great store by the Delivery Unit and was relying on us to drive through the results, the pressure on me felt intense.

Fortunately, by spring 2002 there were early signs that Health, driven mercilessly by Alan Milburn, was at last beginning to make some progress. In late March, at a stocktake, I reminded Milburn that in the January stocktake he had accused me of being excessively pessimistic and, I added, 'it turns out you were right'. The NHS had driven itself hard at the end of the financial year and waiting times had fallen both for outpatients and inpatients, though the maximum wait was still an appalling fifteen months. In addition, winter had passed without a crisis.

Also, the Delivery Unit had reviewed the pilot of patient choice in London and eventually been able to recommend to the Treasury that it go ahead. This was a good example of how we worked. We did not just review how the Department of Health was implementing the choice pilot; we helped it to succeed and became actively involved ourselves. For us it was the result that mattered. In January, when Adrian Masters, the Delivery Unit's recently arrived health wizard, first looked at the pilot, he had been disturbed by the absence of a plan, or even a budget. I emailed Paul Corrigan, Milburn's political adviser, and as a result of his intervention and Masters's skills in planning, some progress was made by the end of the month. Even then, one of our external advisers commented, 'If this were a business proposition, I wouldn't consider investing in it.' By March, though, it was ready to roll. Our assistance and the pressure from Simon Stevens of the Policy Directorate and Corrigan had had its effect.

Even so, the challenge of reducing waiting times to less than six months, introducing choice for all patients, and improving primary care as well as specific services such as those for coronary heart disease and cancer, looked massive that spring. The Budget had provided for a five-year spending settlement with real annual increases of more than 8 per cent, so a lack of funding could no longer be an excuse. The NHS had to deliver, and our job was to help them learn how. When I saw Milburn in late April, he had a spring in his step; after all, no Health Secretary in history had ever secured a better spending settlement. He was very clear what his task was – to drive through the reforms, take on the vested interests, bring in private sector providers where necessary and build on the choice pilot to ensure the results were met.

Once the Health settlement had been made early, the main task for the Delivery Unit, working in close collaboration with the Treasury, before the July spending review was to review the Public Service Agreement targets, remove a handful of badly designed ones, defend some tough ones against departments who sought to get themselves off the hook, and reduce the overall number so that the priorities were clearer and sharper. It was the first time the targets had been reviewed since the Delivery Unit had been established, and it offered an opportunity to clarify and sharpen them. Tony O'Connor and I, and many of the staff, worked hard through a draining series of meetings with departmental officials to make the targets SMART, as the jargon has it: Specific, Measurable, Achievable, Realistic and Time-limited. O'Connor prepared a very witty presentation on how to do this, which he repeated literally dozens of times across Whitehall in a largely successful effort to bring sanity to the process.

Blair was determined to have fewer targets as well as better ones. The Treasury was happy to reduce the number of targets, but only if there was a good explanation for each one that was dropped. So we had a series of meetings with the No. 10 Policy Directorate and the Treasury, in which we ran through the targets, examined progress and wondered whether to keep them (which we mostly did) or drop them (which we occasionally did).* The critique commonly levelled by commentators was that the government either intentionally set targets that were easy

---

*I was delighted when, in one of these meetings, Ed Balls warned of the dangers of 'Hobbesian anarchy'. I had been required to read Hobbes at university and decided he was my favourite philosopher, but I hadn't expected him to feature in spending review negotiations.

to achieve or dropped them if they were inconvenient. This was wide of the mark. In fact, what was striking in these conversations was how the Blair–Brown teams wanted to remain faithful to their commitments to the public, even where they were inconvenient, and often pressed departments to increase rather than reduce their ambition. In the end, the number of targets was reduced from around 160 to around 120 – between eight and twelve per department – while their ambition was sharpened.

I also intervened on a personal interest – education. Given all the attention, and indeed funding, Health had received that spring, I was worried that Education was slipping down the list of priorities. In addition, with Estelle Morris on her own admission struggling to stamp her authority on the department, there was a risk that the Education settlement that summer would be inadequate. Working with Peter Hyman and Andrew Adonis, I wrote Blair a note entitled *Education: Still the No.1 Priority?*, urging him to ensure he gave it personal attention. This, he said in reply, was 'a timely reminder'. In the end, as the settlement was closed in July, the department secured an excellent deal.

Given their importance to all parties, negotiations on the spending review inevitably continued until the eleventh hour and beyond. I remember in one review negotiating the level at which a particular target should be set in a phone call I took at home on a Sunday just two days before the White Paper was published; the decision taken on the spur of that moment made the difference between the target being met or – as happened in this case – missed. On another occasion, I took another call, also on a Sunday, this time in Argos of all places, to contribute to the endgame of a departmental settlement. I can't remember whether I gave good advice, but I know the kettle we bought that day was a disaster.

Given this tendency to finalise the spending review at the very last minute, the quality of the public expenditure White Papers was always a miracle to me. These White Papers explain the state of the economy, the public expenditure projections, each department's settlement and proposals for managing public expenditure. In a parallel text, the PSA targets for each department are published. Not that any of them is a bestseller, of course (they are far too dense for that), but each one is a magisterial overview – a fine example of where the civil service genuinely excels – and one searches in vain for typing errors. For me in 2002, what mattered most was the powerful endorsement of the Delivery Unit in the text:

> The Prime Minister's Delivery Unit was established last year to strengthen the capacity of departments to deliver effectively on particularly challenging targets . . . Working in close collaboration, the Treasury and the Delivery Unit will together ensure that departments have in place effective delivery plans for their new PSA targets. They will ensure that these plans contain robust and clear milestones and trajectories showing how delivery will be achieved.

A year after its establishment, the Delivery Unit had become a vital cog in the government machine.

Change and routine

There were other major changes in 2002 which hugely affected the Delivery Unit, but looking back, it was the unfolding of the routine that mattered most, both in terms of delivering results and in building people's confidence. In one note to myself that year, for example, I recorded a routine round-up with Alan Milburn in which I sensed his growing confidence in the Delivery Unit's role. It was helping him shift the vast bureaucracy beneath him. We moved from a conversation about bureaucracy to the state of the civil service. 'I'm increasingly convinced there are just too many people,' I said. Milburn (and Paul Corrigan, who was also there) agreed. He had that very week received a routine update from some junior official which illustrated the point perfectly. As he put it, 'The sun is shining, it's late May, and some poor sod is still doing a weekly report on the winter crisis!' Incidentally, out of these kinds of conversation, which became increasingly common among ministers, emerged the 2004 efficiency review, which proposed a 100,000 reduction in the number of civil servants. I took the opportunity of this meeting to propose to Milburn that we, the Delivery Unit, should put a project manager in place for a few months to accelerate progress within the London patient choice pilot, which was still not moving as fast as it should have been. In addition to bolstering a high-profile emblem of the reform programme, I wanted to demonstrate that the government machine could move quickly. 'Just do it,' he said, and within days we did.

In another note a couple of weeks later, I decided to record the even more mundane reality of my job:

> I spent the rest of the week shifting along the routine business; preparing for the Education stocktake on Tuesday; working on a proposal to the Health Department on improving hospital productivity; finalising a presentation for Monday's meetings of the street crime ministers with David Blunkett and me; checking the latest train delay figures (which were not encouraging) and the latest street crime figures (which were).

No one in Whitehall was as obsessed as I was with minor shifts on graphs. My staff came to know that, to cheer me up, all they had to do was show me a graph with progress heading in the right direction. Alternatively, if they wanted my approval for action they proposed, they could show me a graph heading in the wrong direction. For my daughters, the fact that I had become the Prime Minister's chief graph drawer was a source of endless amusement; for me it was a daunting reality. While the entire Delivery Unit cheerfully churned out graphs and discussed them, the bottom line in 2002 was that most of the graphs were heading in the wrong direction. We had a burgeoning reputation and some interesting methods, but precious little in the way of results. I knew that, in the end, our reputation depended on changing this single fact. As Blair commented on one of my notes at the end of 2002, 'We can't really afford to miss as many of these targets as seems likely.'

Even so, Blair and others seemed to have developed a disarming faith that his Delivery Unit would somehow reverse this state of affairs. Early in 2002, the Blairs and I had been invited, along with Sally Morgan, for dinner at Blunkett's house.[6] Tony Blair had asked me how I was enjoying myself and offered to come and meet the staff. A few weeks later, he walked across Whitehall to meet us all, gathered in the downstairs room of 53 Parliament Street. Three of the staff presented to him: Tony O'Connor, who showed him how we tracked data; Clara Swinson, who explained how we had built our relationship with the Department of Health; and Eoin Daly, who set out the project planning for the Street Crime Initiative. Blair told the staff, in response, that they were 'the most popular and effective' of any of his innovations in Whitehall, and that he wanted them to press hard for innovation and ambition. For the Delivery Unit staff, many of whom rarely saw the PM himself, this was a great occasion. Blair told me afterwards that he thought 'they were excellent'. I drew on the high expectations Blair had of our team to urge even better performance. I stressed that in the end we would be judged only by the results we delivered.

In fact, inside the Delivery Unit there was a constant debate not just about the techniques we used, but also about our own organisation and how to maximise our impact. My strictures that we had to stay small prevented what would have been the normal tendency in Whitehall for a successful unit – steady growth in the number of staff. For me, one of the best moments of the Blair visit was when he first came into the room and commented dryly, 'Is this really all of you?'

By the first half of 2002, though, we had moved beyond the chaotic early phase when there had been a whirl of activity and everyone simply joined in. Unlike most people, I have discovered that I thrive on ambiguity, even though the Delivery Unit usually conveyed a sense of order. As I said to my management team in a note I wrote them just before I left, 'The job of you as managers is to manage uncertainty . . . You have to persuade people that ambiguity is normal; what holds us together is not structure, but mission. This is not to say structure doesn't matter; rather that it is impermanent.'

For these reasons, perhaps, internal organisation and management had never been my strong point, but by then I had learnt a great deal, not least from the staff themselves. Before Christmas 2001, they were telling me that I had to sort out the organisational chaos and bring at least some role clarity. Rosemary Scully, a management consultant we had on secondment to us in the early days, and William Jordan, a loyal and committed civil servant who was a leading influence in our first three years, were the most insistent about this. I came to agree with them that we needed a clearer structure, but what kind? At this stage, I was against having teams of policy experts on key themes such as health or transport, for the simple reason that there were already plenty of teams of policy experts around Whitehall: in the Policy Directorate, the Strategy Unit and even the Regulatory Impact Unit, not to mention of course the departments themselves. I wanted to employ experts in delivery. The logic this implied was that any of our people should, in theory, be able to work on any of our policy areas. Eventually we developed an organisational plan built around functions, not policy areas. The key function of reporting to the PM and managing relations with No. 10 and the Treasury would be placed firmly with me and my office; an operational research team, led by O'Connor, would gather, analyse and provide data for all of us.* Relationships with departments would be overseen at ministerial and permanent secretary level by me, but depend day to day on 'account managers' – individuals with responsibility for ensuring we had a good relationship with our customers, the departments, as a good bank or advertising agency might have. Then there would be a team of problem solvers who could be summoned by the account managers to whatever the most intractable problems of the day turned out to be. This team would be buttressed by a call-off contract with a consultancy and the panel of outside experts we had appointed so that we could respond to a call for help, as on the Health choice pilot, within days. A weekly meeting would match staff time to emerging problems, thus ensuring flexibility. There would also be a team responsible for developing our techniques and designing and implementing our programme for the top civil servants, a function we came to call capacity-building. A final team provided administrative support and managed our relations with the Byzantine bureaucracy of the Cabinet Office. This organisational model meant we had a flat structure and great flexibility, and it worked reasonably well for a year or so, when we came up with something better.

The model placed the greatest influence in the hands of the account managers, who were generally young, very talented civil servants, since a civil service training certainly helped in understanding how departments worked, including crucial details such as how a minister's office functions. Clara Swinson (account manager for Health), Vanessa Nicholls (Home Office), and a little later Simon Rea (Education) became highly influential. They, more than anyone, represented our brand in the middle and senior ranks of the big bureaucracies. Armed with our methods and the constant backing of myself and the Prime Minister, they performed brilliantly. More than once, their advice to me

---

*O'Connor also organised a variety of statistical games. In 2002, he ran a competition involving predictions of the results of all the games in that year's World Cup. I did very badly, not least because my naïve patriotism requires me to predict an England victory every time.

prevented me from making snap judgements and, crucially, none of them 'went native', the big risk for people in such roles. Indeed, often they were harder on the departments they worked with than I was. Our problem solvers, by contrast, largely came as secondees from consultancies or recruits from regulators such as the Audit Commission or Ofsted. (See Delivery Manual, Document 5 for a chart showing the varied previous employers of Delivery Unit Staff in 2003–4.)

Every now and then in life you come across a group of people that, by some confluence of talent, personality, commitment and mission, become extraordinary. It happens in the arts, in sport, and in both private and public sector organisations. This happened in the Delivery Unit from quite early on, and we sustained it throughout the parliament. Across Whitehall, people, from permanent secretaries downwards, noticed. It was simultaneously inspiring and empowering to be part of it, and it enabled us to inspire belief in the departments with which we interacted. How it happened or why is hard for me to explain. Simon Rea sought to do so when he wrote to me commenting on the draft of this book: he pointed to five factors. 'Your leadership of the unit and your ability to inspire' was his first point. He added, 'For many people who enjoyed working in the unit, this is what made the Delivery Unit the different place it was.' Whether this was a result of my obvious passion for the cause, my idiosyncratic ways of working or my closeness to the Prime Minister I was never sure; I knew for certain, though, that the inspiration I felt came from my staff.

Indeed, 'the enjoyment of working with so many good people and how it developed all the staff' was Rea's second factor. 'What a group of people we had working there! The mix of backgrounds and experience made it such a good place to learn.' His third point was the quality of our working relationships with departments: 'Many of us who had experienced work in the Cabinet Office when these relationships weren't effective relished the opportunity to engage departments constructively to get things done better and more quickly.'

Rea's fourth point related to the quality of management and support. Here he referred not just to senior managers, but to the administrative support offered by Jacqui Matthews and others: 'It was only when I left that I realised how calmly and competently that team had gone about providing an excellent service.' Finally, he referred to the role of O'Connor, our chief operational researcher, who in addition to producing graphs and analysing data, was the social heart of the staff team, organising quizzes, sweepstakes and evenings out. These, Rea commented, were 'all crucial parts of our cohesiveness'.

Another reason was that, from late 2003 onwards, prompted by Peter Thomas, Adrian Masters and William Jordan, my three deputies, we began to actively manage – as an internal document put it – four 'enablers of our mission', which were 'world class tools and processes' (i.e. deliverology), 'excellent relationships', 'brilliant internal Delivery Unit systems' and 'great people . . . with the right experiences, skills and values'. Every quarter, as a management team, we collected evidence on each of these aspects of our work and took decisions about how to improve.

The spirit of the Delivery Unit, Rea said to me in summary, was 'sharing your sense of purpose and creating the right relationships with departments. With the right relationships we could achieve almost anything (and often did), without it we could achieve nothing.' Others who worked there might put it differently, but everyone involved between June 2001 and July 2005 knew that something remarkable had happened.* It was wonderful to be part of it, and I myself don't anticipate experiencing anything quite like it again.

Our capacity was put to the test by that summer's spending review, one of whose outcomes was that we would work not just on the core agenda agreed in 2001, but on a wider set of targets across several other departments. The sensible aim of this was to spread delivery thinking much wider, but I was determined that our focus on the original priorities should not be weakened too much, and that the Delivery Unit should not get bigger. This meant giving account manager roles to a wider group of people. The result was that while we did make an impact on departments such as DEFRA and the Office of the Deputy Prime Minister, we found ourselves sometimes skating on thin ice in terms of the evidence base and unable to deploy problem-solving support with

---

*As time went by, one of the things I monitored was what people went on to do after they left the Delivery Unit. In almost all cases they found it a wrench to leave but progressed to highly influential positions – in departments, agencies, consultancies, No. 10 or the Treasury. My favourite next destination was that chosen by Vanessa Nicholls, who became simultaneously strategy adviser at the Metropolitan Police and a trained special constable, soon averaging more arrests per hour worked than many of her colleagues.

sufficient concentration to make a difference. In the summer of 2003, after a year with this wider agenda, we refocused on the core agenda – the issues that really mattered to the Prime Minister, and where he really needed to deliver results in his second term. That is the story of a later chapter, but it is interesting to observe here that the moment we withdrew our forces from places such as DEFRA was the only time we received a steady series of complaints from across Whitehall. Departments missed us and the fragment of prime ministerial attention we brought with us. They liked working with us, I believe, because they liked being challenged – the only thing worse than being part of the Delivery Unit's agenda, it turned out, was not being part of it.

Meanwhile, outside the Delivery Unit the scene was changing too. Richard Wilson was due to retire as Cabinet Secretary in the summer of 2002, and there was much debate in the upper echelons of government about who should replace him. The *Financial Times* reported at one point that I was running a campaign for Michael Bichard. This was a wild exaggeration, but I was an ardent fan. I had seen the difference he had made in the Department for Education while I was there, and his abrasive streak added to my respect for him. He was not afraid to tackle the tough issues. The fact that he had left government was an advantage too: I thought bringing an outsider in would send a strong message. When Blair consulted me, these were the points I made. Either way, I wanted a bold decision because for once it seemed the stars were lined up. The key figure in the decision was in fact Wilson himself, so I wrote him a private note, importantly making an argument that was both long-term and cross-party. A rare opportunity had arisen, I suggested, for an irreversible reform of the civil service:

- There is the opportunity provided by the huge public interest in the question of governance . . . as people's expectations of services have risen, their faith in government's capacity to deliver has fallen. Levels of cynicism are high, but at least people *are* questioning the status quo and expecting something to happen.
- There is a broad political agreement across the major political parties about the need to ensure successful public service delivery, which means radical reform at this stage of the government machine would transcend party politics. . . .
- The Delivery Unit (and I know I'm biased and passionate about this)

has begun to develop both an effective performance management system for ensuring pursuit of the Prime Minister's (*any* Prime Minister's) key priorities and a set of tools which can be embedded in departments to enable them to strengthen their own capacity to deliver in a very significant way.

- The stage we happen to be at in the electoral cycle means that right now both the time and very probably the political inclination could be found to bring about radical reform. . . .

[These circumstances provide] about 18 months in which a new Cabinet Secretary could bring about the most radical reform of the government machine in recent history. Beyond 18 months, the prospects are much more murky.

Wilson responded with a very short handwritten note. 'What a marvellous minute,' it said, but this was a comment on the way my 'minute' was written rather than acceptance of the argument I had made. When his successor, Andrew Turnbull, was appointed, he asked me, soon after he started, what I thought the central question was. I replied, 'How revolutionary do we want to be?' He said that he did not want to announce a revolution, but hoped that when he retired he would be able to look back on one. But revolution by stealth is close to being a contradiction in terms. Over Turnbull's three years in post I came to respect his achievements, but in the end I do not think we fully exploited the opportunity we had.

Turnbull instituted some changes fairly rapidly, including bringing the heads of the units together in a Delivery and Reform team, although this was little more than a place to exchange (often riveting) information. Certainly it neither delivered nor reformed anything. From my point of view, top of the agenda was ensuring that I had the same degree of both support and freedom to operate from Turnbull as I had had from Wilson – and while I welcomed working more closely with other units, I did not want to be constrained by the need to collaborate, civil service style. I plead guilty to the charge one critic made of me that I was 'a single-issue fanatic'. How else, I thought – in the absence of coherence – would delivery ever occur? I need not have worried though; Turnbull was consistently supportive. In the end, the momentum and strong political support we had already generated enabled us to continue our advance.

Changes on the political front helped too, though I found myself watching carefully so that I could protect Delivery Unit interests if necessary. For example, at one point it was rumoured in the press that John Prescott was going to take direct responsibility for delivery in the next reshuffle, and I raised this with Blair. Blair laughed and told me not to believe what I read in the papers; this had not even crossed his mind. When the reshuffle came, prompted by Stephen Byers's resignation that June, it was much more wide-ranging than I expected and I discovered that, no doubt rightly, I was completely out of the loop. It involved two major developments from a personal point of view. One was that my good friend David Miliband was catapulted into the limelight as minister for school standards. The second was that Alistair Darling became Secretary of State for Transport and brought with him a new permanent secretary, Rachel Lomax, which meant I had some major relationship-building to do in one of our key departments. As became my habit with reshuffles, I called the new secretary of state that day and said I looked forward to working with him. Shortly afterwards, I met Lomax and began to try to exert the Delivery Unit charm on her. In both cases, our relationships with them built slowly and steadily to become very effective.

Mixed progress: delivery one year on

The summer of 2002 finished with the third round of delivery reports. The league table showed further progress since December, but red remained the dominant colour. 'Overall,' I told Blair in an overview, 'progress on delivery is no better than mixed. This will add to the pressure in the next 12 months. We need substantial shifts in outcomes soon to maintain credibility.'

Meanwhile, after a year in post I now felt better able than ever to diagnose the problems and offer advice to Blair on the way forward. The good news, I reported, was that the capacity to deliver had been strengthened and shaped across Education, Health, crime and policing. The tough Railtrack decision had been taken and the targets were clearer and sharper. Even so, the challenges were immense. A real operational approach to planning remained rare, and though the pace of implementation had increased, urgency was not yet a way of life.

Moreover, too often as reforms moved from the ideas phase to implementation, there was a tendency for them to be 'simultaneously watered down and fogged up. As a result, their impact is a pale shadow of the original ambition.' The causes of this fog were, I argued, a willingness to compromise at the first sign of restiveness among lobby groups and bungled implementation which depended on traditional regulatory approaches. Bureaucrats were writing regulations with no thought to what practical implementation would mean on the frontline.

Looking ahead, I advised that the next twelve months would be crucial. I warned (presciently in the light of what happened to NHS funding in 2005/6) that unless changes in public sector pay brought real change in behaviour among employees in the NHS and elsewhere, the government would be in difficulty: 'Any money spent on pay which doesn't change behaviour is money that could have been used to build capacity.' The other key message I offered the Prime Minister was that 2002/3 would be a transitional year, in which we undertook 'the shift from top-down driving of public services to sustainable improvement driven by the pressure of customers'. He described this as moving from 'flogging the system' to 'structural reform'.

Structural reform was the long-term goal for Health, Education and policing of course, but I pointed out that this required a level of sophistication in strategic implementation which was missing in many parts of Whitehall. Both ministers and top officials had a tendency to describe this shift as a matter of 'letting go', implying a relaxation of demands on the frontline. Out among the professions this language was being interpreted as a return to 'a fondly remembered era when there was less pressure on them'. In fact, I wanted Blair to understand the next phase for professionals would involve going forward to a time dominated by consumer pressure, extensive publicly available data, choice and innovation. 'It will be more demanding [for them], not less, than the era of centrally driven reform,' I concluded in bold type. When he and I discussed my note up in his flat at the start of the parliamentary recess, it was clear that he fully understood this analysis intellectually, but I never felt that the government as a whole fully came to terms with its daunting implications.

I also wrote to permanent secretaries about these complex issues. To Nigel Crisp, at Health, for example, I said:

Your reform programme is so bold, so wide-ranging and so rapid that ensuring that the various strands combine to ensure a coherent transformation is immensely difficult. You need to strengthen your capacity to oversee and manage implementation . . . otherwise you run the risk . . . of a building which has all the essential elements but doesn't have either the resilience you would want or the elegance which we should aim for.

Looking back, I feel even more strongly about this set of issues than I did then, and I blame myself for the failure to embed this kind of thinking sufficiently among the political and official leaders of the time. For example, I attribute the loss of pace on education reform during the second term more than anything to a failure to understand sufficiently the nature of the challenge. What happened too often was that, rather than replacing government pressure with customer pressure, departmental officials simply returned power to the professionals. The argument was that this was handing over leadership of reform to heads and teachers, but without a corresponding empowerment of the consumer – in this case parents – there was a risk of reinforcing the inadequate status quo. The practical effect was that there was a loss of pace and direction.

The lesson for reform on this scale is that you have to invest immensely (and I mean immensely) in selecting and developing the senior people – both ministers and officials – responsible for delivery. Bold, sustained leadership is a prerequisite of transformation; professions left to themselves rarely advocate more than incremental change, though of course there are always individuals forging ahead. There is no doubt that the Blair reform programme had a major beneficial impact on the quality and performance of the public services, but more would have been achieved had there been a wider and deeper appreciation of the scale and nature of the challenge and the sophistication of the strategy. Too often it felt like a revolution without enough revolutionaries. The issue this raised for Blair personally was why, after eight years as party leader, and well into his second term as Prime Minister, this was still the case.

In the early summer of 2002, as part of a radically revised approach to communications, Blair began to give the monthly press conferences that since then have become a feature of the political landscape. In these unscripted appearances, he wears the journalists down by answering their questions until they choose to leave rather than keep on asking more. Also in 2002, he began his routine appearances at the Liaison Committee, where the chairs of parliamentary select committees are able to grill him, for two hours or more, on any subjects they choose. He set a new standard of competence in these arenas that his successors will have to match.

Someone – I think Alastair Campbell – decided that it would be a good idea at the second of these press conferences, in July 2002, for me to present on how we approached delivery. At first Blair was cautious – 'It might be a bit nerdly,' he thought – but then decided to go ahead. With the excellent support, as ever, of Tony O'Connor and Kate Myronidis, I prepared for this seminal moment in my usual obsessive way. The presentation, refined endlessly and tested repeatedly, described how we approached delivery and gave some examples. It was agreed that I would present it in a low-key way. The best way to signal that it was unspun was to be deadpan. Thus was born what became the most high-profile part of the Delivery Unit's routine – that every summer, I found myself stepping out in front of the world's media to present – in a steady monotone – a series of graphs and charts on delivery. My beloved graphs at last reached global audience. The crucial message was conveyed unscathed: that Blair himself was heavily involved in securing delivery and not even the momentous events on the international stage had deflected him.

*

On the evening after my inaugural press conference appearance, I happened to run into – one after the other – Darren Murphy, Alan Milburn's tough-talking press adviser, and Ed Balls, both in the environs of the Red Lion pub. I was slightly daunted by both encounters because I had not informed any of the departments about the press conference, even though we were presenting their data to the world. As it turned out, both were relaxed; perhaps the advent of the summer recess had had its effect, or perhaps they were just faintly amused by the ordeal I had been put through.

During the recess, I read American history books and walked in the Lake District hills. On one long walk, which ended in Kentmere, I reflected on the impact my work had on the wider family. At my sister

Lucy's fortieth birthday party that summer, I had found myself defending a mass of unpopular government policy from brothers I adored and wondering if my time in government was making me more realistic and acute or just hardbitten and limited in perspective. I was more at ease being run ragged by my nephews at football, but made a mental note to keep asking myself the moral questions at the heart of the delivery agenda: to what extent was our work making Britain more prosperous, more equitable and more socially cohesive? I made a point of raising these issues all the time with staff, individually and collectively. I wanted to be sure we never lost sight of what our real mission was: to enable the Prime Minister to effect the changes to public services for which he had been elected. Prime ministerial power in itself is morally neutral, but used in a moral way for a moral purpose it becomes a force for good. In a democracy, of course, people's views of what good is can change over time – but for the sake of democracy itself it is important that elected governments make a good fist of doing what they said they would do, otherwise trust in government and politics is worn away.

Less profound in a general way, but more profound for me personally, was a call I had taken before the summer break, which was also on my mind as I came down into Kentmere. The switchboard told me that a persistent fellow called Templeton wanted to speak to me very urgently but wouldn't say why: would I take the call? Curiosity got the better of me, and I said I would. 'Hello, Michael, it's Guy,' came the voice: now I knew who it was – my daughter Naomi's boyfriend. But why was he calling me at work? 'I wanted to ask for your permission to marry your daughter,' he said. I was happy to take on this additional delivery challenge, and reflected on the fact that the present young generation were so much more polite than we had been.

From the Lake District, I drove to Manchester for a two-day 'retreat' with Andrew Turnbull and the Cabinet Office leadership. Back to the long, grinding haul. Stocktakes, notes, training for civil servants, delivery reports, Cabinet presentations, press conferences: all these routines, established during 2001 and 2002, were in my view by far the most important contributory factors to the progress we made over the next three years. At the time, though, we had little to go on in terms of results. In any case, unless we could show that deliverology helped to tackle the inevitable crises that periodically engulfed the government's public service reform programme, it seemed unlikely our reputation would survive. All organisations – whether the Trans-Siberian Railway, the England football team or individual families – face crises from time to time. These become a test of their strength, a measure of the resilience the routines have built. This is the subject of the next chapter.

5

Crises

Should I, after tea and cake and ices,
Have the strength to force the moment to its crisis?
T. S. Eliot, *The Love Song of J. Alfred Prufrock*

Street crime

On Monday 11 March 2002, Tony Blair and I rushed back to No. 10 from an early evening event with Cabinet ministers and permanent secretaries, for an urgent meeting with David Blunkett on street crime. Blunkett had already been shown into Blair's office by the time we arrived. Immediately, Blair began to advocate some really dramatic initiatives to quell the explosion of street crime across our big cities. Almost everyone you met in London at the time knew someone who had been mugged recently, if they hadn't been mugged themselves, usually for their mobile phone. Home Office data showed that, far from falling in line with the trajectory, street crime was skyrocketing. No wonder the press were screaming about it. Blair said the proposals he had seen so far were just not radical enough. He was not against fluffy partnerships between agencies, but he didn't think they matched up to the scale of the immediate problem. Earlier in the day, in a cry of frustration, Blair had told me he had been going on about this for three years! My reply that I was working up proposals with the Home Office that would be ready within six weeks did not satisfy him.

Now, in this meeting, Blunkett readily agreed with Blair that the state of affairs was unacceptable. He and Blair had spoken on the phone the evening before on the subject, and Blunkett himself had not been convinced by reassurances from his officials either.* Out of the blue,

*In his diary, Blunkett says: 'I think the week beginning Monday 11 March should go down as one of the worst weeks that I have had since I came into government – and that's saying something.' (*The Blunkett Tapes*, p. 361)

Blair hit upon what he wanted: 'Why is it that when we have a real crisis like foot-and-mouth or the fuel crisis we get the job done? Perhaps we should call together COBRA [the Cabinet Office emergency committee] and deal with robbery through that mechanism.'

With quiet enthusiasm, Blunkett said, 'I'd be up for that.' And the deal was done. Blunkett saw the leadership opportunity this would offer him; I saw potentially how the Delivery Unit could demonstrate its effectiveness on a new level; and Blair had the chance to prove a point he had previously made on a Cabinet awayday – that there are lessons for delivery in the way government handles crises. As Paul Romer, an economist at Stanford, put it acerbically, 'A crisis is a terrible thing to waste.'[1]

Later that evening, John Gieve, the thoughtful permanent secretary of the Home Office, rang me anxiously, seeking clarification and perhaps fearing a loss of control.* I simultaneously challenged and reassured him. 'We've got to treat this as an epidemic, not as a remorseless rise,' I said, remembering Blair's comparison with foot-and-mouth; 'it's got all the characteristics of an epidemic and needs to be dealt with as one. That way, if we do the right things, we will get it under control. In any case,' I added, 'it's a real opportunity for you. We can get Whitehall lined up behind you as you've always said you wanted.'

With Blunkett and Gieve now driving the department forward, the Home Office officials began to work closely with us to prepare for this dramatic new process. The first impact of Blair's new approach, however, came the following morning when there happened to be an Education stocktake. I presented a hard-hitting graph which showed the 500 per cent increase in the number of robberies committed by 11–15-year-olds in the previous decade and drew – literally – a sharp intake of breath from Blair, Estelle Morris and the others around the Cabinet table. Blair pressed Morris very hard to get a grip on behaviour and truancy and especially to ensure police had access to schools wherever necessary.

Meanwhile, in No. 10 we began to make plans for the first meeting of COBRA the following week. All Cabinet ministers or top officials

---

*According to Alastair Campbell's diaries, while Gieve and I were talking, Blair was having dinner in the No. 10 flat with his political advisers to review the state of affairs. He told them 'his main focus was always domestic – specifically crime' (Alastair Campbell, *The Blair Years* (London: Hutchinson, 2007), p. 610).

with the slightest connection to street crime, along with top police people, were to be invited. At the suggestion of myself and Jeremy Heywood, Blair agreed to have the first meeting in the COBRA meeting room itself, in the bowels of the Cabinet Office. We felt this would symbolise clearly the crisis management approach Blair and Blunkett wanted to see.

The next Sunday, Blunkett announced the initiative on *The Frost Programme*, and a blizzard of media coverage ensued, which high-lighted his admission that people did not feel safe on the streets, rather than his plans to tackle the problem. Even now, Home Office officials had not grasped how much their world had changed. Blair and Blunkett were talking about very regular meetings of COBRA, as had happened the previous year with foot-and-mouth, while the officials were talking about fortnightly meetings at most. At a pre-meeting before the seminal first meeting of COBRA, Blair hesitated and asked me, 'So you really think this will work, do you?' Before I could answer, his phone rang and he had to take a call from a foreign head of state. The truth was, I really thought it would – and in any case I knew that someone had to exude certainty. Part of my confidence came from the fact that in the Delivery Unit we had been exploring the street crime issue with the Home Office and the police for several weeks and much of what needed to be done had already become clear.

Following a stocktake in December 2001, when Blair had already pressed for more vigorous action on street crime, we had decided to pilot a new piece of deliverology on the street crime issue. That same month, I had recruited Richard Page-Jones from Ofsted, the school inspection agency, and he rapidly became one of the leading influences in the Delivery Unit. His engaging character and constant enthusiasm matched his expertise in the design of inspection and review processes. From the outset, I had wanted to develop in the Delivery Unit a capacity to rapidly review how effective implementation was, priority by priority. I knew it was a risk to depend solely on the data, however good it was: somehow we needed to feel and see delivery at the frontline as well as examine the data. Moreover, I wanted us to model across Whitehall the need for senior civil servants – in modern slang – to get out more. While at the Department for Education, I had visited on average a school every two weeks, which meant I really knew what teachers were thinking, saying and doing. Yet I had discovered that in other parts of Whitehall such regular visits were rare.

Government was, of course, littered with inspection and review processes. For organisations such as Ofsted, the Healthcare Commission, Her Majesty's Inspectorate of the Constabulary, the National Audit Office and the Audit Commission, this was core business. The approaches these organisations took varied, but they all shared one important flaw from a Delivery Unit point of view: they were far too slow. Ofsted, for example, would review the implementation of a policy in October but not publish its report on it until the following April or May, by which time, of course, the world had moved on. Similarly, the Audit Commission wrote superb investigative reports but took two years to complete them. Two years! That's an age in this period of extraordinarily rapid change. For the Delivery Unit, I wanted an approach which was much faster and, since we did not plan to produce reports for publication, we did not need to dot every I and cross every T.

The conceptual breakthrough for me came in a conversation with someone who had worked on Audit Commission reports. 'After how long', I asked him, 'did you know 90 per cent of what was in the final report?'

'A month,' he replied.

At that moment I decided we would design a process which took a month, made proposals which were 90 per cent right, and then drove action. Page-Jones, drawing on his deep experience of school inspection across Europe, designed a process which came close to meeting this demanding specification. For any given target, a joint review team of five or six people from the relevant department and the Delivery Unit would be established. They would rapidly pull together all the data they could assemble on the issue and generate some hypotheses and answer the key questions: Were we on track to deliver the target? If so, what were the risks? If not, what could be done to fix the problem? Armed with the background analysis and their hypotheses, the team would then go and see for themselves the reality on the ground. Often they would visit a place where progress was good and ask why, and a place where it was poor and ask the same question. They would ask everyone they met the same questions: Is the target understood? What are the successes? What are the barriers? And what action is needed to strengthen delivery? Finally they would invite interviewees to identify their top three messages for the Prime Minister – an invitation few could resist. This way the team could test and refine their hypotheses. In effect, they checked every link in the delivery chain to see how it could be strengthened.

Once the field work was done, a short, crisp report with some practical recommendations for action would go to the relevant Cabinet minister and permanent secretary, and to the Prime Minister. Almost always, as it turned out, the process was incredibly revealing. It would rapidly show what needed to be done. The departmental officials involved in these review teams usually started out anxious – after all, they would likely discover flaws in their implementation – but soon became enthusiasts, partly because it helped them solve their problems, and partly because the process was genuinely riveting. They learnt so much so fast. Most importantly of all, in most – though not all – cases, once the actions proposed in the reports were taken, performance improved significantly. These priority reviews (see Delivery Manual, Document 1), as Page-Jones christened them, turned out to be an immensely powerful tool in the delivery toolkit.

However, in early 2002, when we first tested the concept on the street crime issue, we had yet to learn all that. Moreover, to start the process we had to persuade first the Home Office and second the police that this was worth doing. The Home Office officials were understandably a little edgy about focusing the spotlight on an area where results were spiralling out of control. However, John Gieve was happy to accept any help from us he could get. The police were more sensitive still. Chief constables rightly guard their operational independence jealously. On the one hand, the thought that the Prime Minister's people might be reviewing how they were tackling street crime seemed at first glance to be a threat to this independence. On the other, it dawned on them that our involvement might open up options to achieve policy changes the police wanted and to exercise influence over other parts of Whitehall – education, for example – which seemed beyond their reach. I spoke to senior officers in the Metropolitan Police and to Her Majesty's Inspector of the Constabulary, Keith Povey, to open the way. (You can always tell when top police officers are sensitive about an issue because they turn up to the meeting in full uniform and regalia; when they relax, this form of intimidation becomes unnecessary.)

Shortly after these consultations with the Home Office and police, there was a further complication which might have blocked progress. Someone leaked the key facts to the *Sunday Times*, which ran a front-page story (on 10 February 2002) saying:

> Street crime is running out of control . . . The increase has so alarmed Tony Blair that he has ordered one of his top Downing Street officials into the Home Office and Scotland Yard to try to sort out the crisis. He has instructed Professor Michael Barber, head of the No. 10 Delivery Unit, to draw up a blueprint for combating the crime wave. It is expected to be completed within a month.

As I repeatedly made clear to my staff, leaks about Delivery Unit activity were always bad news for us because inevitably the story would appear to undermine the relevant Cabinet minister. In fact, in this case, David Blunkett was doing all he could to drive radical action and had enlisted our support, but the story gave the impression that Blair had ordered us in. When, characteristically, Blunkett rang me that morning, he accepted readily that the leak had not come from me or my staff and that potentially it damaged the Delivery Unit as much as the Home Office. If this sort of thing happened often, he said, 'none of us could stand it'.

I knew that was true, and this was one of several moments that graphically reinforced my view that we in the Delivery Unit needed to be extremely careful about confidentiality, even if this sometimes frustrated my staff. As I wrote to them in a farewell note:

> We live in a world where leaks occur. I always took the view . . . that three leaks [like the one mentioned above] would kill the Delivery Unit . . . It never crossed my mind that anyone in the Delivery Unit leaked [anything], but others wouldn't necessarily take the same view, and the damage to the Delivery Unit is the same in either case. Once suspicion is established in this strange world we live in, it is almost impossible to erase, and indeed generally it becomes ever more poisonous as one self-fulfilling prophecy begets another.

In this case my excellent relationship with Blunkett saved the day, and even though the Monday press echoed the *Sunday Times* ('Gun Crime Horror,' screamed the *Daily Star* on 11 February), the priority review of street crime went ahead. The police relaxed and the Home Office officials really enjoyed discovering for the first time how the policies they were responsible for were perceived by police and youth workers in the rougher parts of north London. Through this work, we were able to describe the problem accurately, and through our conversations with the Metropolitan Police about their new 'Safer Streets' campaign we rapidly understood what needed to be done.

We discovered that street crime – in effect mugging – involved theft of a mobile phone in 50 per cent of cases. More than 40 per cent of the country's street crime was in London. The robbers were increasingly young, and among a minority of young black males it had almost become a leisure pursuit. The victims were increasingly young too. In London, only 26 per cent of offences resulted in an arrest, and just 4 per cent in a conviction. In short, there were easy pickings and the chances of getting away with it were very high indeed. Moreover, the variation in performance between different basic command units (BCUs) within London was huge. If only the laggards could learn from the leaders, real progress would be made.

Of course, at the beginning, many in the Home Office and even some senior police officers were sceptical about whether the problem could be brought under control. They thought that, if they were lucky and had some extra resources, they might be able to reduce the rate of increase. They argued that, given the exploding number of mobile phones, especially among young people, even this would be a triumph. I knew Blair did not see it this way. I also knew that I personally had to express complete confidence that the situation could be turned round. Furthermore, I had read former New York police chief Bill Bratton's autobiography, so I challenged the assumptions on which this counsel of despair was based – there were increasing numbers of mobile phones in New York City too, I pointed out, but there street crime was falling. In a change programme as dramatic as the one needed here, 'Someone', as I put it to my staff in my farewell note, 'has to be the unreasonable one.' If you start accepting the excuses, however plausible, it is a slippery slope. As I look back on four years in the Delivery Unit, I regret a number of cases of giving a department the benefit of the doubt; I can't remember a single case of regretting being too tough.

The Met's Safer Streets campaign, helpfully, seemed to indicate a practical way forward. In the BCUs where it was operational, it was beginning to deliver results. Moreover, what worked was relatively simple to put in place. The location of every robbery had to be rapidly mapped. Once this was done, the 'hot spots' became obvious. In those locations, police presence was made highly visible. Plain clothes police and unmarked cars were used to identify suspects and with any specific robbery the key was to act as rapidly as possible after the incident. This is known as intelligence-led policing, but might be better called plain common sense.

The priority review also revealed weaknesses in the way the criminal justice system dealt with those perpetrators who had been arrested. There were weaknesses in the way police prepared evidence to pass on to the Crown Prosecution Service, victims and witnesses were often reluctant to come forward because they felt threatened, police support for them was inadequate, and identity parades often took a long time – several weeks – to organise and then, sometimes at the instigation of defence lawyers, the defendant would refuse to show and the whole process collapsed and began again. Finally, the review revealed a lack of strategy to prevent robberies occurring in the first place. Truancy was tolerated, pupils who had been expelled were left to roam the streets, and police presence in schools was minimal.

The report therefore recommended strengthening policing across London and the major cities along the lines of Safer Streets, improving the management of cases through the criminal justice system, better support for victims and witnesses, and much more effective crime prevention. It had been completed just days before the Prime Minister and Home Secretary decided to embark on the COBRA process, and it meant we had the analysis to underpin a radical way forward. Having skimmed our priority review report, the Prime Minister commented characteristically: 'All this confirms my view that we need a tough response now, advertised and followed through. We must get cracking on it.'

*

The first meeting of COBRA on street crime took place on Wednesday 20 March 2002. With Tony O'Connor and Kate Myronidis, I arrived at about 7.00 a.m. to check all the arrangements and the presentations. Then, from just before 8.00 a.m., the dingy basement room began to fill up. For one reason or another, most of the Cabinet were there, along with an army of officials and heads of relevant agencies and, of course, the top brass from the police (in uniform, needless to say). It was a case of standing room only.

There were due to be three presentations, two from the Home Office and then one from me, but the first two overran and Blair was itching to take control, so all my preparations were for nothing. It didn't matter, because Blair eclipsed all that had gone before – this time he was on top of all the data, challenging, sharp and persistent. Each of the Cabinet ministers was tasked to sort out their contribution to solving the problem and return, ready to act, to a follow-up meeting within days. Blair's main argument throughout was that the criminal justice system had come to accept the unacceptable because the alternative – dealing with the problem – looked too complicated, and because there were so many different players – from police to schools – that no one was in a position to take an overview. 'This is classic,' cried Blair in response to yet another lame excuse. 'Instead of solving the problem, we are accepting an inadequate state of affairs.'

The police rapidly began to see the potential of the process. Through Blair, they could at last begin to get the changes in the criminal justice system that would enable them to make real inroads into crime. Indeed, as the Street Crime Initiative developed, it became not just a means of reducing robbery, but also a way into more radical reforms of a criminal justice system which was in danger of losing its integrity.

That afternoon, under the chairmanship of John Gieve, the relevant officials met to decide how to put into action the decisions taken at COBRA. Taking the advice of Jeremy Heywood, who had often acted on behalf of the Prime Minister on foot-and-mouth the year before, I knew exactly how I needed to behave in John's meeting – like a Bolshevik commissar after the Russian Revolution, urging greater rigour and more urgency, and rejecting any excuses or backsliding. The senior police officer from the Met, representing the Commissioner, Sir John Stevens, beamed at me across the room.

At the end of the meeting, I offered Gieve the full-time support of one of my most talented young staffers, a secondee from a major consultancy. He became the linchpin of the strategy in the next few weeks, applying his incisive mind to each of the problems as they arose, and working excellently with the Home Office officials. Above all, he produced a brilliant one-page summary of the necessary action which from then on Blair used as a checklist at each COBRA meeting.

The meetings of the Street Crime Initiative began weekly and then stretched out to longer gaps, but the officials group, chivvied along by Gieve and the project manager he appointed, and assisted by myself as commissar, catalyst and terrier, always met weekly and real momentum was quickly generated. The key – as so often in delivery – was making sure that we got weekly data from each of the ten forces involved (covering most of the big cities). Of course, all the usual objections were trotted out – it would be bureaucratic to collect and would not always be perfectly accurate . . . but it was crucial. Every Friday, David Blunkett and Blair saw the figures for the country and for each of the ten forces. Acting on their behalf, we were able to question relatively poor performance and challenge excuses. Soon we made a point of inviting chief constables from relatively poor-performing areas to attend the COBRA meetings and explain. Miraculously, the data began to move in the right direction between the invitation being sent and the meeting being held, showing, incidentally, that providing the right incentives is vital to delivery.

Occasionally I offered informal advice to Gieve, who was always open-minded, on the organisational challenges of delivering the necessary results. I was particularly anxious that in each of the ten areas there was proper co-ordination of the effort and that it was clear who was in charge and accountable. I wrote to him within days of the initiative being launched to urge him to have his own people on the ground in each area, who were able to report in at least once a week. I had in mind the excellent advisers I had installed in failing local education authorities in the previous parliament, people who because of their experience and credibility exerted significant influence in the turnarounds that followed. 'We need a machine which, within three weeks or so, is a smooth-running Mercedes. We can't afford to let ten flowers bloom,' and then sort out the ones that wilt, I argued. 'I strongly advise you not to compromise on the early decisions you make about this.' Later, ministers were appointed to work with each of the ten areas and, where the minister put the time in on the ground, they had a significant impact.

Meanwhile, various absurdities of the criminal justice system came to light and were tackled: witnesses often waited in the same rooms as friends of the accused, and not surprisingly felt intimidated. Video identification could replace identity parades and massively speed up the process of identification, but simple technological barriers stood in the way; magistrates refused to give custodial sentences because, even though they thought they were appropriate, they were worried about the size of the prison population; court sessions fell apart because the accused wasn't delivered to the court on time by the contracted-out transport service; and so on. On each of these (and many other nineteenth-century practices which were unearthed), Blair wanted instant action and my job was to press for it, however unreasonably.

At the end of the first week of the initiative, I was round at Gieve's house. We had just watched Arsenal crush Sunderland 3-0. His son, listening to the radio, called from upstairs that the Queen Mother had died, an occasion for which the permanent secretary of the Home Office had to be prepared. A few minutes later, Gieve's office rang and told him – in strict confidence of course – what the rest of the world already knew from Radio Five Live. Gieve was hugely amused, and I left assuring him that I would not let the Street Crime Initiative drift while he was distracted.

In the early April meeting of COBRA, Blair pressed the Department for Education very hard for progress on the truancy which fuelled street crime as well as urging the Home Office and police to sharpen their impact. Blunkett said, typically, 'We need more urgency about every-thing.' By the late April meeting, more than 2,000 police officers nation-wide had been shifted onto street crime. Sometimes they were taken off other duties such as traffic management, but since the overall number of police officers was rising, and at record levels, this was not unduly problematic. Senior police officers told us, of course, that as and when the street crime numbers began to go in the right direction, other crime figures would go into reverse. The implicit assumption here was that they were already working at maximum efficiency and that therefore if officers were transferred from one task to another, any gain on one would necessarily result in a loss on the other. I did not accept this for a second because the premise was not credible – the police, like many other public services, were functioning far below optimal efficiency.* Nevertheless, we agreed we would track the data on all major crimes

---

*At the time the average Met police officer made five arrests per year.

clearly so that if there were perverse consequences we would know.

By then the police had signed up to a target that by September 2002 (i.e. within six months) street crime would be back down to the pre-epidemic levels of the previous summer. This would represent meeting Blair's very public commitment during Prime Minister's Questions that by September street crime would be 'under control'. Once they were engaged, Ian Blair in London and other senior police officers provided impressive leadership. With the Met leading the way, the data, which we were watching weekly, finally began to shift steadily and substantially in the right direction. Better still, the perverse consequences did not occur; in fact we were able to show that those forces which achieved the biggest reductions in street crime often had falling burglary and car crime too. We had destroyed an urban myth.

Blunkett remained impatient for more substantial results, and in late May he expressed his frustration that it was not going fast enough. His restlessness, I knew, was a real quality and I assured him – using a phrase which, from our education days, I remembered he did not like – that we now required not more initiatives but 'relentless implementation'. When the numbers continued to fall through the summer, I knew we in the Delivery Unit, as well as Blunkett, had passed a crucial test. The profile of the initiative, the strong application of deliverology and the huge commitment of prime ministerial time and energy had raised the stakes to a very high level. In fact, meeting the September target successfully was only part of the gain; a much-needed new momentum had been brought to criminal justice reform too, the relationship between government and police was strengthened (Sir John Stevens commented on one occasion that we had achieved more in a few weeks than in the previous twenty years), and across the range of institutions responsible for bringing integrity to law, order and justice, new and constructive relationships had been forged. It was no accident that in the ensuing two years nearly all the indicators of criminal justice system performance began to shift in the right direction, though admittedly they only moved – to use a phrase I shall come back to – from 'awful' to 'adequate'.

In the spring of 2002, Tony Blair's restlessness about public service reform and delivery had been evident, and a cause of anxiety to me. When we discussed a presentation I had made to Japanese leaders on delivery, I told him that they had a lot to learn. He replied tartly, 'We've got plenty to do ourselves too.' In March he wrote a note to me and others: 'The truth is, for all the progress, we are not focused sufficiently on key priorities.' Yet by that summer, with street crime coming under control, his confidence in us had grown: it was no longer a case of us simply talking a good game; in partnership with the Home Secretary, we had delivered results. Deliverology was beginning to prove itself.

Levels of intensity

It was these results more than anything that led Blair to invite me to present at his second monthly press conference that July. I was able to show the press the dramatic falls the Street Crime Initiative had brought about. The entire experience also led us to reflect in the Delivery Unit about how to tailor our responses to different degrees of challenge. From the outset, it had been my intention to ensure that the Delivery Unit provided the Prime Minister with a means of responding systematically when there was a major delivery failure, rather than relying on the ad hoc process of Blair's first term which I thought of – perhaps unkindly – as 'government by spasm'. Especially in that first year of the unit, he and those around him often reverted to the approaches of that first term which, to my chagrin, sometimes left me out of the loop. I thought that if I could develop a system which not only categorised challenges, but also anticipated and managed them before they exploded, this would be a significant contribution to improving government – and would ensure I stayed in the loop. Out of these reflections and in collaboration with the ever-inventive Jeremy Heywood, I developed the concept of 'levels of intensity' and presented it to Blair. Having explained the general concept and gained his approval, I set it out in a brief paper for him. Once the framework was in place, I argued, 'the result will be that when you are anxious about any aspect of delivery we can tell you instantly at what level it is currently being dealt with . . . and whether to escalate it'. I then developed three levels, the key variables being ministerial and especially prime ministerial time.

Level 1 was called 'standard problem-solving'. The routine application of deliverology involved the occasional 'timely nudge from Michael' (as one permanent secretary described it) when the data was marginally off track. If this didn't work, the Delivery Unit and the department would collaborate in diagnosing the problem. Then the Delivery Unit in addition to its routines would commit time and energy alongside the department – perhaps through a priority review – to assist in finding a solution. This was in effect what we did during 2002 on waiting and choice in Health. Action would be reported as usual at stocktakes, but no additional commitment of prime ministerial time would be required.

Level 2 described those problems of delivery which had such significance and required such urgency that 'a more intensive drive' was required. Perhaps they were deeply intractable; often they involved working across several Whitehall departments. Here, in addition to the problem-solving approach of Level 1, there would be an additional injection of prime ministerial energy and focus. Progress would be reported weekly rather than monthly, and a junior minister given political responsibility for driving progress. In addition to stocktakes, it was proposed, the Prime Minister would commit an hour a month to discussing the junior minister's report on the problem.

Finally, there was Level 3, an 'emergency'. For one or conceivably two issues at any one time where the complexity was huge and a sense of crisis had engulfed it, the COBRA-style crisis management was proposed. This applied, of course, to street crime and later to reducing the inflow of illegal asylum seekers, but by definition could only be rarely applied. The downside of the approach was the cost in terms of prime ministerial time – and indeed that of senior ministers – but the gain was the potential to realise dramatic and rapid progress.

Following discussions with Blair, we allocated the various problems to different levels, and for much of the next year I reported to him using this framework. We would discuss periodically which issues to escalate to Level 2 or 3, and which to drop back down. In the case of all of the five issues we allocated to Level 2 in April 2002 (secondary education in London, reducing train delays, Accident and Emergency, the criminal justice system and asylum applications), we made significant improvement over the next two years.

In the case of asylum applications, the problem got much worse before it got better and it was escalated to Level 3 by the end of the year. One aspect of the problem was solved sooner, though. As part of monitoring Level 2 intensity issues, one night that spring I visited

Dover, Coquelles and Fréthun to see what the asylum problem looked like, literally at the frontline. By then, Eurotunnel had built a huge, well-lit fence around Coquelles, and the flow of asylum seekers onto Eurostar had dried up, but at the goods marshalling yard in Fréthun, it was a different story. Asylum seekers could easily climb into the yard, board a goods train and make it to the UK. As I pointed out to Blair in a note: 'The fencing at the SNCF goods marshalling yard . . . is pathetic, about as tough as that round an Islington Council tennis court.'

In four years working for Blair I never hit on a comparison more likely to fire him to action than this one. I suggested we should press the Immigration Directorate to pay for a fence if the French wouldn't, since it would cost no more than £4 million, a sum we would rapidly recoup in savings many times over. 'Absolutely,' he replied. The most striking aspect of the visit for me was the visible impact of brutal and lucrative people trafficking. While the liberal Establishment was wringing its hands back home, here in northern France, Afghans or Iraqis who had been charged perhaps £10,000 by a ruthless operator were searching for any way in they could find, only to risk, if they succeeded, a life of effectively indentured labour while they tried to earn enough to pay off their 'fare'.

This visit and my report to Blair were early evidence that the new levels-of-intensity approach was beginning to work (and also, incidentally, the value of getting out to the frontline). The framework was powerful because, for the first time, we had developed an effective early warning system. By the second half of 2003, we were no longer using the language of levels of intensity, but the process of escalation remained. One of the reasons why none of our programmes reached Level 3 after street crime (2002) and asylum applications (2003) was that we were able – in the case of Accident and Emergency, for example – to solve problems and remove blockages before they reached crisis proportions. A general capacity to anticipate and prevent crises would have substantially enhanced prime ministerial power. Of course, outside the Delivery Unit programme, government was, as ever, faced with crises from time to time. In any case, we might just have been lucky with our programme, but I think we were on the brink of a significant innovation.

For me, though, a personal crisis that was off this scale altogether was about to engulf me.

Anja

During the four years I worked in the Delivery Unit, I visited Russia for three or four days twice a year, with Blair's approval, to assist with education reform. One of these visits took place between 15 and 19 May 2002, when the street crime data was at last beginning to shift in the right direction. The visit involved seeing a school in a neglected small town north of Moscow where the only factory had closed down. Now there was mass unemployment and in the school a handful of heroic teachers were trying to pull a community up by its frayed bootlaces. At the end of the visit, I met the Education Minister in Moscow and then, on the Sunday before flying home, had time to visit the magnificent Novodevichy Monastery in which Peter the Great had incarcerated his sister. Shortly after that, while I was in the park in Moscow where all the fallen statues of Stalin, Dzerzhinsky and other despised former heroes lie strewn among the grass, I called home and Karen told me that our daughter Anja, then aged twenty-five, had had a 'very bad' accident, breaking her back in two places, after being thrown by a horse. She was in hospital. I was numb, frozen to the ground. How could I have been so far away when I was needed?

I was home in time for the major operation the next day. Karen and I saw Anja come round after the pins had been put in her back. Mercifully the spinal cord itself had been spared, and she had feeling everywhere. The surgeon was hopeful that in time she would make a full recovery. Later that evening, when we were home, relieved the operation had gone well, but drained, Blair rang and expressed his sympathy: 'I'm having dinner with David Blunkett and Sally [Morgan] and we all send our love.' The next day Blunkett wrote Anja a brief, very warm letter.

For the rest of the week I was semi-detached at work, dropping in and then rushing off to visit Anja in hospital. After a week or so, she was able to come home, but at first she needed assistance with everything. Karen became a devoted full-time carer. Slowly, slowly, the back began to heal and Anja began to be able to move around. We celebrated the first time she walked to the local shop, then to the Angel, Islington . . . The following year she had a further major operation and after that depended largely on her inner reserves of courage and the love of her family, especially her mother, for her recovery, and her capacity to cope with the pain that will always be with her.

With the accident, her career had gone too. She had lived at a riding stables and trained cross-country horses for a living. Ever since she had been tiny, it was all she had wanted to do. So alongside the physical recovery, there was a social and psychological recovery to make, and in the quiet, profound way which is so characteristic of her, she made that recovery too. Now, five years later, she is working part-time, living independently again at last, and an inspiration to me, her family and no doubt others too.

Accident and Emergency

The NHS always performs brilliantly in a crisis, whether it affects many, as in a train crash, or just one, as in Anja's riding accident. In dealing routinely with the bulk of patients who arrive at Accident and Emergency departments, it has historically performed rather less well. In the 1990s, almost everyone had a story about how long they or someone they knew had waited for treatment. The press loved to highlight lurid stories of all-night trolley waits, but for many of the twelve million who use A&E each year, it was the miserable wait in a plastic chair in dilapidated surroundings that was the more serious problem. The ten-year plan for Health, published in 2000, proposed a way to tackle this problem. Major capital investment would help, walk-in centres would be established in busy locations, and GPs' surgeries would be encouraged to deal with the more routine cuts and bruises. The centrepiece of the plan, though, was a promise that by the end of 2004, no one would wait more than four hours in A&E to be seen, treated or, if necessary, admitted to hospital. While four hours still seems a long time, achieving this target would mean an average wait of much less than this, and put UK performance ahead of most other countries. During 2002 we in the Delivery Unit were monitoring progress on this target monthly and one central fact became plain – nothing was happening. From the moment the target had been set, the data showed that around 80 per cent of patients were dealt with within four hours, which obviously meant that 20 per cent were waiting longer, sometimes much longer. That's how it stayed right through to the summer of 2002. Unacceptable.

After the success of the priority review of street crime, we decided to try the method again with A&E. Clara Swinson, our Health account manager (who hid behind her gentle manner immense determination) persuaded the department a priority review would help them, and Richard Page-Jones – having become an instant expert on street crime – now transferred his focus to A&E. The team made its field visits in August (summer holidays or not, I had promised 'delivery never sleeps'), and by September had stunning evidence of the problem and a clear idea of what needed to be done. The data showed the way, but the field visits discovered the solutions. The team visited one A&E department which was doing exceptionally well – in fact it had as good as achieved the target – and one which the data revealed to be very poor. The poor A&E department had weak management which was in conflict with the chief executive of the NHS trust. Here the situation was so dire that patients waiting on trolleys had become pawns in a game of hospital politics. Managers in A&E condoned trolley waits and indeed drew attention to them to strengthen their case for additional funding. Our team was genuinely shocked by the immorality of it. At the good site, by contrast, management was excellent and a new approach had been introduced which had radically speeded up the process. This new best practice, called 'see and treat', was demonstrably effective. The traditional approach in the A&E department had been for people to see a triage nurse who decided how urgent each case was. If a case required urgent attention, it got it; if not, the patient was asked to sit on one of those plastic chairs and watch a grainy-screened television, sometimes in the company of the Friday night lager louts who would add to the dismal atmosphere by throwing up periodically. 'See and treat' stood this approach on its head. Urgent cases were still dealt with urgently, of course, but those with minor injuries were treated immediately at the triage point and sent home. Like all revolutionary ideas, it was so simple that you wondered why no one had thought of it before.

The fastest possible spread of 'see and treat' to all 200 or so A&E departments became the central recommendation of the priority review. There were other practical recommendations too. Health Service staff knew there was a target, but they did not believe the government minded about it very much, so we recommended that Alan Milburn and Nigel Crisp (the permanent secretary) take urgent steps to raise its profile. Also, hospital performance on A&E did not feature in the published hospital star ratings, so senior managers often neglected it.

We recommended that, from 2003, A&E performance should be taken into account in the ratings. Finally, the report recommended that the Department of Health begin to manage performance on a regular basis, examining weekly data from A&E departments around the country and, where performance was poor, challenging it and offering assistance from external experts. The truth was that until then, even in the department, A&E had not been a high priority. I was told in 2002 that more civil servants were working on hospital music than on A&E performance and, whether or not it was true at the time, it seemed all too plausible.

The report itself solved nothing, of course. We and our allies in the department, such as Paul Corrigan, had to persuade ministers and key officials to act. Vital decisions had to be made and communicated. By the end of the year, while the data remained firmly on a plateau, there were real signs of hope. The message that A&E performance really was a priority had been clearly conveyed to the NHS by Milburn. The decision to include it in the star ratings had been taken, and the department had set up an operations room and staffed it. It became exemplary – a mini-Delivery Unit focused on meeting this single target and fired with enthusiasm for the cause. Meanwhile 'see and treat', the key to improving performance on the ground, stalled. The task of spreading it across the Health Service had been given to the Modernisation Agency, which had done good work in the past but which also had a strong cultural resistance to the concept of best practice. Like many organisations led and managed by professionals, it was obsessed with securing their 'buy-in' to all its activities rather than imposing ideas, however good. This in turn meant not finding best practices and disseminating them but creating circumstances in which groups of professionals discovered these practices for themselves. They even had a name for this process, which told you everything you needed to know: it was called 'assisted wheel reinvention'. This approach had proved effective in encouraging the spread of improved practice in cancer and coronary heart disease care, but it had a major flaw from the point of view of A&E: it took time – several years – to spread, which we did not have. The due date for the target was now only two years away. After months of frustration with the slowness of progress at the Modernisation Agency, the department took the plunge and imposed a 'just do it' approach. 'See and treat' spread rapidly across the country.

Sometimes even professionals prefer simple, clear direction, especially on a high priority. It certainly beats endless bureaucratic regulation and an absence of focus. This is what we had discovered with literacy and numeracy in primary schools in Blair's first term, and what the police had learnt in relation to street crime in 2002.

From January 2003, the weekly data began at last to move in the right direction. It spiked up from just above 80 per cent of patients being seen within four hours to over 90 per cent in the last week of March, which was a 'census' week for the star ratings. It looked momentarily like a classic perverse effect of the measurement system, but it wasn't – performance never slipped back below 90 per cent. The department began to celebrate its impact. The target, however, was that 100 per cent (with the exception of those for whom this would be clinically problematic) should be seen within four hours, not 90 per cent, and, as is often the case, the nearer to success they came, the harder it was to eke out each additional percentage. During the summer of 2003, the plateau was explained away by the Health Department as normal for the time of year, but when it continued into the autumn we began to press for renewed action.

The growing success of 'see and treat' across the service was obviously constructive but, not unusually, the implementation of one best practice simply revealed the need for others at a deeper level. Achieving the target in full required more than just 'see and treat'; it required effective management of the whole hospital. For example, if an A&E patient needs to see a specialist consultant, the management needs to ensure that this is possible within the time limit. Similarly, if a patient needs to be admitted to the hospital, the management needs to ensure a bed becomes free within the time limit too. In fact, in many hospitals, patients were staying in beds much longer than they needed to, simply because the relevant consultants did not do their ward rounds until late morning. Likewise, once a hospital pays attention to the data, it can see when the peak times (such as Friday evening) are and change its staffing patterns accordingly; again a management issue. During 2003, the Department of Health, assisted by the Delivery Unit, codified best practices in these areas too and then, on the basis of the weekly data, despatched teams of experts to the relevant hospitals to solve these problems. In fact, as many hospitals themselves proved, once the management was resolved and the hospital set out to focus on providing the best service it could for patients, the target could be met and clinical outcomes improved.

However, simply spreading best practice together with the threat of accountability that came from star ratings might not have been quite enough. An additional ingredient, a personal favourite of the Prime Minister's, was required. At a stocktake in the autumn of 2003, he asked John Reid, who had replaced Alan Milburn that summer, 'What are the positive incentives to meet the target?' There were none, we all agreed, and Reid, always practical and focused, said he would go and work up a package. By December 2003 I was able to tell Blair, at one of my monthly round-up meetings with him, that Reid had developed a package which would provide financial rewards to A&E departments which met milestones during 2004 on the way to achieving the final target itself in December of that year. Blair was delighted, and as the incentives package rolled out, progress towards the target followed.

At the last stages, along with officials from the Department of Health, we held meetings with the leadership from a few big trusts which were falling short to have them explain how they planned to reach the target. As with the chief constables and street crime, performance improved in the week before the meeting so when they arrived we could congratulate them and offer the necessary assistance to complete the task. Pragmatically, Blair and Reid did not want us to be religious about meeting the last decimal point of the target. They knew by then – late 2004 – that the A&E service had been dramatically improved. This was evident not just in our data on the target, but in the surveys of patients' perceptions. Blair therefore urged me to be pragmatic. In response I said that we in the Delivery Unit had to be the people who took targets literally, but of course we would also apply common sense.

The A&E story represented powerful evidence of how thoughtful reform combined with effective management of performance could radically improve results quite rapidly. It also illustrates, incidentally, the importance of consistent political leadership. Milburn had been an effective Secretary of State for Health, and his surprise resignation, resulting from family pressures, seemed to leave a gaping hole in the government. In fact, Reid, with the experience of numerous Cabinet posts behind him, stepped into the role smoothly. By keeping the same group of advisers – especially Paul Corrigan, Simon Stevens and Dominic Hardy – around him, he ensured there was no loss of momentum. One of the unsung benefits of targets was perfectly illustrated in this case: in contrast to what often happened under his predecessors, under Blair when a new secretary of state was appointed, it was hard to move the goalposts because the targets were public commitments which belong to the entire government. Milburn to Reid was the most seamless transition I saw in government, a credit to them both and extremely important in relation to delivering the A&E and other waiting times targets.

As it happened, I had a personal insight into this moment of transition. On the day of the reshuffle, I dropped in to the gents' in No. 10 across the corridor from Blair's office and happened upon Reid, who asked me what I thought of Milburn's resignation, announced that morning. I said I would miss him and that 'he's the best Labour Secretary of State for Health since Bevan'.*

'That's kind,' he replied. 'Who do you think will replace him?'

'You're more likely to be in the loop on that than I am,' I said lightly, and was on my way. Only later, when I discovered that Reid had been given the job, did it occur to me that while I was talking to him he was waiting for the crucial conversation with the Prime Minister. When we met for an introductory briefing early the following week, he was convinced I had known all along, and I was tempted to leave him with this impression, because if top people thought I was in the reshuffle loop – the loop of loops as it were – it would enhance my influence, but a surge of honesty got the better of me: 'I'd like to say I had,' I told him, 'but in fact I hadn't a clue.' He was in post a little under two years, and delivered every single major target. I often wonder whether my comparison of Milburn to Aneurin Bevan that time in No. 10 inadvertently set Reid an ambitious personal target – or whether, more likely, he forgot it before the day was out.

There is another codicil to the A&E story. Steve Kelman, a professor at Harvard, gathered all the data, trust by trust, on A&E and subjected it to all the analysis that the Kennedy School of Government could bring to bear. He was able systematically to destroy all the urban myths that critics of the target hurled at it – there were not more admissions to hospital, there was no increase in return visits to A&E and therefore no

---

*I believe this because he had the courage to break producer monopolies and began the process of empowering patients.

indication that service standards slipped, there was no evidence that hospitals focused specifically on those who had been waiting between three and four hours at the expense of others, and no evidence that results were falsified. Overall, he showed conclusively that the focus on the target led to better performance and 'produced efficiency-enhancing improvements in treatment technologies'.[2] This is Harvard-speak for 'the service improved dramatically'. Many staff celebrated their success of course, but a few cynics in the Health Service – inevitably given greater attention in the press – who hated government targets, not to mention the successful achievement of them, did their best to shoot the service they purported to defend in the foot.

January–February 2003: war on all fronts

Elizabeth I called it 'the midst and heat of battle', Churchill described it as 'the hinge of fate': the moment in a great enterprise when the storm is at its height and the key is not to relent, but rather to persevere and wait for the clouds to lift. Blair described early 2003 as 'war on all fronts', and demonstrated his resilience and boundless capacity to drive the agenda forward. For him, with the possibility of war in Iraq looming, of course there was much worse to come, but looking back to early 2003, I can see it was the turning point for delivery on the domestic front. Until then, most of the data we were tracking was heading in the wrong direction, but from then on, led by street crime, which had turned the previous year, one by one the trends turned positive. For those crucial months, the key was to hold your nerve, even at the most unlikely moments, as when, on Saturday 25 January 2003 at 9.00 in the morning, my phone rang at home. I had been up just ten minutes, but there are some sentences which are guaranteed to wake you up, even after a night out: 'It's the switchboard here. I have the Prime Minister for you.'* Blair rapidly got over the pleasantries and began firing questions at me about the number of asylum applications. He had seen my weekly note of the day before which suggested the

---

* When the switchboard called, often but not always I answered the call myself. On one occasion my daughter Naomi answered, and when they said, 'It's No. 10 here,' she replied, 'It's No. 62 here, how can we help?'

figures would be dire again. Blair suggested we should go into COBRA mode – or in Delivery Unit jargon, treat it as a Level 3 emergency – and on Monday acted on that decision. He cleared his diary, summoned the relevant officials and began to go through the entire process an asylum seeker would experience, detail by detail, looking for loopholes forensically, like the lawyer he was trained to be. It was a good example of how an assertion of prime ministerial authority can bring about interdepartmental collaboration.*

Working with the Immigration and Nationality Directorate (IND) of the Home Office, we had in fact already systematically examined the impact that the 2002 legislation and the closure of Sangatte would have on the numbers over the next year or so. In short, we had developed a trajectory. At first glance, the trajectory looked impressive. From the peak of over 8,000 asylum applications per month in November 2002, it showed a steep plunge during the first six months of 2003 to less than half that by the end of the summer. Blair had seen this and was obviously pleased, but one somehow doubts he gave it any credence: after all, his experience of the IND over several years was of false promises, constant excuses and inadequate results. However, at the height of the public furore over asylum – driven in part by the numbers which appeared out of control, and in part by the middle-brow tabloids (which had discovered that putting hysterical asylum stories on the front page significantly increased circulation), Blair went on *Newsnight* and announced live that he intended to halve the number of applications by September 2003. Perhaps somewhere in the back of Blair's mind that plunging trajectory had been lodged. As with street crime the previous year, this seemed to be an example of what Margaret Thatcher had described to Kenneth Baker as 'a calculated bounce'.

A bounce certainly, but was it calculated? Shortly afterwards, I was giving evidence to the Public Administration Select Committee and found myself being quizzed abut this *Newsnight* interview. I was asked whether it was a new target. No, I replied somewhat disingenuously, it was 'an aspiration'. I explained that if the Prime Minister wanted to be

---

* Alastair Campbell's diary for this period is, perhaps not surprisingly, almost entirely focused on foreign affairs and the media. There is one brief reference to the rest of the agenda: 'Iraq was totally dominating but at TB's morning meeting it was the usual whinge about asylum, crime, health and all the dreadful figures that were coming out. He was really fed up with it all.' (Monday 24 February 2003).

publicly held to account for an aspiration that went beyond a published target, 'that is a matter for him in exercising leadership'. Then I was asked the killer question: had I advised the PM to make this announcement? No, I said, thus having to admit I was completely out of the loop. 'Were you upset?' came the next question. 'No, I am confident that the aspiration . . . will be achieved,' I replied, remembering the trajectory.

Later that day I saw Blair himself in No. 10 and thought I had better mention this exchange to him in case it became a news story. I told him I had been forced to admit I did not know he was due to make this announcement. He was unmoved; 'I don't see why you should have known,' he commented dryly, suggesting that it had only occurred to him on the spur of the moment.

By then, after a series of meetings in No. 10 driven by him, and further refinements to the plan, the data had begun to fall in line with the trajectory. The major influences at work were the implementation of the 2002 legislation pushed through by David Blunkett in the teeth of opposition, his coup in agreeing with the French the closure of Sangatte, and the tightening of the border with France. The emergency level of intensity helped Blunkett keep the pressure on other government departments, especially the Foreign Office, which until then had been slow to see the resolution of the asylum issue as a major foreign policy goal, in spite of Jack Straw's collaborative approach.

Asylum was the emergency delivery issue of the day, but the most striking aspect of January 2003 was the overwhelming array of challenges. The year had begun for me with a genuine escape. I had been invited to speak at a conference in Sydney in early January and, arriving a day early, dashed to the Sydney Cricket Ground where to my delight I watched England move remorselessly towards a test match victory over the mighty Australians. Along with the Barmy Army, covered in sunscreen and wearing a bright yellow sunhat, I belted out the song 'We're Going to Lose 4–1', which in the years before the 2005 Ashes miracle seemed as much as we could hope for. A correspondent of the *Financial Times* was tipped off – by a Treasury official, I discovered later. The result was the most favourable piece of press coverage I have ever had. Under the heading 'Good delivery', the *FT* diarist (7 January 2003) wrote: 'Observer hears the head of the Prime Minister's Delivery Unit was in Sydney to see a remarkable turnaround as England's cricketers thrashed the Aussies. Coincidence? England's revival could be short-lived: Barber certainly won't be watching them [in the World Cup] in Zimbabwe.'

This idyllic start to the year did not last long. On my last day in Sydney, I had a message from the switchboard to ring No. 10. I finally got hold of the duty press officer to discover that the contents of our December delivery report on Health had been leaked to Nick Timmins of the *Financial Times*, whose front-page story was headlined 'Extra NHS cash may be squandered, PM told' (8 January 2003). The confidential report's striking (and true) phrase, 'the risk is immense', inevitably caught the public eye. The next day the tabloids made hay – 'Blair's £40bn health gamble is going down the pan' was the *Sun*'s graphic interpretation of my report.

Once I had the facts from the press office, I knew what I had to do, but can't say I looked forward to doing it. I rang Alan Milburn. I was in Darling Harbour, Sydney; it was late morning with temperatures in the high twenties, the sun was shining, the water sparkled, England had just won a test match and the Australians were recovering by buying ice creams and sitting in cafés. For Milburn, when my call came through, it was nearly midnight in London, it was snowing and the *Today* programme wanted him to go on the next morning and account for my report. Even so, to his credit, he answered through gritted teeth: 'First of all, Happy New Year.' Then he explained it was a major problem. All I could do was apologise profusely and wish him the best of luck. 'Enjoy the rest of your stay,' he concluded cheerlessly.

Back in London after the long flight home, I whirled round Downing Street to check with Peter Hyman, Jeremy Heywood and others how they had responded. In fact, the press office had come up with a brilliant – and very accurate – line for the lobby: we in No. 10 were not in the habit of sending self-congratulatory letters around Whitehall, they said, claiming this was a sign of strength. Alastair Campbell was more interested in hearing about the test match and explaining away the three depressing performances by Burnley he had witnessed over the holidays.*

Nevertheless, I knew there would be sensitivities in the Department

---

* His diary does not mention the health story at all – or the three poor performances by Burnley.

of Health and, in any case, trust in the Delivery Unit was at stake. I promised Milburn I would investigate what had happened and review our procedures. It turned out that the report had been circulated by Department of Health officials to all 300 trust chief executives and that this was the most likely source of the leak. The next time we circulated delivery reports, we warned permanent secretaries that they were personally responsible for deciding circulation.

When I was not watching cricket, dealing with leaks or prime ministerial calls on asylum, I spent much of January 2003 routinely meeting permanent secretaries to ensure they acted on their delivery reports. In addition, I kept checking the data on the key indicators, especially the weekly data on street crime and asylum. In early February I wrote myself a quirky note:

> Liverpool were dumped out of the FA Cup by Crystal Palace on Wednesday night . . . Cycling into work on Thursday, the gloom of a football fan when the team has lost dominated. Cycling home that evening, though, I had the equivalent of a spring in my step. Why, I wondered . . . I was amazed. The street crime figures and the asylum applications figures were much improved [and] were more important to me than Liverpool's results.

By far the biggest challenge in following up the delivery report was the Home Office. David Blunkett's political leadership had been immense and John Gieve as permanent secretary had steadily strengthened the organisation, but beneath him management remained fragile and the mix of challenges – crime, drugs, bulging prisons, counter-terrorism, asylum, immigration – seemed to become more challenging with every passing week. Blunkett invited me to address a meeting of his ministers and top officials. He urged me to be very hard-hitting. As agreed, at the meeting I set out a stark contrast between organisational reform on the one hand and major crisis on the other, which I predicted could come from an explosive mixture of drugs, immigration and terrorism, and might result in the loss of a minister. Later, a top official rang and asked me whether my contribution had been 'an ultimatum from the Prime Minister'. I knew the Prime Minister would have supported my remarks, but I had not consulted him: 'No,' I replied, 'it's an ultimatum from the real world.' I promised to do everything I could to support Gieve and his colleagues in further strengthening his management team. Two appointments of senior people, given permanent secretary status, followed. It was an ad hoc solution, but provided Gieve with some of the additional resilience he needed.

In addition to meeting individual permanent secretaries, I also reported to them collectively, setting out the lessons of delivery so far and identifying Blair's top ten delivery challenges – the ten issues escalated to the higher levels of intensity. These were, at that moment:

- street crime
- asylum applications
- volume crime (e.g. burglary, car crime)
- drugs
- A&E
- waiting times in the NHS
- primary school literacy and numeracy
- secondary education in London
- rail performance
- road congestion.

Many of these were the same as had been identified a year earlier, and we had made progress on several of them, but the agenda remained daunting, especially for the Home Office, which explained the emphasis that it had been given. The permanent secretaries collectively were extremely supportive of the Delivery Unit by then. They could see that, in addition to monitoring, it offered practical assistance. On street crime, drugs and asylum, it had also facilitated effective collaboration between departments, the much-discussed but elusive 'joined-up government' to which everyone purported to aspire. Our capacity to anticipate problems rather than just respond to them had also been noticed. As one permanent secretary explained, 'We aspire to be one step ahead of the Delivery Unit, but so far we haven't achieved that.'

For Blair, 'war on all fronts' took him far beyond this delivery agenda. On domestic policy he was preparing the ground for the break-through on top-up fees for universities – a policy which was deeply controversial in the party and the country until it was implemented, when suddenly everyone discovered it had saved the universities' bacon, as the vice-chancellors later admitted to Blair. On the international stage, diplomacy in Europe and at the UN, as well as with the United

States in the run-up to the Iraq War, was dominant, and not something that Blair could delegate. When he and I were guests for dinner again at Blunkett's on 20 January, Blair quizzed me vigorously on how I saw the delivery agenda and was reassured that I saw real prospects of progress by the summer.*

As the international crisis developed and then the conflict began, Blair clearly had less and less time to devote to the delivery agenda. In the long run, of course, the Iraq policy cost him dearly, but for me, the impact of the crisis was immediate. I had to maintain the drive for delivery while the Prime Minister's attention was elsewhere for an extended period. For my staff, this inevitably caused anxiety, but in the monthly staff meetings I stressed to them that this was precisely why we existed – to ensure delivery never sleeps. Even in the most difficult of circumstances, it was our job to sustain progress; it was a challenge to rise to, not a barrier to run into. I also took repeated opportunities in these monthly meetings to explain that our mission was not the Prime Minister's political future – that lay in the hands of others; rather it was to secure real improvements in the quality of services to citizens and to ensure that the vast sums of money being invested in the public services yielded a return to the taxpayer. To senior civil servants in Whitehall who saw in the Prime Minister's distraction a weakening of the drive for delivery, we issued a challenge: the Prime Minister has developed the view, we said, that when he stops paying attention, the drive for reform and delivery slows down; this is your chance to prove him wrong.[†]

Meanwhile, on a practical level, when Blair could not make stocktake meetings we did not cancel them. Instead, we stood the ministers down and I chaired a meeting, with the relevant permanent secretary and top officials being held to account. We still sent the briefing to Blair in advance, and the note afterwards. Wherever possible, we even held the meetings in the Cabinet Room itself to convey the formality.[‡] As far as possible, we maintained the appearance of 'business as usual' and the optical illusion of unstinting prime ministerial interest. In fact, to my

---

* See Blunkett, *The Blunkett Tapes*, p. 441. Blunkett describes that week as 'just relentless', which captures the spirit of the time.
[†] See Alastair Campbell's diary for 24 February 2003, where Blair is reported to be 'in a rage at departments who he felt took their feet off the accelerators once we were all occupied with something else'.
[‡] This was when I first had the experience of sitting in *that* chair (see Chapter 1).

surprise, even at the height of the international crisis, Blair did find time periodically to comment on the routine notes that we kept sending him. On one occasion that spring, I passed him in the No. 10 lobby and he asked, 'How's the Home Front?' There had been no loss of momentum, I replied. He smiled and vanished, not unlike the Cheshire Cat.

Oddly, one consequence of the war was that I had more time to spend working through the details of data and delivery with my staff because there were far fewer meetings to attend in No. 10. Being in the engine room of the Delivery Unit was always invigorating – the staff were excellent and the problems fascinating. In the week of the dramatic parliamentary debate which preceded the Iraq War, for example, I spent hours trying to understand why health waiting times and the waiting list were not falling as fast as they should have been. I debated with the Home Office their complacency over the burglary figures – yes, they were falling, but they had not fallen far enough to make people feel that crime was low, as had happened in New York City. And with my team, we challenged the Department for Education to strengthen its plan for education in London, a plan which ultimately delivered impressive results.

'And the war came,' as Abraham Lincoln famously put it.[3] Soon it was over. I watched the scenes of the statue of Saddam being dragged down on the television in Andrew Turnbull's office, while simultaneously updating him on the Delivery Unit's impact. For Blair the damaging traumas of the post-war period were about to begin, but in the short term he was back on the delivery case. The optical illusion had been maintained long enough, though I knew at the time we had been severely stretched. In fact, the data Blair returned to was more encouraging than ever before; a tipping point had been reached, although at the time, it had not yet become apparent.

The future of targets

In that same period of early 2003, prompted in part by Gus Macdonald, Gordon Brown began to give serious thought to the future of targets. Inevitably, they were a constant source of political controversy, with some professionals seeking to denigrate them and some politicians worrying about whether they would be met. The most damaging critique was that they had generated the explosion of bureaucracy that headteachers, Health Service managers and police chiefs complained about.

Macdonald raised this theme with me, suggesting it was time to reflect, well ahead of the 2004 spending review, on how many targets government should have and how success and failure should be explained to the public. Is 'success', for example, meeting all the targets? If so, doesn't that betray a lack of ambition? My view, which I put in a reply to him, was that departments should have a mix of ambitious and less ambitious targets, and that they should be relatively few in number. For some aspects of performance, I suggested that what was needed was not targets but transparency: in other words, the public interest would be satisfied by data being published regularly rather than by setting a future performance goal. I had been influenced by reading former New York mayor Rudolph Giuliani's book on leadership, in which he rejected targets as too politically risky, but argued for transparency, with weekly data on crime being published precinct by precinct across New York City, and a similar approach applied to prisons and social services.

Brown took up this theme in January 2003 in preparation for a major speech he delivered to the Social Market Foundation the following month. Much of the speech was about where and when he believed markets were appropriate, but the part I was most interested in surveyed the future of targets. Nick Macpherson, my Treasury counterpart, and I provided Brown with a series of briefings on the subject. I ensured that Blair – however distracted – was fully informed, and we began to hammer out a serious policy position on the future of targets.

National targets would be fewer in number and used to inject ambition and direction. Then there would be a series of indicators on which data would be public, and beyond that, at local level, institutions would be able to add local indicators to which transparency would apply. In effect, the deal for an NHS trust or a school would be increasingly devolved decision-making in return for greater transparency. The theory, for which Giuliani's book supplied the evidence, was that this approach would be a non-command-and-control, but also non-market, means of driving continuous improvement. Government, meanwhile, would retain and use as necessary the right to intervene where performance was poor. This was important because although command-and-control could work in some circumstances, and quasi-markets in others, there were still others where neither were appropriate – policing, criminal justice and road congestion spring to mind. Equally, where quasi-market models were rejected as a matter of principle, this offered an alternative approach. Later in the year, at the Chancellor's request, Macpherson and I sent a small joint team to New York City (and Baltimore) to see what Giuliani's approach looked like in practice. In this way, Brown prepared for the 2004 spending review, which reduced the number of targets and increased devolution of funding to the frontline.*

Shortly after the Brown speech, Macpherson and I gave evidence on the subject of targets to the Public Administration Select Committee, chaired by the witty and effective Tony Wright MP. We prepared well. I had read in Robert Reich's marvellous book about his time in Clinton's Cabinet his account of preparing for his Senate hearing. The staff in the Labor Department put him through a trial run which they called a 'murder board'. They kept throwing him the most difficult questions they could think of and he kept answering, he felt, rather well. Then one of the department's old hands stopped him and said it just wasn't working. Reich asked why not, and was told that the point at a Senate hearing was not to answer the questions, but to 'demonstrate your humility'.† I asked my staff to set up a murder board for Macpherson and me, not just because, as ever, I wanted to prepare obsessively, but also because I saw an opportunity for some of the staff, especially those seconded in from consultancies, to learn about parliamentary procedure. Macpherson and I were put through our paces and prepared to demonstrate just how humble we could be. The team did such a good job that our appearance before the committee itself felt straightforward by comparison.

Wright began by asking about press reports that the Delivery Unit was being relocated to the Treasury. The truth was that the Delivery Unit staff were moving into the Treasury building, but our status was

---

* The full benefits of the analysis done in 2003 are seen in the much more radical and creative design of the targets framework undertaken in 2006 for the 2007 comprehensive spending review.
† The advice Reich got that day on surviving a hearing has never been bettered: 'They are interested in how you respond . . . Deferentially. Good-naturedly. If they are nasty, don't be nasty back. If they are sarcastic, refrain from sarcasm. Never get angry. Never lose your balance. Never take the bait.' (Robert B. Reich, *Locked in the Cabinet* (New York: Alfred A. Knopf, 1997), p. 39.) Simple, really.

unchanged. The press, needless to say, saw it through the only prism they could think of, and reported it as Brown swallowing Blair's unit, which was entirely untrue, but not at all unexpected. I assured Wright that the move signified business as usual and was evidence only of growing co-operation between the Cabinet Office and the Treasury.

Most of the debate, though, was about targets. We were challenged on whether there were good and bad targets. I denied flatly ever saying that 'the government had never set a bad target', a quote the *Independent* had attributed to me in January. I looked across the room at the relevant journalist, Andrew Grice, who smiled, as if accepting it was a fair cop. Then, in response to a question, Macpherson made the crucial point about targets and ambition:

> I very much agree with a lot of your witnesses from business that if we had a system where every single target was achieved, I would actually think that maybe the Treasury was not doing its job and we would need a bit more stretch in the system . . . It is very striking that in relation to a number of the best targets where departments have just fallen short of them there has been huge success. Michael mentioned literacy and numeracy . . . '[4]

Macpherson was also challenged on why, by February, some departments had still not produced their autumn performance reports, and he displayed his disarming wit to perfection: 'It is an interesting question', he said, 'when autumn ends.'

A few weeks later, we moved into the splendidly refurbished Treasury building and began to enjoy the open plan, good coffee, the company of Macpherson's team and – when we discovered it – the table tennis table in the basement. There I could treat some of my younger staff to an induction into the true art of spin.

The railways

In October 2000, there had been a rail crash at Hatfield, in Hertfordshire, after which the entire rail industry suffered a collective nervous breakdown. The incident had revealed the profound flaws in the structure of the privatised industry, and performance had plummeted. Faith, according to the Book of Hebrews, is the evidence of things not seen.[2] For some reason, throughout the 2001–5 parliament, I kept faith that eventually (and in spite of the evidence) we would begin to see sustained improvement, from the low post-Hatfield base, in the percentage of trains arriving on time. I was not sure how, and soon discovered that – as one of its former governors said of New Mexico – approaches tried and tested elsewhere failed on the railways. I had just one moment – in November 2003 – when my faith failed, despair set in and I suddenly resigned myself to the fact that the Prime Minister had been right all along: with the railways I was banging my head against a brick wall, and no amount of attention would make any difference. Worse still, this was a rare occasion, perhaps the only one in four years, when I admitted my despair to my own staff. Here, it seemed, was an impossible problem that really was impossible. The indefatigable Lucy Chadwick, who had been ploughing the Delivery Unit's lonely furrow with the railways, looked crestfallen. In fact, she soon turned the tables on me. The darkest hour had been just before dawn and, for every month after that November, performance advanced steadily for the next three years.

The central act of the parliament was the replacement of Railtrack with Network Rail in autumn 2001. Though for Stephen Byers it became entangled with the controversy over his special adviser Jo Moore, he had done what any good politician should do, and taken an extremely tough decision early in the parliament. Then he made the sensible decision to appoint, from Virgin Rail, the young but talented Richard Bowker to lead the Strategic Rail Authority (SRA). Neither of these bold steps, though, helped him through the winter crisis of 2001–2. That January,* a combination of unusually bad weather, including heavy snow, and a series of strikes on South West Trains created a metaphorical snowstorm in the media. The fact that, at the time, one in four trains was arriving late fuelled the sense of crisis. It was his bad luck that the height of the controversy happened to occur while Byers had snatched a few days' holiday in India. Arriving back with a tan while commuters were pictured huddling on crowded platforms in

---

* Almost every January begins with a government delivery crisis. Journalists recovering from their Christmas hangovers are more gung-ho than usual. The difficulty in government is predicting which service area the pack will descend on. In 2007, for example, it was the Home Office and prisons.

the cold was never going to be easy. The press had decided by then that he was their first potential scalp of the parliament, and the mix of frustration about the railways, Moore and the accusations and counter-accusations of Martin Sixsmith, the head of his press office, eventually provided the media with enough vitriol to bring him down.*

Alistair Darling, who replaced him in June 2002, bringing a new permanent secretary (Rachel Lomax), sensibly decided to lie low. Transport was separated from Environment, and he focused on the basics. When summoned before the media, he dealt with them as Mike Atherton dealt with West Indian fast bowlers. Then, behind the scenes, he built on the foundations that Byers had laid. The Delivery Unit, meanwhile, sought to build a working relationship with Transport officials. Needless to say, they were sensitive, having taken a battering. We sought, in parallel, to connect directly to Bowker and the SRA. To begin with, he sought to fend us off; he understandably wanted to keep his distance from the political mayhem and build his credibility among the train-operating companies (TOCs). In the end, though, he accepted my argument (using language that I thought someone recruited from the private sector would understand) that he should see the Delivery Unit as representing his major shareholder, the government, and we began to work collaboratively to put in place a means of managing the performance of the twenty or so TOCs.

The data showed that while Network Rail, the new organisation which owned the track, was responsible for half of the delays, the other half were attributable to the TOCs. If Bowker could use monthly data to challenge their performance and encourage them to learn from each other, perhaps, however slowly, performance would improve. In 2004, Darling introduced the plans to overhaul the governance of the railways, abolishing the SRA (which, while it had contributed to improved performance, had been, the Department for Transport and the Treasury believed, insufficiently effective in controlling expenditure) and extending the influence of Network Rail. Network Rail meanwhile brought routine maintenance work back in-house. These changes laid the foundations for further improvement after 2005, but were not the

---

* Alastair Campbell's diary records (Monday 27 May 2002): 'He [Byers] asked me if I thought he should have gone earlier. I said probably, yes. But I was like him, I really didn't want those fuckers to get a scalp.' I thought at the time that Byers's character assassination by the media was absolutely brutal.

drivers of the steady gains in performance from November 2003.

With the railways, as with other areas, the gains in performance were attributable not to one big thing, but to countless small things. The pressure on those who ran the railway to develop a trajectory is an example. In February 2003 I reported to Blair:

> I met Richard Bowker last week to emphasise the importance of the industry collectively driving at least incremental improvement . . . over the next year . . . We had a good straightforward exchange . . . and he has now accepted that [performance] ought to improve by at least 2–3 per cent year on year.

A modest hope admittedly, but at the time performance was flat. With this cautious aspiration in place, Bowker's persistent persuasion led TOCs to establish joint control centres with Network Rail for busy sections of the railway, which meant they could act promptly and collaboratively when something went wrong (which was often). Incredibly, only in 2004, 174 years after the very first passenger train journey, they decided that the whistle for departure of a train should be blown one minute before departure, enabling people to get on board so that the train could depart on time. Above all, from 2003 onwards, they answered our most repeatedly asked question: How come every year autumn takes you by surprise? The data, by the way, was very clear: leaves on the line – at least wet ones – really do cause delays because they make the line more slippery, thus requiring drivers to slow down. What was inexcusable was that, until 2003, no planning took place to minimise the detrimental effects of the dreaded leaves.

The turning point was a disastrous night – 18 October 2002 – when in a mighty storm millions of leaves fell across the country, and the next day rail performance was execrable. Someone told me 40 per cent of all the leaves in the country fell in that single night, but I wondered how on earth they could know. The following autumn, taking a leaf (as it were) out of the NHS book, they planned for autumn just as the Health Service had begun to plan for winter. Performance improved. For autumn 2004 they planned again, learning the lessons from the previous year. Performance improved again. When I described these modest gains to the Cabinet in the summer of 2003, I misused the old Fabian slogan, which I knew Labour ministers would recognise: 'I was going to call this progress Fabian, but decided not to because although it's gradual, it's certainly not inevitable.'

Other oddities abounded in this strange world. For example, we were told routinely that the introduction of new rolling stock always led to a drop in performance. When we asked why this counter-intuitive consequence occurred, we were always told the same thing: 'teething problems'. Only after we had been able to show that new rolling stock provided by the same supplier to railways in some other countries did not have the same baleful effect was action taken. The supplier was summoned and informed that what had been accepted in the past would from now on be seen as intolerable. Quite rapidly, performance of the new rolling stock improved, demonstrating one of the major weaknesses in government – that contracted-out services are often managed poorly. This weakness is often used as an argument against outsourcing; in fact it is an argument for getting better at it.

During 2004, working closely with all the stakeholders, we carried out two priority reviews on the railways, and by the end of the year each of the TOCs and Network Rail had agreed how much – in 'delay minutes' – they would contribute to reducing delay. A monthly meeting chaired by a minister of state – Kim Howells, then Tony McNulty – held them to account and, month by month, performance improved.

Shortly after I had left the Delivery Unit, I received a message from Deborah Heenan, who had taken over from Lucy Chadwick, telling me that the March 2006 target that 85 per cent of trains should run on time had been hit early. That still left 15 per cent being late, but four years earlier it had been 25 per cent, and since each percentage point represented a million passenger journeys, this was serious progress. Matching the metronomic reliability of the Trans-Siberian Railway, however, still lay in the future.

Literacy and numeracy in schools

Between 2001 and 2005 the Delivery Unit successfully worked in partnership with the Department for Education and Skills to bring about significant improvements in GCSE results, where Simon Day, a colleague in the Delivery Unit, helped prepare the ground not just for increasingly rapid progress but also for toughening the challenge by requiring English and maths to be included in the five-A*–C indicator.* However, as Chapter 1 demonstrates, no delivery problem was closer to my heart than literacy and numeracy in primary schools. Early in the second term, international comparison confirmed what our own tests had shown: primary school reading performance in England was now among the best in the world, although everyone involved in the policy knew how much room for improvement still remained. Two years later, international comparisons showed that primary school maths performance was improving faster in this country than anywhere in the world, but here too there were still far too many children moving into secondary school with an inadequate grasp of the basics.

In any case, as explained in Chapter 1, in 2001 progress faltered and the results plateaued. The following year – 2002 – was the due date of the target that 80 per cent of eleven-year-olds should achieve Level 4 in English (in other words, be able to read and write well) and 75 per cent the equivalent in maths. When performance fell short of the targets again that year, it contributed to the state of affairs in which Estelle Morris resigned. While it was the exams crisis and the ensuing row with the Qualifications and Curriculum Authority that was the major cause, the bigger delivery problem was primary school performance. Morris's resignation was traumatic for everyone, especially of course for her. She was loved wherever she went and was a wonderful performer – so genuine – on the media and at teacher conferences. She had been an outstanding minister for school standards under David Blunkett. I had worked with her closely for five years by 2002, and hated seeing the media destroy her career by chipping away at confidence in her, especially her own confidence in herself.

Though the Key Stage 2 results were not confirmed until September, we had known since July that the target would be missed. I was personally devastated and felt that I, more than anyone, was responsible. I told Morris that the right thing to do was not for her to resign, but for me to be fired. I made the same offer to Blair, but in both cases they dismissed the idea. That left me with the only other option – to do what I could to drive up primary school performance by deploying the

---

* The key indicator for school performance: how many pupils achieved five or more GCSE passes or equivalent at grade C or above.

influence of the Delivery Unit. The problem was that, by late 2002, the system which had worked so well between 1997 and 2000 had lost its edge at every level. Morris had been distracted, her top officials focused on other things, and after I had left there was no one at Education to have those restless, sleepless nights worrying about where the next percentage point was coming from. Moreover, after Chris Woodhead's resignation in the autumn of 2000, the impact of Ofsted inspection – a key lever in the strategy – had been weakened. In addition, with performance at a much higher level than just a few years earlier, it was of course increasingly difficult to make further gains.

The good news was that in the summer of 2002 David Miliband had become the minister for school standards in the department, and sought with our assistance to analyse the problem. But even with so talented a minister in place, the Department for Education was overwhelmed with challenges in 2002–3 and it was hard to refocus the system on literacy and numeracy. In the short term, the exam crisis had to be resolved. Then the huge row over student fees which dominated Charles Clarke's first months in office gave way in the spring of 2003 to a bizarre funding crisis affecting a vociferous minority of schools which pressed the government back onto the defensive in a year when the real terms increase in spending on schools was 6 per cent. (It was a classic case of a crisis born in the small print: funding formulae had been changed and headteachers, who had complained for years about government giving them money in ring-fenced grants, now mourned their passing.)

Added to these strategic distractions were changes within the national literacy and numeracy strategies themselves. In Morris's time it had been decided to combine them into one primary strategy, which on the face of it was sensible, since both strategies affected the same headteachers and teachers. But the name change also signified a change of priority. Ever since Elizabeth I overloaded Justices of the Peace in Tudor times, there has been an understandable tendency to pile additional tasks onto successful officials. Both the leaders of the strategies and the footsoldiers had until then focused purely on literacy and numeracy, but now they found themselves taking responsibility for improving behaviour, promoting the rest of the subjects in the primary curriculum and strengthening the use of information technology. From being single-issue fanatics driven by a mission to improve test scores, they became jacks of all trades. In the schools this was celebrated especially when, in the summer of 2003, the government published a new statement of primary school policy explaining this shift, called *Excellence and Enjoyment*, but for literacy and numeracy it was a setback.

The Delivery Unit itself also contributed to the continuation of the results plateau through 2003. At Miliband's request, we had reviewed the department's approach in the autumn of 2002 and declared it sound. We mistook the obvious competence displayed for a real cutting edge. When the 2003 results showed no progress for a third consecutive year, Miliband instituted a thorough analysis of the data and proposed major changes. There was evidence that offering intensive expert support to underperforming primary schools was working well. This programme was expanded. In addition, Miliband proposed that a thousand headteachers of successful primary schools should play a support-and-mentoring role to 4,000 of their peers who were doing less well. This became the Consultant Leaders' Programme. The successful leaders were to be trained for this task by the National College for School Leadership (NCSL). It was an excellent idea with real potential to drive performance above the high plateau.

In January of 2004, the DfES and the Delivery Unit together began to review the impact of these new measures. We decided to focus on ten large LEAs where, evidence showed, implementation in the past had sometimes been less effective. A visit to schools and education headquarters in one LEA raised alarm bells: literacy and numeracy did not appear to be high priorities there. DfES officials reassured us and their ministers that what we had seen was atypical. Then our alarm was reinforced by a visit to another LEA; was this atypical too? One swallow might not make a summer, but two? We gathered the education officers from the ten large education authorities around a table in the study at No. 10,* set out our anxieties and proposed action. They confirmed both. Most troubling of all was evidence that the training of headteachers by the NCSL for the Consultant Leaders' Programme had given little attention to literacy and numeracy and,

*The study had been Margaret Thatcher's office while she was Prime Minister; no doubt this was where a Prime Minister had first set eyes on a National Curriculum and national tests.

indeed, a read of the materials suggested that this seminal programme, instigated by a minister to improve performance in the national tests, had been heavily influenced by the purveyors of management gobbledegook who are always lurking in the education backwoods, waiting for their moment. Indeed, we had evidence that some of the trainers on the course had even made explicit the view that focusing on literacy and numeracy was actually wrong. My faith in the NCSL, and in the departmental officials whose job it should have been to check every detail of the training programme before it began, was shaken.

By coincidence, I had been asked to speak at a conference in Birmingham in early February 2004 where almost all the trainers and 1,000 mentoring heads were due to gather. Having done my best not to interfere too much personally in a policy I had previously run, I now decided to plunge myself headlong into it, and spent more time on that speech than on any other during the parliament. Knowing the risk of controversy, I decided to write out every word of the speech rather than rely on notes as I would normally have done. I cleared the text in an edgy negotiation with an anxious DfES official the night before. He had little room for manoeuvre because I carefully ensured my speech advocated what was formal policy and then challenged its implementation.

I started with the moral purpose – why literacy and numeracy matter so much.

> Why the emphasis on this core ideal at the moment? Because . . . we, all of us here, want to go beyond talking about equity, something many people did in the twentieth century. We want to deliver it . . . anything else would allow poverty to be cascaded from one generation to the next as it did sickeningly throughout the twentieth century.[5]

Then, having shown that standards in the primary sector stayed the same for fifty years before rising steeply in the late 1990s, I directly criticised the training programme in which the audience was participating: there was a failure to focus on English and maths; a lack of attention to the short term as well as the long term; and above all a loss of precision in thinking about how teachers taught, yet the potential for improvement lay most of all right there in the classroom. I emphasised the importance of ensuring the right teaching methods were applied in every classroom. I took on the mantra, so common in education circles, that somehow there is a conflict between precision on the one hand and creativity on the other:

> Genuine creativity is not leaving each individual to work it out for themselves. In fact, that is not creativity; it's betrayal . . . Precision and creativity are not opposites. They go together. Look at the soaring towers of a medieval cathedral; listen to the chorales of the *St Matthew Passion*; watch a great comedian at work; read a novel by George Eliot . . . In teaching, creativity is a question of learning; learning precisely and profoundly the best practice available and then, in striving to bring one more child up to the standard, going to the next step. Just as in music it's about practising the Beethoven Violin Concerto ninety-nine times, so that the hundredth time is sublime.

Over the top perhaps, but on the subject of literacy and numeracy in primary schools, that was how I felt (and still do). Self-indulgently, I felt I was fighting to save a strategy in which I had invested five years of my life; more importantly, I was seeking to ensure that an excellent ministerial decision was executed properly. The success of an idea such as these mentor-heads depends almost entirely on faithful implementation. In this case, not only had the DfES officials failed to check sufficiently what was happening, they had also, no doubt in response to continuous negative feedback from teachers, become apologetic about insisting on a focus on literacy and numeracy. Once this happens, the government is on the defensive. Yet all the evidence shows that if the government seriously wants to tackle the underlying causes of inequity – such as literacy and numeracy – then it has to be willing to take on professional self-interest and confidently win the argument rather than apologise.

The participants that day were split by my speech. There was a long silence before anyone clapped at all. Afterwards, I copied the speech to all the key people in the DfES, some of whom were moved by it. More importantly, a joint Delivery Unit/DfES team visited the ten large education authorities and helped them adjust their implementation rapidly before the eleven-year-olds took their tests in May. The NCSL was sent away to rewrite the contents of the training and put its house in order.

The speech also had consequences in No. 10. I copied it to Blair, Andrew Adonis and others with a covering note:

> Unless the major flaws in the current programme are tackled urgently . . . the test results could go down this year and/or next. By contrast, if they are tackled with vigour and urgency, it is still possible to get the results up . . . it will depend on whether, beneath ministerial level, the department has the capacity to act with clarity and determination.

Blair called me on the Saturday soon afterwards to congratulate me on the speech, as a prelude to asking me to work with him on his speech for the following week on the reform of the civil service. He also spoke to Charles Clarke to affirm his commitment to literacy and numeracy. Most crucially of all, when the 2004 test results came through, performance in English and maths had improved and the analysis showed that the intensive support programme and the headteacher-mentoring programme were both associated with significant gains. The following year – 2005 – there were further small gains. David Miliband's determination had been vindicated. Had my speech made a contribution? I always felt I could evaluate most of the Delivery Unit's work with a reasonably objective eye, but on literacy and numeracy in primary schools I was far too emotionally invested to be objective, and was at risk – as one minister correctly put it – of 'Barber hyperbole'.

Would it work at Anfield?

On Good Friday 2004, a few weeks before the eleven-year-olds took those crucial tests, I watched my beloved Liverpool lose 4–2 to Arsenal at Highbury. They were blown away by a brilliant hat-trick from Thierry Henry. For some, losing to Arsenal at the height of their invincibility might not constitute a crisis, but for me that day it did. It was not so much the result as the manner of the defeat. Nearly three years into my time at the Delivery Unit, and with most of the key indicators now beginning to shift in the right direction, I had learnt a lot about tackling underperformance and – it being the Easter holidays – I had time to ask myself a wild question: would what I had learnt in the

Delivery Unit work at Anfield? I did what I had never done before and wrote a letter to the chief executive of the club I supported. As it happened, I had met Rick Parry on a handful of occasions, which helped.

> Dear Rick,
>   As you know, I am a passionate fan of Liverpool FC . . . I don't have the time to watch [them] as often as I'd like, but I have seen them three times this year, most recently at Highbury last week. After that match and before the defeat by Charlton (although that reinforced my determination) I decided to write to you.
>   In my work, seeking to ensure delivery of public service reform on behalf of the Prime Minister, I see a wide range of organisations at work . . . While the range . . . is diverse, the characteristics which underpin success or failure are remarkably consistent . . . Repeatedly I've seen the characteristics of failure . . . displayed by our football team. You must think about these issues all the time, but allow me to describe three such characteristics, if only as a form of therapy.
>   **1. The manager [Gerard Houllier] makes too many excuses.** . . . The making of excuses undermines performance in two ways. First, it deflects attention from the many inadequacies which are directly under the control of the manager and the team (including tactics, effort, character in adversity etc). Second, by pointing all the time to the injured stars who aren't playing, the manager publicly indicates his lack of faith in the players he sends out onto the pitch . . . [As] a headteacher who had remarkably turned round a school [put it], 'We took all the excuses off the table.' That is a good starting point.
>   **2. The players don't try hard enough.** . . . Whatever else a fan expects, the bare minimum is 100 per cent effort . . . Delivering to world-class standards is very exacting in any organisation – no place at all for the half hearted . . . (By the way, I exempt the remarkable Steven Gerrard from *all* criticism on this point; how can the others watch him play like that every match and not feel ashamed of themselves?) . . .
>   **3. The Academy is not matching expectations.** . . . The best organisations concentrate hard on succession planning. They blend experience brought in from elsewhere – which prevents insularity and introversion – with home-grown talent which burns with commitment to the brand. Liverpool desperately need some home-grown 18- and 19-year olds who can show . . . what commitment really means . . . none have broken

through into the team since Owen, Carragher and Gerrard.

I know what you want for the club and hugely admire what you have achieved. Now it's time for the players to stand up and be counted. They have to believe in the vision . . . of the club as potential European champions again . . .

Best wishes, etc.

Parry was kind enough to write a thoughtful reply saying he had found my letter valuable and that he accepted my criticism. I am sure, needless to say, that my letter had nothing to do with the fact that the following week Jamie Carragher was quoted in the *Times* as saying that the team had been taken to task for not trying hard enough; nor with the fact that they went on to win three and draw one of the last four games that season and scrape into qualifying for the Champions League; nor with the fact that within weeks Houllier left and was replaced by Rafael Benitez; nor, of course, with the fact that the following season in Istanbul, against all the odds and having been 3-0 down at half-time in the final, Liverpool did in fact become Champions of Europe again . . . but football fans as passionate as I am live in a fantasy world.

Fantasy it might have been, but among Delivery Unit colleagues, especially those who followed the beautiful game, which furnished so much of our corridor conversation, the impact of my letter to Parry acquired mythical status. It added to our growing belief that applied deliverology could turn around almost anything. This is the theme of the next chapter.

6

Momentum

There is a tide in the affairs of men,
Which, taken at the flood, leads on to fortune.
                    William Shakespeare, *Julius Caesar*

July 2003

In July 2003, with the Delivery Unit now two years old, I had the opportunity for the second time to present to the Cabinet. The presentation looked ahead to year three of the parliament, drew out the lessons of our experience so far and argued that the challenge for year three was to make 'early progress irreversible'. Certainly by then there was growing evidence of this progress. The Health Service had met its milestones for March 2003, and no one was now waiting longer than twelve months for an operation. Accident and Emergency performance had also significantly improved (for the reasons given in the previous chapter). Burglary and car crime were falling, and street crime had been brought under control. The number of asylum applications had, as a result of Tony Blair's intervention earlier in the year, fallen from the peak of well over 8,000 per month to under 4,000. In Education, while literacy and numeracy performance was still on a plateau, school failure was being systematically reduced. And we had the first – albeit very modest – signs of improvement in the railways. My overall conclusion to the presentation was: 'Early progress is visible across the public services, but is far from irreversible, and time is short.' I had chosen to emphasise the shortage of time because, in the year ahead, I knew we had to step up the urgency. I pointed out that although it was a five-year parliament, two years had already gone and parliaments in the previous thirty years had run for five years only when governments were in trouble (Wilson/Callaghan 1974–9, Thatcher/Major 1987–92 and Major 1992–7). Moreover, in the last few months before an election it would be much harder to take radical and unpopular decisions, and therefore year three – which had already begun – was the last full year they would have to bring about irreversibility. I then defined irreversibility: structure (and incentives) changed; leadership transformed; culture shifted; visible results achieved; credibility established.

I also took up the debate about the future of targets. There had been some indications that one or two ministers thought targets and delivery were no longer necessary, but I argued this was to miss the point. Every government had to have goals – in this case, visibly improved quality of service and greater equity; the targets were merely a measurable representation of whether those goals were being achieved. The central messages of the presentation were what I called the ten key lessons, which I summarised afterwards in a note for the Cabinet and permanent secretaries. Even now I sometimes find them quoted back at me (the full text with challenging questions is in the Delivery Manual, Document 6).

Lesson 1
A week may be a long time in politics but five years is unbelievably short.

Lesson 2
Sustained focus on a small number of priorities is essential.

Lesson 3
Flogging a system can no longer achieve these goals: reform is the key.

Lesson 4
Nothing is inevitable: 'rising tides' can be turned.

Lesson 5
The numbers are important but not enough: citizens have to see and feel the difference and expectations need to be managed.

Lesson 6
The quality of leadership at every level is decisive.

Lesson 7
Good system design and management underpin progress.

Lesson 8
Getting the second step change is difficult and requires precision in tackling variations and promoting best practice.

Lesson 9
Extraordinary discipline and persistence are required to defeat the cynics.

Lesson 10
Grinding out increments is a noble cause . . . but where progress is slow, it's even more important for people to understand the strategy.

The presentation also pointed to a number of areas where the outcomes had not shifted, including school attendance and road congestion, and urged Cabinet ministers to give personal attention to driving delivery when they returned after the summer break. I made sustained use of the 'year three' concept, reminding ministers and permanent secretaries in a letter later in the year that 'half of year three is gone'. The truth was, though, that it was a difficult time for Blair personally and for government. The dominant theme of political debate was the aftermath of the Iraq War; David Kelly, the government scientist, had just committed suicide. This dramatically exacerbated the usual frantic atmosphere in late July.

Nevertheless, the key fact had been lodged with the Cabinet: delivery was beginning to happen and Whitehall was beginning to learn the lessons. In order to convey these messages to the wider public, I was asked for the second time to present to a Blair press conference – in this case, the final one before the summer break. After Blair had introduced me, I provided – with PowerPoint graphs and a deadpan tone – a plain-speaking appraisal of the government's performance. On health, for example, I pointed out the progress on waiting times, but also the scale of the challenge ahead. On crime, I pointed out the overall reductions, but also the rises in more serious violent crime and antisocial behaviour. Similarly, worsening road congestion and the plateau in primary school results were highlighted. It was painstakingly honest, and it is worth recording that the No. 10 press people, contrary to their reputation, encouraged me to be so. My overall conclusion was that 'demonstrable progress has been made, but it is not yet irreversible'.

Blair invited the assembled throng to ask me questions if they wished, but they predictably focused on Iraq and international affairs. One journalist asked Blair about whether he planned to stay or go. In reply, Blair gestured to the PowerPoint presentation, and said: 'You've seen the scale of the challenge ahead. My appetite for the task is undiminished.'[1] Despite all the pressures upon him at that moment, no one in the room could have doubted his intentions.

The press coverage the next day (31 July) made much more of my presentation than it had a year earlier, taking up three broad themes. One was a significant reporting of the progress I had described and acceptance of the balanced report card I had presented. The *Guardian* editorial agreed with the judgement I had reached, and became carried away with a metaphor: 'The wire is high and the roar of the crowd below may be less positive than before, but this is no time to wobble.'

The second theme was to imply that Blair had set me up because he wanted to avoid talking about David Kelly and Iraq. As Anne McElvoy put it in the *Evening Standard* that afternoon (30 July), 'Whenever there is a danger of things getting too hot around Mr Blair, he calls on Professor Barber to calm us down with his graphs.' This critique made entertaining reading without letting the facts get in the way of the story. After all, Blair stayed for well over an hour after I had finished, and answered all their questions about Iraq (and everything else) without them laying a glove on him.

The third theme was to mock me mercilessly for being dull. Damien Whitworth in the *Times* wrote that 'Barber droned on about "trajectories . . . milestones . . . top-down incentivezzzzzzzzzz . . ."', but he like many others picked up Blair's determination to see delivery though. The harshest critic was Simon Jenkins, writing in the *Times* on 1 August, who said I was 'a mole-like figure . . . sat in a corner hunched over a PowerPoint screen reading from a text in pure New Labour mandarinese' and, in case that was not enough, added that I was 'a control freak's control freak . . . a Great War general sitting in his chateau counting "targets" as they go over the top and then counting them back'. My staff were hugely amused, not least, I think, because they sensed he might have had a point.

But 1 August was, in any case, the start of the summer holidays, and the presentation had done its job. Moreover, the most important step that July, as ever, was the now-routine delivery report, which had conveyed not just the general messages of the Cabinet presentation around Whitehall, but also the specific messages on particular departments and programmes. The gains made were recognised, as they had been in the Cabinet presentation – and again there had been a modest shift from red to green – but the real value of the delivery reports lay in the detail. To take just a couple of examples from the Education report, we pointed out the need to strengthen the relationship between the Department for Education and agencies such as Ofsted and the Qualifications and Curriculum Authority and raised questions about whether the leadership incentive grant was really bringing 'decisive change' in the quality of leadership (i.e. resulting in poor headteachers being replaced).* We also urged the importance of anticipating risks and then managing them, which had clearly not happened in relation to the education funding crisis earlier in the year.

Even as we evaluated others, we were also evaluating our own performance that summer. We decided in retrospect that our delivery reports had become too wordy and wide-ranging. Moreover, the agenda was too broad and our efforts spread too thinly. The truth was that if we were to assist the government with the challenge of year three, we needed to reform ourselves again and refocus, even though we were only two years old.

Refocusing the Delivery Unit

I wrote myself a reflective note about future of the Delivery Unit late that hectic July:

> If year three of the parliament is as important as I said it was, then . . . we should review every key programme to check that it is comprehensive and sufficient . . . surely we should prioritise ruthlessly the things that really matter and drop everything else . . . Can we do this? Have we, have I, got the discipline?
>
> I asked a business person . . . yesterday whether he knew of companies that had gone for broke, that had to hit a deadline . . . He said the keys

---

*DfES officials claimed great success for this policy because 9 per cent of headteachers were replaced in the year after its introduction – but in response to our questions they were forced to admit that 10 per cent was the normal turnover rate most years.

198 INSTRUCTION TO DELIVER

would be ruthless prioritisation, a top team absolutely disciplined about those priorities and a staff energised rather than exhausted by the scale of the challenge.

This is precisely what we proceeded to do. In fact, in coming to these conclusions I was following rather than leading some of my Delivery Unit colleagues. The previous summer, following the 2002 spending review, we had expanded our remit to cover all the targets in the four original departments rather than a selection of them; we had also taken on a selection of targets in other departments such as Environment, Food and Rural Affairs; Culture, Media and Sport; and the Office of the Deputy Prime Minister. Part of the arrangement was that we would still work most intensively on the original core remit while working with a lighter touch on the wider remit. The main argument for the expansion was that in this way we would spread deliverology across Whitehall to the parts – to steal a phrase – that other methods had not reached. Our presence was welcomed and we had some limited impact, no doubt, but we were also spread thinly and in danger of reaching superficial judgements on a thin evidence base. So while I enjoyed my fleeting acquaintance with, for example, farming after the foot-and-mouth crisis and with the Department of Trade and Industry's mission to improve services for small businesses, the case for refocusing firmly on the government's top priorities was strong. It was reinforced by the strong sense – conveyed in the Cabinet presentation – that progress would need to be accelerated if key targets in health, education and crime (not to mention the railways) were to be achieved.

Moreover, from within the Delivery Unit – with the three deputy directors in the lead – the model of dividing the staff into account managers and problem solvers was being questioned. Surely, they argued, now we had developed powerful aspects of deliverology such as the priority review, we should build teams around individual departments and apply these methods systematically to every major issue, not just those where the results so far were disappointing. Furthermore, the case continued, we needed to become much more systematic in planning our work ahead. Then our delivery reports could become not only a retrospective comment on progress so far, but also a sharp, clear agreement with the department on what needed to happen in the next six months.

So between August and the end of October we reorganised along these lines. Having praised the staff for their achievements, I said to them in a summer holiday note:

> When we look ahead, we can see just how much there is to do before the public services are delivering the outcomes citizens want to see and the standards necessary to make this country the place we'd like it to be . . . We need to accelerate and intensify our drive for delivery.

Shortly after I'd sent this note, I pulled together the jottings I had gathered over months, if not years, on another subject altogether and worked them up into a speech on which I spent even longer than a Cabinet presentation. I wanted it to be the best speech I'd ever made, even though I anticipated, somewhat unusually, an entirely sympathetic audience. My eldest daughter, Naomi, was getting married and, believing strongly in both the tradition and the man she was marrying, I wanted it to be the best occasion it could be.

Meanwhile, Peter Thomas, one of the deputy directors, took the lead in this reorganisation, and through a series of consultations arrived at a new model. There would be four thematic teams (Health, Education, Crime and Criminal Justice, and Transport/Asylum) and two cross-unit teams (Data Analysis and Administration) (see Delivery Manual, Document 5). Each team was headed by a senior manager. Within the thematic teams, someone would be responsible for delivery on each target in our portfolio. These people would be called joint action leaders – 'joint' because they needed to establish a good relationship with the relevant departmental officials and ensure they had in place plans which were 'comprehensive and sufficient'. The senior managers leading each team would provide internal challenge and problem-solving, pressing the staff in their teams to be as ambitious and as effective as possible. This would free some of my time, enabling me to focus on strategy and relationships. Meanwhile, we agreed with Blair and the Treasury to drop all the targets outside our core areas and refocused sharply on Blair's top priorities. In a note to him in early September, I argued for 'more ruthless prioritisation, deeper collaboration (with departments) and more vigorous challenge'.*

---

* Blair agreed this readily. As Anthony Seldon makes clear in *Blair Unbound*, Blair had much more complex issues on his mind following the departure of Alastair Campbell the previous week (Anthony Seldon, *Blair Unbound* (London: Simon & Schuster, 2007), pp. 218–27).

Looking back, this sentence might be as good a summary as any of how to ensure prime ministerial power has real impact, and underpins the proposals I make in Chapter 9.

We proposed increasing the intensity of focus on school performance, waiting and choice in health, crime reduction, asylum, drugs, rail performance and road congestion; close monitoring of some other targets where current performance was adequate or better; and dropping altogether all the additional targets outside Health, Education, the Home Office and Transport we had taken on the previous year. Acknowledging the pressures on Blair's time, we reduced the number of stocktakes he would need to participate in by instituting more between myself and permanent secretaries. Blair accepted these proposals, agreeing that 'we have worries in all . . . key areas, don't we?'

I arranged to meet all the Cabinet ministers and permanent secretaries in September or October to explain the new phase of our work. As I have often said, there is nothing more powerful than a good idea taken literally – and we took the idea of a drive for results in year three literally. It was, in fact, counter-cultural in Whitehall. Instead of steadily expanding our focus, we narrowed it. Instead of increasing our numbers, we limited them. Instead of seeking permanence, we set out to achieve the agenda we had been set in 2001 and let the future take care of itself. Our rigour in relation to ourselves reinforced the strength of our message to the rest of Whitehall.

I had said constantly to the staff that the keys to our success would be humility – we should always underplay our position as representing the PM and rely on our personal qualities and mastery of the evidence – and our capacity to learn faster than anyone else in Whitehall.* While the culture in the unit strongly reinforced the first, the second had been achieved more by accident than by design. Because we could all fit in one room, it was possible to keep everyone informed, while the positive atmosphere encouraged sharing of information, but until mid-2003 we

---

* One talented young colleague, who had got carried away in a meeting with senior officials in a department and been accused of arrogance, came to see me and said he needed humility training. We found a three-day course for him (somewhere in Oxfordshire, I think). It worked. He came back humble. For a contrasting example, see the arrogance in the Nixon White House. Apparently Henry Kissinger's reply to a woman who congratulated him on 'saving the world from nuclear war' was, 'You're welcome.' (Robert Dallek, *Nixon and Kissinger: Partners in Power* (London: Allen Lane, 2007), p. 93.)

had not been really systematic about giving and receiving feedback, about planning each person's learning and development, and about collectively managing, sharing and applying our knowledge. Thomas, who had studied the business planning of successful companies, reinforced by secondees from management consultancies, now proceeded to build this internal capacity systematically. Staff began to expect feedback on how they had performed in, for example, a meeting with a department, and they wanted more than vague compliments. Regular 'knowledge-sharing' sessions were timetabled; each element of deliverology – from stocktakes to priority reviews – was reviewed internally and the outcomes of the reviews debated and then applied. Each element of deliverology therefore became a focus for continuous improvement. The senior management team was driven by Thomas to become systematic in monitoring our overall progress on a quarterly basis. We also began to seek feedback systematically, from within and without, every six months. I would select ten people randomly from the Delivery Unit staff telephone list, and interview them each for an hour about what the Delivery Unit meant for them, what their ambitions were in life and work, and how being at the Delivery Unit could assist in their fulfilment. Meanwhile, we arranged for external people to interview our key stakeholders in departments – permanent secretaries and top officials – and feed back to us what they thought about what we did and how we could improve it. We asked for feedback from departments on individual members of our staff and drew on this in their performance reviews. In short, we took personnel management to – for the civil service at any rate – an entirely new level. In this I was learning from my management team; it did not come naturally to me but I was overwhelmingly impressed by the positive impact it had on our organisation and our effectiveness. The result was that we really did learn faster about delivery than anyone else.

We were assisted in this by another innovation, which Blair himself brought about. In the reshuffle of the summer of 2003, Gus Macdonald stood down from his post as Chancellor of the Duchy of Lancaster. He had been a constant source of advice and support throughout the two years I had known him. In our regular Monday meetings, after we had reviewed the weekend's sporting developments, we also reviewed the state of the government and the agenda of the Delivery Unit and, especially at the beginning, he helped to steer me through the shoals of micro-politics that characterise the centre of government. When he retired, Blair replaced him with Douglas Alexander, but explicitly indicated that the Delivery Unit would be outside his remit. In effect, we now worked solely for and directly to Blair. The consequence was – and I used to point this out to my staff (particularly those without previous experience in government) when they compared departments unfavourably to us – that we did not need to spend time on servicing a minister. Nor, very often, did we have to deal with parliamentary questions or enquiries from the media. Nor did we have to deal with letters or calls from the public. Nor – because we always insisted they went through departments – did we deal very often with the mass of interest groups that clamoured round all our policy areas. We really were – unlike most of the government machine – able to devote our attention all day, every day, to our core business. This was a privilege and put an onus on us to be mightily effective.

Civil service reform

By October 2003, therefore, our radical reorganisation was complete and we were ready for the drive for results which took us through not just to the summer of 2004, but all the way to the election in May 2005. Though there was some grinding of the gears as we put all this in place, the benefits of it were soon felt both by us and by departments.

One issue our work constantly raised, and we equally constantly debated in the Delivery Unit, was the reform of the civil service as a whole. As previous chapters have illustrated, there were serious weaknesses in the capacity of the civil service to deliver in the terms now being asked of it, and very often we were left asking ourselves how to proceed. The issue raised two major dilemmas for us. One was a question of mission: was it our job solely to ensure targets were met, or was it also part of the mission to build into government departments the underlying capabilities that would enable them to deliver in the future? The truth – looking back – is that we never fully resolved this in those four years. I was clear that, if we had to choose, delivery of targets came first and that our mission was not to reform departments but to strengthen government's ability to deliver its priorities, which meant both ignoring some parts of departments and also examining all the organisations involved in the delivery chain out to the frontline, not just the civil service. Even so, we invested substantial time and effort in trying to educate Whitehall and contributing to the evidence base on which Blair based his belated but increasing determination to reform the civil service.

From 2003 onwards, there was extensive public debate about civil service reform generated by thoughtful commentators such as Ed Straw, with whom I had a number of conversations on the subject. After one of them, he sent me Norman Dixon's excellent book from the 1970s, *On the Psychology of Military Incompetence*. 'The answer [to civil service reform] is definitely somewhere in here,' he said. I read the book and was able to write back that he was right: the answer was on pages 152–3, where a list of the failings of the military over the previous two centuries seemed a highly appropriate commentary on the modern civil service, including, for example, 'a serious wastage of human resources', 'a fundamental conservatism', 'a tendency to reject or ignore information which is unpalatable' and 'an obstinate persistence in a given task despite strong contradictory evidence'.[2]

That autumn of 2003, we ran another of our annual conferences on delivery for the top 300 civil servants across Whitehall, and messages such as those in Dixon's book featured significantly. The previous year, Blair and Gordon Brown had both addressed the conference. This year, Blair and David Blunkett were the main speakers. Blunkett was disarmingly honest in his critique of the civil service, saying, for example, in reference to the rapid turnover of staff in ministers' private offices: 'I used to think that ministers' private offices were there to support them, but now I've discovered they are a training scheme.' To conclude the event by trying to convince the assembled company that the Delivery Unit really would do anything to help them deliver, I walked across two metres of broken glass in bare feet. A floor-level microphone conveyed audibly the crunching and splitting of the shards under me. I reached the far end without a single cut, received a sustained and rapturous round of applause and will no doubt be remembered in Whitehall for this moment of madness long after deliverology is forgotten.

But conferences, however inspiring, do not change the culture of any organisation, still less one as large, amorphous and steeped in tradition as the civil service. That autumn, Blair took personal control of the civil service reform programme, urged on by John Birt, his strategy adviser, and assisted by Andrew Turnbull. Blair's personal attention had, as prime ministerial attention does, injected urgency and radicalism into this vital question. He clearly regretted not paying attention to it sooner. Indeed, it was in relation to this question that he remarked reflectively to me on one occasion that 'in some ways, my second term has felt like my first'. Hoping, somewhat optimistically, to make up for lost time, Blair pulled together his thoughts on civil service reform in a speech in February 2004 at a Docklands venue. The occasion was the 150th anniversary of the Northcote–Trevelyan proposals, which laid the foundations for the modern civil service. He called me on the Saturday before, and asked me whether I would write the speech, incorporating some text he himself had written. How could I refuse?

While I waited for the material from No. 10 to arrive at home, I did what my history degree had trained me to do. I read the key sections of Roy Jenkins's biography of Gladstone so that I understood the Northcote–Trevelyan reforms and their context. Then, with Blair's draft and the excellent work that others had already done, I wrote a revised draft. Blair called again on Sunday evening and asked me whether I had used the text he personally had written. I told him – rather brazenly, I now realise – I had used about a third of it in completing the new draft. Quite sternly (for him), he said, 'When I write part of a speech myself, I expect it to be incorporated as it stands.' The following morning he reinstated all his original text and made some other improvements. The drafting of a speech forces you to clarify policy as well as language, and I enjoyed the debates with Turnbull and the Prime Minister that resulted.

In the speech, Blair acknowledged the many qualities of the civil service, including its impartiality and integrity. He also paid tribute to the calibre of the people and acknowledged that, unlike in a company, civil servants can't usually pick and choose their clients; they have to deal with all of them regardless of how challenging they might be. The argument he made for reform was nevertheless powerful: 'The world has changed, and the civil service must change with it.' We needed, he said, enabling government, government that helped people to help themselves in a period of ever-rising expectations. The principal challenge therefore was 'to shift focus from policy advice to delivery . . . outcomes . . . project management . . . and the ability to take risks'. He emphasised a radical point which was barely picked up on at the time.

On foot-and-mouth, he said: 'The blunt truth is that it was the armed forces' intervention that was critical to delivery. Why? Because they didn't take 'no' for an answer; they used rules as a means to an end, not an end in themselves.'

The speech made a series of proposals which included a smaller, strategic centre for government as a whole and in each department, greater professional and specialist skills, bringing in more outsiders from business and the voluntary sector, more rapid promotion for successful civil servants, an assumed tenure of a maximum four years for anyone in a senior post to open up opportunities, and further developments in leadership, management and delivery. With sufficient rigour in implementation, this was a radical agenda.

While the Delivery Unit approach did not do enough to strengthen departmental capability, through helping to promote the programme described in Blair's speech we had at least put the issue on the agenda. As the programme was implemented, it also helped prepare the ground for the more radical reforms being taken forward by Gus O'Donnell, the Cabinet Secretary who succeeded Turnbull in 2005. In addition to accelerating much of this agenda, O'Donnell expanded the Delivery Unit's remit to carry out capability reviews of departments, resolving finally the debate we had throughout the 2001–5 parliament about whether this was or was not our core business. These reviews have proved to be a powerful driver of civil service reform, not least by laying bare the scale of the challenge department by department.

Strategies

In parallel with the drive to reform the civil service, Blair had also asked all the major departments to prepare five-year strategies. Not only would these show how the government planned to take forward its reform programme well beyond the end of the second term, they would also inform the spending review of 2004 and clarify the ends for which reform of the civil service, departments and the public services were the means.* Blair had set out in a series of speeches his vision of reformed

*See Chapter 9 for commentary on the lack of articulation between the five-year strategies and the spending reviews.

services: much higher standards of performance, much greater customer responsiveness as in the best businesses, and much more tailoring or personalisation so that the services were built around the customers rather than the producers. The means to achieve this, in addition to the substantial increases in funding, included, he argued, extending choice, introducing competition in the form of new providers from the private or voluntary sector, and more generally 'freeing up' those at the frontline, whether headteachers, police chiefs or NHS managers and doctors. He was determined to cut drastically the bureaucracy and red tape which he said were 'killing' people at the frontline and were a political Achilles heel. This was a programme to which I felt personally very committed, and increasingly the evidence from Delivery Unit data supported it. We had seen how choice for patients in London had not just been popular, but also helped reduce waiting times. Its extension across the country had a powerful impact on results. Similarly, new providers – the independent treatment centres – brought competitive pressure in health just as private prisons and contracting out local education authorities had in other services. Meanwhile, in education, the evidence showed specialist schools, a programme being rapidly expanded under Charles Clarke, outperforming the rest of the system.

Even so, a major part of my job during 2003–4 was to identify the risks to delivery this reform programme presented. An obvious risk was a loss of attention on the targets for 2005 as senior politicians and civil servants focused increasingly on the emerging agenda for the next parliament. The relentless routine of stocktakes, monthly notes, delivery reports and priority reviews in the end proved resilient in this respect but as the pressures not just of reform but also of the Hutton report and the aftermath of the Iraq War built up, it was harder to get Blair's attention than it had been earlier in the parliament. The Policy Directorate often wanted stocktake time to discuss reform issues and we were always happy to agree, provided the routine data was discussed too.

There were also risks at a more profound level. While everyone agreed that there was too much bureaucracy and it needed to be reduced, there was not always agreement on how to do this. For example, one popular way to have reduced bureaucracy would have been to reduce the impact of inspection across the public services, but I also knew that inspection was one of the most powerful levers of change available. I argued for sharpening inspection rather than reducing it. Similarly, it became almost universally accepted that ring-fenced grants (which gave schools, local authorities or hospitals specific money for specific purposes) were a cause of bureaucracy and therefore a bad thing. I agreed that there were too many of them and many had been badly implemented, but also argued that in some cases, implemented properly, they were a powerful lever too. In short, I worried that in the drive to reduce bureaucracy we would inadvertently reduce our capacity to deliver and, as I reminded a Policy Directorate meeting, however much ministers devolved responsibility, in the end the public and the media would hold them to account for delivery. 'Ask not with whom the buck stops; it stops with thee,' I explained in a pastiche of John Donne and Harry Truman.

The reform programme also presented the Delivery Unit with the not inconsiderable challenge of actually delivering system reform. The whole of deliverology was designed to deliver specified outcomes. Targets themselves, while beneficial, were not necessary; what was essential was a clear definition of success and some way of knowing whether it was being achieved. Organisations as diverse in their objectives as the Foreign Office, GCHQ and the Meteorological Office had invited us to present, and found deliverology extremely useful, they said. But system reform – changing the structure, incentives and relationships in a large system such as the NHS or schools – presented a rather different challenge. Increasingly what Blair wanted to know in addition to progress towards targets was whether the steps necessary to reform the system were being taken in the right sequence with the right rigour, even though the benefits in terms of outcomes would only be seen in the long term. For example, introducing new school suppliers and thus creating competition should be beneficial in the long term, but it won't affect test or exam results this year or next.

With our Health team under the profoundly knowledgeable Adrian Masters – 'the one true professor in the Delivery Unit', as I called him – in the lead, we began to explore how we would monitor system reform. In the summer of 2003, at the suggestion of the Treasury, we had carried out an assessment of the 'affordability' and 'deliverability' of extending choice across the service. We had strongly recommended it, but the major value of the work was that for the first time we were assessing deliverability in advance of the decision being taken, so we could identify the risks and suggest ways of managing them. We were also edging our way towards a means of assessing progress with system reform.

Finally, the issues of strategy became central to the political debates within Whitehall, sometimes causing controversy between departments and individuals. The Strategy Unit and the Policy Directorate, of course, led for Blair on these issues while we were on the fringes. Nevertheless, as part of the No. 10 team, we had to work hard to maintain our relationships sometimes. The hardest area for me personally was education, where, as an expert with a track record of publications, I had known views, which were not always consistent with what Charles Clarke wanted to do.

During the autumn of 2003, part of me was tempted to throw myself into the debate about the education five-year strategy – but I was aware this could have fatally distracted me from carrying out my instruction to deliver. So I chipped in my views in meetings at No. 10 or at Chequers, but otherwise left the consistently impressive Andrew Adonis to lead. As with all the strategies, in education the risk was that complexity would drown out the central thrust of policy. I summarised my own approach to education as having three prongs: a renewed and much sharper focus on standards, especially for the disadvantaged; letting the market rip while protecting equity; and a tough 'rights and responsibilities' agenda on behaviour and discipline. I knew that Blair wanted much the same, but what came back from departments on all the strategies was always hedged about and qualified. Of course, sometimes there are good reasons for qualification, but often it's merely the innate conservatism of the system or a lack of confidence in taking risks. As Blair put it to me once, 'The thing I've always wanted to be in a position to do but never actually been in the position of doing, is to be sat in the Cabinet Room holding someone back!'*

Largely I avoided the temptation to bury myself in these fascinating strategy debates although the Delivery Unit reorganisation had freed up some of my time. My main contribution was to prevent the attention on, and conflict over, future strategy deflecting the government from

---

* This is eerily similar to Margaret Thatcher's assertion that 'I so often had to act as a lone opponent of the processes and attitudes of the government itself' (quoted in Simon Jenkins, *Thatcher and Sons: A Revolution in Three Acts* (London: Allen Lane, 2006), p. 54). Perhaps it's something in the nature of the role.

delivering its current programme. For the Delivery Unit as a whole, active involvement in these reform issues largely lay ahead, when decisions had been made and we could monitor implementation and solve problems as they emerged. In the meantime, with our structure, our increasingly effective methods and an outstanding team of staff, 2003–4 was a relentless slog as we drove for results.

The slog

The Delivery Unit was a marvellous place to work: talented people committed to a mission and excited, even intoxicated, by the potential impact we could have. I had made a point of personally involving myself in the appointment of every single member of staff, whatever their role, largely because I wanted to build a strong team spirit as well as to secure talented people. Going into work every single day was a genuine pleasure, and the feedback from departments consistently highlighted the quality of our people and their 'can do' spirit. The corridor conversation sparkled, not just about delivery, but also about the latest political gossip and the weekend's football results. Often Tony O'Connor had provoked conversation too, by organising one of his bizarre games, which in addition to quizzes and Grand National sweep-stakes also included an appalling weekend pub crawl involving half a pint in each street or station represented on the Monopoly board.*

Even so, the work was often very hard. In spite of the huge burdens he faced, Blair still restlessly questioned the progress on delivery and never seemed satisfied. Without the Delivery Unit, he commented in September 2003, delivery would have gone off the rails altogether, but he wanted more. The workload was monumental; I often arrived at work by 8.00 a.m. and didn't get home until eleven at night. If I was home by 8.00 p.m., I considered it early. Meanwhile, the content of each day, while fascinating, was challenging. These were major issues of concern to millions. There were challenges facing my family too in 2003–4, so that I went through periods of utter exhaustion which I hid

---

*For the record, in the quizzes, although I repeatedly revised the answer to 'Which six countries border Chad?', the question never came up; I never won the Grand National sweepstake; and in relation to the pub crawl, for me discretion overcame valour, and I stayed at home.

at work but which led Karen to say to me one evening that autumn, 'You've lost your sparkle.' That felt true.

Narrowing our agenda back down to the core priorities had the huge benefit for me that I could carry the whole programme in my head. This meant that when my monthly one-to-one with Blair came round, I could list a series of bullet points on one or two sides of A4 in the hour before I saw him and then take him through it in rapid-fire fashion. So, just to take one of these meetings as an example, in my thirty-minute meeting with him on 15 December 2003, I briefed him on five Health issues (cancer and coronary heart disease, primary care, booking and choice, waiting times and A&E). I also responded to his comment on the most recent monthly update on Health, where he had said we needed to get the overall waiting list down as well as waiting times (which we eventually did during 2004). In the same meeting, we ran through five Home Office issues, including asylum, delivery of justice, police performance, drugs and crime. On the last two, I was urging a need to step up the pressure. We went on to discuss three major Education issues (including attendance and behaviour, where I thought progress was insufficient), and both rail and road congestion. We also touched on the overall reform programme and the future of targets. We could cover so much ground so fast because we both knew the context and much of the detail well, and so had quick exchanges specifically on what needed to be done next.

'One-to-one' was sometimes true and sometimes a euphemism. On this occasion, Jeremy Heywood, who was about to leave, and his successor, Ivan Rogers, were present. Their presence often helped because it meant a note recording actions could be rapidly injected into the machine. It also meant that others at the vortex knew what was going on. As I ran through my agenda, Blair would chip in, emphasising his chief concerns and steering our efforts where he felt they were most needed. On this occasion, as the meeting broke up, he said, 'It's crime I'm most worried about.' Statements such as these were gems from my point of view. As I noted to myself just after this meeting, 'A half-hour conversation such as this gives me immense strength. At meetings throughout the week I was able to say with confidence "the Prime Minister thinks this" or "he's most worried about that".'

Of course, the meetings strengthened Blair too because, in effect, they enabled me to spread around Whitehall what was on his mind. Even with the narrowed agenda, though, the range of issues we faced were huge. Just to illustrate, during these same few months (September 2003–February 2004), my activities included the following:

- Having consulted Blair, I wrote to all permanent secretaries urging them to think about how the services they were responsible for were being internationally benchmarked and what they could learn from this. International benchmarking and learning from international best practice would become ever more important, I argued, as globalisation unfolded. Departments should compare their performance to other countries and draw on the experience of the most successful. Moreover, some other countries were already thinking explicitly in this way, whereas we tended to await the results of international comparisons with trepidation, pat ourselves on the back if we came out well, explain the results away if we came out badly, and then forget about them until the next time.

- At Gordon Brown's request, I presented to representatives of the IMF on how we monitored delivery in order to ensure we got value for money (and learnt from their response that our approach was at the global cutting edge).

- I joined colleagues to welcome England's World Cup-winning rugby team to No. 10 and experienced the knuckle-crushing handshake of Lawrence Dallaglio.

- At the invitation of the newly elected government in Ontario, in early January 2004 I spent twenty-four hours there (where the temperature, with the wind chill factor, was -33°) to present to their Cabinet on our approach to delivery.

- Immediately on my return, I updated Blair and senior ministers at Chequers on progress on delivery as a way of introducing a further update on the five-year strategies.

- On Monday 12 January I met Blair for a round-up of Delivery Unit business in the morning and an Education stocktake in the afternoon. A note I wrote then conveys well the flavour of that time as I saw it: 'I saw a great deal of Blair at first hand as we moved towards his moments of crisis on tuition fees and the Hutton report . . . He was relaxed, good humoured and focused more than anything on political and government strategy through to 2005. You might have expected mounting tension . . . but

Blair's focus was elsewhere – on delivery and strategy . . . the [Education stocktake] revealed exactly why a delivery unit was worth having. Without us and our processes, any meeting between the PM and the Secretary of State for Education would surely have focused on the tuition fees controversy. Instead, it was barely mentioned.' We dealt with literacy, numeracy, behaviour and school leadership.

- I debated with top officials in the Department for Education the theory of best-practice transfer, which might sound obscure, but is in fact one of the central issues of delivery. My main objective on this occasion was to try to prevent – unsuccessfully, as it turned out – the government spending money on the education establishment's latest fashion, which was networks. On the basis of the excellent work of Sir John Oldham in the Health Service, I argued that networks would only be successful if, at their heart, there was a clear definition of the best practice they were intended to spread; if there was a dedicated project manager; and if rapid, real-time, comparative data was used to assess impact. Since none of these conditions were in place, I predicted the networks the Department for Education proposed to fund would fail. (They did.)

- In the midst of all this, my parents, in their eighties, decided to move house, a decision which divided my brothers and sisters. I equivocated, in part I know because I was too exhausted to give the issue the attention it deserved.

If I was close to exhaustion, Blair must surely have been tired too, but most striking were his resilience and increasing focus on the agenda for a third term. On the day he was reported as having been in hospital for a heart murmur (20 October 2003), he was back in Downing Street later that morning saying, 'I don't want anyone to ask how I am!' From January 2004 onwards, as Hutton and the vote on top-up fees left him unscathed, he gave more and more attention to radicalising public service reform, both because he believed it was essential and because he saw it as a means of dominating the political scene.

Momentum

Demanding it might have been to achieve, but the longer 2004 went on, the more it became clear that we had that intangible but vital force of change – momentum. Indeed, in modern government – as with aircraft – the only alternative to moving forward is falling out of the sky. Advance or fail. Momentum or drift. Here there is no middle way. With our new team structure in place and our focused agenda, we were able to review thoroughly every area of delivery in our portfolio and assist in removing blockages and generating results. In 2004 (as seen in Chapter 5), we saw breakthroughs in delivery on primary school literacy and numeracy and on the railways. Assisted by a golden autumn in 2003 in which the leaves swirled slowly down and landed on miraculously dry ground, but mainly because of better planning and management, rail results began a steady improvement which continued for the next three years. A&E performance improved, and health waiting times fell in line with trajectory. One of our reviews showed that the biggest risk to achieving the six-month maximum wait for surgery was in the area of orthopaedics (mostly hips and knees, in layperson's language), where waiting times had been static. By persuading the Department of Health to break their data down by type of operation in this way, we had helped them understand their challenge better. As a result, they put in place a specific contingency plan to deal with orthopaedics, and here too at last the data began to move in the right direction.

On the criminal justice system too, the data began to shift positively. The number of offences being brought to justice rose steadily, and the percentage of fines and community penalties being enforced also began to rise, though from a very low base. Crime continued to fall, although because of rises in violent crime the public did not notice. Even anti-social behaviour, that most intractable of issues, was demonstrably falling by mid 2004.

In the Delivery Unit it dawned on us that by 2004 we had moved from having a good theory (in 2001–2), to a good theory with a few supporting stories in 2003, to a demonstrably successful methodology that was improving performance wherever we applied it. In May I was able to report to Blair that on almost all the key domestic indicators we were monitoring, performance was better, often much better, than it had been when he became Prime Minister. There were three exceptions:

street crime, which had risen steeply in 2001–2, but was now back under control, though plateauing; rail performance which at least was now steadily improving; and road congestion.

By 2004 we had even begun to come to terms with road congestion, at least on the motorways and A-roads. This is not to say that congestion was about to fall; on the contrary, simply due to the rising number of cars and the increasing desire to travel that always occurs when the economy is growing, congestion was due to worsen. Alistair Darling, though, had accepted that in these circumstances he could at least take two major steps; first, he could develop a long-range plan for road pricing, and without taking the decision to introduce it could begin to prepare the ground both logistically and politically. He moved cautiously forward on this agenda. Second, and more relevant to the Delivery Unit's work, he could improve the capacity to manage the road network. Legislation early in the parliament had shifted responsibility for managing the major roads from the police – allowing them to focus better on crime – to the Highways Agency. In the past, the Highways Agency had in effect been a manager of road-building contracts, and was most famous for John Major's Cones Hotline. Now it became an active manager of the road network under its energetic and focused new boss, Archie Robinson, who took the job just after the agency had been crucified in the media for failing to anticipate and manage a massive snowfall which closed, among other roads, the M11, trapping numerous drivers overnight. This, as it were, provided him with a burning platform.

His colleagues in the department had now developed and begun to apply a sensible way of measuring traffic using satellite technology. (Rather than the thirteen hapless drivers mentioned in Chapter 2 – what became of them, I wonder? Are they still out there, like those Japanese soldiers you hear about who carried on fighting the Second World War for decades after it ended?) They piloted the new approach – active traffic management, as it was called – on the motorway system around the urban sprawl of the Midlands, known to traffic fanatics as the Birmingham Box. Working with the Highways Agency and the department, we reviewed its implementation, including identifying all the causes of congestion on a particular stretch of the M6 during the review period to assist the traffic managers in prioritising. Accidents and spillages were among the most common while, by contrast, only once during the period was congestion caused by an elephant crossing the motorway. In any event, the experiment was a great success and the approach was then – in the time-honoured phrase – rolled out across the country, starting with the M25. Congestion was still getting worse in 2004 and 2005, but the management of it, the provision of information to drivers, the use of hard shoulders and minimisation of the impact of roadworks all improved. Meanwhile, the opening of the M6 toll road – the final implementation of a decision taken in the Major years – and the introduction of London's congestion charge radically reduced congestion in two notoriously frustrating localities. Variable road pricing – still at least a decade away – will be needed for a serious, sustainable, national solution.

Congestion illustrates a point that applies more generally to delivery issues. The fact that the majority of these issues were improving and nearly all were better than in 1997 did not mean they were good or even – as inspectorates love to say – satisfactory. Often, because the base performance had been so poor, even after significant improvement they were still unacceptably bad. Waiting six months for an operation is still a long time; only just over half of sixteen-year-olds achieving five higher grades at GCSE is not good enough; and a fine enforcement rate up to 75 per cent from 50 per cent, while a huge improvement, is still an embarrassment. Nothing illustrated this problem better than the government's sterling efforts during the 2001–5 parliament to implement a national drugs strategy. In the first Blair term, a drugs tsar, Keith Hellawell, had been appointed, and while he had talked a good game, he had made little headway. By 2004, though, with consistent attention from David Blunkett and the Prime Minister to ensure that any drug user who came into contact with the police or courts should be tested, there were signs of progress. Interdepartmental collaboration had improved, the amount of treatment available had increased and the indicators showed both that drug use among young people was beginning to fall and that the rise in drug-related crime had been reversed. This, however, was no cause for celebration. There were still a quarter of a million 'high-harm-causing drug users', as the jargon describes them, and around half of all crime was still caused by these addicts. Moreover, for the individuals and families caught up in it, the misery was appalling.

This came home to me on a visit I made early in 2004 to see how delivery looked when far from Whitehall. In one small town in the north of England, I discovered graphically the misery that about 175 drug users could cause on a single housing estate. Research there had shown that each drug user cost the state £200,000 per year. Meanwhile, police raids to arrest the occasional dealer were – incredibly – welcomed by the drug-using community as creating 'promotion opportunities'. The drug users on this estate had been in and out of prison on average six times – a classic case of the revolving door. Needless to say, the law-abiding families who lived there, especially those with children, were terrified.

Yet because government programmes were (rightly) targeted on the areas with the most serious problems, which did not include this particular town, they were having no impact here at all. In short, there were good policies beginning to make an impact, but they simply fell far short of the scale of the problem they were tackling. Blair himself wanted more and there were those around him who wanted a much more draconian approach to drugs policy, but a combination of risk and potentially very high cost stood in their way. Yet without dramatic change, it was hard to see how the government's approach would do more than mitigate a devastating social problem.

For reasons such as this, the government's progress on delivery did not necessarily translate into popular enthusiasm. There was much talk in Downing Street about this perception gap, and some interesting data produced by polling organisations. The evidence showed that most people were much more enthusiastic about their own local service, especially if they used it, than about the equivalent service at national level. In part this was because they were influenced by the media, which focused relentlessly on the negatives. In part it was because, as improvement occurred, people's expectations rose. The good news was that, especially on health and education during 2004, there was growing public recognition of genuine progress.

Preparing for the next parliament

In May 2004, we also sought feedback from departments, especially permanent secretaries, on their views of the Delivery Unit and how, if at all, its agenda or approach should change. This was in part because we were beginning to think about the next parliament, and in part because

I was determined to honour the promise I had made to the permanent secretaries back in 2001 that, if possible, I would like to abolish the Delivery Unit before the end of the parliament. I opened my conversation with each of them by making this offer but, not surprisingly, each of them rejected it. They said they valued the Delivery Unit because it had clear priorities and would not be deflected from them; had excellent people; employed simple, clear, practical methodologies; worked on the basis of rigorous analysis and hard evidence; adopted a partnership approach to working; assisted in sharing best practice across departments; and provided a constant, sharp external challenge which helped them to do their jobs. Disarmingly, one or two of them mentioned that they found it useful to be able to say within their departments that even though they had doubts about doing x or y, it had to be done because the Delivery Unit wanted it done. In other words, where their courage failed, they could substitute ours. This, I replied, was all part of the service. Looking ahead, they did not want radical change in the way the unit worked, but they did want to extend the range of priorities we worked on. This provided a central part of the evidence base when, later in the year, we came to review the role and function of the Delivery Unit.

Outside government, mid-May 2004 was dominated by the aftermath of war in Iraq and the fall of Piers Morgan, editor of the *Daily Mirror*, for publishing fake pictures of British soldiers torturing Iraqi prisoners. Inside, Blair's focus was on the culmination of the five-year strategy process. Increasingly confident of delivery in the short term, he was now looking forward to irreversibly changing the public services so that, as he would put it, they could become self-sustaining, self-improving systems. One after another, ministers brought their plans before the Cabinet for debate, refinement and approval. Blair was always on the radical side of any argument – independent state schools in education, freed up as far as possible from bureaucracy and held to account for their results; healthcare free at the point of use, offering patients choice and provided by any provider, public or private, who could do so at the tariff set; crime broken down into three types – serious and organised crime, volume crime and anti-social behaviour – and each type dealt with differently both by the police and the courts. When he saw drafts of five-year plans, he almost always insisted on greater clarity, increased sharpness and reduced bureaucracy. The five-year strategies that emerged from the process that summer of 2004 of course involved contributions from many hands, but they were also a personal triumph for Blair. His constant cajoling, driving, persuading and urging pushed most of his ministers to be significantly more radical than they would otherwise have been, and dramatically more radical than departments would have been if left to their own devices. The single most important lesson he had learnt from his years as Prime Minister was summed up in the refrain, 'we should have been bolder'. He constantly asked his favourite question as a way of radicalising discussions: 'If there were no constraints or if there were a national emergency, what would you do?' A process which had begun in September 2003 and which was at first not taken seriously in several departments had resulted in an agenda for the public services which would dominate the next parliament. Moreover, Blair had also driven the departments to reorganise themselves and reduce their staff numbers in order to be able to deliver the radical new agenda. It was a very personal achievement for him, and one was left to wonder how much more he might have achieved had we put in place a coherently organised centre of government and developed an approach to strategy which was better integrated with the Treasury.*

On 20 May 2004, I had a rare unscheduled opportunity to review the entire domestic policy scene with Blair. I was in the private office collecting some mail, when he emerged from his office and summoned me in. I reviewed the progress on delivery with him in a pretty upbeat manner.† All the health figures, including both waiting lists and waiting times, were heading in the right direction. The combination of choice and extra capacity was making the difference. On asylum applications, I told him they were now below 1997 levels and still falling. On crime, progress was shifting in the right direction but still not perceived to be so. I told him my top three worries were violent crime, school test results and the drugs strategy. Blair congratulated me on the impact of the unit and said he was going to give his ministers a tough time on the subject of bureaucracy in the meeting we were both about to go to. I had a theory that on this subject junior ministers were the key; rather than

---

*See Chapter 9 for further discussion of these issues.

† Anthony Seldon says that after a troubled spring of 2004, in which he considered quitting, 'Blair's mood went into an upswing in late May' (Anthony Seldon, *Blair Unbound* (London: Simon & Schuster, 2007), p. 275). I like to think my report cheered him up.

spending their time in departments, they should be out in hospitals, schools or wherever, learning how the government's programme looked on the frontline, interpreting it politically and then discussing the implications with their secretary of state.

When Blair pressed them to do this for just one week, they were reluctant to because, of course, they were busy. But how much of this work really needs ministerial attention? Compared to most other countries, we have far bigger ministerial teams, and departments will always create work for ministers if only, as they see it, to keep them out of trouble. Surely they could add more value by looking back at government from the other end of the telescope and keeping their secretary of state and the government as a whole firmly in touch with the real world?

In the meeting on bureaucracy that followed, I argued that collecting data was not part of the problem but part of the solution: once the data told you a policy was working, you could cease to regulate altogether and free entirely those parts of the system that were delivering excellent results, instead focusing efforts on the underperforming parts. By contrast, if you did not have the data, you would end up having to regulate everybody. This was consistent with the work the Delivery Unit had done jointly with the Treasury on the future of targets and with the agenda emerging in the five-year strategies, but it required a change of culture in departments on a scale far beyond what would be achieved by the following year.

There were two specific areas of the five-year strategies on which either I or the Delivery Unit had been specifically asked for advice. The first was on waiting times in health, where we had been asked how much lower they could go between 2005 and 2008 and still be 'deliverable'. Adrian Masters led an outstanding piece of work on this subject and recommended a new maximum 'end-to-end' target. Instead of the then existing separate targets for the outpatient phase and the inpatient phase (with any diagnostic phase in between not counting at all), Masters proposed, prompted by John Reid's determination to cut out the ambiguity, a target of eighteen weeks, including the outpatient, inpatient and diagnostic phases. He was able to show that if this was the maximum, the average would be well under twelve weeks and that, on the evidence of international comparisons, this would remove waiting as a concern among patients and the public. Moreover, it could be afforded within the spending allocation that the Department of Health had already been given. I happened to meet Reid just after he had taken the Cabinet through this major commitment. He said he had told them he knew it could be done because the Delivery Unit had said so! 'Just to be clear,' I asked him, 'if it works, you get the credit; if it fails, I take responsibility?' 'Exactly,' he smiled.

The other issue was school funding. The 2003 funding crisis had shaken confidence both in the Department for Education as an organisation and in the way in which funds were allocated. In his March 2004 Budget, Gordon Brown had brought forward the Education spending review settlement (as he had done with Health in 2002) and allocated further large increases. One of the key questions in the reform programme was how to allocate that funding. As an education reformer, I had long been in favour of reforming school funding so that the money for schools went straight from Whitehall into the school budget. The money that local authorities needed to carry out their functions could be in a separate pot. In this way, the argument between schools and local authorities about whether the latter were 'holding back' money and wasting it on bureaucracy would be ended, since everything would be transparent. I had advocated this as long ago as 1999 when I had been in the DfEE, and the funding debacle of 2003 provided a new opportunity for me to revive the idea. Moreover, in Health, funding had just been allocated out to the frontline on a three-year basis. Imagine if schools knew what they were entitled to, not just for one year, but for three! That would be the logical next step in advancing Blair's aspiration to free up headteachers, who in turn could be held to account for delivering continuous improvement. Indeed, their last excuse for not delivering would have been removed.

I promoted the idea with everyone who mattered in No. 10, the Treasury and Education. Almost everyone agreed that, from the point of view of schools, this was both radical and sensible. Andrew Adonis, the tireless radical at Blair's side, led in developing the detail. For local authorities, of course, it did mean a reduction in their discretion, and their leaders, with allies in government, lobbied to prevent it. In 2003 they had carried the day, but in 2004, after the new spending settlement had been announced and the need to resolve on a permanent basis the system of allocating school funding became apparent, three-year funding for schools was approved by the Cabinet. In many other countries, where three-year funding, even at national level, is seen as an unimaginable advance, three-year funding of individual schools is seen as one of the Blair government's most remarkable achievements. As far as I know, no other country has even proposed it.

That July, the spending review allocated funds for government for the years 2005 to 2008. Since Health had already had a five-year settlement in 2002 and Education's settlement had been announced in March, the emphasis was in part on the further increases in Home Office expenditure, but also on some of the wider aspects of the spending review. The number of targets had been reduced again from around 125 to around 100 for the whole of government, through the now-routine process involving the Treasury and ourselves. The major new development was the announcement of efficiency targets on the basis of Peter Gershon's review of government efficiency. The goals of saving up to £20 billion of public expenditure and reducing the number of civil servants by up to 100,000 over the next three years were set out. The Office of Government Commerce, in collaboration with the Treasury, set up an operation, which it sought to base on the Delivery Unit model, to deliver these savings.

In July 2003, I had emphasised to the Cabinet how important year three of the parliament would be. The year to July 2004 had been very gruelling indeed, but it finished with the emergence of a radical agenda for the reform of the public services, the allocation of substantial funding to deliver it, a bolder agenda for reforming the civil service and individual government departments, and a welcome new emphasis on efficiency. Most importantly from my personal point of view, the year had also seen the development of real, perhaps unstoppable, momentum towards the delivery of the targets the government had set out to achieve back in 2001.

July 2004

As in the previous July, I found myself responsible for presenting to Cabinet, issuing delivery reports and, once again, sharing with Blair the delight or ordeal, depending on your viewpoint, of appearing at his monthly press conference. This time, the Prime Minister wanted my presentation to the Cabinet (on 1 July 2004) to do more than show the results: he wanted greater emphasis on what explained the progress we had made. He was in the thick of completing the five-year plan process, and wanted the Cabinet to see the empirical data that underpinned the case for reform; helpfully the evidence did indeed support the view that the best delivery had occurred where the reforms had been boldest.

Harking back to the previous year's presentation, I called this one 'Delivery in Year Four: Time for Results'. I demonstrated, on the basis of the data from rail, crime, asylum, health and education that 'the most impressive delivery is a result of a combination of bold reform and effective performance management'. For example, on asylum applications, reforms such as the introduction of freight search, the closure of Sangatte and juxtaposed controls in northern France (that is, UK immigration officials working on French soil), combined with much better management of performance against trajectory, had made a massive difference. Similarly, on health, which had seen the most impressive progress, the reductions in waiting times resulted from a similar combination, in this case choice, competition, delegated three-year funding and incentives, allied to constant checking of the data, publication of the results and constructive intervention in under-performing locations.

I also argued that there would be 'a major opportunity in the next year to build on the foundations which have been painstakingly put in place over the past few years'. In short, the results so far were only the beginning. My report concluded by demonstrating the gains made just in the past six months. In December 2003, we had estimated that 47 per cent of the programme we were monitoring was on track to deliver; by July 2004, the figure had risen to 62 per cent and was still rising. There were, however, issues such as school attendance and alcohol-fuelled violent crime on which the data had not improved, and these needed urgent attention. I stressed the importance of each minister personally continuing to pay attention to delivery – whatever the distractions – over the next six months. To emphasise this, I thought of quoting Bertolt Brecht and saying, 'The red dawn of socialism will not come after a night of sleep,' but decided that it did not sound very Blairite.

The ministers directly involved with the Delivery Unit were probably very familiar with our philosophy by then, though even they, consumed in their own departmental affairs, probably rarely saw an overview. For the others, such as the chief whip, Hilary Armstrong, or the Secretary of

State for International Development, Hilary Benn, much of this was new and reassuring, since in the end the government's prospects as a whole depended to a significant extent on delivering improvements in the core public services.

The following week, the July 2004 delivery reports were sent to departments. As we had done the previous year, we ensured that the messages they contained were consistent and indeed integrated with the messages that the Cabinet had heard. We had also arranged meetings with the permanent secretaries during July, at which we could discuss the challenges to delivery in the next six months and also the new agenda for the Delivery Unit which was emerging from the five-year strategies.

One way I sought from time to time to promote the Delivery Unit brand was to write letters around Whitehall of a kind that would be quite out of the ordinary. Since I knew from the consultations in May that we had the full confidence of the permanent secretaries we worked with and that the new emerging agenda would be very challenging indeed, I decided to write them my most expansive letter yet (the full text is in the Delivery Manual, Document 7). I based my argument on a metaphor.

> We collectively were asked in 2001 by the Prime Minister to write a thriller on the theme of the public services. Could we, within one parliament, [deliver] results of . . . substance? . . .
>
> Our thriller has had its twists and turns. We've had moments of writer's block and once or twice, like Dostoevsky with *Crime and Punishment*, we have felt like throwing the whole script on the fire and starting again . . . but, especially over the past six months, we've discovered that our text is coming out rather well . . .
>
> Now, three-quarters of the way through this, our first book, an insight of stunning importance has occurred to us . . . it's the end, that final sequence, which decides whether we have a bestseller or a remainder on our hands. All that work and now everything depends on a few months! . . .
>
> In the meantime, the Prime Minister has developed sufficient confidence in the likely success of our first novel that he has commissioned the second. This too will be on the theme of public services, but now the question is whether, through . . . bold reform . . . we can

achieve a further step change in the quality of public services and thus ensure they are among the world's best.

Then the letter set out what we expected departments to do in the next six months to deliver their priorities and prepare for implementation of their five-year strategies.

The day I completed this letter, Andrew Turnbull asked me to present to the permanent secretaries collectively so they would hear the same message as the Cabinet. I delivered the same presentation with the addition of the full league table of delivery. I contacted each of the permanent secretaries we worked with beforehand so that they were not taken by surprise. In David Normington's case, I had dinner with him. Needless to say, the league table in PowerPoint on the screen (but not handed out on paper to minimise the risk of a devastating leak) was fascinating to the gathering – like the whole class seeing the end-of-term reports on a handful of individuals. It was most challenging for Normington because down at the bottom, in a swathe of red, was 'attendance and behaviour in secondary schools', where there had been no progress and we had felt for almost a year that we were banging our heads against a brick wall.

Normington himself had not been directly involved in the issue up to that point – no permanent secretary can do everything. What was impressive was his reaction. When we met him and his top team a couple of weeks later, he took personal control. He said he did not want to argue about the details of the Delivery Unit judgements; he wanted the problem fixed. He said he thought the actions we were proposing were broadly right and he would like to chair another meeting soon at which his colleagues would present on the way forward. From that moment, the blockages were removed and by Christmas 2004 there were already early signs that attendance was improving, especially in the schools which had previously had the worst track records. This was evidence indeed of the power of a permanent secretary when he or she focuses on something and, of course, of the value of a league table presented to a group of peers.

The same day, I assembled my staff for an end-of-term briefing too. I congratulated them on getting the delivery reports and league table done. These were always a huge task, not so much in the writing of them, although that was substantial, but in coming to hard-headed, evidence-based agreements with officials in departments about the state of play and the actions needed in the next six months. Also, within the unit a great deal of work went into moderating judgements so that they really were comparable and fair across departments. Then, in addition, the staff had to submit drafts to me on consecutive weekends and deal with the flow of feedback. I always devoted a full day at the weekend to the task of reading the delivery reports because I knew I would have to defend the judgements with ministers and permanent secretaries and because, even more importantly, if they were good, clear and practical, they would have an immense impact on progress in the six months ahead.

In editing the delivery reports, I saw my chief functions as bringing in consistency, combating management jargon and above all ensuring plain speaking in the judgements we made and clarity and ambition in the actions we set out. On those July 2004 draft reports, for example, I had made comments such as:

> It's worth remembering . . . that every marginal improvement in your text could potentially benefit thousands of citizens by December. It's a daunting and empowering thought.

> The 'key actions' specified . . . need to be clear, with a date and a person responsible.

> Can everyone edit through and check spelling, grammar and excessive use of jargon . . . ? Remember we need the PM to be able to read and understand these reports.

> Can this be even crisper and more hard-hitting? E.g. something about lack of urgency and management grip.

> The phrase 'overperformance' is always inappropriate; from the patient's perspective there is no such thing.

> Why are we happy to settle for what we've got? Surely [the action proposed] can bring further improvement.

These are small details but they are key links between a Prime

Minister and delivery of outcomes. The delivery reports for July 2004 were in some ways the most important of all. Though no one at that point, perhaps not even the Prime Minister, knew the date of the next election, the history of the past quarter-century suggested the very strong likelihood of an election in the early summer of 2005, in which case the six-month period from July 2004 would be the last chance in the parliament to secure delivery and ratchet up the outcomes still further. So in our meeting, in addition to congratulating the staff, I also warned them that the biggest threat to us and delivery in the next six months was complacency – we had to write a brilliant final chapter to the first thriller.

Towards the end of July, as ever, Parliament went into recess and almost everyone began to relax, but Blair and I had the now-traditional press conference to do on delivery. I was not sure what I would be doing by the following July, so I was conscious that this could be the last time I would do this: walking up the famous staircase past all the photographs of past Prime Ministers and into the small dining room; a pause; hearing the hum of the media gathered in the larger room on the other side of the double doors. While Blair checked through his brief opening remarks once more, I mentally ran through my opening lines, which I wanted to do from memory. Characteristically, he checked the buttons on his jacket and then asked, 'Are you ready?' I nodded and we went through.

Blair opened:

> As you will see when you see Michael's presentation, there has without a doubt been a step change in delivery across our public services in the last year. [Here he proceeded to give an array of statistics.] As Michael summarised it to Cabinet earlier this month, there is widespread and significant progress, becoming irreversible . . . Now this is encouraging, of course, but it is nowhere near enough.[3]

Hence he argued the need for the five-year strategies. Then it was my turn. As I had for the Cabinet at the beginning of the month, I provided both data and an explanation of the progress that had occurred. The point was to emphasise the need for continuing radical reform. Wherever possible, I provided independent verification of government data from, for example, the Audit Commission.

The most complicated part of the story was the crime figures. Consistent with our determination not to overclaim, the data I presented showed that although the chances of being a victim of crime were now lower than at any time since the measurement was introduced in 1981, there were real problems with alcohol-fuelled violent crime, which the government was just beginning to tackle, and gun crime, which had risen and then plateaued but was far from under control. As ever, while crime in general was falling, there were significant types of crime that were rising. On the overall programme, I concluded:

> Last year I said to you that there was demonstrable progress in most areas, but it was not yet irreversible. This year I am more optimistic. There is widespread and significant progress which is becoming irreversible. The foundations have been laid for further radical reform. The task is far from complete.*

Blair thanked me and told the media that I was available to answer their questions. Predictably – but faintly depressingly, I felt – they plunged straight in with the questions they had prepared in advance on whether Peter Mandelson would be Britain's new European Commissioner and on the continuing issue of Iraq. I stood silently at the lectern for twenty minutes or so in the sweltering room and then took a seat.

Blair, as always, demonstrated his mastery of the genre, using his blend of fluency, insight and good humour. It was so hot in there on this occasion that after an hour or so the press were longing to be released rather than continue their vain attempts to ruffle him. Then, to wind them up at the end, he said, 'Anyway, just before you go, because I know you really enjoyed it, Michael is going to repeat the presentation.' Amid peals of nervous laughter from the press corps, we were done. Tony O'Connor, who with Kate Myronidis had once again worked tirelessly to produce the graphs for the presentation, sat throughout the press conference next to a representative from a well-known tabloid newspaper. Apparently, as successive graphs appeared on the screen during my presentation, this journalist said, sotto voce, 'Bullshit . . . bullshit . . . bullshit . . . '

*Excerpts from the PowerPoint presentation are in the Delivery Manual, Document 9.

I spent the following day (23 July 2004) at Lord's, but not before I had skimmed through the press coverage. The sketch writers commented on the heat and the dullness ('It was comparable to a lecture from the speaking clock,' wrote Quentin Letts in the *Daily Mail*),* but the news pages generally reported the case I had made without comment. The more serious political commentators such as Peter Riddell in the *Times* took up the debate we had intended to provoke: 'The most important words at the end-of-term Downing Street press conference came not from Tony Blair but from Michael Barber . . . [His] annual update tends to be ignored by journalists as a slightly tedious ten minutes . . . before they can get on to the red meat of politics.' Riddell went on broadly to endorse the case I had made, before asking sceptically but perceptively how far choice and competition would go and what would happen when the growth in public spending slowed down in the years ahead. Meanwhile, the central political message of the day was Blair's assertion that 'we have just been publishing these five-year strategies . . . and I want to see them through'. In the ongoing debate about how long Blair would stay in office, this was an unmistakeable commitment.

Going the extra mile

Shortly after the summer break – in late September – Blair surprised everyone by going even further and saying that if he won the forthcoming election, he would stay a further full term but would not stand for re-election again. I was listening to the *Today* programme when this news came through and stayed at home to hear it all again at 8.00 a.m. to make sure I had understood it. In fact, that September turned out to be extremely demanding for Blair. He had returned in the first week of the month and reshuffled his ministerial team. The most striking aspect of it was the creation in the Cabinet Office of a strong ministerial team led by Alan Milburn – returning from self-imposed exile – and supported by Ruth Kelly. They would drive strategy, and the Delivery Unit, as before, was left to get on with its job.

* Robert Peston says the same comparison to a speaking clock has been made about Gordon Brown (*Brown's Britain* (London: Short, 2005), p. 9). I think it's unfair to both of us, but either way this is company I'm happy to keep.

My only involvement in the reshuffle was tangential. Blair had agreed to a team photograph of himself with the entire Delivery Unit staff as a reward to them for their hard work. We assembled as planned in the No. 10 garden and were able to watch (without being able to hear) Blair's conversations on the terrace with the ministers who came and went. As the photos were taken, Blair said to the Delivery Unit team, 'Not every reform in government works, but the Delivery Unit has . . . it does very good work.' Later he signed copies of the photos for each of them. I mention that this was all the involvement I had because that week Simon Jenkins reported in the *Times* that Andrew Adonis and I drew up lists for Blair of 'beacon Ministers'. To make his story more convincing, he finished it, 'I kid you not.' Whether one consequence of this story was that junior ministers afterwards took me more seriously, I cannot say; I do know it was entirely untrue (I kid you not).

By far my biggest anxiety in the autumn of 2004 was that – in spite of my presentation to Cabinet in July – Blair and his ministers would focus more on the long-term agenda and on the politics of the pre-election period than on grinding out results. In fact, Blair returned from holiday and insisted with his office that the stocktakes had to remain, and while he missed one or two, his continuing attendance sent a strong signal to his Cabinet colleagues.

This was important because, in spite of the huge momentum that had been created in the previous twelve months, there were still major risks, and in any case much of the progress was from a low base, had not gone nearly far enough, and was often not fast enough. I discovered that for myself in relation to the railways when I visited the Joint Control Centre at Waterloo station and then took a train to Woking with key managers, who explained the improvement in performance over the previous year and set out the risks ahead. They said that Network Rail's decision to take maintenance staff in-house, much faster responses to incidents and much better, longer-term planning had all contributed. They were worried that the autumn of 2004 might not be as golden as the previous year's but at least they said they had a plan. Unfortunately for them, in a conversation that was going rather well, the train we travelled on together to Woking was twenty minutes late owing to engine failure on the train in front.

On education, it took time for David Normington's attention on school attendance to bite, and on school behaviour the department seemed to be endlessly scrambling for coherent policy, in spite of Blair's constant entreaties to send a strong, clear signal which would shift the culture. Sometimes only the detail of an individual case reveals the crucial insight. For example, that autumn I made a point of personally following up an individual case I came across of a boy who ceased to turn up to school in east London at age fourteen, and then simply fell through the cracks. When I called his council, they said that since he had not been excluded they could not offer him a programme. I said they had a responsibility to get him back to school; they said that the school he was in was across the borough boundary and it was the school's responsibility. The school said he was no longer on their roll. Eventually the council offered him a place on a scheme for excluded pupils. They suggested improbably that he should turn up at a specified roundabout on a given morning, where a bus would collect him and drive him across London to the scheme. Why did they expect a boy who never turned up to school to suddenly decide to show up on time for a bus ride to a scheme he was hardly likely to relish? And why did no one visit his home? Certainly, no one from the council checked whether he took up the offer (he didn't). A few months later, I heard he had been arrested for grievous bodily harm. It was cases such as this that led me to press the Education Department to require local authorities to have excellent individual-level data on every at-risk young person. I was accused of being bureaucratic: in fact I was making the point that only through sharp, rigorous systems can these kinds of human tragedy – and there are thousands of them – be avoided.

On asylum, the number of applications, having fallen dramatically, now plateaued; the number of removals of failed asylum seekers, always a challenge, remained flat, and Blair's promise that in 2005 the number of removals would exceed the number of applications looked at risk (in the end it was achieved, but only in the early months of 2006). This was an area where I thought the Delivery Unit (including myself) had been insufficiently tough, and too willing to accept the account of the relevant officials. On crime, there were continuing worries about violent crime, and alongside the Police Standards Unit (PSU), the Delivery Unit played a leading part in assisting police to strengthen their performance. The inspiration behind this was the PSU head, Paul Evans, who had previously been police chief in Boston, Massachusetts, and was shocked by the alcohol culture among young people in this country and fearful that the police had lost control. A series of campaigns he organised with the Association of Chief Police Officers, linked to important changes in the law (such as the capacity to close individual pubs) began to redress the balance. It involved, as I found myself explaining to Blair one Monday morning, Delivery Unit staff (though not me, I hasten to add) spending Friday and Saturday nights in some less-than-salubrious venues in northern cities. Though they were far from shrinking violets, they were shocked by what they saw – the quantities of alcohol, the associated violence, and (until Evans's campaigns) the ease with which underage drinkers could buy alcohol. On one occasion, the hotel they were staying in was the site of a stabbing – they really were on the frontline. We were also heavily involved, along with Home Office officials, in sharpening up a strategy for reducing the number of prolific offenders.

Even on health, which had stolen the show in the previous twelve months, not all was plain sailing. While waiting times continued to fall steadily, the plans to offer patients choice over where to have an operation were progressing more slowly than hoped for. Again I felt we in the Delivery Unit had erred too often in the previous few months in giving the department the benefit of the doubt. Internal wrangling among officials in the Department of Health had not helped. In the meantime, the issue of the MRSA 'superbug' threatened to eclipse all the achievements of the parliament and, at John Reid's suggestion, we helped the department plan its response. When I told a senior official in the department that I had been shocked to discover so many people died every year of infections caught in hospital, he shrugged and said, 'Hospitals are dangerous places; 5,000 people have died in this way every year for many years.' It was one of many examples I came across of passive (and, frankly, immoral) acceptance of the unacceptable. How many lives might have been saved if top officials had demanded the problem be tackled without waiting to be asked? How much better might our public services have become if a restless search for improvement was a firmly established part of civil service culture?

Stocktakes and the monthly notes ensured Blair and No. 10 more generally remained actively involved in seeing the progress and resolving these problems, but for the Delivery Unit the pivot of the entire six-month period was an awayday we had at a Docklands hotel in early October. As a result of Peter Thomas's professionalisation of our management processes, we had now instituted quarterly monitoring, which meant that half way between the July and December Delivery Reports, the management team saw the staff's estimates of where we would be on delivery by December. In other words, I was in a position to see whether by December we would see a further shift on the league table from red to green. When I read this quarterly monitoring report the day before the awayday, I was disappointed to discover that the predictions amounted to modest rather than substantial progress. I decided that I would make the entire theme of the awayday intensifying one more time our efforts to shift even more into the green by December – without of course lowering our standards. I focused almost entirely on this theme throughout the twenty-four hours we were there.

Aware of the impact we could have in the next few weeks, on this occasion I wrote down exactly what I said and circulated it to all staff after the event. 'This is the best team I've ever had the pleasure of working with, and given what I know about the new people joining us, I believe the best team is about to get better still.' (There was constant turnover in the Delivery Unit; a core stayed almost throughout, but many people joined for a year or two and moved on, usually to strikingly better things, having contributed to the collective competence and culture of the unit.) I then set out the metaphor of the two thrillers and said that we had two months to finish the first one while starting to plan the second. Before coming to the detail, I highlighted three major successes – our reputation, which we knew from the feedback we had from permanent secretaries and other colleagues in department was perhaps the strongest of any organisation in Whitehall, though 'there is nothing inevitable about [it]. We have to earn it over and over again'; our proven methodology, which was simple in concept but required 'extraordinary discipline to implement . . . consistently'; and our prioritisation and focus on the 'relatively few big things'.

The challenge, though, lay in the quarterly monitoring report. I said I was struck by how much red and amber-red still remained, and by the fact that 'in many cases you are predicting no change at all between July and December and in one or two cases that things will get worse'. An obvious line would have been to criticise the departments, but I wanted us to take responsibility, so I continued:

> [This] can only mean one of two things – either the actions we specified are not being taken, or the [July] delivery report was drafted wrongly.

Then I turn to the section of the quarterly monitoring report specifying action you propose to take between now and December and see phrases such as 'no significant changes are proposed'. This cannot be right . . . Don't get me wrong – I don't want any lowering of our standards. I want the necessary action taken here and in departments.

In short, I believed my own rhetoric. In spite of all we had achieved, everything would depend on what we did in the next two months. 'We need to review, intensify, accelerate and challenge both our actions and those planned in departments . . . Above all, don't flinch, don't compromise.'

Most of the rest of my remarks were about planning ahead for a reformed civil service, but I wanted to finish by dealing with the ethics of our work. 'We are people with a mission. Naïvely or not, optimistically or not, everyone . . . is here . . . to make the world a better place.'

Our ethics came through, I argued, in the way we developed our relationships – honest, plain-speaking, consistent, principled, evidence-based, constructive. The ethics also came through in the mission, which was not the re-election of Blair – that was someone else's problem. Ours was 'the development of public services of real quality, which citizens from all backgrounds want to use, which deliver equity as well as high standards and which make productive use of every penny of the tax-payers' money which is entrusted to government'.

This was important because, in the pre-election atmosphere, party politics was already heating up and I wanted to reaffirm that our mission was to serve the citizens, not any particular party. In fact, the week before, at party conference, the Conservative leader Michael Howard had promised, 'In week one of a Conservative government, I will order the closure of the Downing Street Delivery Unit.' Rather than worry about this, the main reaction of the staff had been pride in the fact that we were seen as worthy of being abolished – or even given attention at all – in week one of a newly elected government. I had already determined that in the event of Howard being elected I would seek to convince him that any Prime Minister of any party who once knew what the Delivery Unit could do for him would want to keep it in existence. Why else were leaders in so many other countries paying such close attention and indeed in some cases seeking to emulate what we did?

In any case, the response to my contribution at the awayday and afterwards was electrifying. The staff rose to the challenge; their energy levels were tremendous and over the next couple of weeks we examined all the red indicators and asked what we might be able to do with the relevant departments to shift them. It is amazing how through a combination of real drive, passion, attention to detail and refusal to take 'no' for an answer, a small, committed band of people can make real improvements in huge systems in just a few weeks.

The week after the awayday, I saw Blair for my monthly update. I suggested to him that he should remind Cabinet ministers of the need to do everything they could to shift their delivery priorities from red to green by the end of the year. He readily agreed because he was worried about – again a characteristic word – 'slippage'. That Thursday, the jargon of deliverology therefore reached the heart of the British constitution. What Walter Bagehot, the nineteenth-century analyst of the British Constitution, would have thought of a Prime Minister urging his colleagues to shift their portfolios from red to green we will never know, but I was delighted.

I reported on Blair's response to my management team too, so that they could state explicitly in conversations with departments that this was what Blair wanted and had said so at Cabinet. I also checked that this remark was in the Cabinet minutes because I knew permanent secretaries read them and this would add to the impact. Resonance is all in the detail.

Having established the platform for the final drive for results, it was a question of delivering. A note to myself at the end of one week that autumn gives a flavour:

> There were a series of [stocktake] meetings with Blair and others on major issues – drugs . . . organised crime, the Tomlinson report [on secondary school qualifications] – and a stream of routine but nonetheless excellent meetings in the Delivery Unit – young people and drugs, choice in health, long-term care, asylum . . . following through from the awayday in which I increased the challenge . . . This is the task – chivvying people along all the time.

Again, from a month later, I have a scrap of paper on which I wrote: 'This was a week of driving forward our core agenda – finalising delivery reports, agreeing traffic light judgements with permanent secretaries, sorting out key messages for my [December] presentation to Cabinet and arguing about all of these things (in the best sense) in the unit.'

Two other major themes dominated our thinking in the run-up to Christmas. One was what part the Delivery Unit might play in a reformed centre of government after the forthcoming election. The debate about this was happening in a variety of more or less secret, more or less informal locations, and rather than wait to be asked, we in the Delivery Unit wanted to have proposals ready (see Chapter 7). The other was how to ensure we could be effective in overseeing not just delivery of targets, but also the implementation of system reform. We designed and tested another element of deliverology to assist us in this task: a review process for the introduction of choice and contestability (details are set out in Document 8 of the Delivery Manual). This development pointed the way towards a professionalisation of the entire policy-making process. Deliverology had made targets, trajectories and delivery planning explicit processes which could then be refined and improved continuously. Why not follow the same logic with system design, the creation of markets and any other key processes?

December 2004

On 9 December 2004, I was due to make my final presentation to the Cabinet. We had all but completed the delivery reports and they were circulated at the end of the week. The most striking aspect of them was the extent to which we had indeed been able to shift more items from red to green. By focusing ministers and key officials on eking out every last ounce of potential – in the same way as a big occasion brings out something extra from top sportspeople – performance really had improved in the space of a few short weeks. The momentum generated in the first half of the year had, after the early autumn slippage, been maintained or even accelerated.

In preparing for this Cabinet presentation I had, at Peter Thomas's suggestion, worked with a small team from within the unit. This was important because I wanted this brief report to do more than show the results and explain them; I wanted it to draw out conclusively the

Figure 6.1: December 2004 presentation slide

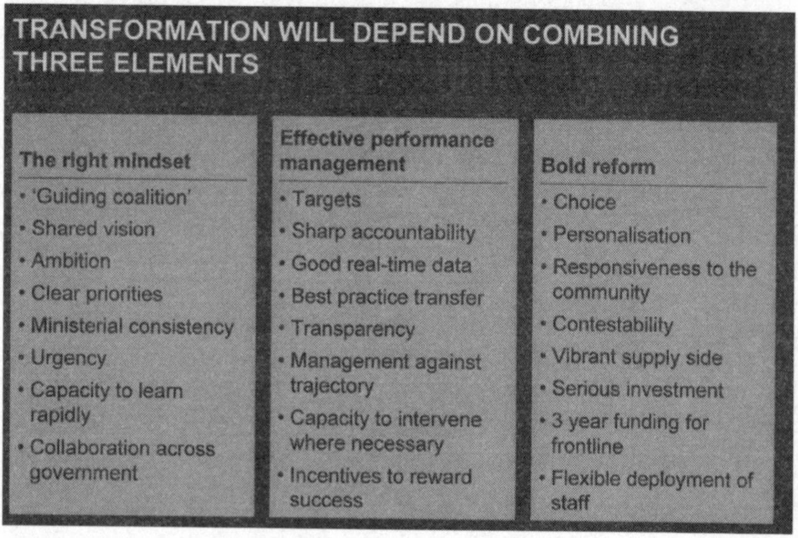

> **TRANSFORMATION WILL DEPEND ON COMBINING THREE ELEMENTS**
>
> | The right mindset | Effective performance management | Bold reform |
> |---|---|---|
> | • 'Guiding coalition' | • Targets | • Choice |
> | • Shared vision | • Sharp accountability | • Personalisation |
> | • Ambition | • Good real-time data | • Responsiveness to the community |
> | • Clear priorities | • Best practice transfer | • Contestability |
> | • Ministerial consistency | • Transparency | • Vibrant supply side |
> | • Urgency | • Management against trajectory | • Serious investment |
> | • Capacity to learn rapidly | • Capacity to intervene where necessary | • 3 year funding for frontline |
> | • Collaboration across government | • Incentives to reward success | • Flexible deployment of staff |

lessons we had learnt over the four years so that, in a conscious way, we could leave them with the Cabinet as a legacy.*

The Delivery Unit team produced a draft which told a series of stories and then showed the overall picture of progress since the previous December. Then the presentation concluded with two analytical sections, one relating to public perceptions of what had been achieved, and the other summarising on a single slide the key insights from our work. Needless to say, we tested the presentation out several times with staff in the Delivery Unit before, on the Tuesday, I shared it with Blair. As I thought often during those few weeks, he looked terribly tired. He made just a couple of minor comments on the report.

The following day, I gave the presentation to the permanent secretaries collectively, singling out for attention David Normington's personal contribution to shifting school attendance off the bottom of the league table and from red to amber/green. Then the next morning I was in No. 10 early. The previous evening, Liverpool had sensationally

---

* Interestingly, Douglas Hurd believes that the Central Policy Review Staff under Ted Heath 'carried out, with great aplomb and elegance, [a] pedagogic role for ministers' (quoted in Jon Davis, *Prime Ministers and Whitehall 1960–74* (London: Hambledon Continuum, 2007), p. 126). This is precisely what I aspired to.

beaten Olympiakos 3-1 thanks to an outstanding Steven Gerrard goal, and I skimmed the back pages outside Blair's office. John Prescott walked past and commented cheerfully that delivery was on the up. When the Cabinet itself assembled, I thought they all looked exhausted too. I had to wait while an early item was debated at some length, then Blair said, 'Right, Michael, you've got twelve minutes.' The presentation flowed, not least because I had memorised what I wanted to say: from 47 per cent on track in December 2003 to 62 per cent in July 2004 and over 80 per cent now in December 2004. Impressive progress. Most importantly, the summary of lessons learnt meant that I was able to convey important and challenging messages (see the slide reproduced as Figure 6.1, and for more detailed analysis of the issues set out here, see Chapter 9); for example, targets had often been controversial during the parliament, even inside government, but no one should fool themselves, I argued; they had made a major contribution to the track record, especially those 'floor' targets that set high minimum standards and therefore helped secure greater equity.

I also pointed out the impact, where it had occurred, of the 'guiding coalition'.

This is a phrase taken from the Harvard management guru John Kotter, and it reinforced an idea I had discussed with Blair and others during the course of the parliament which previously I had put thus: one or two people, even in powerful positions, will always struggle to achieve dramatic change, but seven people in key positions who agree profoundly about what they want to do and how they want to do it can change the world. In government this is not so much a question of management teams as of securing committed (and of course talented) people in the seven to ten key positions that influence policy and implementation – for example, the secretary of state, the relevant minister of state, the permanent secretary, key civil servants, the political adviser, the No. 10 Policy Directorate staff member, the head of the relevant inspectorate . . . or the equivalent. If these people share a vision and an understanding of how that vision is to be achieved, they can make dramatic progress, as had been proved in Blair's second term in health and in his first term in education. For Blair personally and for a Cabinet minister, this is a vital issue; it should be possible to create consciously a guiding coalition, and indeed I have seen it done well in relation to education in Ontario. Reshuffles of the future should be as much about creating guiding coalitions as about juggling individual ministers.

In any case, the Cabinet responded positively to these key messages. I could also tell from the body language around the room that they thought the explanation I gave for the gap between the impressive objective progress during the parliament and sceptical public perceptions of it was the most convincing they had yet heard. My team and I had worked hard on this. Why, we asked, if so much progress has been made on delivery, are the British people not dancing in the streets?

The answer, we said, had a number of elements to it: there is often a time lag between getting something done and people noticing; in some cases the progress had taken a long time; and while there might be general improvement, it was uneven across the country: if – to take one example – you live in a high crime area, the news that crime is falling elsewhere in the country does nothing to cheer you. Added to this is the fact that the scale of reform had angered some public service leaders who grumbled regularly in public. Needless to say, nurses, doctors and teachers are more credible with the public than government ministers. In spite of Peter Hyman's excellent efforts in the first half of the

Figure 6.2: The public is unimpressed by 'adequate'

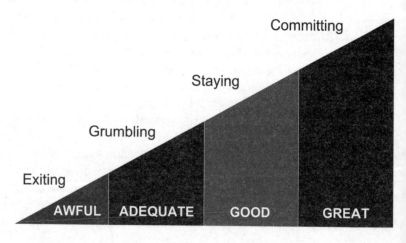

THE PUBLIC IS UNIMPRESSED BY 'ADEQUATE'
...THEY WANT 'GOOD' AND ASPIRE TO 'GREAT' ...

parliament, there had never been a sustained and comprehensive approach to communications about delivery. Then again, the media would inevitably emphasise the negative and shift the agenda so that, to take another example, as health waiting times fell, MRSA would be highlighted. Finally, of course, for all sorts of reasons – not least the Iraq war and its aftermath – by the end of a gruelling and controversial second term, the public were no longer prepared to give the government the benefit of the doubt. Most of all, though, we argued that the answer to the conundrum lay in the diagram shown in Figure 6.2.

Jim Collins, the American business author, wrote an excellent book called *Good to Great*, explaining how a number of companies achieved that transition and sustained excellent performance over fifteen years. However, for our purposes in examining progress in the public services, we needed to extend this two-point scale backwards, and invented the four-point scale illustrated here. In the Cabinet presentation, I argued that often the progress achieved during the parliament was not 'good' to 'great', or even 'adequate' to 'good'. In fact, much of it was 'awful' to 'adequate' – no mean feat, incidentally – but when the public see that a service has moved from 'awful' to 'adequate' they do not dance in the streets. They continue to grumble; they don't even say 'thank you', they say 'why didn't you do that years ago?'

For the Prime Minister and his Cabinet colleagues as they left for the brief Christmas break, therefore, there was plenty to ponder: the significant scale of their real achievement; the low base in performance of the public services they had inherited; the fact that they had not, except in a few areas, made as much progress as they should have done in the first term; the grudging nature of the public's recognition of their achievements; and of course – outside my sphere – the political challenge of turning that state of affairs into the third election victory they craved. As Andrew Grice summarised it in a commentary piece in the *Independent* (11 December 2004), 'Almost eight years since Labour promised it, things really are getting better . . . The danger for Mr Blair is that many people may pocket the improvements without giving credit to a government they feel in no mood to thank or reward.'

Before that, though, there was one of those political crises that absorb everyone's attention for a few days, in this case the fall of David Blunkett. I had worked closely with him for four years in Education and often collaborated with him as Home Secretary. I think (and thought then) he is one of the most remarkable people I have ever met and has been a politician of the first rank; certainly the best Labour Education Secretary in history, certainly an impressive Home Secretary in a period, following September 11, that was one of the most demanding in the post-war era. His fall happened on the day of the No. 10 Christmas party and for me (and no doubt many others) replaced the festive spirit with a sense of hollowness.

7

Endgame

I am very sorry not to be with you on my last day . . . I have enjoyed every minute of my time working with you. You are a *fantastic* team.

Note to my staff, 8 July 2005

Playing to the final whistle

On 2 January 2005 I went on a long walk in east London – through Broadway Market, past the Blind Beggar pub (once a favourite haunt of the Krays) and the somewhat neglected Hawksmoor church of St George in the East, over Tower Bridge, along the South Bank to Southwark Cathedral, then over the Millennium Bridge and back home to Hackney through the back streets of Islington. As I walked, I looked back on a year of trauma in the family and thought ahead to what I wanted to do next in life, sure that once the election (which everyone expected to be in May) was over, I would leave the Delivery Unit, but still unsure whether I would do something else in central government or leave altogether.

The Cabinet presentation just before Christmas had been close to a sign-off. I knew it had been my last chance to present to them. Even so, I have seen too many football matches where last-minute goals have changed everything to be complacent in believing the job was done. We had to play to the final whistle. I knew that the Prime Minister and indeed the entire Cabinet would now be focused on preparing for the election – shaping the politics, writing a manifesto, oiling the machine, creating dividing lines, massaging Achilles heels and reducing risks. This was confirmed for me in a round-up we had at Chequers on 7 January, which focused entirely on the agenda for the third term.

As far as the Delivery Unit agenda was concerned, what Tony Blair wanted was continuing progress wherever possible, but I thought there was more to do than that. Our job, as I'd always explained to the unit's staff, was to ensure the public got results for their investment. This responsibility continued, election campaign or not. Moreover, any impact that the Delivery Unit had in the first few months of 2005 would not be felt on the frontline until some time in the summer, and the incoming government – whichever party won – would reap the benefits.

In the first meeting of the new year with my management team, I stressed that, as the political system geared up for the election to the exclusion of attention on our agenda, we should ensure there was no let-up in the drive for delivery – we owed nothing less to the taxpayer. Our priorities should therefore be to do everything we could to shift any remaining red ratings to green; to work with departments to ensure the plans for implementing their five-year strategies were firmly in place so that, if the government were returned, it could hit the ground running; and to prepare a half-day training programme for the top civil servants of each department through which we would spread what we had learnt over the previous four years, as summarised in the December 2004 Cabinet presentation. This would help embed delivery capability in Whitehall. And that was how I spent my time in the early months of 2005. Instead of looking at the referee to see if he was about to blow his whistle, we kept playing as if the game had only just begun. The fact that the politicians were now playing a different game made our performance all the more important. All our routines, which were key to our success, needed to continue.

So, in January, for example, I spent time with top civil servants in the Department for Education's Schools Directorate, urging them to refocus on improving test scores, to sharpen the accountability system and to relax about introducing choice and new providers of schools. I reminded them that in the mid-1990s intervention in failing schools, such as Hackney Downs, had been hugely controversial. Now it was routine, and the evidence of beneficial impact overwhelming. Going further back in history, I reminded them of the hymn that R. A. Butler had quoted to reassure the churches during the second reading debate on the 1944 Education Act:

> Ye fearful saints fresh courage take
> The clouds ye so much dread

Are filled with mercy
And will break
In blessings on your head.[1]

Exactly the same applied to the extension of choice and opening up supply, I argued. In other words, my main point to them was that the barriers to reform in this case (as so often) were in the mind – and in this case in their minds.

I also found it necessary to continue to challenge the Education Department officialdom on primary school literacy throughout those months. My case for doing so had always been strong because the Prime Minister, not to mention parents, attached a huge importance to the three Rs. With Ruth Kelly's appointment as Secretary of State for Education in place of Charles Clarke in December, my case was further strengthened because Kelly attached a clear personal priority to further improvements in the basics. I pressed the department to reinforce the teaching of phonics, which new research showed could be strengthened, but ran into huge institutional resistance. There were some in the department who felt that changing the 1998 phonics package would be tantamount to admitting an error. I had been the editor of that package and felt the opposite – refining a document six years on in the light of evidence was a sign of strength, not weakness. In any case, we owed it to the pupils to adopt proven best practice. More worrying was the strand of resistance which was based on the fact that some officials in the department were more interested in pleasing the middle-brow strand of the teaching profession than they were in delivering results – a classic case of the producer's interests being put ahead of the consumer's. Under pressure from teachers, and using the excuse that reform was all about 'letting go', some officials in the department had ceased to believe that it should ensure that teachers used proven methods in the classroom or that schools should set ambitious targets.

I nearly choked on my breakfast coffee one morning in April 2005 when I heard the otherwise excellent Stephen Twigg, who had replaced David Miliband as minister of school standards the previous December, talking about phonics on the *Today* programme. As soon as I reached the office, I emailed the official who would have been responsible for briefing him:

Back to my obsession: Stephen Twigg was terrible on the *Today* programme . . . It is the road back to the 70s to say each teacher knows best in their own classroom. Moreover, it isn't true . . . the line . . . that we already do phonics is complacent . . . we do some, but the later evidence demands significant change and we should be preparing to do this.

In fact, with an election looming, it was impossible to make any progress on this in the short term. After the election, with Andrew Adonis now in the Lords and a minister at Education, the necessary review was driven forward.

Kelly's first few months in office were challenging. She had to take prompt decisions on the Tomlinson review and make a series of major policy announcements before the election. As far as short-term delivery was concerned, she had little option but to depend on what her officials were doing. I told her advisers she should look at her time there like a test match opening batsman – see off the new ball without losing your wicket, but don't worry about the score, just make it through to lunch (the election) and pick up the pace as the sun comes out in the afternoon. I have never asked Kelly whether she responds well to cricketing metaphors, but I thought in the end she played a dogged opener's innings at Education, resisting some very hostile bowling.

Another blip on the education front in those same weeks demonstrated that, because of my background, I sometimes interfered in details of education policy in a way I would never countenance in other areas. I made the mistake on 18 February of picking up the *Times Educational Supplement*, which always used to be filled with a mixture of job adverts and professional whingeing and never failed to irritate me when I worked for government.* On this occasion, I discovered, incredibly, that the Qualifications and Curriculum Authority (QCA) was consulting teachers on whether reading and writing would remain basic skills as technology progressed over the next decade. In order to overcome my apoplexy, I emailed key people in the department as follows:

*By constantly reinforcing cynicism, it conveyed the implicit message that transformation was impossible but never acknowledged that the only alternative to successful transformation was the running down of our education service so that it became a safety net for the poor. The *TES* is now under new ownership, has undergone a makeover, and is consciously more positive because it has understood that teachers themselves have become more positive.

Subject: Goodbye Tolstoy

The QCA [in its proposed review] is actually quoted as asking: 'Will reading and writing still be basic skills in 2015? Will the printed book disappear? If most screen reading is in short chunks, how important is stamina in reading and writing longer texts?' . . . This is lunacy . . . it represents a degree of ignorance and irresponsibility that I simply cannot comprehend. I had better be brief given the QCA view of modern attention spans! I am sure you agree with me, but what can we do?

I mention this example because it demonstrates that there is so much being churned out by the government machine at any given time that even for a secretary of state, never mind a Prime Minister, it is impossible to be on top of everything. So much for the control freak argument – the chance would be a fine thing.

These kinds of routine interventions, if not at this level of detail, were mirrored in other areas. This was the time, for example, when we invited to meetings the few hospitals that were falling short on the A&E four-hour target. It was also the time when the performance of the railways suggested we might after all reach our punctuality target. As John Cleese might have said, it was no longer the despair that was killing us; it was the hope. Even customer satisfaction with rail performance was now going up. One time in January, I was in the Department for Transport and happened to run into Alistair Darling. As ever with such a chance meeting with a Cabinet minister, I took the opportunity to quote a relevant statistic. Passenger satisfaction with punctuality is up, I said, and suggested this might be worth mentioning in a speech some time. Darling raised an eyebrow, turned to his private secretary and said, 'Yes, we met one of them yesterday, didn't we?' as though it had never happened before. Come to think of it, it probably never had.

Other parts of the routine continued unchanged. Our monthly notes went to Blair on Fridays and he continued to comment on them most of the time. The March stocktakes also went ahead. I had asked Blair whether he wanted stocktakes in March and he had said he did. On two or three further occasions I reminded him that he had said they were important, but when the time came he simply pulled out. I was deeply frustrated as I had told departments how much store the PM set by them. Nevertheless, we went ahead with them without Blair. I chaired them and the relevant permanent secretary led for the department. At least I had one final chance to conduct meetings from the Prime Minister's chair in the Cabinet Room. I pressed departments not to let up the drive for delivery. There is a real tendency across Whitehall to slacken the pace as an election looms – in fact it becomes an excuse for taking it easy. To me this is morally unacceptable. After all, public money keeps being spent and the public has every right to expect the civil service to strive for the fullest possible value from every pound spent, election or no election.

Meanwhile, during the election campaign we ran the promised half-day training sessions for top teams in all key departments. We asked them to evaluate their own performance in delivery over the previous parliament and then to identify the likely priorities for the next parliament. It was a great opportunity to tell stories of success in one department to top officials in another. As so often happens when sharing best practice, the first reaction is to say, 'Ah, yes, but our circumstances are different.' Our job was to say, 'Maybe, but not that different. Don't look for reasons why you can't learn from this, look at what you can learn.' Overall, there was a real can-do spirit about the events, which were a good way to make use of the election campaign, when the absence of ministers frees up the diaries of top officials.

By the end of March, I was confident that performance across the Delivery Unit priorities was marginally up on the December report to Cabinet. In early April, I received confirmation that rail performance had improved yet again, performance on the A&E four-hour target had been sustained for a full quarter, and even the number of removals of failed asylum seekers, the most intractable of all issues, was finally going in the right direction. It was pure coincidence that Blair called the election the following week. I had promised to assist Blair on delivery for a full parliament, and when the election was called I felt I had done my duty – mission accomplished? I felt positive it had been at the time (see Chapter 8 for a full assessment). We had played to the final whistle.

It was a strange Easter, though, dominated by family issues and my own personal attempt to ruin the government's crime figures. Our youngest daughter Alys dropped out of university and came home for a series of heart-searching conversations which for all their trauma were rich and rewarding. I wrote myself a note at that time:

Tired, tired, tired, emotionally as much as anything after getting through the week . . . I felt better after I'd spoken to Alys again on the phone standing in the street near Westminster Bridge in the lovely early spring weather . . . it's a good, strong decision if she now really gets on with life. [And she has, by the way.]

One day, reflecting on all this as I cycled into work, I was stopped by the police for going through a red light. I was torn between my acute embarrassment at being caught and delight at this direct evidence that the new system of fixed penalty notices was operational. Then, a couple of weeks later, I drove Alys back to Norwich, where she had been at university and had now decided to get a job. As I left her outside her house, I said, 'I think our luck is about to turn.' A few minutes later – distracted again – I hit an oncoming BMW and found myself scrambling out of the car, which I thought was on fire. I had gone through a red light again! Fortunately, the driver of the BMW was unharmed too (and generous in nature), and when the police came I accepted full responsibility. They asked me what work I did.

'You don't want to know,' I said.

'Yes, we do,' they replied, so I told them.

The conversation moved from how the accident had occurred to what the Prime Minister should do to reduce police bureaucracy. Needless to say, the law took its course and I (rightly) paid my penalty for the second time in a few weeks. Somehow, though, the event shook me up and reinforced in my mind the need not just to move on, but to make more mental space for my family.

Meanwhile, at work my thoughts, like everyone else's, were on what the election result would be. Everyone knew Labour would win; the issue was the size of the majority.

The start of the third term

In the topsy-turvy world which is modern politics, an election victory for Labour with a majority of sixty-six seats was portrayed in the media (fuelled, it has to be said, by some disaffected Labour backbenchers) as a defeat. The truth was, though, that in top Labour circles there was some disappointment since hopes of a majority of eighty or even 100 had been widespread. In fact, the Conservatives had only marginally recovered (to a position less strong than that of Neil Kinnock's Labour Party in 1987), but the Liberal Democrats had made gains on an anti-war protest vote.

I dropped into Blair's private office on the morning after the election. No. 10 had been almost deserted during the election campaign. Now it was bursting with life. Since I hadn't seen the political team for a while, the conversation immediately turned to the result that mattered most – Liverpool's victory over Chelsea in the semi-final of the Champions League that Wednesday. (Was it a goal or wasn't it? Who cares?) Then we turned to the election campaign. I asked what had been the high and low points. The low point, they said, had been the leak of the Attorney General's advice on Iraq. And the high point? There weren't any high points. It had been very gruelling.

I stayed at No. 10 for the formal moment when the Prime Minister and his family returned to Downing Street. The staff lined the famous corridor from the front door to the Cabinet Room. Tony and Cherie were welcomed with rapturous applause and cheering. They shook hands and smiled, Blair looking utterly exhausted. Later in the day, I was over with my staff in the Treasury and we joined in the similarly rapturous welcome accorded to the Chancellor when he returned to his office there. I thus make the small claim to fame of having been the only person to shake hands with both the Prime Minister and the Chancellor on their return to office that day.

My disappointment on the Friday after the election was, however, with the Cabinet reshuffle. My worry was less with any specific individual than with the lack of change overall. I had never been in the reshuffle loop, but I had expected to see a real sense of a new generation coming to the fore. The reshuffle seemed to betray a lack of confidence and left Blair with a team which looked more like a last gasp than a fresh start. I had expected to see talented and successful ministers of state such as Douglas Alexander, John Hutton, Jacqui Smith and Hazel Blears in major Cabinet delivery roles, joining David Miliband, Des Browne and Ruth Kelly in giving the Cabinet a more energetic and youthful look.* Below Cabinet

*Alexander was made minister for Europe and made it to a frontline delivery job in 2006 when he became Secretary of State for Transport. Hutton was in the Cabinet as minister for the Cabinet Office, and finally made it into a frontline delivery job later in the year when David Blunkett resigned from the Department for Work and Pensions.

level it was much better (I was especially pleased that Andrew Adonis was made an Education minister) but when I ran into the PM on the Monday after the election I told him that I thought he hadn't been radical enough.

'Congratulations on your victory,' I said.

'Apparently we lost,' he laughed, referring to the weekend press.

On the reshuffle, I told him he should have made more use of Clement Attlee's famously economical lines: 'You've had a good innings' and 'Not up to the job'. Blair smiled.*

It was not just the reshuffle that lacked cutting edge in the days after the election. Plans for major organisational changes were shelved. Even the most superficial of the proposed changes – a new name for the Department of Trade and Industry (to focus it on Energy and Productivity) – was dropped after the press ridiculed it. Meanwhile, the appointment of a new Cabinet Secretary was delayed for a month. Since the appointment of new permanent secretaries and the various possible moves of existing ones could not happen before the new Cabinet Secretary was in post, vital momentum was lost. In fact, the building of the new permanent secretary cadre was not completed until January 2006, eight months into the third term. My own vigorously argued proposition had been for the new Cabinet Secretary to be appointed provisionally in the spring before the election campaign. The incoming Prime Minister, whoever it might have been, could then simply have confirmed it in week one and let him or her get on with the job of sorting out the top of Whitehall, thus generating momentum. If the incoming PM had really had a problem with the selected individual, he could simply have restarted the selection process. At least in the end the appointment was a good one. Gus O'Donnell had set out radical plans for overhauling Whitehall and built strong relationships with both Blair and Gordon Brown. He also had real skills as a communicator on a platform and in public, not just the capacity to operate behind closed doors, for which traditional mandarins are famed.

Paul Corrigan once said to me that a major problem with the British

---

*It is true that there are aspects of creating a Cabinet that are not visible to even well-informed insiders such as myself. 'The construction of a Cabinet . . . belongs to a branch of the fine arts . . . [It] requires a delicacy of thought and subtlety of perception, secured only by experience,' one newspaper advised Abraham Lincoln in 1861 (quoted in Doris Kearns Goodwin, *Team of Rivals: The Political Genius of Abraham Lincoln* (New York: Simon and Schuster, 2005), p. 318). *Plus ça change.*

constitution is that you have to do the second most difficult thing in politics (win an election) and then start immediately, without even a night's sleep, on the most difficult thing (run the country). It is a fair point – why couldn't a returning Prime Minister receive the traditional rapturous welcome from the No. 10 staff and then tell the press that he or she was going to take Friday afternoon off, get an early night and start on the reshuffle on Saturday morning?* Either way, on the central domestic issues – education, health and so on – the third term began with a stumble and a loss of pace.

It is easy to forget that what saved it was foreign policy. Before May was out, the voters of the Netherlands and France had firmly rejected the proposed European constitution. Thus, at one bound, Blair escaped from the trap he had set himself by promising a referendum on it. Of course, the promise of a referendum had enabled him to come through an election for the European Parliament and a general election unscathed, and now he wouldn't have to pay the price (a classic example of the high-risk strategy, sometimes essential in politics, of taking a risk and hoping something will turn up). Shortly afterwards, the decision on the 2012 Olympic Games, the Gleneagles G8 summit and his response to the suicide bombings in London reinforced Blair's unexpected new mastery of the scene.

Organising for the third term

From late 2004 onwards, Tony Blair and those around him had given thought to preparations for the third term. The five-year strategies, the 2004 spending review and then the manifesto gave expression to the policy agenda while the reshuffle represented the (disappointing) outcome of reflections on political personnel. Less visible but equally important was the question of what organisational changes to make in preparation for a third term. This question was germane for me, partly as a trusted adviser on such issues in general, and partly as head of the Delivery Unit, which was always likely to be at the centre of any set of changes.

* The nearest thing to a historical precedent for this is Vice-President Gerald Ford's reaction when Nixon suddenly resigned, which meant Ford became President: 'My feeling is you might as well get to sleep' (quoted in the *Economist*'s obituary of Ford, 4 January 2007).

I had begun to think seriously about these questions in the summer of 2004. Given that the Delivery Unit was by then seen to be a success, there seemed to me to be three options for its future, all of them plausible. The first was to extend its remit by connecting it more organically to the Strategy Unit; in fact a strong case could be made for a strategy and delivery function which developed options for overall strategy on government priorities in consultation with departments, put them for decision to the Prime Minister and/or Cabinet and then, through its delivery arm, checked that they were implemented. The second option was to integrate the Delivery Unit with the Treasury public expenditure function so that the allocation of public funds, the monitoring of delivery and the pursuit of efficiency gains became a combined, coherent function. Again the case for such a function, which would mirror the Office of Management and the Budget in Washington, seemed strong. The third option was simply to leave the Delivery Unit as it was, since no one in Whitehall wanted to take me up on my oft-repeated offer to wind it up.

I discussed these three possibilities with my staff and found them open to all of them. While there was some natural anxiety about the degree of change, most people had confidence that whatever happened, the future was likely to bring an enhanced role. My personal view on which option was best changed over time. At first, in the summer of 2004, at the time of the spending review, I favoured the second option, integration with the Treasury. I thought this would be the best way to put public service productivity on the agenda. The Delivery Unit, working with departments, had been able to secure improved outcomes, but this did not answer an even more important question: were the improvements in outcomes commensurate with the scale of investment the government was making? In short, were we securing better value for every pound of taxpayers' money spent? Only by integrating delivery, spending and efficiency would we put this question – which remains an Achilles heel for government – at the centre of attention. There were, however, downsides to integration with the Treasury. One was that it would risk departments defaulting to their standard relationship with the Treasury (telling them as little as possible) rather than continuing the open and challenging dialogue with us that was so central to our impact. The other was that it could only work if Blair and Brown could genuinely share ownership of the new function so that the Prime

Minister would gain influence over public expenditure in return for ceding influence over delivery – and in the summer of 2004 they were not ready to do that.

By the end of 2004 I began to consider the benefits of the first option, the connection with the Strategy Unit. We had always had good relations with its successive directors, Geoff Mulgan and Stephen Aldridge, but we had not worked in an integrated way with them. They were thinking three, five or ten years ahead while we focused on delivering targets in the short and medium term, but as we looked at the agenda for the third parliament and the outcomes of the five-year strategies, the possibility of closer collaboration looked attractive. Delivery of the five-year strategies would require reform of whole systems so that patient choice drove the NHS and parental choice the schools. This was a much more complex and profound challenge than hitting the PSA targets, however demanding they might be. It would involve not just strengthening planning and delivery, but redesigning entire systems and paying attention to the sequencing of reform. For example, should payment by results be introduced before or after reform of primary care trusts? If power and responsibility is to be devolved to headteachers, how can government ensure that the best practice in teaching phonics happens in every primary school classroom? On questions like these you could see how an integrated function could manage an overall approach which connected strategy to design, design to planning, and planning to delivery.

Besides the three options I had considered, there were two others which had strong advocates. One was that the Delivery Unit should be expanded to drive delivery not just on key prime ministerial priorities, but on all the commitments in the five-year strategies. In short, it would become a machine for imposing Blair's will in key departments. While this might have had superficial attraction, I do not believe Blair ever considered it seriously. It would have produced all the flaws we had so carefully avoided in 2001: the sense of prioritisation so crucial to the Delivery Unit's success would have been lost; worse still, a large bureaucracy would have been created in place of the fleet-of-foot and flexible unit we had at the time.

The other possible option was that the Delivery Unit or its successor might have taken responsibility for civil service reform, which had belatedly risen up the agenda following Blair's speech in 2004 and was clearly central to securing reform of the public services as a whole. In the end, while this option was not pursued, in September 2005 Gus O'Donnell did make the Delivery Unit responsible for reviewing the capability of all departments and thus the key driver of progress in civil service reform. This turned out to be the most significant change in the Delivery Unit's role made following the 2005 election, and indeed the capability reviews became its dominant function, making it harder to sustain the focus on Blair's priorities.

I set out all these options and my views on them in a Christmas note for Blair, and early in January 2005 discovered the note had been returned without a comment, without even the characteristic Blair tick which indicated that at least he had seen it. Jonathan Powell told me this was because he was still mulling the options in his head and did not want to commit himself, but I suspect he had simply decided not to read it, no doubt weighed down with other Christmas reading of more immediacy or significance.

Either way, the debate around Whitehall rumbled on occasionally in formal meetings and often informally in quiet corners. I changed my approach to the dialogue I had with Blair on the subject. Rather than try and set out what I thought was the answer, I decided to describe the criteria which any solution would have to meet. This had the advantage of leaving final decisions on structure to the incoming Cabinet Secretary and to my successor at the Delivery Unit. At the time, of course, I did not realise quite how long it would take to get those appointments made.

The criteria were set out in a private note I sent to Blair on preparing for the third term in which I urged that he take key decisions before the election campaign began. Central to my argument was that 'a fast start is essential . . . You should work on the basis that at least 50 per cent of everything you want done in a third term needs to happen in the first year.' My unstated assumption, since borne out by events, was that after the first year his power would ebb away as the focus shifted to his departure and the succession. If this argument were accepted, then he needed to be clear before the campaign what he wanted done in each department between the election in May and the summer recess in July. I also urged him to decide prior to the election what organisational and people changes he wanted so that they could be announced immediately after he returned from the campaign, if he won. 'Experience shows that it is all too easy to spend months working through reorganisations, appointing people, etc. at just the time you need to be building momentum,' I said, predicting, as we have seen, exactly what happened in practice.

Finally, I urged him to set up some kind of transition team as they would in the United States and to bring these people together to give them their marching orders before the election campaign began. There was an obvious objection to the comparison with the US. There, unlike here, there is a gap of two and a half months between a President being elected and actually taking office, but I thought this made my point stronger. 'The fact that in the UK there is no transition period and therefore an incoming government needs to act fast under great pressure only reinforces the case for a team of this kind.' (Obviously, given civil service impartiality, any transition team for Blair would have had to be mirrored by one for the opposition.)

A few days later, I had the opportunity to discuss this note with Blair himself at my monthly update meeting. I found him receptive, and set out the case. I urged him to think about the key people – ministers, permanent secretaries, political advisers – in teams. The best progress would be made, as I had pointed out to Cabinet in December, in departments where there was a guiding coalition at the top, connected to No. 10 and the Treasury, which readily understood what needed to be done and how. At the end of my lecture, Blair said, 'Thank you, doctor.' I never knew whether this was a reference to my faded academic qualifications or to his having felt like a patient being asked to take some strong medicine for his own good.

A few weeks later, acting on my advice (and no doubt that of others too), Blair had a final summit at Chequers before the election to go through the 'how' questions just as his summit in January had addressed the 'what' questions. In preparation for this meeting in March, I prepared Blair a further note, this time setting out what I called 'the Delivery Unit success factors'. I knew others were in the lead in making preparations for the third term, but I wanted the key lessons from my experience to influence what happened. There were five key lessons:

- The leader of the Delivery Unit or any successor function should have regular and direct access to the Prime Minister.
- Ruthless and sustained prioritisation would be vital – any idea

that the Prime Minister could have a function which monitored everything was undesirable and in any case a mirage.

- The Delivery Unit benefited from smallness; its successor should too.
- The partnership approach developed by the Delivery Unit would need to be built upon – rather than a reversion to traditional dysfunctional relations between the Cabinet Office and departments.
- Simple, clear methodologies need to be developed and adopted. (Here I had in mind all the key aspects of deliverology, which by this time were well understood and reflected across Whitehall.)

Blair commented that these were all sensible lessons. He was clearly considering wide-ranging reforms of the centre of government at the time of the Chequers meeting. These were discussed there and broadly approved, but with Blair a positive response to a change did not necessarily signal that he really wanted to do it. It all depended on his tone of voice and the expression on his face. If he said with alacrity that this is what he wanted, looked you in the eye and urged you to get on with it, you could be sure he wanted it done. If, on the other hand, he was unfocused, looking into the middle distance and said yes in a vague kind of way, it meant he wanted the work to go on but he was reserving the right to change his mind at a later date. Moreover, any radical change of the centre of government involved Gordon Brown, both because of its implications for the Treasury and because of Blair's public commitment to stand down before the end of the next parliament. Decisions such as these could only be taken by Blair and Brown having a private conversation.

There is another factor in deciding these organisational issues – the personality of the Prime Minister himself. Of course formal systems and processes matter hugely, but so does the way the particular individual who is Prime Minister works. The virtue of the flexibility of the British constitution, as Peter Hennessy has pointed out, is that it allows each Prime Minister to shape the role to suit him or her; its vice is that all form can be lost. There was a good example being debated in the weeks either side of the 2005 election. Leading civil servants had decided that formal Cabinet committees needed to replace stocktakes as part of re-establishing the traditional order. This would mean that instead of Health stocktake there would be a Health Cabinet committee. As with other Cabinet committees, this would mean not just the Prime Minister, the relevant secretary of state and the chief secretary attending, but also other ministers including the Chancellor and the Deputy Prime Minister. Moreover, it would mean establishing an agenda which covered reform as well as delivery. When Blair – eyes in the middle distance and speaking vaguely – said yes, there was much delight in the Cabinet Office that traditional control had been restored. It was pointed out as a matter of celebration that at last we would return to the norms of the Major era. I remained sceptical throughout, not least because the Cabinet of the Major era hardly seemed to represent best practice. At one point I even challenged Blair privately: 'Do you really want all these committees?'

What happened in practice after the election was that the committees did have a value, particularly to other participants. However, they did not offer the Prime Minister what he really wanted (and what suited his individual way of working), which was a sharp, informal, genuine exchange with a secretary of state about what was happening and what was planned. The stocktakes, when they worked well, gave him this. After the first of the new Cabinet committees, which took place shortly before I left, Blair exclaimed in exasperation, 'What's happened to my stocktakes?', exactly as I had anticipated.

As a consequence, stocktakes were reinstated but the Cabinet committees, because they had been established, were maintained too. The result, in my view, was a waste of prime ministerial time and a classic example of solving the wrong problem. The stocktakes, after all, had been one of the great successes of the second term, so much so that everyone wanted to replicate them. Moreover, though they weren't formally Cabinet committees, they were entirely formal and systematic in every other way – carefully prepared for, well used, well followed up, and considered by all participants as a good use of time. However, the fact that I felt secretly pleased that the first Cabinet committee had not gone well was a sure sign that it was time for me to leave. Had I been staying, I am sure I would have thought about how to make them work.

Time to go

From the second half of 2004 onwards, I had begun to think about what I might want to do after the Delivery Unit. I had committed myself for a full parliament, and never regretted sticking to that commitment. Equally, though, I was clear that I did not want to run the Delivery Unit through another parliament. As anyone who has founded a successful start-up company or charity knows, it is easy to slip into the mindset that no one else can do the job, and then slip further into 'I've seen all this before'. I hadn't reached that stage and I wanted to be sure I left before I did. In any case, I was ready for a new challenge. One possibility was a new task in government, and I was seriously tempted, not least because I had loved every minute of being there (including the stress), but in the end I decided to leave government altogether, at least for a while. I was swayed partly by the attraction of thinking about, and trying to solve in other countries, the problems I'd worked on in the UK, and partly by Karen's view that, fascinating though the ins and outs of the Labour government were, there was more to the world than that, and it would be nice to talk about something else occasionally! I was also swayed by the possibility of being able to buy Anja a house and finally establish her as an independent adult again, three years after her terrible accident. So I chose to become a consultant, helping governments around the world improve their performance. (As a cab driver remarked to me recently, 'You're unlikely to run out of work in that line any time soon.')

I discussed all this with Blair a number of times in the run-up to the election and found him (and his team) consistently supportive. He would have liked me to stay, but also completely understood. With individuals on my staff, I sometimes debated my dilemmas, and I'd been clear all the way through that my commitment to them, as well as to Blair, was only until the 2005 election. Four years earlier, after the 2001 election, when I set up the Delivery Unit, I had quit the Standards and Effectiveness Unit abruptly, leaving it in some disarray, which had had negative consequences for both people and policy. I wanted to avoid making the same mistake again.

Having made my decision by mid-April, I broke the news to one or two trusted colleagues and then the whole management team on an awayday a week before the election. Once they had got over the shock, they began to plan together how they would manage the transition between my departure and the arrival of a new leader. From that day onwards I began to reduce my input into management of the unit, even within a couple of weeks to the point of not attending management team meetings. Instead, I provided advice when asked for and access to key people in No. 10 and elsewhere when necessary.

Also, of course, I had to tell the whole staff, which I did on the Monday after the election. I told them that the departure of the pioneer was an opportunity to achieve new heights and that I'd stay until early July to secure both an orderly transition and the Delivery Unit's place in whatever new constellation of power emerged in the next few weeks.* Inevitably there was some uncertainty. I decided to allay this by persuading first Andrew Turnbull and then Blair himself to write notes asserting how important the Delivery Unit would continue to be. Turnbull wrote me an email which I circulated to the staff:

> It is clear the DU has made a lasting impact . . . the methods are so familiar now it is easy to forget how much intellectual capital they embody . . . Looking forward, the work of the DU will remain important, indeed more so as we enter a period of slower growth of resources.

This was heartening but of course everyone knew that Turnbull too was leaving. More reassuring was the fact that I had spoken to each of the candidates to be his successor, and they had all emphasised the importance of the Delivery Unit. Blair told me that in their conversations with him, each of them had said they saw the Delivery Unit approach as demonstrating the way forward: 'They thought you were on their side,' he explained. Blair understood immediately that the Delivery Unit staff would want reassurance from him, and, rather than sending a note, promised to come and talk to them just before I left.

I began to relax in that last month. There is only so much you can do once people know you're on your way out. I offered advice to staff about their careers, and made it through to the quarter-finals of the Treasury table football competition before choking on the brink of glory, unlike Liverpool, whom I watched miraculously defeating AC Milan in the European Champions League Final in Istanbul. I also spent time writing down some random thoughts for my staff, which I called '(Possibly False) Pearls'. Some of the points I've made about leaks, being

---

*If he had said it at the time, I would surely have quoted Michael Owen's explanation of why he has never watched a video recording of his famous goal against Argentina in 1998: 'You have to feel like you are always working towards your greatest achievement' (*Times*, 28 October 2006).

the unreasonable one and sharing credit are referred to elsewhere in this book. A few additional points are worth quoting here because they go to the heart of the culture we tried to create in the Delivery Unit:

> Always push the credit either out to departments . . . or up to the PM and the Cabinet Secretary . . . This has a double benefit – people like us better . . . moreover, the more we push it out the more credit we get in the long run. It is not a zero sum.

> I've worked hard at learning to ask questions; at getting better at listening; at monitoring the amount of time in a meeting I contribute (to see if I can reduce it . . .). Anyway, I read somewhere that experts answer questions; leaders ask them, which I think is true and a very demanding thought.

> Presentations to top officials and above all to ministers and the PM, especially at stocktakes, need to be really clear and simple. The presentation [on Health] this week was a classic example. Paul and Tom [two members of the Delivery Unit Health team] produced an excellent presentation – but we went through it again and again stripping it down so that each slide made one point and had no clutter. This takes time, but it's well worth it . . . We in the Delivery Unit should be the great simplifiers.

> Someone will need to be the guardian against management jargon and for plain English after I leave. Sometimes I've been overwhelmed by an incoming tide of it and failed completely, but it is an issue all the time . . . it poses a particular threat to relations with politicians. By the way, civil service jargon is just as bad. [Also] who will be the guardian of good grammar – conditionals, subjunctives and reported speech . . . Maybe I'm descending into 'Daily Getsmuchworse' mode, but I think grammar matters. It's all about conveying an impression.

Looking back, I can see that I was beginning to sound like a grumpy old man, even though I was still a few months short of my fiftieth birthday. It was definitely time to leave.

The day of Blair's visit to the Delivery Unit, 21 June, arrived. It was preceded by the last stocktake I ever attended and was followed by my final meeting in post with Blair. Appropriately, the stocktake was on education. My biggest fear, as with every stocktake, was that the PowerPoint technology wouldn't work, so for one last time Tony O'Connor and I arrived early in the Cabinet Room to check that all was set. Blair passed through on his way to the terrace, deep in conversation about foreign policy. Then Ruth Kelly and her team assembled. Blair returned and heard them present first on what standards they expected to reach in that year's tests and exams and then on their plans for implementing the radical proposals in the manifesto – more academies, allowing good schools to expand, encouraging new providers, and local authorities as commissioners of schools rather than managers of them. Behind the scenes, during the election campaign while the politicians were away, as we have seen, the department had been slow to advance this agenda, fearful of its consequences; we had been pushing them to be bold and urging them to put numbers to it – how many academies by when, how many schools would expand by when, and so on.

With the election out of the way, Kelly, assisted by Jacqui Smith and Andrew Adonis, had pressed her department for a more radical package and Blair was clearly pleased. He urged them to be ready to remove the barriers that he knew local authorities and the education establishment would put in their way. With support from Blair, I urged them to establish a national agency which would ensure recalcitrant local authorities could not block progress. (This became the Office of the Schools Commissioner.) In the meantime, returning to my perennial theme, I pointed out that no amount of radical legislation would affect the test results in the next twelve or even twenty-four months and they needed to maintain a steely gaze on literacy and numeracy performance in primary schools. I was happy that my last contribution to a meeting in the Cabinet Room was on exactly the same issue as my first had been in May 1997 – over the eight years significant progress had been made, but to their credit no one round the table thought the job was done.

Following the stocktake, Blair came over to the Treasury with me to meet the Delivery Unit staff. We walked from Downing Street through the Foreign Office and into the Treasury. It was a hot midsummer's day. Blair said he had enjoyed the education stocktake and I briefed him on the messages to convey to my staff. They were gathered in a Treasury meeting room not far from the Chancellor's office, which I pointed out to Blair. He decided to drop in unannounced. Gordon Brown intro-

duced the Prime Minister to his private office and special advisers. It
was a very cheerful moment.

From there, Blair came with me into the meeting room where the
Delivery Unit staff were assembled. He complimented them on their
achievements and said the Delivery Unit was the most successful change
he had made to the machinery of government. He was sad I was leaving,
he said, but that did not make the role of the Delivery Unit any less
important. He said he routinely read their reports, liked the stocktakes
and appreciated the fact that they didn't just monitor performance but
pitched in and helped. He told them that departments liked the way the
Delivery Unit related to them. At one point I chipped in to say, 'These
people are your streetfighters.'

'Yes,' said Blair, 'but they do it with such charm . . . I could do with
some lessons in how you do it to help with my negotiations in Europe.'*

Then he answered their questions and left them in no doubt that their
future was secure. As he got up to leave, he looked at the awful modern
art on the walls and asked if the room belonged to the Delivery Unit. I
told him that this was the Chancellor's meeting room. 'Did Gordon
choose the artwork?' he asked sceptically. On the way out, he dropped
in once more to see Brown, who joined us for part of the walk back to
No. 10. The artwork wasn't mentioned and the two of them were
entirely at ease discussing Europe – their shared view was that Europe
needed to be less introverted and much more focused on its place in the
wider, rapidly changing world.

When we came back into No. 10 I wasn't sure how much time I
would have for my final one-to-one meeting with the Prime Minister. It
was my good fortune that his diary was, for once, relatively free. We
walked through to the Cabinet Room, where he suggested I be
photographed sitting in his chair at the Cabinet table. From there we
walked out into the garden where children were playing cheerfully, and
sat down on a bench. Blair said he had been impressed by the staff and
their devotion to me. I said they were the best team I'd ever had the
pleasure of working with.

We talked about education, health and wider issues such as the
nature of the role of Prime Minister and his preparations for the

---

*Incidentally, all the Delivery Unit staff had been trained on principled negotiation
techniques and would have been happy to offer some advice.

forthcoming G8 summit, which he was due to chair at Gleneagles. We discussed how easy it is for Prime Ministers to become obsessive or even paranoid – Wilson and Major spring to mind – something which Blair had managed to avoid. He said that having school-age children while he was in No. 10 helped keep his feet firmly on the ground. I had prepared a list of delivery issues for Blair as I did for all our routine meetings, but had accidentally left it in the private office. I had also thought of a number of messages I wanted to leave him with at the start of his third term. For once he had time on his hands and, on the brink of leaving, I had the opportunity to be as blunt as I liked . . . but my mind went blank. Somehow, it didn't seem to matter. I had done what I could for him and, on a lovely English summer's day, any pearls of wisdom I had dredged out of the corners of my mind would no doubt have floated away on the breeze.

Back in his office, I gave him a book to read in his summer holidays: Edmund Morris's outstanding biography of Teddy Roosevelt as President, *Theodore Rex*. There were two reasons for the choice, I said. First, Roosevelt was my favourite President; second, I thought he was the politician in history who most resembled Blair – each propelled into leadership by an unexpected death, each dealing with globalisation at the turn of a new century, each persuasive and charismatic in public, each with young children while in office, each with a tendency towards activism in foreign policy, each committed to a pro-business, pro-competition policy in the economic sphere and each in favour of social policies which would reduce the burdens on the hard-working poor.

'Wasn't he a great hunter?' Blair asked, perhaps considering a new hobby. 'And how many terms did he serve?' came the next question.

'Two. He decided not to run for a third term in 1908 and always regretted it,' I replied, thoughtlessly missing the obvious parallel.

As I left Blair's office I thanked him for the opportunity to serve: 'It has been absolutely fantastic.' He agreed and said I should fix to see him once more before I left, but I knew that with his visit to Singapore where the decision on the 2012 Olympic Games would be made, and then to Gleneagles for the G8 summit, this would be impossible.

*

My last week in the Delivery Unit did not go according to plan. Until the Thursday morning it was a smooth, if sad, routine. I spent time packing books into crates, clearing out files and chatting with my staff. I had virtually no formal commitments. At lunchtime on Wednesday 6 July, the decision on where the 2012 Olympic Games would be held was due to be made public. I had made a bet (only for a Mars bar, I hasten to point out) with Keiran Brett on my staff, months earlier, that London would win. We all gathered round a television in the room shared by the Education team and the data analysts in the Delivery Unit* and leapt with delight when the result came through: London had beaten Paris to the great prize.

'Why did you think London would win?' Brett asked as I took delivery of my Mars bar.

'Give our Prime Minister an election to win and he wins it,' I said, 'whereas Chirac . . .'

That morning there had been more good news. Liverpool football club had announced that Steven Gerrard wasn't going to Chelsea after all. So when people gathered for my leaving party in the Treasury that evening there was a festive spirit. There were former colleagues from my time in the Department for Education as well as from the Delivery Unit. Several ministers and permanent secretaries as well as the outgoing and incoming Cabinet Secretaries were there. David Blunkett, back in the Cabinet, made a funny and touching speech which included the line 'He is New Labour down to the soles of his very expensive shoes': high praise indeed from him, if somewhat inaccurate.[†]

I replied, reminding Blunkett that I would always be grateful for the fact that he'd always given me space in which to work, while never being less than demanding. I thanked lots of people, but finished with advocacy on behalf of three groups to whom I was very attached. The first was bean counters:

> Why do they get such a bad name? What's wrong with counting beans? No one pretends that counting things is sufficient, but it is certainly a

---

*I asked them once why they had a television. They said it was there so that we could watch videos related to delivery. I asked what they had in fact watched, and they said, 'The World Cup 2002, the Rugby World Cup 2003, Euro 2004, the Athens Olympics and the 2005 Ashes Series.' Clearly they too were single-issue fanatics.

[†]My shoes were cheap Doc Martens from Kenny's on Kingsland Road, E8.

264 INSTRUCTION TO DELIVER

good start. Our Delivery Unit bean counters – who prefer to be called operational researchers or statisticians – have transformed the extent to which policy is informed by evidence and regular data is used to monitor progress. Journalists might mock sometimes, and professions might complain, but this is absolutely basic. No serious business would seek to run without these basic disciplines, so let's hear it for the bean counters.

Secondly, politicians – another breed which unfairly gets a bad name. We often get told they lack courage and are only interested in the short term. This was not my experience, I said, either in the present government or in the case of the Conservative politicians I had worked with in the mid-1990s. Many of the targets that they had set and we had been working on were ambitious and long term and had resulted in major improvements in performance from which citizens had benefited. Sometimes, in fact, setting these targets had been courageous, bordering on the politically foolhardy.

Finally I turned to my staff. They were multi-talented and very committed. I asked everyone in the audience to cherish them after I had gone. The party went on, at least for the hardcore of the Delivery Unit, well into the night. When I left, two colleagues were, appropriately enough, arguing (though with less cogency and more heat than usual) about how best to influence the Department of Transport.

The following morning the world was a different place. As I was coming out of the Cabinet Office through No. 10, I noticed a number of the top people involved in national security rushing in the other direction. Also, a Cabinet meeting was just breaking up. The television was saying that some 'power surges' had affected the Tube, but conveyed only a sense of confusion. I rushed back to the Treasury and piece by piece the story of the 7/7 suicide bombings began to emerge. Kate Myronidis began methodically to track down every member of the Delivery Unit staff to check they were OK. Karen rang from home and we checked up on each of our daughters. At lunchtime the Cabinet Office personnel department finally rang to suggest we accounted for our staff, but Myronidis had long since completed the task.

London was eerily quiet – a quiet punctuated occasionally by sirens. I encouraged people to go home early. I cycled as usual, but the atmosphere was quite different from ever before. No traffic and only the sound of Londoners walking, walking, walking. It was very moving. I found myself recalling those wartime broadcasts of Londoners waking up after a night in the Blitz and simply getting on with the day.

That evening my sister Lucy rang. The previous week my mother had had a stroke. We all thought she was recovering well, but that day Lucy had visited her in Warwick and thought she had taken a serious turn for the worse. There was no point trying to get to Warwick that evening, but early the next day I drove up. My mother had a chest infection; her breathing was strained, her skin was dry and cracking like parchment paper. For the first time I realised she was dying. So I missed my last day in the Delivery Unit – which would have been my 1,470th (Tony O'Connor counts everything) – and, absorbed in thoughts about my mother and my family, I only had time to send my staff the briefest of emails:

> I am very sorry not to be able to be with you on my last day . . . I have enjoyed every minute of my time working with you. You are a *fantastic* team and I look forward to hearing about your success in the future.
>
> Thanks for the friendship and commitment, and good luck.

8

Mission accomplished?

> Don't waste your second term like I did.
> Bill Clinton to Tony Blair, quoted in Anthony Seldon,
> *Blair*, p. 629

That summer I had two months off after I left the Delivery Unit before starting my new job. I spent much of the time with my mother as she almost literally faded away, and with my father and my family, but I also found myself thinking about what my previous eight years of working life had been about. What had we actually achieved? In relation to the public services, what was Tony Blair's legacy? How would history see it? I would love to have discussed it with him, but at that point he would have brushed it aside. Now I had left, I wanted to give some meaning to the project of which I had been a part.

The public services: history's verdict

Of course political legacies are very difficult to assess until long after a government has left office, so making judgements when a government's reforms are still in mid-flow is doubly dangerous. The fact is, though, that many commentators have already made these judgements. For example, in October 2005, the doyen of Whitehall watchers, Peter Riddell, published a book called *The Unfulfilled Prime Minister*, the title of which is a judgement in itself. His actual conclusions, certainly in relation to the public services, are muted although somewhat more positive than the title implies:

> [Blair] has paid the price for the earlier mistakes and the overselling of minor changes in public scepticism about later achievements. Even when there was clearcut evidence of improvements in health and primary schools, many voters believed the government was all spin and no

substance. While in the first term New Labour overpromised, and under-achieved, in the second term it was given insufficient credit for its much more firmly based achievements.[1]

Polly Toynbee and David Walker of the *Guardian*, with caveats, were more positive: 'Blair's era was a better time to be British than for many decades.'[2] Anthony Seldon updated his Blair biography to cover to the end of the second term, and described Blair's 'vast unfulfilled potential'.[3]* Others are even less sympathetic. Matthew Parris, who wrote an entertaining article about Tony Blair – so entertaining in fact that with a tweak here and there he published it again and again – dismissed him long ago. 'Such a store of early idealism, early trust . . . And all rotting away,' he wrote in one version of this single transferable article (*Times*, 16 March 2006). Meanwhile, Max Hastings in the *Guardian* (16 May 2006) called Blairism 'an unmitigated disaster' and Simon Jenkins concluded that the state under Blair 'was riven with inefficiency, waste and misdirected effort. It was not working.'[4] In short, the debate on the Blair legacy began even before he left office, and as a participant – obviously not an impartial one – I feel bound to join the fray, at least in relation to the public services.

The first point to make is one of context. The steady growth of the British economy, low unemployment and low inflation – a shared achievement of Blair and Gordon Brown – made possible steady and substantial increases in investment in health, education, policing and the other public services. Critics point to the fact that Blair and Brown inherited from John Major and Kenneth Clarke a reasonable legacy, which is true, but they took it and built upon it, which was not the story of previous Labour governments. Others say they have been lucky, but the truth is they rode major economic crises in Russia and the Far East, for example, as well as the dotcom crash without creating major financial imbalances or falling into recession for even a single quarter.† Other major economies, the United States, Japan, Germany and France among them, did not manage this.

* In *Blair Unbound*, published in the autumn of 2007, Seldon is distinctly more positive in his assessment. 'Blair became a more impressive figure in 2001–07 . . . notching up achievements at home and abroad . . . until the very end.' (Anthony Seldon, *Blair Unbound* (London: Simon & Schuster, 2007), pp. xii–xiv.)
† We will discover during 2008 whether they are able to ride the current 'sub-prime' crisis which originated in the USA.

This provides the backdrop to the discussion of public services because it was Brown's prudence in the early years in office, when there were many pressures to go on a traditional Labour spending spree, that allowed what came later. By paying off large chunks of the national debt and reducing unemployment, Brown made it possible by 2000 to spend 80p of each tax pound on the public services, whereas just three years earlier 50p of each pound went on debt repayments and the social security costs of unemployment. The combination of this added impact of each pound on the public services with the real increases in expenditure sustained over the decade from 1998 to 2008), has provided the greatest opportunity to transform the public sector since the Second World War.

But the growth in investment is not the central issue: that is common ground across the spectrum, with Blair's friends pointing to it as an achievement and his critics as a waste of taxpayers' money. What is at issue, therefore, is whether the government's reforms really have exploited the opportunity provided and delivered improved performance and transformed service commensurate with the scale of new investment.

So, how does it all measure up? The first point to make is that if you look at the hard numbers, results on almost every aspect of the public services have improved, and in some cases dramatically improved. Primary school pupils can now read and write and do mathematics much better than their predecessors a decade ago and probably much better than any previous generation. Children's spelling in 2005 was shown to be twelve to eighteen months ahead of their predecessors' in 1975.[5] They also compared well on reading and maths standards with the rest of the world. Relative performance on these indicators slipped after 2001, but performance in global terms in 2007 was above average although short of world class. Secondary school pupils achieve better results in GCSEs, A-levels and vocational qualifications, and there is significant evidence that schools in disadvantaged circumstances have narrowed the gap between themselves and the rest of the country. Certainly results in the five most challenging inner London boroughs have improved much faster than the national average. In addition, the extent of outright school failure has been massively reduced. If we want our schools to be world class there is more to do, and much greater consistency of quality at school and classroom level will be required, but nevertheless the progress over a decade is substantial.

In health, waiting times are dramatically reduced for all kinds of surgery and in Accident and Emergency departments. Mortality rates are dropping steadily and care for patients with cancer and coronary heart disease is often now exemplary. In the case of crime, the large-volume crimes – vehicle crime and burglary in particular – have fallen steadily, and the chances of being a victim of crime in 2005 were the lowest they had been since records began (in 1981). There are problems too though, with street crime, after the falls in 2002–3, now rising again. Some types of violent crime may be on the increase and are certainly too high, and anti-social behaviour, while it might now be declining, remains a blemish on many localities. Meanwhile, in spite of the periodic media orgies, the criminal justice system is also performing better than it used to. Trials are more likely to take place on time, and fines and community penalties are more likely to be enforced. The percentage of crimes being detected is up, and police are more visible on the streets.

With railways, after the disastrous first term, which culminated in the system's collapse after the Hatfield crash, there has been a slow but steady recovery. Punctuality is the highest it has been since 1999–2000 and is still rising. There is a great deal of new rolling stock, and the major challenges now are those of excess demand, with too many passengers and too few trains on a network that for forty years was starved of investment. A similar picture emerges in the case of road congestion, where the problem is being better managed, but the remorseless rise, even in a period of expensive fuel, in car use will lead to higher congestion in the long term unless more and better roads are built and road pricing is introduced.

In spite of the vast increase in pressure on the asylum and immigration system, even here there is evidence that its capacity to process applications, prevent illegal asylum seekers getting into the country and remove those that are here has improved.

Before anyone accuses me of giving a starry-eyed account, let me make it clear that I believe it goes without saying that much of this progress, while important, is not enough. My message to the Cabinet in December 2004 is still valid – much of this improvement was from 'awful' to 'adequate' whereas what people want is 'good' and 'great'. There are aspects of our public services which really are good and great

– plenty of individual schools and hospitals, for example – but overall our public services still fall short of what the 21st-century public rightly demands. If the numbers were all we had to go on in judging Blair's track record, we would have to say that, while they are to his credit and are still mostly heading in the right direction, they do not add up to the transformative change he promised.

However, there is more to the argument than these numbers. There are some positive and fundamental changes behind the numbers which are rarely commented on, but which will have major significance in the long term; there are also some open questions. Let me list four of the former and two of the latter.

1. A *new strategic framework for the public services*

The entire strategic framework for the public services has been radically changed for the better. Again there is much more that could be done, as I shall set out in Chapter 9, but five-year strategic planning, three-year funding settlements, the publication of targets and results, and the independence of the Office of National Statistics have entirely changed the rules of the policy game. No Prime Minister and Chancellor in history have been as willing as Blair and Brown to be judged on measurable results. Gordon Brown as Prime Minister has gone still further in this direction, insisting that all local authorities, as well as central government, publish results on 198 indicators of interest to citizens, while Ed Balls, the Schools Secretary, has plans to establish a new independent school standards watchdog. At times, particularly when being publicly chastised by the media, they must wish that they had not been so transparent, but the overall consequence has been extremely beneficial. The message has been that everyone, government included, is accountable for the results they deliver. Thus David Blunkett was the first Education minister in history to have his performance judged by how well children did in schools on his watch. Alan Milburn's track record in Health depended similarly on demonstrably reducing waiting times. As Toynbee and Walker point out, 'New Labour . . . deserved to be known as the most scrupulously self-monitoring government ever.'[6] This new framework has brought much-needed discipline to policy-making by ensuring that, more than ever, hard evidence is taken into account in preparing policy proposals, which makes long-term success more likely. Moreover, it will be a lasting legacy; it is hard to imagine any future government choosing to return to one-year spending settlements or not publishing results. It might not choose to have published targets, depending on how courageous it is, but the shambolic amateurism that used to characterise public service policy-making is unlikely to return.

2. A transformed public sector infrastructure

The public sector infrastructure – buildings, broadband and the like – has been utterly transformed and barely commented upon. The vast majority of school buildings have been radically improved, with thousands of schools being built or rebuilt, and the same is true of hospitals, GPs' surgeries and police stations. As if to emphasise the point, on 18 August 2006 there was a media controversy in which, according to the *Times*, public health specialists responded 'with fury' to government approval for a further six new hospitals as part of the largest hospital-building programme in history because they thought the money could have been better spent on other things. That single announcement proposed more new hospitals than were built in the entire Thatcher era. Doctors' leaders back then would have shaken their heads in disbelief had someone told them that within twenty years their successors would be complaining that too many hospitals were being built!

Moreover, most of the public buildings being built in this current phase are aesthetically pleasing and built for the long term, unlike the products of the previous big building programme in the 1960s, which even twenty years later were often looking tawdry and beginning to crumble. We can add to this the electronic whiteboards, broadband connections and major investment in IT equipment and capability. I fully expect that in twenty-five years' time people will look back on the Blair–Brown capital investment programme and see it as marking the moment when a whole new standard was set for the public sector infrastructure, an achievement comparable with social security in the 1909 Budget and the establishment of the NHS in 1948.

3. A transformed public sector workforce

Similarly, the growth in number and increase in quality of the various public sector workforces will prove to be a lasting achievement. In 2006, doctors who started medical training as a result of its expansion in the Blair first term began to join the Health Service. Of course, they have yet to make much impact on its performance, but from now on and for perhaps thirty years they will be making an impact. As described in Chapter 1, in 1999–2000 there was a major problem of teacher shortage. This is no longer true. Recruitment to teacher-training is up, even in traditional shortage subjects such as science and maths. Many people in the 25–35 age bracket are switching to teaching. (Indeed in this age group, remarkably, teaching is the first choice for career switchers; in 2000 it was the ninety-second choice!) Again, this large new intake has barely had time to impact on the results of the education service, but many of them will do so for the next 20–30 years. There are also record numbers of police, and in all these areas – health, education and policing – there are growing support workforces too: more nurses and healthcare assistants, more classroom assistants, more community support officers. The training and development of all these groups have also been demonstrably improved. The December 2007 announcement that newly trained teachers will have the opportunity to gain a master's qualification to further enhance their classroom skills is a case in point. In short, underprovision in all these areas, which characterised these services for much of the post-war era, as the result in part of policy and in part of economic weakness, is now a thing of the past. Future governments of whatever political persuasion are unlikely to want to undo this new settlement.

4. A new public expenditure settlement

The new buildings and the growth in numbers of public service professionals and other staff are only possible because of the new public expenditure settlement. Spending in health and education now matches or exceeds OECD levels as a percentage of GDP. Most of my generation grew up implicitly aware that Britain was running its public services on the cheap. If we were activist about public service issues, it was to fight 'cuts'. Suddenly we find ourselves in an entirely new era where our services are well funded, our doctors and teachers are well paid and the buildings they work in rather impressive. To take just one example: in relation to the provision of under-fives education, this country went from being one of the world's laggards to one of the world's leaders in just eight years. Sometimes, though, our ingrained mental models have not caught up with the new reality. For example, you can almost hear the relief among public service union general secretaries when they have the chance to leap on a temporary funding crisis such as that in education in 2004 or in health in 2006, because they know how to do victim status.

This leads to a central aspect of the Blair-Brown legacy. In the mid-1990s one of the underlying dilemmas of British politics was whether we wanted on the one hand to spend around 40 per cent of GDP on the public expenditure and make public services so good that the growing number of well-off people would still choose them, even though they could afford the private alternative, or on the other to spend around 30 per cent of GDP, encourage those who could afford the private alternative to take it, and merely provide safety net public services for the poor. This debate is now over for a generation and it might turn out to be as substantial an achievement historically as Attlee's welfare state, not so much because of what happens but because of what does not. At the 2005 election, the Conservatives promised to match the government's public expenditure commitments in health and education, and David Cameron has even promised to increase expenditure on the public services if he is elected. Anatole Kaletsky, one of the shrewdest political commentators, identified this as a defining characteristic of modern politics during the run-up to that election:

> The core idea of modern Conservatism as reinvented by Margaret Thatcher and Ronald Reagan – that state intervention even when well-intentioned is rarely a benign force and that great social challenges can be met by reducing the role of government, instead of increasing it – is simply not on the political agenda . . . Mr Blair, whatever his other failings, has one great achievement to his credit. After 20 years of Thatcherite reform designed to reduce the size of the public sector . . . Blairism has restored faith in government as a creative and essentially benign force . . . Until the Tories are ready to rejoin this debate in earnest . . . Blairism, rather than Thatcherism, will be Britain's dominant political creed.[7]

The point has been reinforced by developments since the 2005 election. As Peter Riddell has argued in the *Times*:

> For Mr Blair the extension of parental and patient choice and increased diversity, are meant both to help children in deprived areas (where most academies are being set up) and persuade the middle class to use the state

system. This strategy is now producing results and has the backing of the Conservatives.[8]

Meanwhile, in the *Economist* a week later, Bagehot argued: 'The three main parties have thus converged on a common position, endorsing a tax burden of two-fifths of GDP . . . That is much higher than in America, but a bit lower than in the euro area.'[9]* In short, the argument is, the political landscape has been transformed. As a result, the political debate has now shifted, legitimately and helpfully, to the question of how to achieve the most impact with that 40 per cent of GDP. In other words, the biggest threat to the new settlement is not so much from pure politics as from a failure of those who work in the public sector – including future governments – to deliver results. Leaders within the public services – to put it bluntly – need to put victim status behind them and begin to strain every muscle not just to deliver improved performance, but to demonstrate it to the taxpaying public.

Incidentally, if there were a future government that proposed cutting public expenditure, it would find it much harder than in the past for another reason, namely that funding has far more than previously (and more than in most other countries) been devolved to the frontline – the school, the primary care trust, the basic command unit. The vast bulk of schools funding is devolved to schools themselves, with headteachers and governors deciding how to spend it. Similarly, primary care trusts have extensive discretion. Any cuts, therefore, would be immediately apparent to parents, patients and citizens, who could be expected to protest loudly.

Even if all we did was accept the conclusion in Riddell's book, which I think is far too cautious, we would have to agree that Blair has had a positive impact:

> There have been obvious pluses – the stability of the economy, low inflation and interest rates; the rate of job creation; the reduction in child and pensioner poverty; definite evidence of improvement in the NHS and, more ambiguously, in schools; the big expansion of pre-school and

---

* Just over a year later the *Economist* argued that 'the time is right to ditch the long cross-party consensus about taxation (broadly that whatever level Mr Brown set – now some 40% of GDP – is correct)' ('The emperor's new clothes', *Economist*, 13 October 2007). This seems improbable but the fact that the argument is being made will add to the pressure to deliver results.

nursery provision; the beginnings of a credible long-term funding structure for universities; and a partial, though uneven shift, to a more pluralist and less centralist structure of government. And, despite the terrorist attacks of July 2005 and worries over street crime and disorderly behaviour, Britain is generally a safer place in which to live.

In many of these areas there are as many qualifications as unequivocal verdicts . . . it would be premature to say, for instance, that secondary education policy is yet a success, even though there are many positive signs in school results and in the recruitment of teachers. No one can say that transport policy is yet more than an ambivalent work-in-progress.[10]

Even on this account, Blair's achievements are substantial. Now to the two open questions.

5. New operating models?
The biggest question mark over the legacy is whether the new operating models for the major public services, especially health and education, turn out to be effective and resilient. Much of the debate earlier in the book has been about the transition from the top-down approach of the early Blair phase, when the aim was to establish basic minimum standards, to the more sustainable but also more complex model which depends on devolution, transparency, choice and quasi-markets. This transition – which Matthew Taylor, one of Blair's key policy advisers until 2006, has called a Copernican revolution because it shifts the user to the centre of the public service universe – is not complete. The trials and tribulations of the Health Service in 2006, to take just one example, are testament to how difficult it is to bring about, and illustrate perfectly how at the first sign of difficulty those who want to turn the clock back to the (inadequate) past leap at the chance. In addition, it remains to be seen whether, at the top of Whitehall, there are sufficient people with the capacity to implement strategies so challenging. Clearly, too, mistakes have been made on the way – as preceding chapters have described – and these add to the challenge. Finally, the plans remain politically controversial both within the Labour Party and within the public services. For all these reasons, the reforms are not yet irreversible. Whether they become so depends on sustained momentum in the years ahead.*

*See Chapter 9 for further discussion of the factors involved.

Personally, I am optimistic that these reforms will ultimately work well but it is no wonder that Blair regretted the lack of progress during his first term and the time he lost before he came round to reforming the civil service.

6. The start of something?
The final point is raised by the previous one. The judgement of the Blair legacy will ultimately depend on – as they might put it on *A Question of Sport* – what happens next. Take an example: during his second term, Blair's higher education reform, including the introduction of variable fees, scraped through Parliament at substantial political cost to him. Now universities are saying they would have sunk without the change, but supposing in a few years' time a government keen to pander to middle-class sensibilities and students unwinds that reform rather than extending it. Then the Blair reform would look like an aberration or missed opportunity, depending on your point of view. It certainly wouldn't be the first major step in a radical transformation. Ultimately, therefore, the judgement of Blair's public service reforms will be affected by the extent to which his successors build on them. As Bagehot accurately put it shortly after the 2005 election:

> It took the best part of a decade before the full impact of Margaret Thatcher's economic reforms was felt. Because Mr Blair took a while to get into his stride, his public service reforms are still very recent and only now gaining some momentum. Frustratingly for him, he is likely to be long gone from office before he really knows whether he has a legacy that is any kind of match for Lady Thatcher.[11]

In relation to the whole public services area – even in education and health, where they are furthest advanced – Bagehot's point is valid. I think the progress Blair made already compares well historically, and all the evidence suggests that the Brown administration will build on this progress rather than reverse it, but it will be some time before the true extent of the legacy becomes clear.

Society: history's verdict

If this is the profit-and-loss account on the public services, what about the wider issue of whether the public service reforms, combined with other major strands of reform such as the attack on child poverty, have made Britain the more cohesive, fairer society that Blair has promised? There is a great deal of evidence that they have. Lest I be accused of bias, let the case be made by none other than Matthew Parris, one of Blair's fiercest critics, who at the end of 2006 finally wrote an entirely new article about Blair.

> The truth is that there is just one good thing I can say about this Prime Minister, but that it is a very big thing indeed. Britain is a nicer place than when he entered Downing Street nearly ten years ago. His premiership has placed his personal stamp on a genuinely new era for Britain – an altered culture, a permanent change in our national mood.
>
> Without any shadow of a doubt, Mr Blair will leave a happier country than he found. Something tolerant, something amiable, something humorous, some lightness of spirit in his own nature, has marked his premiership and left its mark on British life . . .
>
> The association of New Labour . . . with what we might call the spirit of the age has been very strong. Head and shoulders above the rest of his administration, Tony Blair, the man himself, in himself, has embodied the modernity.
>
> Concrete examples – the way this has been translated into politics – are as slight and individually as seemingly trivial as they are legion. You would expect me to mention civil partnerships, the scrapping of the 'Section 28' prohibition on the promotion of homosexuality in schools, the equalising of the age of consent, and the ending of the ban on gays in the Armed Forces; but this programme of repeals, though bringing big changes for the minority of which I am part, is more significant for the small changes it has reinforced in the attitudes of the majority.
>
> The minimum wage (towards which I was at first sceptical) is another big change for a minority that signals a small civilising of majority attitudes. Many of us now feel quietly pleased to live in a country that cares – and takes legislative measures to show it – about the poorest paid. Childcare provision, the 'social inclusion agenda', relaxations on licensing hours, the reclassification of cannabis, a relentless campaign of

oratory and example of religious tolerance, and a brave opening of the doors to Eastern European labour from the new EU members, are all further examples of a phenomenon for which the term 'raft' of measures has become a dreadful cliché, but which has meaning here. I like this raft. I like its drift. I like its rainbow flag.

And there has been, as gradual as it is signal and (I hope) permanent, a steady reduction in the level of general censoriousness in public life . . .

This is now Blair's Britain: a trite phrase, I know, but the world did change. Mr Blair is associated with that change, but more than associated with it: as our Prime Minister he has been a presiding mind, a presiding imagination. By no means has he created the new mood but he has caught the mood and run with it, and in running with it, validated it . . .

In democratic politics it is no small thing to catch a changed wind early, to let it fill your sails, and to help steer the spirit of a nation into different waters. This Mr Blair has done with a deftness, with a sensitivity to national mood that has been unequalled by any British politician I can remember. And the result has been good. That at least is a legacy of which he should be proud.'[12]

All this is a huge gain, but two serious questions remain to be answered. The first is that, while there is considerable evidence that Britain, especially London, has become a more tolerant, more successful multi-racial society in the past decade, there are some fundamental challenges. The immediate one – rightly receiving extensive attention since 7 July 2005 – involves the relationship between Islam and modern British society and especially the question of the upbringing and education of Muslim young men. This is not the place to open up that debate, but it is doubtful whether there is a coherent strategy yet in place to tackle the issue, though Ruth Kelly and other ministers began to open up the debate. More fundamental in the long term may be the wider question of whether British society has really come to terms with the change in its make-up in the past decade. We have experienced the biggest wave of immigration since the 1950s and 1960s, indeed perhaps ever, and while the economic benefits are apparent, the wide-ranging social implications for the long term have barely been touched on. Indeed, because much of the immigration has been illegal, the government has sometimes preferred to narrow the scope of the debate. Yet 30 per cent of London's present workforce was born outside the UK. As

Trevor Phillips, chairman of the Commission for Equalities and Human Rights, has argued, 'We desperately need immigrants to sustain our workforce. But in this new world of more rapid and more diverse immigration, coupled with an unprecedented threat to global security, we cannot pretend there are no costs.'[13]

What we know from post-war history is that a failure to open up and confront promptly the issues raised by immigration in the 1950s and 1960s caused major social dislocation in the 1970s and 1980s – Brixton and Toxteth spring to mind. If we are to avoid similar long-term consequences of the much more diverse immigration of the past decade, as government ministers among others have indicated, we shall have to do much better than the tepid combination of liberal relativism and hand-wringing which characterises much of the present public response. This is why the emphasis placed on Britishness by, among others, Gordon Brown and David Blunkett, is so important and far from purely theoretical. It is also why it is important to deliver demonstrable results – in education, health and crime reduction, for example – for all citizens, regardless of their background.

The second underlying social issue which remains unresolved in spite, in this case, of numerous attempts to tackle it, is the really tough end of poverty and social exclusion, especially in decaying urban areas. In some ways, in fact, the problem is exacerbated simply because of the steadily growing prosperity of the majority. Liverpool – my home town – is significantly transformed and in 2008 is European Capital of Culture. The city centre and the Albert Dock heave with shops and restaurants. Similar, and in some cases even more dramatic, transformations have affected Manchester, Newcastle and Cardiff, to mention just three great cities. But in each case, within walking distance of those thriving city centres are blighted estates, urban decay and people trapped in miserable lives. And among that group is a minority of truly dysfunctional families for which the state has, as yet, no answers.

For all the talk, money and even action in relation to social exclusion – and here the government deserves credit for putting it on the agenda – the results have fallen short of expectations. I was there in the south London school for the launch of the Social Exclusion Unit in 1998. It had a great mission and a glorious first phase, but when its flamboyant founding director, Moira Wallace, left, it followed the trajectory of most Whitehall units and became a backwater, absorbed in the name of tidiness into the quagmires of bureaucracy. (Belatedly, Hilary Armstrong tried to rescue its mission after she was given her new Cabinet Office role in the 2006 reshuffles, and her work has been built on since by Ed Miliband.) The New Deal for Communities, Neighbourhood Renewal and other initiatives each had their moment in the sun and then disappeared from sight, though the money kept being spent. In my view, the reason why these programmes delivered insufficient in the way of return was that they were too loosely defined, gave money to local authorities and other partners at local level without any assessment of whether they had the capacity to spend it well, and failed to put in place a system for learning from experience what worked so that best practices could be adopted and spread. Where the money found its way into the hands of talented social alchemists, it brought benefits, but often it did not. Even with popular programmes such as SureStart, which provides support and advice to parents of very young children, there have been real problems in relation to equity because it relies on parents to turn up voluntarily. Aspirant parents lap up the service, the professionals who offer it generate a feel-good factor around it, but the parents who really need the service – the very young, the drug-using, the downtrodden and the crushed – often don't bring their babies and toddlers along. Why, given the lack of self-esteem they feel, would they choose, without persuasion, to spend time with the educated professionals and super-confident mums they would meet there? Again, after bravely evaluating SureStart's impact, the government is now refocusing the programme constructively, but it will need hard-headed consistency in implementation if it is to maximise its impact.

All too often, the programmes aimed at the most socially excluded were based on a combination of good intentions and plenty of money, which was never likely to work. As a result, the Blair government's impact on social equity was blemished. Now, there have been major gains as a result of the minimum wage, the incentivisation of work and tax credits for those who make it into work. The strongest evidence of this is the significant reduction in child poverty, with nearly a million fewer children living in poverty than a decade ago. Pensioner poverty has also been significantly reduced. Most importantly, as John Rentoul argues, 'the overall gap between rich and poor has narrowed under Labour . . . Office for National Statistics data on "the effects of taxes and benefits on household income 2004–5" show the most equal distribution of post-tax income since 1987.'[14] There have also been gains for the lower half of the income distribution, where public service outcomes – as with literacy and numeracy in education and choice and waiting times in health – have levelled up.

However, for a small, significant (and expensive) minority not enough progress has been made. There are programmes for pupils who are excluded from school or have excluded themselves (truants), but they have often been poorly implemented. More than 30,000 pupils leave school every year with no qualifications at all (not even a single GCSE grade E in art*) and find themselves in an unequal struggle in the jobs market with, for example, Polish graduates, and there are swathes of people holed up in housing estates claiming incapacity benefit and watching the world go by with a jaundiced and sometimes desperate eye. Robert Peston has given a balanced account:

> Brown's redistribution . . . has not been trivial. And it has not been confined to helping the working poor, to the exclusion of the unemployed, quite as much as his public statements might suggest . . . almost all the increments in tax credits have been replicated in increases in income support to the non-working impoverished.
>
> On the other hand, the extremely indigent, the absolute poorest, seem to have missed out.[15]

The figures he provides (from the Institute of Fiscal Studies) bear this out. While the incomes of the bottom 40 per cent have indeed risen faster than those of the rest of the population, which when bench-marked against the US, for example, is a spectacular achievement, 'the incomes of the very poorest . . . have actually fallen'.[16] In short, while the bottom 40 per cent have benefited significantly from both economic/fiscal and public service reforms, between 2 per cent and 5 per cent have fallen further behind.

At the start of the third term, the government showed signs of seeking once again to get to grips with these two major problems, which are at once social, economic and moral. Ruth Kelly reopened the debate on

---

*I single out art not because it is easier than other subjects in any general sense but because success in the subject depends less on being literate; therefore it has always been a good option for those whom the school system failed to teach to read and write well.

multi-culturalism. John Hutton proposed the kind of radical reform of incapacity benefit that should have been embarked upon years ago. Hilary Armstrong looked at how to tackle the minority of truly dysfunctional families. Since Gordon Brown became Prime Minister, the social security reforms have been driven forward and the new Department for Children, Schools and Families has sharpened the focus on these issues. This is encouraging, but I think even more radical approaches should be considered.

The lessons of the Delivery Unit experience would suggest a radical departure in tackling social exclusion. The government spends money on downtrodden places through programmes such as Neighbourhood Renewal; it spends money on institutions in those same places through, for example, supporting schools in challenging circumstances; and it spends money on individuals in those same places through the benefits system, especially incapacity benefit. Suppose all that money was unlocked and combined, and a competent entity established at a very local level (much more local than a local authority) to spend it. Surely then major inroads could be made into these deeply intractable problems? To work, such an approach would have to learn some hard lessons from the past few years, such as:

- **Precise targeting**
Precise targeting is crucial. You have to make sure the money is being spent on those it is aimed at.
- **Incentives**
You have to incentivise escaping from poverty and social exclusion rather than rewarding those who wallow in it (which is why Hutton's determination to reform incapacity benefit is so important).
- **Alternative providers**
You need to bring in alternative (often voluntary sector) providers where the state is failing. Talented, idealistic, committed people would be required at ground level to run such programmes.
- **Prescription**
You have to be prescriptive in demanding that all providers gather data, identify best practices, apply them and are then held to account for results.
- **Empowered customers**
You have to empower the customers, even when they are the poorest

members of society, rather than hand them over to the professionals.
• **Check and check and check**
Finally, you have to check and check and check again that the pro-
grammes are being implemented properly.

As the *Economist* pointed out after the government announced its
new, highly interventionist policy on dysfunctional families, 'charities
broadly welcome the new emphasis on early and active intervention . . .
Ministers insist that vulnerable groups need all the help they can get,
whether they want it or not.'[17] Amen to that. This all sounds rather
tough, and might be unpopular in the short term, but tackling gross
inequality always is, because it involves shifting whole swathes of
people – customers and providers – out of their comfort zone.

Interpreting the world

Before concluding this assessment, one further point needs to be made.
Great leaders have the capacity to interpret the changing world for the
people of their country, even if this means conveying some tough and
unpalatable messages. Clearly Margaret Thatcher was able to do this on
economic and labour market issues. She built on the courage that Jim
Callaghan and Denis Healey had displayed – not always with the
support of their colleagues – in the late 1970s. By contrast, among
contemporary leaders, it seems evident that some are less willing to play
this part. Jacques Chirac, for example, completely failed to level with
the French people about the consequences of globalisation. Recent talk
there of 'economic patriotism' only reinforces the lack of realism.
Similarly, as Thomas Friedman argues throughout *The World is Flat*,
many of America's political leaders are burying their heads in the sand,
whether on the right by arguing that America can go it alone, or on the
left by supporting the tariff barriers promoted by some unions to
protect obsolete jobs.

Blair, meanwhile, in spite of the accusation that he is all spin,
measured up well on this test. He levelled with the British people about
the challenges globalisation presents. At Labour Party conference in
2006, he argued: 'The British people are reluctant global citizens. We
must make them confident ones.' Nor did he run away from the security

challenges after 9/11 or 7/7. He was right to convey the unpopular message that 'the rules of the game have changed'. Meanwhile, on the public services he insistently conveyed the message that they would have to change to meet the twenty-first century's exacting demands. One can argue about whether his view was right, or about whether his policies were as good as they could have been, but he told it straight, and Gordon Brown was four-square behind him. As a *Times* editorial put it on 7 June 2006:

> Two speeches, one delivered by Gordon Brown, the Chancellor, on Monday and the other by Tony Blair yesterday, are the starkest evidence yet that the era of excessive public spending is drawing to a close . . . Mr Blair, in effect, warned the public sector that if it could not produce tangible results shortly, the willingness of the public to forgo tax cuts in exchange for supposed superior services could no longer be expected.

It is easy to miss how hard-hitting this message is. After all, it involves a Prime Minister who had been in office nine years at the time pointing out that performance – in services that have been at the heart of his agenda throughout – is not good enough. Many politicians in these circumstances would have chosen the soft option of selling the successes.* (Incidentally, those who say the glass is half empty sometimes have a point which is rarely acknowledged.)

My overall conclusion – and for the reasons I have given, any conclusion at this stage is provisional – is that, in spite of the blemishes and uncertainties, Blair's achievements in relation to the public services and society were substantial and will turn out to be long-lasting. The combination of new investment, improved results and radical reform could, if built upon in future, result in an entirely new settlement of similar scale and long-term impact to that wrought by Clement Attlee in the late 1940s. It is worth remembering that in 1950 and 1951 many

---

*This in my view is why Blair stands ahead of Harold Macmillan as a Prime Minister. Peter Hennessy's judgment on Britain in 1960 makes the point: 'The country should have felt a greater sense of urgency about its relative economic performance, its place in Europe and the wider world. But comfortable societies can be very difficult to invigorate' (*Having It So Good* (London: Allen Lane, 2006), p. 621). I'm not sure Hennessy would agree with me but I don't think Macmillan tried hard enough; in similarly comfortable times, Blair certainly did.

people wrote Attlee off as having failed.

Tony Blair's personal leadership of this agenda was vital and impressive: he consistently advocated the vision, demonstrated a grasp of strategy and learnt from early mistakes, and he constantly led from the front. When many in public services and even some of his colleagues urged consolidation, he always countered by demanding boldness and urgency. While of course more might have been achieved, as the former Prime Minister himself would no doubt accept, the scale of the achievement compares well to similar areas of reform in the past and owes a great deal to the former Prime Minister. Those who are writing Blair off now will, I think, find in twenty-five years' time that history has on the whole been kinder to him.* We shall see. Either way, with reference to the quote at the start of this chapter, it seems clear that Blair avoided Bill Clinton's error.

The Delivery Unit's impact

Whether or not my judgements in the previous section turn out to be correct, it is also important in this book to examine briefly the contribution made by the Delivery Unit. There is no doubt in my mind, and others involved confirm this, that the Delivery Unit made a significant contribution to delivering improved results and meeting the targets for which it was given responsibility (for a table of results, see the Delivery Manual, Document 10).

How the Delivery Unit contributed has also become clear by now:

- Establishing and sustaining clear priorities;
- Applying good, clear, simple methods ('deliverology');
- Ensuring good people were in key positions of responsibility whether in the Delivery Unit or departments;
- Clarifying and checking the strength of all the links in the delivery chain;
- Building good, plain-speaking, honest relationships between departments and the unit so that problems could be identified early and, more often than not, rectified;
- Securing good collaboration between departments on cross-cutting issues such as drugs and the criminal justice system;

---

*As has become clear in the course of this book, I only bet Mars bars, but if anyone would like to take a bet on this judgement and doesn't mind waiting . . .

- Building and maintaining the routines which drive performance.

Much of this is simple and obvious, but then so much of human progress is based on the systematic application of simple truths. Overall, though, there was huge potential in the discipline of delivery – a common language of delivery, an evidence base of what worked which transcended departmental boundaries, and a great deal of that knowledge made explicit and learnable so that it could be applied elsewhere. In these ways the Delivery Unit made a contribution far beyond the progress on the targets for which it was responsible, important though they were. It also developed and then modelled in practice a new way to build relationships between the centre of government and departments. Implicitly this strengthened the relationship between the Prime Minister and Cabinet ministers. Certainly it enabled the Prime Minister and the government as a whole to deliver their priorities substantially better than would otherwise have been the case. The implications of this for the future are the subject of the final chapter of this book, but before turning to them, it is important to be honest about any possible negative impact the Delivery Unit had.

First of all, by forcing prioritisation, it inevitably attracted talent – in terms of the best civil servants, for example – and sometimes money to the issues on which it focused. This is, of course, what it means to prioritise and at one level, therefore, is fully justified. Even so, it has to be recognised that in some cases this had negative consequences for policy areas outside those priorities. The Home Office, for example, made good progress on its PSA targets but, as events in 2006 and its capability review revealed, its underlying fragility as an organisation remained after the targets had been achieved.

A critique, much beloved of public service professionals who wanted to resist targets and accountability in order to preserve the quieter life of the past, was that the Delivery Unit distorted its priorities. Sometimes this led to absurd claims such as those made in the *Sunday Telegraph* on 10 April 2005. Under the headline 'Targets can kill', its editorial quoted a hospital specialist in Epsom, Surrey, objecting to the use of a day surgery unit as an overflow for A&E. 'It is simply not acceptable to be nursing a patient with copious, foul-smelling diarrhoea in an open area with no sluice.' Of course it's not, we would all agree, but the *Sunday Telegraph* wanted to make a point by suggesting a causal connection that did not exist. It went on:

That dangerous and unacceptable practice was the direct result of Tony Blair's policy towards the NHS. Epsom NHS Trust had, only days before, been summoned to give a presentation to the Prime Minister's 'Delivery Unit' to explain why it was failing to meet the Unit's target that no one should wait more than four hours in A&E. The pressure on managers to meet its targets was, and is, relentless.

I plead guilty – almost entirely – to the charge in the last sentence. Hospital managers were invited to a meeting with me and others and the pressure was relentless because meeting the target was a question of establishing a minimum standard which the public had a right to expect. In fact, if you ask most patients, they think four hours is far too long to wait! The part of this charge I reject is the implication that the target could only be met by putting patients' lives at risk. For one thing, it had always been clear that clinical exceptions to the task could be made if there was any such risk; for another, by the time Epsom NHS Trust came to the excellent meeting we had with them, the vast majority of hospitals around the country had demonstrated that the target could be met perfectly well through good management practice. Newspapers should be sharp witted enough to spot public servants hiding poor management by waving shrouds.

Even so, one can reject this kind of hysteria out of hand and at the same time acknowledge that targets could have negative consequences. For example, in 2004–5 a hospital manager faced with either hitting his or her targets or risking a deficit the following year would probably have chosen the former. While it is true that a well-managed hospital should have had no difficulty achieving its targets without running a deficit, in the real world not all hospitals are well managed. Indeed, the fragility of management is an ongoing threat to the success of the Health Service reforms, and in the absence of a comprehensive programme to improve management, these dilemmas are very real. I can argue that deficits in poorly managed places are a price worth paying for the demonstrably improved services that reduced waiting times bring for patients, but I also have to accept that this is a matter of opinion.

A further negative impact is the way nationally established targets sometimes cause confusion at very local level. If the first call on primary care trust managers was waiting times, on school managers exam results and on police reducing car crime or burglary, as the Delivery Unit would have hoped, is it surprising that sometimes it turned out to be difficult to get all three agencies to collaborate on, say, dysfunctional families? I heard this complaint often, and sometimes it had validity: government will need to set fewer but better targets in future (as indeed the Treasury did in the 2007 comprehensive spending review). Often, though, I found the argument used as an excuse for poor performance or turning the clock back to a time when life for public service professionals was admittedly much calmer, but the results they achieved were sadly much worse. If those who identified the problem of conflicting targets had more often proposed practical alternatives, offering even better results, then their objections would have had more credibility.

A further objection relates to other trends in government policy which conflicted, to some extent at any rate, with Delivery Unit philosophy but which were being implemented simultaneously – in another part of the forest – and thus caused a lack of coherence out there. An example will illustrate the point. In the first Blair term, across many policy areas, specific ring-fenced grants littered the scene. In my own area of education, we had more than most: grants for literacy and numeracy, grants for homework clubs, grants for music and so on. There was a similar picture in crime and health. All worthy causes to be sure, but the result was that frontline managers such as headteachers were faced with lots of small sums of money for which they had to account separately – a bureaucratic nightmare. In response to the understandable criticism that came from professionals, the government swung the other way and decided to have no specific grants at all. They were wound up and the money put into mainstream funding, which had two consequences. First, funding distribution changed, resulting in the absurdity in education in 2004 of a funding crisis for a significant minority of schools at a time of rapidly increasing overall resources. Second, some important policies that the government wanted to pursue but professionals did not (such as catch-up classes in literacy for 11–14-year-olds who had fallen behind their peers) didn't happen, and the government was no longer able to make them happen: it had thrown away a key lever. Yet the Delivery Unit was still seeking, through the relevant departments, to deliver the relevant goals such as higher standards of literacy among fourteen-year-olds.

Meanwhile, the very professionals who had complained about the ring-fenced grants now used their abolition as a reason for not doing the things the money had been for – even though they still had the money as a result of overall increases in resources. In 2006, for example, the police claimed that street crime was on the rise again because the specific funding for it had been removed, even though their overall budgets had risen by much more than the specific grant they had lost, and numbers of police were at record levels. Rather than the pendulum swinging from too many ring-fenced grants to their abolition, the government should have used them rarely and judiciously and only in those circumstances where an issue had high priority and the professionals, if left to their own devices, would not choose to tackle it. Either way, the Delivery Unit sometimes found its approach in tension with a swing of the pendulum such as this.

A final negative about the Delivery Unit impact was that it did not do enough to build departmental capacity. There was clearly a need and we increased capacity to an extent, but clearly also what we did was insufficient. I always said to the staff that if we had to choose between delivering results and building the long-term capacity of departments, we should do the former. After all, we were only forty people and we were on a mission to deliver results for citizens. However, the experts urge companies to focus both on performance (results in the short term) and health (the capacity to keep delivering results in the long term). The Delivery Unit focused on the former. We contributed to building the latter, but in fact long-term capacity was the responsibility of others, especially the Corporate Development Group of the Cabinet Office, and I believed – and still believe – that if we had been pulled away into capacity-building, we would not have had the impact we had on the targets. I have to accept, though, that sometimes departments and therefore the government as a whole paid a price for our focus. In 2005, Gus O'Donnell sought to rectify this by introducing departmental capability reviews. They are certainly a step forward; much will depend on how their diagnosis is followed up in departments themselves.

This raises the final comment to make in this chapter, and a major theme for the next one: in 2001 I consciously chose to make sure the Delivery Unit did its job even though the Cabinet Office as constituted was incoherent, and Blair's reforms of it that year – with the creation of a plethora of units – had improved matters but had not resolved them.

To put it bluntly, the Delivery Unit had the substantial impact it did in spite of the incoherence and weakness of the Cabinet Office of which it was a part. It is true that some progress was made on wider reform of the Cabinet Office and the civil service more generally in 2004 and 2005, but it was far from enough. Ultimately, Blair himself, along with successive Cabinet Secretaries, must take responsibility for this state of affairs. Imagine how much more we might have achieved if the drive for delivery had been part of a coherent approach to transforming the performance and the health of the civil service as well as radically reforming the public services. As we have seen, Blair has achieved a great deal as Prime Minister; with a coherent administrative machine firing on all cylinders he would surely have achieved much more. Between 2001 and 2005, we talked about what this would entail often enough. The next chapter describes what it might look like in practice.

Section 3

Learning from delivery

Power is not a zero sum . . . The alchemy of good relationships can turn base metal into gold.

9

Enhancing the power of the Prime Minister

'There must be some way out of here,' said the Joker
  to the Thief,
'There's too much confusion now, I can't get no relief.'
                    Bob Dylan, 'All along the Watchtower'

Imitation

I met John Howard, the then Australian Prime Minister, in a suite of
offices he has in Sydney; they were all dark wood panelling and
spectacular paintings of the Australian outback. We discussed cricket
first, and this being three years before the 2005 Ashes miracle, I
expressed due humility and respect for the magnificent Aussies.* We
talked about foreign coaches of national teams such as Duncan Fletcher,
the Zimbabwean who managed England.

'It's the way of the world, I guess,' he said.

'Yes,' I agreed, 'it's another example of globalisation.'

Then he quizzed me about education reform in England, on which I
had given a presentation the day before. The main comment from the
audience on that occasion was 'you Brits are hard'. Being Australians,
this was meant as a compliment. Howard, though, took my account in
his stride: he is, after all, a hard man too.

After that, he turned to the Delivery Unit, on which he had clearly
been briefed. He listened carefully as I took him through a presentation
of how it worked – the priorities, the assessment framework, the full
works. I explained that it was modelled on how the chief executive of a

*As of January 2007, sadly, humility and respect for the magnificent Aussies are
required again.

business would drive key priorities. He clearly understood it and wanted to know how we had overcome civil service defensiveness. I talked about how we had tried, with some success, to build relationships in a new way. Then he asked what he most wanted to know – does Tony Blair really turn up to all those stocktakes? I told him he almost always did. With that, my time was up. The cab driver who picked me up told me the secret of Howard's electoral success: 'He knows what we're thinking.'*

Within a year, we had a visit from Janice Wykes, an official in the Australian government. Howard wanted to emulate the Delivery Unit. Howard, a great admirer of Blair in spite of coming from the other side of the political spectrum, operates in a different way. More like Attlee, Callaghan and Major in post-war British history, he is a Prime Minister who operates through and with his Cabinet collectively. Issues are taken there, debated, sometimes vigorously, and then decided. Once decided, the now-established Australian version of the Delivery Unit is responsible for checking implementation takes place. Naturally enough, therefore, it is called the Cabinet Implementation Unit, but its function is similar: it's a mechanism for ensuring that decisions are implemented so that citizens notice the difference. Kevin Rudd is likely to strengthen this capacity.

Imitation, they say, is the sincerest form of flattery. If so, the Delivery Unit is the recipient of floods of (sincere) flattery. Howard's Implementation Unit is not the only imitation. In Toronto, after I had presented to the newly elected Ontario Cabinet in January 2004, the province's Premier, Dalton McGuinty, established his version of the Delivery Unit, the Results Office. It has enabled him to keep on top of delivering important promises such as improving literacy in elementary schools and reducing waiting times in health. Antonio Villaraigosa,† the first Hispanic mayor of Los Angeles, has established a Performance Management Unit on 'the Blair model' to drive delivery of the major commitments he has made to his sprawling city. The President of Indonesia, Susilo Bambang Yudhoyono, again inspired by Blair's

*His long run of success ended when he met his match in the 2007 election, which Labor, led by Kevin Rudd, won.
†To add an interesting angle on Blair's reputation: in one conversation I had with Villaraigosa, he said, 'I had a Blair moment yesterday.' I asked, 'What's a Blair moment?' He replied, 'It's when you do the right thing and get pounded for it.'

model, is establishing a Delivery Unit to secure implementation of his economic reforms. The Dutch Prime Minister's office has looked at how it can learn the lessons of the Delivery Unit to assist with implementing the coalition agreement. Meanwhile, learning from the Australian federal government as well as Blair, several Australian states, including New South Wales, Queensland and Victoria, are developing a similar capacity.

International organisations such as the IMF, the World Bank and the OECD have asked for presentations on the Delivery Unit, and a stream of visitors from countries around the world make visits to it to find out how this new invention works in practice.

Of course, through these presentations and meetings less-than-democratic governments learnt about our techniques too. This raised a troubling question for me – was deliverology moral? Or was it a set of techniques that were morally neutral and could be put to good ends or bad? In discussing this question with my staff, I emphasised the importance, morally speaking, of the way we built relationships based on plain speaking and mutual respect and the purpose for which we worked so hard: a better, fairer, more productive society. But as with many technologies, I knew that large parts of deliverology could be put to less worthy purposes.

Meanwhile, within the United Kingdom, all four individual countries learn from abroad, but learning from one another has often been sadly frowned upon. I know because I've been guilty of this mistake myself. However, the new political leaders in Northern Ireland have studied the Delivery Unit story. Meanwhile, Scotland, determined to make its own way in the world after the re-establishment of its own Parliament in 1998 (after a 291-year gap), seemed resistant at first to learning from England. So it is interesting to discover that even there – following a study visit to London – a Strategy and Delivery Unit has been established. Moreover, the Scottish Parliament, far from wanting to ensure the Scottish Executive operates differently from Whitehall, is pressing it to emulate the Delivery Unit more closely. Take this comment from Wendy Alexander MSP, for example, from my appearance before the Scottish Parliament's Finance Committee on 17 May 2005:

> Your presentation suggests that we [in Scotland] can learn something about how to deliver improvements in public services. I hope that you can

> share the . . . information in your presentation . . . It would also be helpful if somebody in your unit could do a bit of work with our advisers and support staff.

In short, if there are English developments that the Scots want to emulate, we must be on to something.*

We are on to something, and there are reasons why. Every government in the world is under pressure to deliver results. Every government bureaucracy in the world is struggling to keep up with the pace of change in the modern world. Few, if any, have developed the capacity to deliver change on the scale the public expects to the standards it requires and at the pace which it demands. As Sir Richard Sykes, rector of Imperial College London, has argued vigorously in relation to the UK:

> There is a clear and urgent choice. Either reform to improve services, keep government affordable and enable tax reductions. Or a continued failure to reform, leading to rising costs, reductions in services and further tax increases. Either economic growth, with all its benefits, or the disaster of low growth and its creeping social and economic cost.[1]

Whether substantial tax cuts are possible in the near future I doubt, but the days of steep rises in investment in the public services are over. As Anatole Kaletsky has argued, 'that taxes and public spending must rise for ever can no longer be taken for granted'.[2] People's tolerance for paying taxes is strictly limited. Moreover, every leader of a government in the world – whether President or Prime Minister, governor or mayor – knows that all that pent-up expectation rests firmly on his or her individual shoulders. Some politicians can hide behind others from time to time and dip out of the limelight, sometimes for long periods. Leaders cannot. The pressure is on 24/7, all year round. In these circumstances, an innovation such as the Delivery Unit, which has simple systems for driving delivery of a leader's priorities and (on the early evidence) can secure significant results, often at quite rapid pace, is bound to be attractive because it enhances the personal capacity of the leader to get things done.

*In addition, since I left the Delivery Unit, the Scottish Executive has asked for one of the new capability reviews to be done.

As Delivery Unit replicas proliferate, we will learn more about what works from the failures as well as the successes. As with John Howard's Implementation Unit, each replica will have to be tailored both to the political system in the relevant country and to the personality of the particular political leader. In design and operation, therefore, they will no doubt vary significantly, but I expect to find a core set of characteristics common to all those that succeed: clear priorities, simple methods, good relationships and steady routines will be among them.

In the meantime the strong message these imitations send to British politicians is that the Delivery Unit or some variation of it is here to stay. I would not expect to see any politician who seriously expects to be Prime Minister of this country proposing, as Michael Howard did in 2004, to do without the capacity provided by the Delivery Unit. Certainly Gordon Brown has made clear the importance he attaches to it.

The central theme of this chapter, therefore, is how a Prime Minister in the future – whoever it might be and of whichever party – might make the most of what the Delivery Unit learnt between 2001 and 2005, both about how the central government machine functions and about how the public services as a whole might be successfully reformed. In short, it is about how, in relation to the public services, a Prime Minister might maximise his or her ability to bring about a transformation of the performance of the public sector. Before turning to that crucial set of questions, however, it is important to consider more closely the issue of prime ministerial power itself, which after all has been the subject of fierce controversy among political scientists and commentators for much of the post-war era.

Prime ministerial power and its limitations

The famous debate

On 6 April 1780, the House of Commons famously passed Dunning's Resolution amid anxieties about George III's approach to politics. 'The influence of the Crown', it read, 'has increased, is increasing and ought to be diminished.' Two hundred years later, the thought behind the resolution was dusted off, amended and applied to the power not of the crown, but of the Prime Minister. The modern version of the debate began in 1960 when the appointment of a member of the House of Lords, the Earl of Home, as Foreign Secretary prompted the celebrated professor Max Beloff to claim: 'Taken together with other Cabinet changes, and in the light of the development of the office of Prime Minister over recent decades, it may well be that it marks a further stage in the evolution of British government from a Cabinet system to what is virtually a Presidential system.'[3]

Heaven knows what Beloff would have said had he known – as Peter Hennessy, the best-informed and most entertaining commentator on contemporary history, has revealed – that a year earlier Harold Macmillan had toyed with and ultimately (albeit reluctantly) rejected the idea of setting up a Prime Minister's Department (of which more later).

Clement Attlee, retired by this time, rejected Beloff's account: 'The essential principle of our British system is that of collective responsibility.'[4] In other words, the Cabinet acting together was a constraint on the Prime Minister's power. John MacIntosh, the peerless academic analyst of the British Cabinet system, sought to resolve this issue in classically British pragmatic fashion in 1962: 'The country is governed by the Prime Minister who leads, co-ordinates and maintains a series of Ministers . . . There is no single catchphrase that can describe this form of government.' In other words, given the famous absence of a single formal written constitution for Britain, the role of the Prime Minister and his or her relationship to the Cabinet has been constantly negotiated throughout history and will continue to be. 'The Prime Minister', MacIntosh continued, 'stands at the apex supported by and giving power to a widening series of rings of senior ministers, the Cabinet, its committees, non-Cabinet ministers and departments.'[5]

This, however, is essentially descriptive. It does not answer fully the question of where power lies, perhaps because the question is unanswerable. Where power lies depends on the particular individuals who make up that 'series of rings' and the circumstances of the time. Nor does it resolve what the trend was when MacIntosh was writing – was the power of the Prime Minister remorselessly rising or not?

Other commentators were less shy of catchphrases and bold assertions. Richard Crossman, who had made a career out of both before becoming a Cabinet minister under Harold Wilson, was very clear about what he believed was happening. 'The post-war epoch', he wrote, 'has seen the final transformation of Cabinet government into prime ministerial government.' Wilson did not always agree with Crossman, as Crossman's riveting diaries reveal,* but implicitly at any rate it seems on this he did: 'The levers of power are all here in No. 10.'[6]

George Jones, writing in the same year (1965) as Wilson made this remark, was more sceptical. He argued that individual secretaries of state wielded immense power in their departments. Of course 'the Prime Minister is the leading figure in the Cabinet whose voice carries most weight. But he is not the all-powerful individual which many have recently claimed him to be . . . A Prime Minister who can carry his colleagues with him can be in a very powerful position, but he is only as strong as they let him be.'[7]

Just over a decade later, Tony Benn, in the self-justifying torrent of writing he published to explain Labour's failure between 1974 and 1979, weighed in firmly on the Crossman side of the debate, but characteristically pushed it to extremes: 'The present centralisation of power in the hands of one person has gone too far and amounts to a system of personal rule in the very heart of our parliamentary democracy . . . [we should] redress the balance of power in favour of the public, Parliament and the party.'[8]

These exchanges, more than a generation ago, have set the terms of the debate ever since. Hennessy has shed light on the question by helpfully defining more precisely the role and powers of the Prime Minister and – drawing on a phrase of Michael Foley's – explaining 'the stretching of premiership', but this clarifies rather than changes the terms of the debate. Crucially to my argument, it must be pointed out that the debate as it stands is between, on the one hand, those who think that the power of the Prime Minister has increased (and the Thatcher and Blair premierships have reinforced this, they say), and that therefore there is a problem, and, on the other, those who argue that Cabinet government is alive and kicking (as demonstrated by the defenestration of Margaret Thatcher that famous evening in 1990), and that therefore there is not a problem. It is important to note that both sides of this argument implicitly agree that any increase in prime ministerial power is inherently problematic and to be disapproved of. But suppose that in

*Wilson compared Crossman's diary unfavourably to that of Harold Macmillan: 'Macmillan's was much less subjective and much more accurate.' (Harold Wilson, *A Prime Minister on Prime Ministers* (London: Weidenfeld and Nicolson, 1977), p. 321.)

the heat of this controversy the central point has been missed? Given the stretching of premiership and the extraordinary changes in the post-war era, which have accelerated since the 1960s, suppose the real problem is not the extent of power the Prime Minister wields, but the lack of it? Suppose the problem is not the strength of the prime ministerial role, but its weakness?

My own experience suggests this alternative analysis is at the very least worth exploring. Before returning to the clearly important question of the checks on the Prime Minister's power, I want to set out the case that the office of Prime Minister is not powerful enough and that – given the challenges of early 21st-century government – it needs strengthening, at least in relation to the reform of public services on which this book is focused.

The changing nature of the role

The starting point for the case I want to make is the changing nature of the Prime Minister's role. The ever-increasing demands of the job suggest the task is becoming more difficult to do. Seen from this perspective, the establishment of the Delivery Unit was not just a personal whim of Tony Blair, but an institutional response to the demands of the time. If this is so, then the trajectory would suggest in future (unless further institutional change is made) a weakening rather than a strengthening of prime ministerial power. The evidence for this over the long run is too extensive to relate here, but a few anecdotes can make the point.

- In October 1793, William Pitt, a Prime Minister in wartime, found himself writing to his colleague William Grenville: 'You need have no scruple in sending me as much business as you please as . . . I have at present nothing to do.'[9] Even allowing for Pitt's voracious appetite for work, it is hard to imagine any of his 21st-century successors writing such words. (The fact that on 27 May 1798 he found time to fight a duel on Putney Heath only reinforces the point.)

- In the same era, on the other side of the Atlantic, John Adams, second President of the United States, was given the responsibility of moving the presidential files and archives from the President's residence in Philadelphia to the newly built White House in the equally newly built Washington, DC. The entire presidential papers of the United States fitted into just seven packing crates. No. 10 probably generates this much paper in a week.

- William Gladstone, as Prime Minister in 1869, writes in his diary during a three-week stay – but not holiday – at his country house, Hawarden, 'Worked six hours on my books, arranging and rearranging: the best brain rest I have had (I think) since Decr last.'[10] Gladstone was another great Prime Minister with an extraordinary appetite for work but, again, the extent of leisure time he found seems quaint by comparison with recent times.

- Shortly after the fall of France, the principal private secretary of another great wartime Prime Minister, Winston Churchill, writes in his diary on 7 June 1940: 'There was very little to do and I sat in the shade most of the afternoon in the garden at No. 10, reading a book of war stories.'[11] In four years in Downing Street, I never remember Jeremy Heywood or Ivan Rogers being similarly absorbed.

- Peter Hennessy reports that Attlee, Prime Minister in the immediate post-war era, found his workload 'heavy but not insupportable' and goes on to describe how 'on one famous occasion he fetched his own tea on the grounds that the No. 10 messenger was "probably busy"'.[12]

Compare these scenes with Margaret Thatcher's comment in her memoirs:

> The hours at No. 10 are long. I never minded this. There was an intensity about the job of being Prime Minister which made sleep seem a luxury. In any case, over the years I had trained myself to do with about four hours a night. The Private Office too would often be working till 11 o'clock at night.[13]

Or listen to James Callaghan commenting on how he felt exhaustion impaired his performance in the final throes of his premiership: 'I really did understand until the last few months when I had gone to sleep a bit because I was very tired.'[14] The turning point might indeed have been under Wilson. Hennessy points out: 'There had quite plainly been an explosion of activity since the late 1950s.'[15]

There is no doubt that the role of Prime Minister in modern Britain has become hugely demanding. I remember once being in Blair's office when, as often, his diary secretary came in to remind him that his next meeting was supposed to have started already. On this occasion, an exhausted Blair looked up and decided to find out what the rest of his day entailed: 'And then what have I got?' She told him. 'And then what have I got?' said Blair with growing exasperation. She told him again and, as he repeated the same phrase seven or eight times, she ran through the long series of commitments, finishing late at night. As Hubbard Elbert said of life, sometimes being Prime Minister turns out to be just 'one damned thing after another'.

The demands of the role come in part from the lack of constitutional definition, which means the limits are ill defined, and in part from the nature of the modern world. Not only has the volume of business expanded, but the pace of decision-making has accelerated. To give just one example of this acceleration (which is rarely commented on), while researching a previous book, I decided to look up what the National Union of Teachers (NUT) had said during the consultation on the Hadow report, one of the seminal statements of education policy between the wars. The librarian at the NUT answered my enquiry a few days later – they didn't comment at all, she said. I expressed surprise; the biggest teacher union of the time had nothing to say about the most important report of the era? I asked her to double-check. She replied again a day or so later. The NUT had indeed commented on the Hadow report of 1926 . . . in 1928. A two-year consultation phase was perfectly normal eighty years ago. (Incidentally, full implementation of Hadow's main recommendation – the ending of all-age elementary schools – took forty-five years.) This leisurely pace is a far cry from the modern world in which, to pick a single startling statistic, 5,000 alterations are made every day to the Ordnance Survey map of the United Kingdom.

Hennessy lists the many functions of a Prime Minister under several headings:
- procedure and constitution
- appointments
- the conduct of Cabinet and parliamentary business
- organisation and efficiency
- budgets and market-sensitive economic decisions
- foreign and defence functions.

He acknowledges that, thanks to Gordon Brown's pre-eminence, the penultimate one of these was a reduced burden for Blair, but the rest have grown. There is no need to set out the detail. Hennessy points out that, in addition, as party leader, a Prime Minister is responsible for the management of politics and political strategy. Thatcher believed she was the guardian of the strategy, a view Blair would certainly have reiterated; and no doubt John Major wished he could have been. Indeed, for both Thatcher and Blair, their talent as strategists was the well from which their mastery of the political scene was drawn. The political demands, of course, reach far beyond strategy – the tasks of managing the party and managing (sometimes sensitive) colleagues, not to mention securing party funding, all require time and energy.

On top of all this come the relentless, ever-growing demands of what Alastair Campbell called the 24-hour media churn. In all ministerial posts, the media makes demands, but in many it comes and goes in waves, while in others the challenge is exciting media interest rather than fending it off. For a Prime Minister, it is an unending pressure: he or she must have a view on every issue, and every statement he or she makes is crawled over for consistency or lack of it with everything else he or she has said, and everything else every relevant minister has said on that issue. The search among journalists for hairs to split is a constant one. Long gone are the days when Clement Attlee could conduct a television interview early in the 1951 election campaign as follows:

> *Interviewer:* On what will Labour take its stand?
> *Attlee:* Well, that's what we shall be announcing shortly.
> *Interviewer:* What are your immediate plans, Mr Attlee?
> *Attlee:* My immediate plans are to go down to a committee on just that thing as soon as I can get away from here.
> *Interviewer:* Is there anything else you'd like to say about the coming election?
> *Attlee:* No.[16]

The voracious appetite of the media, driven by technology, competition and globalisation, presents a huge challenge. Its caustic, often cynical and destructive style, which helped, for example, to destroy Major's personal confidence, is a constant factor too. To some extent this is true everywhere, but there is good reason to believe – not least from the comments made by foreign visitors, especially politicians – that the British media is particularly vitriolic. There are those who argue that, especially in its early days, through its approach to media management (always called 'spin'), the Blair government brought problems upon itself. This argument has validity and mistakes were made, but no one should miss the underlying trend evident before and after that phase. The Blair team's mistake was to believe that, through their media management skills, the remorseless trend could be bucked. Once his team realised this was not possible, they responded to the challenge of the modern media by setting new precedents that future Prime Ministers will have to follow – the monthly press conferences; the regular appearances before the Liaison Committee; the on-the-record briefings of the lobby; the live mea culpa appearances Blair did on *Newsnight* and other programmes, sometimes painful to watch but always brave. Some might have debated his response, but few questioned the extent of the pressure. Blair's excellence as a media performer means these events were taken for granted, but a moment's reflection suggests that some of his predecessors would have struggled to survive in this daunting new world.

Cocooned too in the necessary protective bubble that modern security demands, a Prime Minister is inevitably sheltered from the experiences of ordinary everyday life. Even with a war on, Neville Chamberlain, during his time as Prime Minister, routinely took a morning walk in St James's Park, chatting to members of the public as he went, before returning to No. 10. Such ordinariness is no longer available, and the growing threat of international terrorism will ensure that the Prime Minister's security arrangements will become tighter and tighter. As a result, formal time has to be made to find out what is happening in the real world. Because this is crucial to the exercise of judgement, Blair made a huge commitment of time to visiting hospitals, schools and businesses, but every visit required meticulous planning and preparation. All spontaneity has been removed from the job.

And indeed this is what the job comes down to in the end: the management of time. Given the vast number of demands and the limited number of hours, on what should the Prime Minister focus? Which meetings and engagements should he take and which refuse? How can he find time for himself? For the modern premier, a huge amount of the week, month and year is spoken for even before you begin to make these choices. I know because I've been there at the vortex with the diary secretary trying to squeeze in my monthly half-hour one-to-one meetings and two dozen or so stocktakes over the course of a year. In all, I was asking for just over thirty hours of Blair's time out of more than 8,800 hours in the year. Yet even though these were meetings Blair was committed to and I had established an excellent working relationship with his heroic diary secretary, it was tremendously difficult. There are dozens of people hungry for prime ministerial time.*

There are so many commitments that cannot be delegated. There are the routine weekly meetings such as the audience with the Queen and Prime Minister's Questions, the latter demanding substantial preparation on a Wednesday morning. There are the regular monthly meetings such as the press conferences. There are the crucial parliamentary occasions such as the Queen's Speech or appearances before the Liaison Committee. There are ceremonial occasions such as the State Opening of Parliament. There is the growing number of international summits with the EU and the G8, for example, as well as bilateral meetings with other heads of state in their countries or here. Many of these meetings require preparation, pre-meetings, calls to colleagues in Europe and conversations with Cabinet colleagues who need to be consulted. We have not yet even begun to find time for issues of massive substance in public service reform, such as getting your head round the complexities of the Health Service, working through how the government should relate to the professions, dealing with spending reviews . . . the list goes on. The consequence is that a Prime Minister often has to make a decision with extremely limited time or on the basis of a short written briefing with, at the end of it, the inevitable question: 'Do you agree?'

This is not a matter of expecting sympathy for those who take on the role of Prime Minister. As James Callaghan – who had an extremely challenging time in the role – explains: 'It is never a misfortune to be Prime Minister . . . it is absolute heaven.'[17] The issue is effective government; the use of power to deliver results. The Prime Minister certainly has extensive power, but the nature of the role in modern Britain has made it harder and harder to use it effectively.

*Listen to the ageing Churchill reflecting of the role in his final years in office: 'You must remember that the office of Prime Minister is not a dictatorship, certainly not in peacetime. I am surrounded by hungry eyes.' (Quoted in Peter Hennessy, *Having It So Good* (London: Allen Lane, 2006), p. 271.)

Meanwhile, since the great debate on the power of the Prime Minister in the 1960s, further underlying constraints which have crept up almost unnoticed are nevertheless profoundly affecting the role. Here, let me identify just three.

- The growing use in the past two decades of judicial review, which has often constrained Prime Ministers – including in Blair's case his preferred policies on asylum, immigration and security.

- The emergence of hugely influential international bodies such as the European Union and, to a lesser extent, the World Trade Organization, not to mention the rise of global capital markets which – as Norman Lamont remembers better than most – can make and unmake careers and governments in the time (to adapt an old Tibetan phrase) it takes a cup of Downing Street tea to go cold. In short, the shift identified by Philip Bobbitt, in his magisterial account of recent history (*The Shield of Achilles*), from the 20th-century nation-state to the 21st-century market state makes a practical difference to a Prime Minister's power.

- The introduction of Freedom of Information is beginning to have an impact. The increasing difficulty which results, in developing policy, discussing options and generally operating confidentially, might be a benefit to democracy, but it certainly makes the Prime Minister's job harder. Even before the new legislation took effect in January 2005, the Butler report, with its painstaking revelations of internal No. 10 email traffic, was a harbinger of things to come. (As the implementation of Freedom of Information approached, in paying attention to detail as ever, I urged my staff to avoid using email as an alternative to conversation and ensured training for them all in what to archive and what to delete.) Certainly the internal workings of No. 10 are going to be revealed as never before – in close to real time – as the implications of Freedom of Information work their way through, again constraining a Prime Minister's power.

Here I am not arguing for or against any of these – simply pointing out their consequences for Prime Ministerial power. To summarise the argument at this point, a set of underlying trends over the past generation is simultaneously focusing attention on the Prime Minister's ability to deliver and eroding his power to do so.

Blair's constraints

In Blair's personal case, there were other personal or self-imposed constraints. A major one was that, prior to becoming Prime Minister, he had never run a government department, or even been a junior minister. Neither did he have experience of running a major organisation outside government in the way that David Young, one of Margaret Thatcher's favourite ministers, or Alan Johnson in Blair's (and Brown's) Cabinet had done. Of course, he had successfully transformed a political party, but this is not the same thing as managing a business, a local authority or a major trade union. As a consequence, as Prime Minister he had a huge amount to learn about how organisations, especially large bureaucracies, work. He always had a tendency – which at one level is a strength because it means he took on intractable issues – to believe that in the end, through an act of his own personal will and the exercise of his own formidable powers of persuasion, he could achieve almost anything: pass a law, change a system, stop a revolt by backbenchers or bring a conflict to an end.* More often than his critics would like to admit, the optimism to which this characteristic gave rise proved justified. The Good Friday deal was secured, his higher education reforms came through, and so on. But sometimes it didn't work, and Blair felt lonely and let down by his colleagues and the system as a whole; at these times a deeper understanding of organisations and the motivations of those who work within them might have delivered a better result. As a result, Blair's style of operation did not always maximise his influence. When he complained that his ministers and officials rarely brought him ideas more radical than his own, he should have recognised that, in part, this was a consequence of his own unique style of management, which sometimes involved urging people to be radical, only to retreat when his own exceptional political instincts suggested he should.†

A further constraint on Blair's power that applied uniquely to him was

---

*I recognise this characteristic in Blair, incidentally, because on a different level it's one I suffer from myself; as Lindsey Olliver in my office used to say in an exasperated tone: 'Why do you always think everything is amenable to an act of your own personal will?'
† Douglas Hurd recalled that Ted Heath as Prime Minister 'needed people around him who would have constant original ideas and he wasn't getting that out of the machine' (Jon Davis, *Prime Ministers and Whitehall 1960–74* (London: Hambledon Continuum, 2007), p. 149). If two such different people as Heath and Blair, thirty years apart, felt so similarly, it would appear to be largely an institutional problem.

the relationship with his Chancellor, Gordon Brown. At one level, of course, the successes of both the New Labour political project and the New Labour governments are a joint achievement, and together Blair and Brown achieved far more than either could have alone. As Jim Naughtie says in *The Rivals*, 'No pair of politicians in our modern history has wielded so much power together.'[18] But here we are dealing with the role of Prime Minister, and there is no doubt that by agreeing to concede so much power to his Chancellor, Blair constrained his own influence. Brown was the master of the Budget and management of the economy. Spending reviews were a matter of a hard-fought card game (more canasta than poker), in which the Treasury held the trump cards on timing and information. Meanwhile, major strategic choices on policy, especially health, were the subject of ongoing negotiation. Contrary to much of the press comment, the areas of agreement were overwhelming, but while the gaps that occurred, often over crucial details such as the precise role of markets in the Health Service, might have been narrow they were deep. Sometimes they were based on limited information or straightforward misunderstanding as partial information swilled between 'seconds' in each team and between both teams and the department concerned. I know because, rather haphazardly over a six-month period, at the request of both the Prime Minister and the Chancellor, I chaired a group that examined some of the sensitive areas of health and education. On health, once we had finally had the necessary thorough meeting with all the key people from the department, No. 10 and the Treasury, agreement turned out to be relatively easy to achieve (and certainly much easier than getting the meeting in the diary).

Moreover, when Blair and Brown talked with each other, they no doubt often got along famously, but rarely was a record kept – their relationship is intensely private – and as the details emerged, a Chinese-whispers effect sometimes occurred. The major cost to Blair as Prime Minister was not the power ceded to Brown (indeed, in part this could be seen as a gain since it gave Blair time for other issues) nor was it the need to spend the energy hammering out these hard-fought agreements on policy and spending; it was the dilemmas and the sometimes down-right confusion it sometimes caused in the key departments on which Blair depended to deliver the transformation of the public services he craved.

Secretaries of state had to decide whether they were predominantly in the Brown camp or the Blair camp or whether they would seek to be in both. Much of the time they might not have had to choose, but when one of those narrow but deep divides occurred they did. For officials, the tension might have been less acute, but the confusion was often greater. Reading signals not just from their own ministers but from their interaction with No. 10 advisers and Treasury officials, they sought to pick their way across a minefield but, understandably given that they were often basing their views on incomplete and third- or fourth-hand information, they lost their way. In fact, often they found themselves forced to rely on those unattributed soundbites in the press which, even in the best of times and the best of newspapers, are rarely a good basis for policy-making. Often officials would explain to me that x or y was not possible because either 'the PM' or 'the Chancellor' had a different view, which I knew perfectly well wasn't the case. It was tempting in such circumstances to dismiss the official as ill informed, but I had to recognise that the system of dual power at the top and, more particularly the way it was played out in practice, caused real problems. Richard Holt, in his sharp and witty survey of chancellorship in the post-war era, concludes his analysis of the relationship between it and the Prime Minister thus: 'A Prime Minister usually has power over a Chancellor's career and reputation; the opposite is less true . . . When things go wrong, the Prime Minister usually outlasts the Chancellor.'[19]

The Blair–Brown relationship requires a rewriting of this aspect of history. There is nothing unusual in there being tensions periodically between a Prime Minister and a Chancellor (think of Margaret Thatcher and Nigel Lawson or John Major and Norman Lamont). What was unique in the case of Blair and Brown was the relationship enduring for so long (Harold Macmillan by comparison had four Chancellors in seven years; Thatcher three in eleven years); its basis throughout, contrary to Holt's correct conclusion about their predecessors, was mutual interdependence and the sheer scale of the shared achievement. In the end, it was a genuine case of that overused phrase 'creative tension', and the result was huge positive impact along with periodic confusion. Either way, it certainly constrained the power of the Prime Minister. As Blair's power ebbed away during his third term, this constraint inevitably became greater.

Thus, challenged by the remorseless stretching of the job, scrutinised as never before by Parliament, the public and the media, and living with some additional self-imposed constraints, Blair carried a far heavier burden than any of his Cabinet colleagues. Yet, ironically, he was the only one who did not have a department or a ministerial team to share his burden. Instead, he had the No. 10 operation and a less-than-coherent collection of units and functions in the Cabinet Office. In power for just over a decade, of course, Blair himself bore part of the responsibility for this state of affairs, as did his successive Cabinet Secretaries. My own experience – described in earlier chapters – points to the dangers of either being sucked into endless 'keeping-in-touch' meetings or sinking in the quicksands of incoherence which were part of the Cabinet Office landscape. Meanwhile, in No. 10 itself, while the people were extremely talented, a pleasure to work with and devoted to Blair personally, they were certainly not organised in a structured team. A former colleague likened them to the Real Madrid squad with its *galacticos*: imagine, he said, if they played the whole squad at once.

Blair thrived on this because it suited his style of work. For major prime ministerial speeches he wrote his own, but loved to draw on the diverse opinions around him, as Peter Hyman describes so brilliantly in *1 out of 10*.[20] On policy again Blair liked to hear diverse views and while each of us hoped he'd say 'I agree with . . .', none of us indulged in rivalry or point-scoring. To use Tom Peters's phrase, Blair thrived on chaos. As Peters argues, this might be the way to manage in the modern world, but one wonders what Clement Attlee would have made of it all. Not averse himself to playing off those around him while maintaining a silence, Attlee nevertheless imposed order. He himself said: 'The essential quality in a PM is that he should be a good chairman able to get others to work,'[21] and Peter Hennessy suggests Attlee 'probably ranks with Peel and Gladstone as one of the tidiest-minded men to have filled the office of Prime Minister'.[22]

Blair cleared his boxes promptly, worked consistently hard, rarely if ever panicked, kept on top of the immense demands of his job, and was a pleasure to work for, but no one, least of all Blair himself, would call him either an outstanding chairman or the tidiest-minded of men. It is tempting to take the Peters line about chaos to justify the way the centre of government ran under Blair, but in truth it would be an excuse. It is also tempting to place the blame for it solely at Blair's door, but that too would not be fair. If a given Prime Minister has prodigious talents, but not necessarily for tidy administration, then, at least in part, it is up to those around him to make effective arrangements. We could and should have been more effective. I personally bear some of this responsibility: perhaps instead of focusing so intently on ensuring that the Delivery Unit succeeded, I should have put more time and energy, with the Cabinet Secretary, into coherence-making. Either way, Blair's successors deserve better. The next section but one outlines how that might be done, but first, in case anyone suspects that this is an argument for elective dictatorship, I want to examine briefly where the limits of the Prime Minister's power should lie.

Limits to prime ministerial power

The Prime Minister's job is becoming more demanding all the time and he or she needs more power to do it well: this is the nub of the case I am making, but I am not arguing that the Prime Minister's power should be unconstrained. Far from it. Just as it has become fashionable to talk about better regulation rather than deregulation, so my argument here is for better constraint rather than no constraint.

A good place to start the argument is with the historical evidence. It is not at all clear from the record that the country has been better governed or its public services more effectively managed or reformed, in those periods where the Cabinet has been to the fore and the Prime Minister merely 'first among equals'. To take just the past four Prime Ministers, it is hard to make the case that James Callaghan and John Major, both of whom invested heavily in Cabinet government, had more or better impact than Margaret Thatcher or Blair. Quite the reverse in fact. The school reforms of the late 1980s, for example – a decisive turning point in post-war educational history – bore the strong imprint of Thatcher's personal attention. Indeed, Duncan Graham, the first chairman of the National Curriculum Council, swears that the statutory order for English was returned to him from No. 10 with Thatcher's marmalade on its corners. Moreover, the biggest implementation error on education – overloading the National Curriculum with too much content – came from the department in spite of strictures from No. 10, suggesting additional prime ministerial power might have helped.

Similarly, for all the implementation challenges, it is evident that

312 INSTRUCTION TO DELIVER

Blair was far more radical and effective in health reform than any of his three immediate predecessors and in education too, in spite of Thatcher's powerful finish. Callaghan, who was so determined to be an education Prime Minister, failed, beset as he was by problems and, with his attention diverted, frustratingly dependent on ineffective Education ministers such as Fred Mulley and Shirley Williams. Major's record in the public services is similarly uninspired, though the Citizen's Charter is underrated. If there is a rule, then, it suggests that the more powerful the Prime Minister, the better their reforms of the public services. Clement Attlee is the stellar exception to this rule, but not only was he an exceptional chairman able to exercise leadership with very few words, it is also forgotten that when he became Prime Minister, he had behind him the extraordinary experience of having been Deputy Prime Minister and of having managed domestic affairs for Winston Churchill in the wartime coalition.

Nor does the historical record show that the more powerful recent Prime Ministers – Thatcher and Blair – have been unconstrained. In the end, after all, it was Thatcher's Cabinet and MPs who overthrew her in what John Cole called 'a very British coup'; Blair's Cabinet and MPs could, had they wished, have done the same at any time.* The fact that Blair's party did not overthrow him has a number of explanations. His mastery of political strategy and exceptional track record of electoral success were obviously crucial. Another explanation – so obvious it gets missed altogether – is that they largely agreed with the direction in which he led the country; the Blair Cabinet did not see the deep ideological rifts that were apparent, for example, over trade unionism under Harold Wilson, over public expenditure under Callaghan, or over Europe under Thatcher and Major.

A less remarked (but perhaps in some ways more profound) reason is that, for most of the time under Blair, the Cabinet was made up of people whose politics were forged in the struggle for the soul of the Labour Party of the 1980s. (My small part in this struggle is described

---

*As the *Times* argued in its editorial of 9 September 2006, at the end of the frenetic week in which Blair was forced to name his departure date: 'There has been much chatter about "presidentialism" in Britain's political life and how Blair has marginalised the government and the House of Commons. What this week shows is how facile that generalisation is in practice ... A Prime Minister must retain the backing of his MPs ... Britain is not a permanent elective dictatorship.'

in Chapter 1.) David Blunkett, Tessa Jowell, Paul Boateng, Jack Straw, Charles Clarke and of course Blair and Gordon Brown had seared into them during those conflicts both the importance of relating their politics to the common sense of the British people on the one hand, and the concomitant dangers of division and conflict on the other. When collectively they gained power, therefore, they acknowledged the political triumph that Blair and Brown had wrought and were deeply reluctant to rock the boat. From Labour's most disastrous decade, they learnt discipline, which – with the exception of the resignations of Robin Cook and Clare Short over Iraq – only became periodically frayed in relation to the leadership question, not ideology.

In any case, the Cabinet has the power to constrain the Prime Minister, and implicitly uses it all the time. As proposals are prepared, consideration of whether they will 'get through' Cabinet is constant: it is therefore not surprising that proposals which finally reach Cabinet tend to go through. This is not necessarily a sign of Cabinet weakness; merely that its influence has been taken into account in preparation for the meeting.

One example, in which I was personally involved, was the introduction of three-year funding for schools, which Blair wanted to introduce in 2003. I had been arguing for something along these lines for years, so urged him on, but could not hide the fact that it posed challenges to other parts of government, especially local government. Fearing strong opposition in Cabinet, he decided not to go ahead . . . until the following year, when he judged, correctly as it turned out, that he could now push it through without significant conflict. The judgement here was not one about principle – Blair was equally in favour in 2003 and 2004. It was about the Prime Minister's power relative to Cabinet; how much political capital would he use up to get his reform? In short, those who fear the increasing power of the Prime Minister sometimes underestimate the often latent power that resides in Cabinet, which is as it should be. Incidentally, the example illustrates the contingency of prime ministerial power – it ebbs and flows month by month, sometimes even week by week. In the summer of 2003, Blair was more dependent than usual on Cabinet colleagues; a year later with an election approaching and his personal triumphs on five-year strategies, he was (and felt) strong.

Of course, the Cabinet collectively is not the sole constraint: individual secretaries of state are also sometimes a constraint. As

George Jones pointed out in the 1960s, they can, if they choose to, be highly influential in their own departments. Many decisions can be and are made by individual secretaries of state with minimal or no consultation with No. 10. Moreover, secretaries of state can also control the flow of information to No. 10 and the access that the Prime Minister's people have to their departments. Some ministers (Charles Clarke would be an example) took a traditional view of how government should work: Prime Ministers, they believed, should appoint powerful secretaries of state and leave them to get on with it. Needless to say, such ministers give short shrift to bright young things from No. 10. We in the Delivery Unit invested thought and time in changing such attitudes and building strong relationships. We were usually successful, but even then often heard complaints about 'interference' from No. 10 and the Cabinet Office.

In my experience, for Cabinet ministers to seek to operate alone and independently is not the best way to get things done, let alone to create coherence across government. Add into the mix the No. 10/Treasury issues set out above, and muddle was a real risk. I never understood those stakeholders in the education system, for example, who complained about the Prime Minister 'interfering' in the Department for Education's approach. If a Prime Minister puts education at the centre of political debate and nails his personal colours to the mast, if a Prime Minister secures the biggest increases in funding for education in history, he has every right to be actively involved in shaping, and even directing, education policy. If, in these circumstances, an individual minister tries to act alone it might be a constraint on prime ministerial power, but a high price in terms of policy muddle and sometimes bruised relationships will inevitably be paid. In the end, to remove such tensions, the Prime Minister is likely to exercise the power of patronage during a reshuffle, but secretaries of state know that this option can only be exercised rarely, and that some of them have enough clout to make outright removal difficult.

Generally, the secretaries of state who did best in my view invested carefully in their relationships with Blair and Brown and earned the right to significant autonomy by demonstrating their competence and instinct for finding the invisible dividing line between where they needed to consult and where they did not. They also understood that they were part of a government team and, while they led in their appointed department, others, not just the PM and Chancellor, had a legitimate interest in the direction of policy in their area. Overall, in the political sphere, the best constraints on a Prime Minister are the Cabinet acting collectively and individual ministers thinking corporately. What might be called the UDI approach, by contrast, is a crude constraint that more often than not ends in tears.

At the official-administrative level, better constraint is also possible. In theory, the civil service should exercise constraint by setting out the consequences of different policy options and where necessary fearlessly stating views that, though unpopular, are believed to be right – telling truth to power. All too often, though, constraint is not applied this way but through other means – excessive risk aversion, exaggeration of the likely difficulties, refusing to believe that what the politicians have said they want is what they really want, slowing down or watering down implementation and, last but not least, simple incompetence.

This might sound harsh, but the evidence is there. Party-political impartiality is not in question; the problem is one of clarity, openness to risk, and competence. Nor is the problem new. In his diaries, Richard Crossman is critical of what he believed were selective records made by civil servants of Cabinet decisions. More powerfully still, he recorded the influence senior civil servants exercise not just as individuals, but more especially as a network which upheld the 'official view'.[23] Ironically for one so suspicious of Prime Ministers, he concluded that unless a minister has the backing of the Prime Minister or another very important colleague, 'the chance of prevailing against the official view is absolutely nil'. While any conclusion based on Crossman's view must be tempered by his relatively modest impact as a minister, his point here is nevertheless important.

At my much less prominent level, I found evidence of similar problems. In the summer of 1997, for example, I explained to officials that the government would want the Schools Bill then being drafted to include powers to intervene in poorly performing local education authorities. I had no doubt that this was what Education ministers and the Prime Minister wanted. Indeed, the government had just published a White Paper which stated this intention. Time and again draft clauses for the Bill came back to me hedged with qualifications and clearly prepared by people who did not believe in these powers. Eventually, a ministerial meeting was convened and the importance of the powers explained in no uncertain terms. I kept a copy of the note of the meeting. A year later, with the powers now on the statute book, I was responsible for preparing their first use in Hackney and Islington. Even then I was warned, given the nature of the legislation, not to use the powers and told that it would be very difficult and perhaps they would not stand up in court. I pulled the note of the meeting a year earlier out of the filing cabinet and said the intention had been clear and we would proceed. As it turned out, no one challenged the powers in court – but the legal foundations were weaker than they should have been, and without my personal pursuit of the issue at each stage they would not have been there at all.

Another example from my early days in the Education Department illustrates the vigorous attempts departments make to defend 'the official view'. In September 1997 I commented in a speech that after the introduction of the GCSE exam in 1988 there had been some grade inflation in the first few years before the Major government tightened up marking procedures. It turned out I was the first person representing the department to admit that this was the case, and headlines followed, such as 'Officials admit – exams have got easier' (*Daily Telegraph*, 17 September 1997). I came under immense pressure in the days that followed, not from ministers, but from officials, to put out a statement denying I had said this, or that it was true. I refused. Even though I had the backing of ministers, officials continued to pressurise me and also to try to persuade ministers to contradict me. Their line, sustained for a decade, had been that there was 'no evidence' that grade inflation had occurred. They even drafted a letter for me to sign and send to the *Telegraph*. Again I refused. Eventually, an official who had been there at the beginning of GCSE broke ranks; he sidled up to me and, with a faint smile, began, 'I don't suppose it does any harm to tell the truth now and again.' Then he told me that, in order to ensure the new exam got off to a good start, grade inflation in the early years of the exam had not only occurred, but had been actively encouraged. In other words, the official view, which the recently elected government had no interest in defending, had been untrue all along. I was glad I had resisted the pressure.

These are two relatively minor examples of how 'the official view' can be deployed to constrain prime ministerial power. In what sense, if any, did it enhance the quality of decision-making or of administration?

And in what sense, if any, could the exercise of constraint in this way be seen as more democratic than allowing the stated policy of a newly elected government to be implemented cleanly and crisply? As it turned out, the policy of intervening in local education authorities was extremely challenging to implement. With better law it might have been easier, but it would always have been a stretch. Even so, its consequences – documented by the National Audit Office among others – were significant and beneficial. Interestingly, though, after David Blunkett, Michael Bichard and I moved on from Education in 2001, the official view prevailed once more, and the powers in the Act have not been used since.

Clearly, this way of working within the civil service can certainly be considered a constraint, but surely even those most anxious about prime ministerial power cannot see this as a good way, still less the best way, to exercise constraint. Surely the civil service's power to constrain a Prime Minister would be much greater, and the results of its interaction with the Prime Minister significantly more productive, if it had a reputation for excellence in execution, for innovation in thinking and for quality in the evidence base on which it draws. In short, the more confidence politicians had in civil service competence, the more effective a constraint it would be when it was genuinely necessary.

To conclude the argument I am making in this section, then, a clearer, sharper, more effective prime ministerial function would enhance the power of the holder of the office to successfully do a job which is becoming steadily more demanding; the best constraints on that power would be the Cabinet acting coherently, ministers acting corporately, and a civil service acting with such evident competence that when it seeks to constrain the Prime Minister, he or she treats its advice with the utmost respect.

In other words, the aim should be to bring about both a strengthening of the power of the Prime Minister and a sharpening of the constraints on the holder of that office, in the interests of increasing the effectiveness of governance in the early twenty-first century.

A new Prime Minister, a fresh start*

These reflections lead me to the following wholly personal view of what might work in the future. To achieve this combination of stronger power and sharper constraint, Blair's successor, should, immediately on becoming Prime Minister, learn a lesson from the Australian government and establish a Department of the Prime Minister and the Cabinet, incorporating No. 10 and the Cabinet Office. Whenever this happens, there will be those who will condemn it as an unwarranted extension of prime ministerial power, but at the moment of appointment, any new Prime Minister has an extraordinary (if fleeting) honeymoon period which it would be a shame to waste.

A new department would be a sensible response to the problems described earlier in this chapter. The incoming Prime Minister should unapologetically justify it on the grounds of effectiveness and coherence. Clarity will replace fudge, blunt will become sharp. Moreover, he or she should argue that the intention is for the new department (PMC, to use the Australian abbreviation) to have fewer people in total than No. 10 and the Cabinet Office had in the past, so there would be an efficiency gain too.

Alongside the announcement of this important change in the machinery of government, the new Prime Minister would also of course announce the appointment of his or her new Cabinet. While the membership of the numerous Cabinet committees might not be announced for a few days, one important new Cabinet committee should be announced right away because of its significance. Called Public Service Policy and Expenditure (PSPE), it would be chaired by the Prime Minister, with the Chancellor of the Exchequer as deputy chair. The Chief Secretary to the Treasury, the minister for the Cabinet Office and the Secretaries of State for Health, Education, the Home Office and possibly Transport would also be members. Other Cabinet ministers would join its meetings as appropriate. The secretariat of the committee would be provided jointly by the new PMC and the Treasury, where there would also be changes. The Public Services Directorate of the

---

*This section was written for the hardback edition in early 2007, before Blair completed his term of office. Rather than alter it I thought the reader would benefit more if I commented in the new Postscript on the extent to which these proposals have been taken up by Gordon Brown.

Treasury would incorporate all the efficiency functions currently in the Office of Government and Commerce (OGC, which would refocus on delivering the government's most important capital and IT projects). A second permanent secretary in the Treasury would head this important new function, to be called Productivity and Public Expenditure (PPE), reporting on a day-to-day basis to the Chief Secretary.*

'The establishment of this powerful new committee', the Prime Minister should explain, 'is a signal of intent to put the reform of the public services at the heart of the new administration.' After all, the central issue of modern politics is how to secure constantly improving performance and better customer service standards across the public services without raising taxes. 'Under the previous administration,' the new Prime Minister would say, 'Britain's public services improved and the historic underfunding of them was corrected; that improvement needs to continue and indeed accelerate, but no one should be under any illusion that, in future, annual increases in resources will match those of the previous decade.

'Driving through successful reform,' he or she will continue, 'building on the undoubted achievements of successive administrations, exploiting the new resource levels in both capital and revenue, and securing the best possible value for every pound of taxpayers' money will require the government to act corporately, hence the new committee. Crucially, it requires effective collaboration at the centre of government, hence the new secretariat. Finally, it requires an administrative machine that is sleek, powerful and highly competent, hence the proposed PMC and the changes in the Treasury.

'Now, colleagues,' the Prime Minister will beam at the journalists who for the moment cannot help but give him or her the benefit of the doubt, 'if you will excuse me, there's work to be done.'

*

Before turning to the organisational implications of this startling announcement, one caveat and one general observation need to be

*In the autumn of 2006, the Treasury merged its Public Services Directorate with its wider work on productivity, a significant step in the right direction. Some weeks later the efficiency functions of the OGC were returned to the Treasury, a second step in the right direction.

made. The caveat is this: there are parts of the Cabinet Office that deal with aspects of foreign and security policy and a range of other things that I do not intend to deal with here. Rather I will stick to my knitting, since this is a book about how a Prime Minister and government can reform the public services. The general observation is this: there is no organisational structure in the world that will work without a shared sense of purpose or a commitment to collaboration from key personalities. Oversized egos and destructive factionalism can undermine even the most perfect structures. This is the reason, Jim Collins argues in *Good to Great*, that the first characteristic of great companies is that they get the right people on the bus and the wrong ones off it.[24] It is why Clement Attlee said in 1961, 'A fairly egocentric Cabinet minister can get along, but an egocentric Prime Minister can't.'[25] It is why Kenneth Stowe, a senior civil servant of the 1960s and 1970s – who for our purposes now needs to be forgiven his sexism – said, 'It's all about good chaps. 'Fraid so.'[26] And it is incidentally why I was so careful in selecting staff for the Delivery Unit.

Above all, it is why a new Prime Minister should give the utmost care to appointing a new Cabinet and should think, in relation to the public services, about building a team of ministers who will drive the project forward. The liberal writer John Morley said, over a century ago, that 'the Prime Minister is the keystone of the Cabinet Arch'.[27] At least in relation to the public services, this should be true, I am arguing, and furthermore the arch should be robust and, if possible, elegant. Too often in the past couple of decades the Cabinet Arch has looked either precarious or clumsy. Famously, Blair's reshuffles were not well executed.* I think the entire process needs to be treated as worthy of the application of the best modern personnel management techniques. The people who are appointed should be strong, trained and prepared to work in teams. Furthermore, succession planning should be taken seriously – where are the high-potential junior ministers? How are they being trained and developed? Who is planning their careers? Of course

---

*In his diary Alastair Campbell observes (27 May 2003): 'These reshuffles, like pregnancy, dentistry and exams, were further proof that pain has no memory. I didn't know how many we have done now, but until a new one starts, you forget how awful the process is. First the usual and occasionally random discussion of who should go where. Then the unstructured remembering . . . why such-and-such a move was unwise or even impossible.' Well, maybe, but why 'random'? Why 'unstructured'? If they had done so many, why hadn't they professionalised the process?

day-to-day politics will disrupt the best-laid plans, but that is not an argument for not having a plan at all. The planning also needs to go a stage further. The new Prime Minister needs to create 'a guiding coalition' (see Chapter 6) at the top of every department so that the relevant combination of ministers, special advisers and top officials in every department is cohesive – and within each department the secretary of state and the permanent secretary need to give time to building the coalition.

The Prime Minister, in relation to his or her overall public service reform programme, needs to build a guiding coalition too. Thus, as he or she creates the new committee, simultaneously, with assistance from the Cabinet Secretary, he or she needs to ensure that the relevant permanent secretaries and No. 10 political advisers are built into the wider team that has the responsibility for delivering successful reform and outstanding results without remorselessly raising public expenditure. This is what the public wants, not just in this country but across the developed world, and it cannot be left to chance.

The Department of the Prime Minister and the Cabinet (PMC)

Given the chaotic history of past decades, it is also relatively straight-forward to agree that a new department would be a major step forward. It is harder to describe what the new department's organisational structure should be and how it should function. There are always several plausible ways to cut a set of responsibilities and – reinforcing the point made in the previous section about the guiding coalition – to some extent the design of the organisation should be built around the people. Nevertheless, in relation to public services, it is worth sketching out one potentially effective way to organise it and then examining how some of its key processes might work.

Heading the new department would be the Cabinet Secretary, a post which should continue also to be Head of the Home Civil Service (as the task is still somewhat quaintly described). Beneath him or her (although so far it has always been a man), there should be two permanent secretaries, one responsible for strategy and performance, the other responsible for the underlying capability and capacity (or what management consultants call 'organisational health') of the civil service and the government machine (see Figure 9.1).

The permanent secretary for performance would oversee strategy (long-term policy thinking), the co-ordination of short and medium-term policy thinking (requiring a close working relationship with the No. 10 Policy Unit) and delivery (securing the implementation of already agreed policy on key priorities). The current Strategy Unit, Delivery Unit and Economic and Domestic Secretariat would all come within this remit.

The permanent secretary for organisational health would be responsible for all people issues (top appointments, performance reviews and so on), the overall structure of governments and departments (what the jargon calls 'the machinery of government') and securing improvements in the capability of the civil service. Crucially too, this person would need to drive the change in civil service culture – its ambition and urgency for example – which throughout the preceding pages I have argued is necessary. The key to this in turn is appointing the right people, often from outside the civil service, to the top jobs. As Blair

Figure 9.1: Structure of the proposed Department of the Prime Minister and the Cabinet

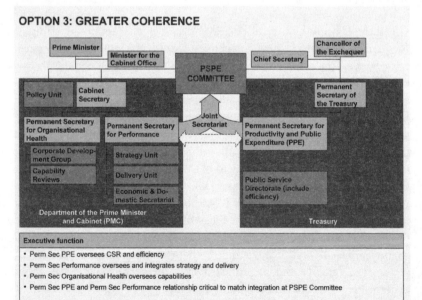

OPTION 3: GREATER COHERENCE

Executive function
- Perm Sec PPE oversees CSR and efficiency
- Perm Sec Performance oversees and integrates strategy and delivery
- Perm Sec Organisational Health oversees capabilities
- Perm Sec PPE and Perm Sec Performance relationship critical to match integration at PSPE Committee

remarked to me once, 'The leadership team at the top is absolutely crucial . . . you cannot leave that to chance.' The permanent secretary would also have responsibility for the current Corporate Development Group of the Cabinet Office and all the machinery of government people, and would also include taking responsibility for the capability reviews which Gus O'Donnell, the present Cabinet Secretary, instituted in 2005.* In the first instance, it was right for O'Donnell to ask the Delivery Unit to develop and implement the capability reviews because of its reputation, but now they have been developed it makes sense for the Delivery Unit to return to its single-minded focus on performance and for the reviews to be transferred elsewhere. This permanent secretary would be responsible for strengthening and, where appropriate, standardising key civil service processes such as preparing policy advice to ministers as well as the development of innovative processes – for example considering how responsibility for policy advice itself might sometimes be contracted out or contested in some way.

Just as in 2001 the Delivery Unit had to build crucial relationships in sometimes difficult circumstances, so each of these permanent secretaries would have to work out how to secure excellent working relationships inside government, based on a win-win deal with each key stakeholder. Just two examples: the permanent secretary for performance would need a close and trusting working relationship with the Treasury. Together they would service the powerful new Cabinet PSPE Committee, and together they would need to think about strategy and long-term expenditure. The 'win' for the PMC would be better, more up-to-date information on public expenditure and a strong influence on major spending decisions. The 'win' for the Treasury would be the capacity to begin to manage public sector productivity, which is now the central issue in managing public finances.

The same permanent secretary would need to develop a similarly effective relationship with the No. 10 Policy Unit. Given that, under these proposals, there would be a powerful strategy function under his or her aegis, the Policy Unit could be small and powerful and staffed by political appointees who are both heavyweight in their fields and really know the Prime Minister's mind, people such as Paul Corrigan and

*These have examined, department by department, capability in three areas: leadership, strategy and delivery. All departments had gone through the process by December 2007 and the reports were published.

Conor Ryan in Blair's third-term Policy Unit. The permanent secretary for performance would need to invest in the relationships with these people. The 'win' for him or her would be a much better understanding of the politics behind an issue and a deeper understanding of both the Prime Minister's personal thinking and that of the key secretaries of state, with whom these political advisers would interact on a regular basis; the 'win' for them would be the ability to exert influence over the implementation machinery on which, ultimately, everything depends. The permanent secretary for organisational health would need excellent relationships with the Treasury too, not least in relation to reducing the number of civil servants. Relations with departmental permanent secretaries and their personnel functions would be important too; there's no need here to labour the point.

It is, however, worth touching on whether the much closer working relationship implied between the Treasury and the new PMC is within the realms of credibility, since if traditional institutional tensions between the Cabinet Office and the Treasury are so great that they could never be overcome, then my proposal falls. In fact, I do not believe this would be the case. Crucial, of course, in the first instance is the relationship between the Prime Minister and the Chancellor, and the parallel relationship between the Chief Secretary and the minister for the Cabinet Office. Whatever the recent experience, history shows that a good relationship between the two titans in any government is both perfectly possible and often achieved. Listen to Denis Healey, for example, reflecting on being Chancellor under Jim Callaghan: 'In my opinion, Jim Callaghan was, for most of his time, the best of Britain's post-war Prime Ministers after Attlee . . . the political skills he had perfected . . . were now just what his office needed. Without them the government would never have survived the negotiations with the IMF.'[28] Note how Healey gives credit to Callaghan for an achievement he might have claimed himself. Later, Callaghan offered Healey the post of Foreign Secretary, but to his relief Healey turned it down: 'I had broken my back in planting the tree and I wanted to be there to gather the fruit,' said Healey.[29]

About twenty years later, this is what John Major had to say about his relationship with Kenneth Clarke: 'I saw the Chancellor each week, and his pivotal position in the government ensured that we discussed every issue and its financial implications . . . Our meetings were relaxed affairs laden with political gossip and, if in the evening, rounded off with a drink.'[30]

At the level of the Chief Secretary and minister for the Cabinet Office, the holders of these offices would no doubt take their cue from the titans. In any case, in my time I saw Andrew Smith and Paul Boateng get along well with Gus Macdonald and later, at the start of the third term, Des Browne with John Hutton. Equally, at the official and institutional level, there is no reason to assume tensions cannot be overcome. The Delivery Unit, as we've seen, was so popular with the Treasury that they invited us to cohabit. The collaboration was genuine and, when necessary, so was the independence. In the present parliament, Gus O'Donnell as Cabinet Secretary has maintained an excellent relationship with Nick Macpherson at the Treasury, building on their long and productive working relationship in that department.

Public Services Policy and Expenditure Committee (PSPE)
Supposing the PMC was established as I have described it, let me briefly touch on the parallel changes mentioned in the new Prime Minister's announcement. The new committee (Public Services Policy and Expenditure, or PSPE) would demand the time and attention of the Prime Minister and the Chancellor and be attended by other key ministers, but what would it do? I'll come to how it would monitor performance and productivity, set strategy and shape spending later in this chapter, but here let me describe its key task: to receive updates on progress from departments on a rolling basis. Each key department might be in the spotlight quarterly. When it was a department's turn, in discussion with the permanent secretary for performance it would generate a report on overall progress using a standardised framework. In response to suggestions from the Prime Minister or the Chancellor, one or two issues for deeper inquiry would be selected either because of their importance or because there were problems. The named top official responsible for these issues, along with the relevant minister, would attend – and the committee would grill them. Prior to the meeting, the relevant official might be expected to have a sleepless night because it would be a thorough going-over. Imagine the possible outcomes – recognition (perhaps leading to reward), assistance (enabling the job to be done) or, where there was evidence of sustained poor performance, consequences such as transfer to a less challenging assign-

ment or even, in rare cases, losing the job (and why not?); for a talented and ambitious civil servant, this is a positive ratio of opportunity and threat.

The state of South Australia has recently instituted a process of this kind to secure delivery of its ambitious strategic plan, which includes more than seventy published targets, some of them very ambitious. They have brought a further innovation to the process: the involvement on a committee of this kind (chaired by Mike Rann, the Premier) of two outsiders, one of them a businessman, the other a campaigner against social exclusion. These two don't play by the polite rules of the traditional civil service; as you might say, they play Australian rules and make it very challenging for those in the spotlight. Again, why not? Spending large sums of public money to deliver vital social outcomes is an extraordinarily important responsibility.

The benefits would be immense. Like traditional Delivery Unit stocktakes, they would create a regular routine and a set of deadlines. They would also ensure that the most precious of commodities in any organisation – an honest conversation about performance – happened with all the key players in the room. Crucially, the existence of the committee would ensure that, between its meetings, a constant, honest conversation went on between PMC and the relevant department. You can be sure, for example, that if the permanent secretary of a department knew there were real problems in a key area, he or she would want to resolve them before accounting for them at PSPE and would therefore open up the dialogue in a purposeful way with PMC well in advance of the meeting. As a result, problems, instead of being allowed to drift, would be resolved.

There would be other advantages too. Think how much the ministers present at PSPE meetings would learn, not just about the policy issues in other departments, but about delivery problems and how to resolve them. Since at present no one thinks consciously about how to ensure ministers learn, this would be a major step forward, the benefits of which would be ploughed back rapidly into performance.

Before moving on, let me deal with one possible objection, namely that inner Cabinets have been tried before and have never worked in peacetime. One answer to this is that while it might have been true in the past, that does not necessarily mean it would not work now. Much more importantly, though, the real answer is that I am not proposing an inner

Cabinet. I am proposing something new: an admittedly powerful Cabinet committee to deal with public services policy and expenditure. To those who say the members of this committee would have much more influence over this central area of government responsibility than other members of the Cabinet, I would answer bluntly that they would anyway, but without the committee. The difference my proposal would make is that they would be powerful together. The net result would be more significant impact, I believe, and surely the entire government would sign up to that. In any case, if the Prime Minister chose, the committee could report periodically to the full Cabinet, setting out both progress made and challenges ahead, as I did as head of the Delivery Unit.

The Treasury and public sector productivity

Then there is the need for further change in the Treasury. The Treasury has advantages over most other departments: it has fewer people, and generally they are younger and more talented. I remember when we moved into the Treasury in 2003 being struck in the (excellent) canteen by how young the average age seemed to be. The one downside of this comparative youth was that I was never able to get beyond the quarter-finals of the table football competition, but in every other respect it brought benefits, as the quality of the best Treasury work demonstrates. Moreover, the Treasury has already been significantly modernised. As Robert Peston says: '[Gus] O'Donnell [Permanent Secretary of the Treasury 2002–5] and his senior management team strove to encourage teamwork and break down the traditional hierarchical barriers to communication . . . Like a business . . . these days the Treasury's senior echelon . . . even hold open days during which anyone can fire questions at them about anything.'[31]

I can vouch for this as occasionally I was asked, as a friendly outsider, to chair these sessions. However, as I have argued, public service productivity is now the central issue of domestic politics. The Treasury, therefore, needs a function that can manage productivity (i.e. both outcomes and inputs) with the same hard-headedness it applied to expenditure before 1997, when cuts were the order of the day. To do this, it needs all the tools at its disposal, hence the proposal outlined above to integrate the management of efficiency into its Public Services

Directorate and create a new PPE Directorate while freeing the Office of Government Commerce to focus firmly back on its core business of overseeing major projects (where progress had been insufficient and there are still major problems).* Hence also the proposal to build the kind of relationship between this part of the Treasury and the permanent secretary for performance in the PMC that existed between the old Public Services Directorate and the Delivery Unit when Nick Macpherson and I were there (and which no doubt still exists).

At the moment, public sector productivity is much talked about in government circles, and not just in the UK, but no one anywhere in the world as far as I know has yet found a way to manage it effectively. In fact, because of its experience with PSA targets, the Gershon efficiency review and the Atkinson review (of public sector productivity), the UK Treasury could credibly claim to be the world leader already. The new part of the Treasury I propose could be the powerhouse that achieves the intellectual breakthroughs in this area which are just over the horizon: most crucially the need to find a way to measure productivity across the public services, not just at national level, but at the level of the institution (school or hospital, for example). If the Delivery Unit can define an effective measure of 'likelihood of delivery', no doubt the Treasury could do the same for public sector productivity.

Now, to illustrate how these three institutional reforms – PMC, PSPE and PPE (no reform is complete without some new abbreviations) – might transform some key processes of the centre of government, in addition to the new kind of stocktake already described, let me take two examples.

1. The Public Service Agreement Framework

Each department has, since 1998, signed up to a public service agreement with the Treasury. The PSA sets out the targets the department will seek to deliver in return for the public money it receives from the Treasury. By connecting outcomes to inputs for the first time, this was an important innovation and the first step towards managing productivity. Tucked away in the PSAs there are some value-for-money targets, another good idea, but these have not received the same attention as other targets: there is, for example, no tailored deliverology for them.

*Since this paragraph was drafted these steps have been taken, one of the advantages perhaps of sharing a draft of the book with the Cabinet Secretary.

Also, it has to be said, some of them are obscure, bordering on the bizarre. In addition, in 2004, following the Gershon review, departments were given efficiency targets to meet, another good idea but separated from the PSA targets and monitored by the Office of Government Commerce rather than the Treasury or the Delivery Unit. Finally, in the Cabinet Office some good work was done between 2001 and 2005 on public perceptions of public services, another good idea resulting in another stream of data but not connected in any way to the PSAs (although some PSA targets did specify customer or citizen attitudes as outcomes). Confused? Of course you are, and so was government. Here were several major innovations in search of coherence.

Crucially and conveniently, there was a coherent idea waiting for just these ingredients – public value. The classic text on this subject is Mark Moore's *Creating Public Value: Strategic Management in Government*. Moore describes public value thus:

> The definition . . . equates managerial success in the public sector with initiating and reshaping public sector enterprises in ways that increase their value to the public in both the short and the long run. . . . Sometimes this means increasing efficiency, effectiveness, or fairness in currently defined missions. Other times it means introducing programs that respond to a new political aspiration or meet a new need in the organization's task environment. Still other times it means recasting the mission of the organization and repositioning it in its political and task environment so that its old capabilities can be used more responsively and effectively. On occasion it means reducing the claims that government organizations make on taxpayers and reclaiming the resources now committed to the organizations for alternative public or private uses. This is clearly the proper conceptual definition of managerial success: to increase the public value produced by public sector organizations in both the short and the long run.[32]

This is an advance, but short of being clearly measurable. However, tied up in this definition of public value are a number of key elements:
1. delivery of results
2. organisational health of the institution or service
3. efficiency
4. public perception of the institution or service
5. expenditure.

The central question – in effect the productivity question – is how much of the first four are you getting for the fifth? Turning this into a ratio is not the most complicated of mathematical challenges. By developing an assessment framework, similar in nature to the Delivery Unit's framework for assessing likelihood of delivery (see Delivery Manual, Document 8), but built around these five aspects, each of which is relevant to every public service, a measure for public service productivity could be derived. It might at first be too crude to meet the justly exacting standards of national statistics, but it would certainly be good enough for PSPE to use as its means of monitoring departmental progress on the public services. Moreover, if the PSAs were revised to incorporate all these five strands instead of just the first and last, they would provide a coherent framework within which to think about the overall progress not just of each service, but of government as a whole. The Treasury's proposals for PSAs, published late in 2006, shift thinking helpfully in this direction, but could go further.

Let me address, though, one challenge before it inevitably arises. Assessing public perception of public services is a key aspect of public value and should not be confused with tracking opinion polls for political purposes. Here I am thinking of data that would tell us, for example, whether the public in Newcastle valued their police service more than people in Bristol or Nottingham. Or the equivalent data for the Health Service. This kind of benchmarking data would raise questions at both national and local level and, through requiring answers to them, lead to improvement. In addition, it is important to point out that significant aspects of public services can be improved faster and more profoundly if the relevant members of the public are willing to actively engage. Reading standards, for example, will improve if, as happened in 1998–9, there is a significant increase in the percentage of parents who read to their children at bedtime. This is not an alternative to teaching children well in school, but a reinforcement of it. Similarly, if citizens are more willing to be active in their local community, they, with police, can significantly reduce anti-social behaviour. In health there are numerous examples: everything from obesity to smoking, in the end, depends on the actions of individuals which government can advocate, facilitate or incentivise, but cannot mandate. For these reasons alone, understanding public attitudes to public services is vital; in fact, the more the public values a service, the more public value it will have and the more its results will improve. A coherent centre of government would seek to set this virtuous circle in motion.

2. Strategy and expenditure

The second example of how the reforms I propose would improve government performance relates to the connection between strategy and expenditure. Under the Blair government, strategy for the public services was largely the domain of each department interacting with No. 10, sometimes the Policy Unit, sometimes the Strategy Unit, and sometimes both. The Treasury too had a strong and legitimate interest. The result was more or less messy, multi-stranded negotiations. One should not exaggerate the problems, for there were major positive strategic developments, but no one, least of all the participants, would argue that this was the most efficient or elegant way to arrive at a strategy. The five-year strategies published in 2004–5 might have been impressive documents (I'm biased, I know), but the process for arriving at them was draining and painstaking.

Meanwhile, the major funding decisions were made every two years (1998, 2000, 2002 and 2004, and then a three-year gap until 2007). The process for a spending review usually involved departments preparing a set of proposals by December, connecting the proposals to specific funding requests by February of the following year and then entering into a negotiation with the Treasury at both official and political level. No. 10 was a major participant alongside the Treasury in the latter stages of this process, and the result was a messy three-way negotiation or, even worse, three messy two-way negotiations which sapped energy and demanded huge amounts of time, but usually somehow resulted in sound agreements which were published – accompanied by one of the Chancellor's magisterial statements to the House – in early July of the spending review year.

In 2003–4, both the strategy process and the spending review process described here happened at the same time, but largely separately, which was utterly exhausting and, though the outcomes were, miraculously, usually sensible, no one believed they had been maximised. The question is whether, under the new arrangements I propose here, government could do better, and the answer must surely be 'yes'. The process could unfold as follows.

Spring 2007	Departmental and cross-departmental spending proposals to Treasury with proposed targets
Autumn 2007 (or earlier if departments choose to settle early)	Departmental spending allocations agreed along with targets
April 2008	New settlement agreed in 2007 comes into effect
Spring 2008–spring 2009	Entire government machine focuses on delivery results
Spring 2009	Departmental strategy reviews launched in collaboration with both PMC and PPE; stakeholders consulted
Autumn 2009	Updated departmental strategies agreed as PSPE: implications for government as a whole assessed. Summary strategies published and consultation on targets begins.
Winter 2009–10	Nature of next round of targets established in context of the overall public value framework
Spring 2010	Departmental and cross-departmental spending proposals to Treasury etc.

A start down this road has been made. This way, a department would review its strategy and then its priorities, that is, the areas in which it wanted to set targets (across the five aspects of public value set out above). It would then agree the kinds of target it would set, but not yet put a value to them. Now clear on strategy and priorities, it would make its spending proposals and relate these to the specific timetabled targets it thought it could deliver. Finally, after a negotiation, the spending allocation and the new PSA incorporating values for each of the five strands of public value would be agreed and published. PSPE would oversee the entire integrated process. The permanent secretary for performance and his or her counterpart in the PPE part of the Treasury would drive the process collaboratively. Its leadership would lie with the former until the strategy and priorities were identified and then shift to the latter once it became largely a question of money but of course, through regular reports to the PSPE, both would be well informed throughout.

The result would be a single, integrated, three-year cycle. Better product from more elegant process: well worth having and perfectly plausible. Clement Attlee considered and ultimately rejected the idea of a Prime Minister's Department, but he was always keen to bring 'greater cohesion to the machine of government'.[33] The proposals I have made in this section are designed to do exactly that in these much more complex times. Future Prime Ministers and Chancellors would be much better served than Blair and Brown were in my time in government if these proposals were adopted.

A new understanding of public service reform

A new, coherent centre of government will also need a new, coherent understanding of how to reform the public services. As the preceding chapters have illustrated – graphically in places – reforming the public services over the past decade has been a struggle. It should also have become clear that the struggle was not just about delivery – it was conceptual. For example, the conversations I had with Blair about inspection, with Gordon Brown about targets and with numerous ministers about relationships with professionals are all vital conceptual questions. And, of course, the conceptual challenges are integrally related to the delivery challenges because lack of conceptual clarity results in mixed messages and confusion both in government departments and in the public services beyond Whitehall. The debate about devolving responsibility – whether to consumers and citizens or professionals – is a classic case in point.

Blair himself often talked about the transition in his own reform programme, from a first phase which was largely top-down ('flogging the system' in his terms) to a more sustainable reform based on quasi-markets through which the incentives in the system drive continuous improvement. The other parallel transition is the one from a first term where reform was slow or non-existent in large parts of government to a second term where, in domestic policy at any rate, it became the central issue for the government. To understand these transitions, though, it is necessary to step back for a moment and see a wider, more profound transition in the nature of the state which is affecting the entire developed world, for only with this perspective can the Blair–Brown programme be fully understood and the challenge ahead accurately described.

In his extraordinary analysis of the course of history and its implications for the twenty-first century, *The Shield of Achilles*, Philip Bobbitt argues that, following the end of the Cold War, the nature of the modern state itself is in transition. The conflicts which dominated the twentieth century were fought by nation-states – a concept familiar to Clement Attlee and still familiar to Margaret Thatcher. However, with the fall of the Berlin Wall and the final collapse of communism, globalisation became the dominant factor in shaping the modern world and, as a result, Bobbitt says, we are witnessing the emergence of 'the market state, which depends on the international capital markets and, to a lesser degree, on the modern multi-national business network to create stability in the world economy, in preference to management by national . . . political bodies'. This is the trend that Brown and Ed Balls understood when passing control of interest rates to the Bank of England. Moreover, Bobbitt argues, 'whereas the nation-state justified itself as an instrument to service the welfare of the people . . . the market state exists to maximise the opportunities enjoyed by all members of society'.[34] Alongside this transition from welfare to opportunity, the market-state will, he argues, also bring about a transition from an emphasis on rights to an emphasis on security, as it is required to respond to the threats associated with globalisation, such as 'the monitoring of epidemics and diseases, of international migration, of terrorism, of espionage and of threats to the environment'.[35]

As it responds in these ways to the demands of the emerging global market, Bobbitt argues, the market-state will need to become significantly more effective, which will result in an increase in its costs. However, because globalisation makes it harder to enforce high taxes (they drive companies and talent elsewhere), in order to keep its costs under control, government will have to do less, better. This is the underlying explanation for Blair's emphasis on the enabling state. As he put it towards the end of his time in office:

> Globalisation is profoundly changing the nature of our society. It forces businesses and people to step up a gear simply to keep abreast with the pace of change: commercial transactions are completed without delay;

communications happen instantly; goods can be moved rapidly across huge distances.

Government is not immune to these changes. For it to continue to maintain its legitimacy, it needs to change its outlook radically. The technological innovations driving global change have not just opened up new opportunities for delivering services, but increased people's expectations of what they want from those who serve them.

To meet these challenges the State must provide the same level of customer service as the public have come to expect in every other aspect of their lives. To achieve this, the role of the State is not to control, but to enable. Making modern public services the cornerstone of the enabling state – where the State provides strategic direction not micro-management – requires a transformation of how we deliver our services.[36]

In his lecture to the *Guardian* Public Services Summit (26–27 January 2006), Matthew Taylor, at the time a key figure in No. 10, went further:

What is different about the period we are living through is the combination of two powerful sets of factors. First are the demographic shifts such as population ageing, mass migration and growing ethnic and cultural diversity, the rise in women's employment and declining dominance of the traditional family form. Second are trends in public expectations and attitudes: declining deference . . . a rights-based culture . . . [This is] a heady mix driven and reinforced by a 24-hour mass media.

This explains convincingly why the old left's demands for the reinstatement of the public services of the nation-state era are not just unpopular, because the public services of that era were not good enough, but also forlorn, because there is no going back.

It is against this background that public service reform needs to be conceptualised. The more governments of the future are able to clarify both the ends they seek to achieve through public service reform and the means by which they seek to achieve them, the greater their chances of success. For much of the Blair era, ministers, including the Prime Minister, were necessarily learning as they went along. In a sense, this book is an account of how that learning took place. If, as Bobbitt argues, this is a transitional era and the transition is happening at an unprecedented pace, then it is not surprising that governments in many countries have found it difficult to be clear on their approach. What is undoubtedly true is that elsewhere in the world Blair's approach was viewed with a mixture of admiration and awe; the UK is currently seen as the most significant laboratory of learning at the cutting edge of public service reform anywhere in the world.

Given the experience of the past decade, though, it is now possible to set out a conceptual model of public service reform which codifies what we already know and could guide future action and ensure greater clarity (see Figure 9.2).

The most obvious approach to reforming public services is what Figure 9.2 calls command-and-control. It involves a top-down implementation of a change the government wants to bring about. Examples mentioned in this book include the approaches to literacy and numeracy in primary schools and waiting times in the Health Service. It has become fashionable to criticise command-and-control, both because it is not popular with professionals, who, generally speaking, do not warm to being told what to do by governments, and because, it is

Figure 9.2: Making sense of large-scale system reform

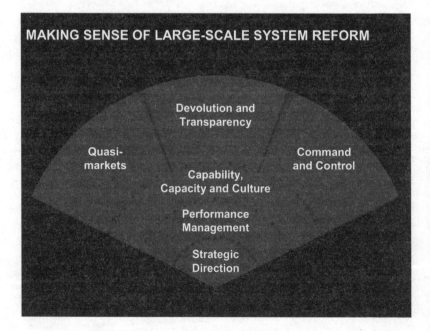

argued, it is 'unsustainable'.

In fact, in some circumstances, it is the right approach to take – for example where a service is failing or seriously underperforming, or where there is a very high priority which is urgent. If a government chooses to adopt the approach in these circumstances, then crucially it is obliged to execute it excellently. It should go without saying that command-and-control done badly is disastrous. As it happens, in the cases of both literacy and numeracy and NHS waiting times, the services were poor, the priority was high and – admittedly with mistakes on the way – government did a very good job. As a result, in both cases, the services improved significantly in a short space of time. While the approach is indeed unsustainable because of the energy and attention it requires at all levels in a service, the results it delivers can be and – in both examples quoted – have been sustained. To pick up the argument I made to Cabinet in December 2004, command-and-control done well can rapidly shift a service from 'awful' to 'adequate'. This is a major achievement, but not enough because the public are not satisfied with 'adequate' – they want 'good' or 'great'. But command-and-control cannot deliver 'good' or 'great' for, as Joel Klein, chancellor of the New York City School System, puts it: 'You cannot mandate greatness; it has to be unleashed.'

In seeking to do exactly that, Tony Blair, especially in relation to Health and Education, turned to the second paradigm, quasi-markets. The argument for introducing market-like pressures into the public services is clear – people like choice; also competition drives productivity improvement in other sectors of the economy, so why not in the public services? Moreover, as Julian Le Grand argues, however committed the professionals are, 'they can never have the degree of concern for users that users have for themselves'.[37] The potential benefits for government of putting the user in the driving seat include not just improved performance, satisfaction and productivity, but also the possibility that the system constantly improves itself and therefore no longer has to be driven ('flogged', as Blair would say) as it does under the command-and-control option. As Blair put it in a conversation with me once, 'Innovation should come from self-sustaining systems.'

The quasi-market option works well in many situations, but certain conditions have to be in place. Consumers of the service need to be able to exercise choice as, for example, they can in much of health and education. At least a degree of diversity of provision has to be desirable, for example in relation to school ethos or specialism; and a range of different competing suppliers needs to emerge. There are also dangers which need to be avoided. The greatest is that the quasi-markets, like pure markets, will militate against equity, yet for most public services equity is a highly desirable outcome. It is for this reason, above all, that the quasi-market is 'quasi' and not pure. So in Blair's education and health reforms, unlike a pure market, the price (of an operation or a school place, for example) is fixed by government rather than by the laws of supply and demand. Moreover, the evidence shows that if quasi-markets are to promote equity, the government needs both to regulate more and to intervene more than it would in a pure market. In the school reforms, for example, the government has severely restricted selection by academic ability because the evidence shows this harms equity. For the health quasi-market, the government has provided advice and assistance to patients to enable those with low confidence or low incomes to exercise choice. Through this combination of market forces and evidence-based regulation, the aim is to reap the benefits of a market in terms of innovation and productivity while enhancing equity and the other values which are central to the public services. As Blair once explained to me, a fundamental problem with the debate about the public services has been that

> people fail to distinguish between outcomes or ethos, which are distinctive for public services, and a lot of the management of a public service, which is actually identical to business and [to which] best business practice . . . is central. So the National Health Service at one level is values driven but at another level of course it is a business.

The third paradigm is the combination of devolution and transparency. This is necessary because there are some services and some circumstances where neither command-and-control nor quasi-markets are desirable. This is why Gordon Brown, in his important speech to the Social Market Foundation in February 2003, emphasised the need for 'non-market, non-command-and-control models of public service reform'. Where, for example, individual choice does not apply, as for example in policing, prisons or the court service, it is impossible to create quasi-markets. The pioneer of devolution and transparency is the New York City Police Department, which devolved operational responsibility and resources to each precinct commander and then created transparency by publishing weekly crime data precinct by precinct. Precinct commanders were held to account for their performance by the chief of police. The model, though, has wider application and its influence can be seen in, for example, the reforms of the court service or police here. Given the Brown spending reforms, which allow devolution of three-year budgets, devolution and transparency has great potential in the UK. As with quasi-markets, it unleashes frontline managers to do the job and holds them to account for their performance. Also like quasi-market models, it allows for services to be contracted out. Thus a small number of privately run prisons or privately provided local education authority services have been commissioned, resulting in a boost to the performance of the whole system, through contracting out. In other words, beneficial competitive pressure can be introduced even where individual choice does not apply.

I have described these three approaches to reform as paradigms advisedly. They are theoretically different models. In practice, in any given service a combination of the three can be adopted. Thus, for example, in the school system, failing schools are required to improve under pressure from government (command-and-control), parents exercise choice and funding follows their decisions (quasi-markets), but also funding is devolved to school level, headteachers have extensive operational authority and their results are published (devolution and transparency). The key, though, is for those overseeing the reform of a system to be conscious of the paradigms and how they combine.

This leads us to the three core functions at the base of the fan in Figure 9.2. Whichever of the paradigms a government chooses (or if it chooses a combination of them), it retains responsibility for these three major aspects of reform, which cannot be delegated. The first is the capacity, capability and culture of the system. For example, an individual hospital cannot ensure a continuing supply of good doctors or nurses. Neither can it secure the overall hospital-building programme. Nor can it set the legal framework within which doctors practise, nor shape the overall relationship between that profession, the state and society. For a public service only government can do this, albeit in consultation with others. A similar case could be made for education and policing.

The second is managing the overall performance of the system. While an individual hospital is responsible for its own performance, it is not in a position to set the objectives of the system, nor to decide how progress will be measured and what data will be published. Nor can it decide who intervenes (or when and how) when the performance of an individual hospital falls below an acceptable standard. Again, only government can decide these issues; again, the same applies in other public services.

Third, in each public service and for the public services as a whole, a strategic direction is required: future trends need analysing and understanding; the various steps in a reform programme need to be sequenced and their combined effects understood; and the values that underpin the reform need to be stated and their impact secured. Again, only government can do this. In the reformed centre of government I have described here, each department would carry out these crucial functions in its area of responsibility. The reformed Treasury and PMC would provide these at overall public service level, and political direction and management in relation to all three would come from the Prime Minister and the new Cabinet committee, PSPE.

This latter point should not be underestimated. The reform of public services is always intensely political, as the history of the post-war era makes clear. Successful reform therefore requires successful political management. As Blair put it to me in conversation once,

> don't think you can simply have a good idea and not manage and build stakeholders who will support it . . . [also] don't back away from the thing you know is right, because in the end you'll have to come back to it. [Finally,] don't always feel you have to change the entire system overnight, as opposed to building an empirical evidence base for your change programme. In other words, I think you can go step by step.

He often quoted Margaret Thatcher's employment legislation as an example. The proposals I have made here would strengthen collective political strategy and management.

In various places throughout the preceding chapters, it has been made clear that – partly because this has been an era of transition – the paradigms have not been as clear as they might have been, and the role of central government not as sharply defined as it should have been. Moreover individual departments as well as the centre of government have lacked the capacity to carry out these crucial functions which only government can do. As a result, mistakes have been made, some of them illustrated in Figure 9.3. Success in the future will depend upon learning from these mistakes and avoiding them.

If a new Prime Minister established the PMC and the other reforms

Figure 9.3: Common errors in large-scale system reform

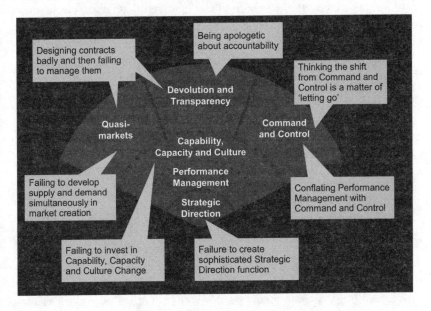

set out here, and learnt the hard lessons of the past decade through candid, self-aware analysis, a step change in the performance of both the public services and government could be brought about. This would both inform and demand a fundamental reshaping of the civil service along the lines this entire book has advocated. Then the legacy of the Blair years would not just be the substantial achievements set out in Chapter 8, but also a government machine and the experience and evidence on which to base the next step change in performance.

342   INSTRUCTION TO DELIVER

Conclusion

The earlier parts of this chapter showed how the job of Prime Minister has been stretched and become extremely demanding. I have argued that, contrary to much of the commentary on prime ministerial power, it should be strengthened not weakened. The later parts of this chapter suggest in outline how, in relation to the public services, this might be done. I am not wedded to the specifics of every aspect of what I propose and, as I have argued, I believe that in building new structures one should take account of the individuals involved. I agree that holders of the office of Prime Minister can make of it what they will. As Harold Wilson put it: 'No. 10 is what the Prime Minister of the day makes it.'[38] I agree that this is a strength. My point is to set out plausibly, specifically in relation to the public services, how the role might be done differently and better by strengthening the Prime Minister's capacity to exercise his power. Anyone who anticipates holding the office should think very hard about how best to meet its many demands. Here I have set out some ideas intended to provoke aspirant Prime Ministers and their advisers and indeed every interested citizen (since it is in all our interests that Prime Ministers and governments are effective) to think about and debate the vital issues involved.

My final point is this: I believe the proposals I have made here would not just strengthen the Prime Minister, they would strengthen the Chancellor, the Cabinet and the top civil servants too. How come everyone gains and nobody loses? Well, this is not quite true because there is some loss of autonomy – for example, the Delivery Unit in my time had huge autonomy and used it well, but all of us in the Delivery Unit would have agreed that we could have achieved better outcomes if we had been able to give up some of that autonomy in return for becoming part of a coherent and powerful PMC. However, this is not the main point. Many more key players would gain power under what I propose than would lose for a profound reason, which is simple: power is not a zero sum. By enhancing the crucial relationships at both political and official level, these proposals would generate additional power, making it possible to enhance the quality, speed and impact with which reform is implemented. The alchemy of good relationships can, as the Delivery Unit showed, turn base metal into gold. That – and the routines.

Postscript

Second thoughts:* reflections on the journey to world-class public services

> Central government . . . must entrust the execution of its will to agents, over whom it frequently has no control and whom it cannot perpetually direct.
>
> Alexis de Tocqueville, *Democracy in America*[1]

Perhaps the most rewarding outcome for me of publishing *Instruction to Deliver* was how much I learnt, from people who read the book and responded, about what it will take for our public services to become world class. Of course I was pleased that (most) people enjoyed the read, but the feedback, rich and informative, was more important. In this postscript, I comment on the feedback in three sections. In the first, I respond – in spirited and constructive fashion, I hope – to the published reviews. In the second, I examine the extent to which the proposals I made for the reform of the centre of government were adopted by Gordon Brown when he became Prime Minister. In the third and longest section, in response to some thoughtful commentary from people inside government and the public services, I refine and deepen my analysis of the three crucial relationships – those between ministers and civil servants, between central government and local government, and finally between government and the professions. I don't claim to have resolved all the complex issues, but I hope I have at least advanced my thinking and that, as a result, this postscript will prompt further debate over these central elements of public service reform.

---

* The title is borrowed from the spectacular foreword written for the second edition of A. J. P. Taylor's *The Origins of the Second World War* (London: Hamish Hamilton, 1963)

Blunt and sharp

When the hardback edition of *Instruction to Deliver* was published in May 2007, it provoked exactly the kind of response I had hoped for – a public discussion of how to get things done in government. The *Times* (14 May 2007) said the proposal I made for a new Department of the Prime Minister and the Cabinet was 'a bold plan and ... bound to prove controversial'. The *Guardian* a few days later suggested that some might dismiss my case as 'delusional' (indeed some did!), but that it was 'at least a debate worth having' and that establishing a Prime Minister's Department might be seen 'less as a centralising move than as one designed to foster efficiency in a more devolved system of delivery' (17 May 2007). There was widespread acceptance that the current Whitehall machine was in need of radical reform. The *Times* finished its editorial by stating that 'unless there [are] constant and concentrated efforts in reforming the bureaucracy, the bureaucracy will win every time', while the *Guardian* argued that this was 'an important opportunity to shape a modern system of democratic government that responds to and delivers for citizens'.

Many commentators liked the insights into the workings of government I had provided and (almost) all enjoyed the story. (John Rentoul was glowing but also apparently surprised in describing it as 'an astonishingly good read'.) Many went on to provide critical comments, the main themes of which are examined in turn in the next few paragraphs.

An inveterate centraliser?

One line, represented best by Simon Jenkins's review in the *Sunday Times* (27 May 2007), was that the whole account, not to mention the proposals for the future, was that of an inveterate centraliser. In fact, Jenkins described me as 'the last shamelessly unreconstructed Old Labour centralist on the planet'. I could introduce him to a number of people – none of them leading lights in the Blair and Brown administrations incidentally – with better claim to that title than I, but the accolade had its uses. When I was quizzed by the Public Administration Select Committee on my proposals, and the veteran (Old) Labour MP Kelvin Hopkins attacked both Blairism and my adherence to it, I was able to remind him of Jenkins's comment and suggest to him, possibly irreverently, that 'perhaps we have something in common'.

Jenkins's review goes on to castigate both the entire approach of the Delivery Unit and its impact ('a grease-spattered engineer [who] takes everything to bits in the boiler room with no clue how to reassemble it') but, when we debated the issues in good-humoured fashion at a think-tank and I challenged him on what he would do, he pointed out simply that he is an inveterate localist and concluded, as does his review, that government – divorced from political direction presumably – should be 'left to get on with its job'. Of Prime Ministers since Stanley Baldwin in the 1930s, only Harold Macmillan might be said to have taken this view (and even that would be unfair), and in relation to domestic policy what stands out from his period in office is complacency and a failure to address the country's underlying weaknesses. To be fair to Jenkins, when he is not getting carried away with his own prose, he also quotes the experience of European countries in support of his case, but what is striking in this respect, as I discovered when I debated delivery with the Dutch Prime Minister and Cabinet in 2007, is the huge admiration among European political leaders (across the spectrum) for Tony Blair's reforms of the public services. They don't necessarily want to adopt every aspect of them, but they admire the vision, the boldness and the real progress. As if in confirmation, one leader of a major global business told me recently that the two countries he hears about as leading innovation in the public sector are the UK and Singapore.

More fundamentally, as I argue in the book, the Delivery Unit approach is not synonymous with centralism. Rather, it provides a Prime Minister with a relatively simple but demonstrably effective means of tracking the progress of his (or her) programme. It would work just as well if the Prime Minister's priority was to devolve power (as indeed Blair did to schools and primary care trusts); all it requires is the Prime Minister to have a clear definition of success, and any Prime Minister without that is surely one lacking ambition. I suspect Jenkins's real disagreement with me is that over the past three decades – as he argues in his own book, *Thatcher and Sons* – he wanted to see a minimalist state, and a central government with a programme of, to annex a phrase from across the Atlantic, 'massive inaction'.[2]

A related, more subtle critique with a different historical perspective came from Christopher Hood, Gladstone Professor of Government at

Oxford University. A professed admirer of the book, he is nevertheless sceptical about its emphasis on driving progress from the centre and suggests I would have done well, at the outset of the Delivery Unit, to examine the history of targets and data in government and to have learnt lessons, for example, from wartime production targets. He makes an important point. Some of what we in the Delivery Unit thought we were discovering had in fact been learnt before. With greater historical insight we might have made faster progress and avoided some errors but, for all that, Hood himself accepts that our approach did break new ground and assist in bringing progress.

Balanced about Blair?

A second line of critical commentary was that I was too positive about what was achieved under Blair. For example, John Crace in the *Education Guardian* (12 June 2007) described the memoirs as 'rose-tinted'. However, his article suggests that his real frustration was that the book did not include revelations about 'where the bodies are buried'. Certainly his comment that I was reluctant 'to concede . . . that there were some parts [of the reforms] that could have been done better' suggests a less-than-careful reading of the text. For example, on page 36 in Chapter 1 above, I said: 'We made mistakes. Certainly I did. We took on too much . . . we failed to design some programmes properly: education action zones was the classic case.' Three pages later, I own up to sowing the seeds of the plateau in primary school results, and so the account goes on.

Others argued also that I was insufficiently critical of Blair himself. I would debate this too. In the preface, I admit my bias and suggest that the account that follows will be positive, so the book – as the saying goes – does exactly what it says on the tin. However, as Peter Hennessy says in his foreword, this is not a 'soft treatment' of Blair. I am unsparingly critical where I believe it to be appropriate, and as the story unfolds, Blair is indeed criticised for poor reshuffles, for having insufficient revolutionaries to drive his revolution, for failing to reform the civil service soon enough, for creating a plethora of competing units rather than a coherent operation . . . and more. Again, I suspect some reviewers were disappointed not to find a searing critique of the invasion of Iraq or other unpopular Blairite acts, in which case their mistake was to read the wrong book.

In any case, published as it was during Blair's last few months in office, the book emerged at a time when most commentators were at best bored of the Blair show, and at worst hurling rotten vegetables in the hope of hastening his departure from the stage. Indeed, one publisher remarked to me during the year before Blair departed that there was no market for books that were positive about Blair, which reveals just how short term some publishers' thinking has become. For, of course, once he had gone, it was entirely predictable that views of him would become more positive. Certainly Alastair Campbell and Anthony Seldon have had no trouble selling many copies of portraits that are broadly positive. The shift began, in fact, in the days before his departure, with the *Economist*, for example, arguing that 'for all the disappointments, posterity will look more kindly on Tony Blair than Britons do today' (12 May 2007). By the autumn, the *Times* was arguing: 'For now Mr Blair is about as fashionable as kipper ties or flared trousers. Fashion, though, has a habit of turning full circle. It will do so in this case.' (17 November 2007.) What I have attempted to do in *Instruction to Deliver* is not merely to tell the story of the struggle for reform, but also to attempt to judge Blair's impact on the public services as history will come to judge it. Nothing in the year since the book was published has changed the views I set out in Chapter 8. Indeed, that informed opinion has shifted in a positive direction and the fact that the public service reforms have continued under the new administration reinforces my views. Even *Private Eye* seems to believe that Blair's legacy will be long-lasting: 'Do you think Blair's changes will stand the test of time?' one cartoon character asks another. 'Yes,' comes the reply, 'they'll be causing problems for years to come.' (27 April 2007.)

The spirit of the age?

A more profound critique was that the proposals the book makes are out of tune with the times we live in. The *Times*, in an otherwise broadly supportive commentary, suggests that 'although the Barber scheme is cleverly constructed so that it could be presented as a cost-cutting measure, it does not fit with the spirit of the times' (14 May 2007). Similarly, Vernon Bogdanor, in a highly positive review in the *Financial Times* (11–12 August 2007), suggests that 'there is a profound contradiction between Barber's approach and the programme of decentralisation to which New Labour is committed'. This commentary has significant support within Whitehall among top civil servants, not to mention among local government leaders and some ministers. Either because of, or in spite of, my best efforts, I have become associated with the top-down approach to reform which, during Blair's third term (and continued since) became unfashionable while the idea of 'letting go' took hold. Throughout the book this theme is debated, and one of my criticisms of the Blair reform programme is that we failed to establish sufficient conceptual clarity among ministers and civil servants on the central issues of public service reform. I seek to address this in the final pages of Chapter 9. I have not changed the views expressed there, though I have added to them, as will become clear.

On key aspects of this issue, I have had time and cause to reflect further since the first edition of the book was published, and two of the three sections in this postscript address them (see below). At this point, though, I want to reinforce my central case. Even with conceptual clarity about reform, and therefore a drive towards (the right kind of) devolution, the argument for a sharper, smaller, more effective Prime Minister's Department, far from being weakened, would be strengthened. Indeed, this would be the case even if Daniel Finkelstein's conclusion from reading my book (with which I have some sympathy) – that we need smaller government altogether – were to be accepted. This is because the case I make for a Department of the Prime Minister and the Cabinet is not about size or scale, but about effectiveness. Indeed, it is about doing less, better. In arguing that the spirit of the age is against my proposals, critics have conflated centralisation and top-down reform of the public services on the one hand with the proposed creation of the new department on the other. I tried to clarify this in my hearing at the Public Administration Selection Committee on 19 July 2007, when the erudite chairman, Tony Wright MP, put the case this way:

> Your book is completely . . . counter-intuitive to the age. The story of the age says, 'The Prime Minister is becoming too powerful: Cabinet is being bypassed. Sofa government has arrived. This is outrageous. The civil service is being bypassed. Something has to be done about it.' You pop up and actually reverse all of that.

My reply accepts his final point:

I do try to reverse all of that because I do not think the analysis is correct . . . [My] argument is that the role of Prime Minister has become more and more difficult . . . I am not arguing that the Prime Minister should become more powerful in relation . . . to Cabinet, still less . . . in relation to Parliament; I am arguing that the Prime Minister needs an effective machinery to deliver results. After all, Prime Ministers lead governments, governments have been elected to do things, and confidence in modern politics depends on those who are elected into power being able to deliver [their] programme.

This is indeed my point, and it would apply whether the programme was for centralisation or decentralisation, for bigger government or smaller. As I suggest in Chapter 9 (p. 318), my case is that 'clarity will replace fudge, blunt will become sharp'. That, surely, is an argument that would appeal to any worthwhile Prime Minister with any worthwhile programme. This might be why my proposals generated interest across the political spectrum.

A reformed centre?

Much of what Gordon Brown did to reform the government machine in June and July of 2007 was far more radical than anything I envisaged in Chapter 9 of *Instruction to Deliver*: the ambitious reshaping of departmental boundaries and the changed relationship between executive and legislature, for example. The appointment of ministers with an explicit role in more than one department – such as Liam Byrne, who is responsible for immigration in the Home Office and border taxes in the Treasury – is also innovative, as is the establishment of ministers for each of England's regions. These changes seem to have been broadly welcomed. In the case of the new departmental boundaries, it will inevitably take time for the benefits to accrue, but there is already a sense in, for example, the schools and children's arena that having one department (the Department for Children, Schools and Families) responsible for all government policy relating to children, young people and their families is leading to more integrated thinking about policy and to consideration of all the outcomes that matter – well-being as well as school standards. My proposals for reforming the centre of government, based on my four years in the Delivery Unit and set out in Chapter 9, were radical and extensive. As pointed out in the previous section, they were based on the view that the Prime Minister's task had become much more difficult to do and that comprehensive reform of the public services required a more coherent, aligned operation around the Prime Minister, especially since the productivity of public services had become (and remains) the central issue of modern British politics. The centrepiece of my proposals was a new Department of the Prime Minister and the Cabinet (see pp. 32–7). When Brown became Prime Minister last June, he did not set up a department with that name, preferring to keep No.10 and the Cabinet Office separate but connected, as they had been under his predecessors.

While of course I would have been happy to see my advice taken in this regard, I could see the problem of appearing to centralise at a time when the main shift was towards more Cabinet government and a greater emphasis on Parliament. What struck me on looking more closely, however, was that many of the specific suggestions I had made had indeed been adopted. The Policy Unit was smaller and staffed with serious policy people trusted by the new Prime Minister, such as Nick Pearce and Gavin Kelly. The appointment in January 2008 of Stephen Carter to oversee both policy and communications in No. 10 should strengthen it. In the Cabinet Office there was a new permanent secretary post, answerable to Gus O'Donnell and filled by Jeremy Heywood, the brilliant principal private secretary to Tony Blair during my time at No. 10. The post did not have the title 'Permanent Secretary – Performance' as I had proposed, but its responsibilities were almost identical to those I had set out. In January 2008 Heywood was made permanent secretary of No. 10; the position he left behind in the Cabinet Office nevertheless still exists but had not been filled at the time of writing. His appointment as the first ever permanent secretary of No. 10 surely reinforces the case for a Department of the Prime Minister and the Cabinet; in fact it is implicitly a step towards its creation. Though the role held by Gill Ryder does not have permanent-secretary status, it closely parallels the 'Permanent Secretary – Organisational Health' role I suggested. Responsibility for the capability reviews has been located with this function, also as I suggested, leaving a renewed Prime Minister's Delivery Unit to focus on delivery of the government's priorities.

Meanwhile, parallel reforms in the Treasury also closely follow what I recommend in Chapter 9. There is a new permanent secretary responsible for productivity and the public services (John Kingman), and the new PSA framework, with far fewer cross-government targets (about thirty) and a set of indicators on which data will be made public, moves in the direction set out in the first edition. Here there is some way to go to achieve full clarity about public value (see pp. 329–31), but there is growing emphasis in inspectorates such as Ofsted, the Healthcare Commission and the Audit Commission on gathering good data about what citizens and users think of services. It remains to be seen whether the integrated process for shaping strategy and targets and allocating public expenditure will be adopted, but there are reasons to be hopeful.

And what of the Delivery Unit itself? In the first two years after I left in July 2005, it continued to drive delivery, but its biggest impact came through the departmental capability reviews, which – using combined teams of insiders and outsiders co-ordinated by the unit and drawing on one of its now-famous frameworks – examined the effectiveness of departments in relation to strategy, delivery and leadership. The process caused some consternation in the upper echelons of the civil service, but most departments, whether or not they enjoyed the process, found the reviews beneficial. The publication of the reports brought a degree of transparency to Whitehall that would have had many past mandarins turning in their graves. The overall impact has been very positive. By driving this programme forward, the Delivery Unit finally resolved the dilemma we had throughout my time between driving for results on the one hand and building capacity on the other (see pp. 202–3, for example), eventually choosing to emphasise building departmental capacity. An inevitable result was that, in spite of the best efforts of the staff, the unit's original agenda of delivering the government's key priorities gained less attention from its leadership and indeed from the Cabinet Secretary and Prime Minister during that two-year period.

Since Gordon Brown became Prime Minister, he has refocused the unit on the government's delivery priorities. Relieved as it has been of the capability reviews and under the leadership of the engaging and experienced Ray Shostak – a man with an exemplary track record on delivery in the world beyond Whitehall – its task is now to secure delivery of the thirty or so PSA targets at the heart of the new administration's agenda. It has become part of the Treasury and is thus much more closely connected with delivering productivity as well as results, but it is formally required to report jointly to the Chancellor of the Exchequer and the Prime Minister and is exactly where it should be – in the thick of things. In these respects, the unit is attempting to gain the best of all worlds from the three options set out in Chapter 7 above (p. 251). Given the new stage of public service reform the country has reached – we have come a long way since the Delivery Unit was established in 2001 – it will need to develop some new techniques, but if it builds relationships on the same creative basis, there is every reason to believe it can innovate further and help deliver the next phase of reform.

Overall, therefore, I was pleased with the impact of my proposals on the new Prime Minister's arrangements. I was also pleased that there was interest across the political spectrum in the arguments I made in the book. Organising to deliver results need not be a matter of party political debate. My advice to current and future Cabinet Secretaries and Prime Ministers would be to learn rigorously the lessons not only from our experience since 2001 and ongoing, but also from the conscious attempts around the world to build on these innovations and go beyond them. The search for effective systems to drive delivery is never-ending of course, and definitive answers elusive, but we are better placed to get it right now than ever before.

The alchemy of relationships: greater depth

Some of the published reviews were knockabout stuff; others made more substantive points. Much of the most thoughtful commentary, though, came to me in the private notes or seminar discussions that followed publication. Almost all can be routed back to Alexis de Tocqueville's observation quoted at the head of this chapter. Successful delivery in the early twenty-first century, as in the 1830s when de Tocqueville was writing, depends on establishing relationships or partnerships with powerful organisations and groups whom governments 'cannot perpetually direct'. Even though both civil servants and public service professionals are roundly criticised in the book, many confessed both to enjoying the story and to accepting or at least recognising the case that was being made. That does not mean that they necessarily accepted either the argument in full or the proposals for the way forward. Nearly all signed up to the ends proposed (summarised, for example, on page 233): 'the development of public services of real quality, which citizens from all backgrounds want to use, which deliver equity as well as high standards and which make productive use of every penny of the taxpayers' money which is entrusted to government'.

With regards to the means, though, several came back not so much in direct opposition to the argument, but with suggestions which indicated a need for significant refinement. Broadly, these fell into three categories, which might be best phrased as questions.

1. While we might accept your critique of civil servants, don't you pull your punches in relation to ministers and their responsibilities for the lack of progress? As David Walker put it in his review in *Society Guardian*, 'ministerial impatience and ignorance about systems were part of the Blair problem, but Barber is too much the courtier to say so' (20 June 2007).

2. Given that it spends over £100 billion of public money every year, don't you think you underestimate the importance of local government and therefore of establishing a clear role for it and ensuring an effective working relationship between central and local government?

3. While we understand the critique of leaders of the public service professions, isn't your account light – to say the least – on the nature of the relationship between the professions and government? After all, if the results of the Blair reforms are as positive as you suggest, it must surely worry you that professionals themselves remain so disaffected.

These are highly significant questions, and in the rest of this postscript I hope not just to respond to them, but also to show how my thinking has been refined as a result.

Ministers and civil servants

I accept the criticism that the first edition of *Instruction to Deliver* did not explore sufficiently the responsibilities of ministers and how they might best be developed. Nor did it explore sufficiently the ministerial–civil servant relationship, in spite of the emphasis I place throughout the book of 'the alchemy of relationships'. These were omissions on my part.

The charge that I am critical of civil servants but not of ministers does not quite stand up. I checked. Laced throughout the book are numerous criticisms, implied or otherwise, of the political masters in the New Labour years (and of myself). What is true, though, is that the weight of the criticism of the civil service is much greater than that of the politicians. I shall return to whether that weighting is fair at the end of this section, but first it is worth summarising the critique the book makes in each case.

The criticisms of the civil service can be summarised thus:

- more policy than delivery orientated: not always good enough at the former, but certainly lacking the necessary skills for the latter;
- not focused enough on delivering results for citizens;
- too risk averse; too incremental and sometimes even downright resistant to change;
- too caught up in the world of Whitehall and insufficiently in touch with the rapidly changing real (globalising) world;
- not innovative or imaginative enough;
- too willing to concede to lobby groups in order to ensure a quiet life;
- sometimes propounding an 'official' view, even after clear ministerial decisions have been made;
- often poorly managed;
- sometimes grossly inefficient.

All of this appears already in the book, but when it is summarised in a list, the strength of the critique becomes readily apparent. In his powerful chapter in *Public Matters: The Renewal of the Public Realm*, Sir Michael Bichard, the iconoclastic former permanent secretary of the Department for Education and Employment (see above, Chapter 1) provides a similar list:

- a risk-averse culture;
- poorly developed political skills;
- a continuing deficit of leadership, management and procurement skills;
- a disconnection between Whitehall and its clients and communities;
- a perceived reluctance to share information and knowledge which could and should be in the public domain.[3]

It should go without saying that the critique does not apply all of the time to all of the programmes and all of the people. On the contrary, there are many examples of exemplary policy and delivery, some of them (for example, the implementation of Excellence in Cities or the delivery of the Accident and Emergency four-hour target) outstanding, but that is not the issue here.

The charge sheet against (prime) ministerial leadership in the book can be summarised as follows:

- the reshuffles were poor and ministers changed too often;
- tensions between No. 10 and the Treasury sometimes caused confusion;
- conceptual clarity across government as a whole about the public service reform programme was insufficient;
- in Tony Blair's first term there were too many initiatives and too much emphasis on media presentation;
- it took too long for ministers to realise they needed to engage constructively with reforming the civil service machine;
- in dealing with one problem, ministers sometimes made decisions that created others (e.g. doing away with all – as opposed to some – ring-fenced grants as a means of reducing bureaucracy);
- not enough was done to build teams ('guiding coalitions') combining the political and official to deliver major objectives;
- it was too easy to become apologetic about unpopular policies which were right (e.g. published performance data);
- too many were not bold enough.

Here too, of course, the critique is spread throughout the book, which tells a largely positive story, but nevertheless it is substantial. Let us accept that, to a degree, civil servants will have a tendency to blame their political masters who, in turn, will want to point the finger at officials. Both groups know, though, that if this tendency goes too far, it will breed contempt. Most of the time, in my experience, relationships are sound across the divide and there are many examples of excellent collaboration.

One way to think about how to strengthen the capacity of both sides *and* the relationship between them is to examine best practice. If you ask them, civil servants will tell you they like ministers who

- are clear about priorities;
- work hard ('clear their boxes');

- make decisions;
- build good relations on the political network (e.g. No. 10) and work as part of a ministerial team;
- are effective in Parliament and the media;
- know their stuff;
- set exacting expectations;
- are fair and consistent; and
- show the human touch.

Ministers like civil servants who
- work hard;
- provide clear advice;
- know what they are talking about;
- engage in debate and exercise judgement;
- admit mistakes/problems early rather than covering them up;
- command respect among stakeholders;
- don't flap in a crisis;
- demonstrate common sense;
- are well networked; and
- see the funny side.

The research base for these lists of characteristics could be strengthened, but I doubt major studies would change them significantly. Either way, it should be perfectly possible within Whitehall to develop talent management programmes that bring out these characteristics among officials and ministers. There is already extensive training and development provision for officials in Whitehall through the National School of Government (NSG), which could be adapted for this purpose.

For ministers, such provision has been patchy and limited and, as I have argued, I saw little or no evidence of systematic human resource management of ministers and potential ministers (see p. 320–1). Indeed, there would appear to be a gaping hole in providing talent management of and development for ministers. Perversely, it seems to be the case that whereas for any other top leadership job careful selection, development, coaching and mentoring would be absolutely basic, a minister is expected to step fully formed (and informed) into an extremely demanding role on day one.

To be fair, the NSG has begun to address this with induction sessions for new ministers. I have been lucky enough to present to and answer questions at such events. The new ministers feel sufficiently liberated in the confidential atmosphere to ask the really simple questions they hadn't dared to ask elsewhere, such as: 'I need to spend Monday mornings in my constituency, but the private office frowns on this; what should I do?' The answer in this case is simple – just tell them! – but it clearly reveals the need at the most basic level.

Above and beyond this basic level, the curriculum for a ministerial development programme would include learning the following:

- What you might expect of a government department.
- How policy should be made.
- How to stay the course (when the going gets tough).
- How to achieve conceptual clarity (so you can explain simply and easily what you are doing, why you are doing it and how).
- How to ensure you make time for reflection and thinking (don't confuse activity with action).
- How to find time to get to the frontline.
- How to create effective teams (among ministers or across the top of a major policy area, a 'guiding coalition').
- How to make the most of meetings (and especially how to sum up clearly what the key decisions are and whose job it is to implement them).
- How to deal with Parliament.
- An understanding of systems (e.g. health, criminal justice) and how they can be successfully changed.
- Cautionary tales of disastrous pieces of policy-making and implementation in the past (the poll tax, the Child Support Agency, education action zones and many more), as well as crisis management.
- How to manage the media and communications.

Special advisers should also be involved where appropriate. Gerald Kaufman's excellent and entertaining book *How to be a Minister* should be compulsory reading (though it needs updating to deal with, for example, Freedom of Information)[4]. Note that I have left media and communications to the end of the list. While they are often absolutely vital to ministerial success (or even survival in some situations), they are not the be-all and end-all, and indeed there are some junior ministerial posts whose occupant virtually never sets foot in a television studio – but if he or she is doing the job well the contribution to the government's success could be huge.

A serious programme of ministerial development along these lines would surely be valuable and could be highly engaging (and entertaining) for participants if it were delivered well. Some ministerial development could take place in joint sessions with special advisers and top civil servants. It could be reinforced, as it is for many in business, by offering ministers executive coaches or mentors. The recently proposed Institute of Government, to be founded by David (Lord) Sainsbury, could clearly play a significant role. The biggest challenge for ministers would be making the time for such development, but this is true in all top jobs, and the evidence is compelling: making the time for development pays huge dividends. As the American feminist Elizabeth Cady Stanton put it more than a century ago, 'self-development is a higher goal than self-sacrifice'.

*

Some commentators go significantly beyond these ideas in promoting civil service reform. Michael Bichard argues in support of Guy Lodge of the Institute for Public Policy Research (IPPR) for clarifying the different accountabilities of ministers and civil servants in new legislation. This, Lodge argues, would finally solve the problem whereby currently 'ancillary to ministerial accountability is the non-accountability of civil servants'. In other words, the heart of the problem is that the civil service can hide behind ministerial responsibility. There is certainly a case for this; my only hesitation, although potentially a major one, is that drafting the law in this area could be a minefield and it is not hard to imagine that, in making its passage through Parliament, it would become more complex and opaque than anyone at the outset would want, in which case we might end up worse off.[5]

Certainly Bichard's other conclusions are consistent with the case made here. He argues for a civil service which has greater accountability and transparency; commitment to personal responsibility; creativity, innovation and energy; focus on value for money; and better use of information technology, largely through improved procurement.[6]

Either way, note that, on this question of the relationships between ministers and civil servants, I have said nothing about special advisers. This is not because I forgot, but because – in spite of literally one or two celebrated examples – I never saw special advisers as part of the problem. On the contrary, Conor Ryan or Nick Pearce, both former colleagues of mine in the Department for Education, were clearly part of the solution: helping explain to civil servants what ministers wanted, pointing out political pitfalls, thinking about presentation and generating ideas. They also had the ability to point out to ministers when they were paying insufficient attention to civil service advice or mismanaging relationships. Good special advisers help oil the wheels. This was the case with the vast majority of those I met, and this is why I advocated (in the first edition) clearly engaging the special adviser in the guiding coalition at the head of any major policy area, as Paul Corrigan was in Health during Alan Milburn's time, for example.

The final point here is to do with how the weight of responsibility for the successes and failures of the past decade is divided between politicians and civil servants (between what Jon Davis in his excellent book *Prime Ministers and Whitehall* quaintly calls the 'temporary' and 'permanent' parts of the state). Here I accept that in the first edition of this book, the underlying message was that an ambitious government sometimes struggled with delivery – despite the best efforts of the Delivery Unit – in large part because the civil service found it hard to rise to the challenge. Do I want to reverse this judgement? Answer: no; but in the preceding pages I have sought to temper it and moderate it. Overall, while responsibility for success or failure is clearly shared between ministers and civil servants, I think the politicians have by far the harder task and ought to be able to expect the civil service to adapt, change and commit to delivering their programme. There is a simple reason for this: in a democracy, governments are elected to deliver a programme, and people expect them to do so. Cynicism ensues when they fail. Moreover, politicians – not paid more than senior civil servants, and paid far less than their counterparts in business – take enormous decisions on our behalf and are held to account for them more visibly (in Parliament and in the media) than equivalents in other fields.

I once heard of a Danish headteacher who decided to take a two-year sabbatical working in Africa. His school, an age 15–19 community college, had a long internal debate about who should act in his place. As with the Conservative Party before Edward Heath, the assumption was that a leader would 'emerge' from this debate. The person who finally did emerge was an eighteen-year-old student! The staff were stunned and put it to the headteacher before he left that this was impossible. He offered them some simple advice: 'Your job is to make sure she succeeds.' When he came back two years later, that is exactly what had happened. So successful had she been that the returning head said he would join the staff and leave her in post. In the end, she said she'd rather finish school and go to university, so he took up his post again.

I often told this story in the Delivery Unit because it captured our role well – our job was to ensure that others succeeded. Overall, I feel the same about the civil service in relation to ministers – its job is to ensure that ministers and, as far as possible, ministerial teams succeed. In the time I worked for government, the programme was ambitious, and some disappointment was inevitable. As I have documented, there was plenty of success, and Britain has been changed for the better, but with a combination of effective ministers and an effective civil service even more could have been achieved.

I certainly do not share the weary cynicism of Sir William Armstrong as he approached retirement as head of the civil service. When asked, 'What do you go home and say at moments of economic crisis?' he replied, 'Thank God the government's influence is so little.' It is not that I want big government – far from it, as I hope I've made clear – but when government does act, regardless of which party is in power, it is in all our interests that it is effective and that requires the temporary and permanent parts of the state to collaborate successfully.

Central government and local government

The second relationship which serious commentators said I had not sufficiently explored in the first edition was that between central and local government. I think this is fair. While, as I have made clear, I reject extreme localism, for example, this still leaves an onus on me to explain more clearly than I have previously what a constructive relationship between central and local government might look like. There are many reasons for this. While it is true that local government's performance for much of the 1990s was, to put it politely, uneven, it is also true that in the past decade it has improved significantly and the best of local government is now outstanding and in advance of most, if not all, of Whitehall. Moreover, as Thatcher, Major, Blair and Brown all came to understand, there is no alternative to engaging and collaborating with local government, even if they sometimes wished there were. The National Health Service was created in 1948, at the height of 'Old Labour centralism', but no one would recreate it that way now, still less apply that thinking to any other service. There were those in education circles in the 1990s – Chris Woodhead for example – who wanted to write local authorities out of the education script entirely, but successive governments from Thatcher to the present chose instead to seek means of improving their contribution rather than removing it. My own efforts to do so – which I don't regret at all – are recounted in Chapter 1, but under Tony Blair – exaggerating only slightly – local government was often viewed as a necessary inconvenience. Directly elected mayors might make a difference (as Mayor Jules Pipe has done in my home borough of Hackney), but only towards the end of the Blair years did something approaching an intellectually coherent role for local government emerge. (As an aside, it might be remarked that this is historically speaking odd, for the historical antecedents of Blairism lie far more in the municipal socialism of Joseph Chamberlain than in either the Fabianism or trade unionism on which the original Labour Party was built.[7])

Be that as it may, both Gordon Brown and the Conservative opposition foresee a major role for local government in the future, building on the much more constructive relationship that emerged at the end of the Blair years. This relationship had its roots in the thinking Brown did for his Social Market Foundation speech of February 2003 (see pp. 178–9), when the concept of devolution and transparency emerged as the non-market, non-command-and-control approach to reforming public services. The 2006 local government White Paper set out how this might work. Essentially, the 'devolution and transparency' model of reform is now being applied to – and welcomed by – local government. There will be far fewer national targets, replaced by a set of indicators which both local and central government agree are valid and important (in relation to, for example, adoption, carbon emissions, housing and transport) and on which data will be published regularly so that citizens can see how their authority compares to others. Moreover, local authorities will agree with the local leaders of other services – the police or the NHS, for example – what their local priorities for change are and then negotiate a local area agreement with central government. Through this negotiation, central government will seek to secure commitment from local authorities to delivering its key national priorities and in return will provide the flexibility and the bulk of resources to enable delivery. As a recent joint publication from the Department for Communities and Local Government and the Local Government Association puts it, 'the [new] framework brings together national standards and priorities set by government with local priorities informed by the vision developed by the local authority and its partners'.[8] How well this new deal will work in practice will depend on the quality of the negotiation and the capacity to deliver of each local authority, the local government sector as a whole and of course central government.

The negotiation will in all probability be less difficult than might be anticipated because both local and central government are sensitive to public concerns and the public's priorities are remarkably consistent: tackle crime and anti-social behaviour, keep places clean, provide good schools, offer people (especially young people) good facilities, and make it reasonably easy to get around. Climate change is also rising up the agenda. As for means, there is also substantial agreement between central and local government that finding more active, effective means of becoming the 'voice' of citizens, while also where possible offering them 'choice', is important.

How the local government role develops in practice will vary from service to service – in education it will be a question of ensuring that there are plenty of good schools to choose from (and therefore tackling poor schools) as well as securing the necessary services to support children and their families out of school, especially children with special needs. In relation to crime, the role will be one of collaborating effectively with the police and ensuring, for example, that provision of street lights and the design of estates minimise the risk of crime. At the intersection of education and crime it will mean cracking down on truancy, providing services for children excluded from school which resolve their problems and doing whatever can be done to avoid boredom among teenagers (for as Bertrand Russell once observed, boredom, or the fear of it, is responsible for half the sins of mankind). Above all, though, the potential for much-improved results comes from the capacity of local government to combine the strands of policy from different government departments to solve the problems of a particular place. This is what the jargon calls 'place-shaping'.[9] For some policy areas, this place-shaping might be very local – a specific collaboration involving a housing estate, a school and a police team, for example. For others – transport around Manchester, say – it would involve a region larger than any single local authority. Barking & Dagenham local authority, at the cutting edge of these reforms, is building partnerships, not just with the police and the health authority to meet multiple challenges, but also with the local university and employers to make – in the words of its inspirational chief executive, Rob Whiteman – 'a place that can wash its face in the global economy'. Whiteman will be delighted to ensure central government targets are met as long as it gives him the flexibility to shape programmes to the context of his borough.

It is not necessary to discuss all the responsibilities of local government to make the point, which is that after almost two decades of uncertainty (since the poll tax), the role and means of operating for local government are finally becoming clear. It has a great opportunity to deliver, and central government will be hoping it does – since many outcomes which the public want depend on it doing so. Of course, central government will have the right to intervene where performance is poor. It will be interesting to see whether it chooses to do so because, as this book describes (see pp. 36–7 and 315–16), it is difficult to do, though it can be hugely beneficial. To those who say this potential for intervention demonstrates that central government has not really let go, my reply is twofold: one, if local government delivers what citizens want, intervention from central government will never arise; two, it is worth remembering that around 80 per cent of the money spent by local authorities comes from national, not local, taxation, and he who pays the piper surely has the right to ensure the tune is played well enough for the audience to enjoy it.

Those who want a less conditional form of localism would need to propose a means of raising a much higher proportion of taxes locally, and since the poll tax, most politicians have understandably flinched from doing so. Many argue that policy should rise to this challenge. Dermot Finch of the IPPR argues that, in addition to the new partnership of local and central government described here, 'greater local revenue-raising capacity . . . is absolutely critical'.[10] The question may emerge onto the political agenda in the next few years; so far, though, there has been little evidence of public demand.

Summarising, I accept that in the first edition I did not do justice to the potential role of local government. As it happens, this second edition is being published at just the time when the whole local government sector has the chance, as a result of the new settlement I have just described, to demonstrate that it can deliver in the way the pioneers such as Richard Leese in Manchester, Simon Milton in Westminster or Jules Pipe in Hackney, did in the past decade or so. It would be good for the country if they succeed.

One codicil though – the new settlement does not make it less important for those responsible for delivery in central government to worry about delivery plans, delivery chains, trajectories or all the other central elements of deliverology. On the contrary, doing so will become more important than ever, since in order both to liberate those who are succeeding and intervene where there are problems government needs to be well informed, with regular, real-time data. As I argued in the first edition, the next phase of reform, in this case adopting devolution and transparency, is not about 'letting go' and worrying less about delivery; it is about building more effective relationships so that better results can be delivered, hopefully faster and more efficiently.

Government and the professions

The third relationship critics say I failed to explore sufficiently is that between Government and the professions. The famous blues song says: 'If you're so smart, how come you ain't rich?' The equivalent question put to me on the basis of the first edition is: 'If the government did so well for the public servants, how come they're so miffed?'

And while it does not apply by any means to all public service professionals, it is certainly true that there is frustration. You see it in polls of doctors* and other public servants and you find it in the headlines in newspapers, but I was struck how deep it went when I read one of those circular letters that some families insert in their Christmas cards. After cataloguing the heroic achievements of their children and singing their praises, this one came to the mother's year at work as a GP.

---

*MORI data suggests that, in private conversation, 70 per cent of doctors are negative about the NHS (Presentation by Ben Page at the Guardian Public Services Conference, 8 February 2008).

In a paragraph written less as a newsy update and more as one of those campaign leaflets we all drafted in the heady left-wing university days of the 1970s, it reads: 'More expletives . . . about the political pressures and general hassle from Government thrown at GPs these days . . . Why do politicians get away with introducing tiers and tiers of admin . . . rather than genuinely helping those that do the job on the ground?'

Even though the note was sent in the season of goodwill, there was no mention of the fact that GPs in this country are among the best-paid doctors in Europe. Perhaps the pay increase did not 'help those that do the job on the ground'. What about the modernisation of thousands of GPs' surgeries? The major investment in drugs, training and technology? The opportunity for GPs to take on a specialism? The shift of many services from hospitals to primary care? The much greater provision of practice nurses? None of these things helped? Of course, if politicians are the problem, as her note implies, you might expect this GP at least to leap for the simple solution – privatisation – but she doesn't, and nor do GPs collectively. In her rant there is no policy solution, only a vague sense that everything would be all right if GPs were left to themselves: in effect, 'give us the money and get out of the way'. The only problem is that when this was tried, it wasn't all right. When it was tried, noble professions, once organised, became vested interests. Altruists became monopolists. That explains why both Tony Blair and Gordon Brown have encouraged new providers into the public services. For example, it can only be for the convenience of GPs (and virtually no one else) that it is so hard to find a GP surgery open in the evening or at weekends (whereas the vet who attends to our dogs and is crucially dependent on satisfying customers is open until 7.30 every evening and on Saturdays and Sundays).*

The status quo ante was unacceptable. However, rightly in my view, few people in this country really want full-scale privatisation because it cannot deliver the fairness British people expect from their services, so public service reform, combining transparency, devolution, choice and

---

*On 4 February 2008 the Health Secretary, Alan Johnson, wrote to GPs, urging them to extend opening hours to include (some) evenings and weekends. The British Medical Association responded in traditional bargaining mode but, interestingly, the NHS Alliance spokesperson, Dr Michael Dixon, said: 'Almost every GP in the country accepts . . . that we are not open as much as we ought to be.' (Quoted in Adam Brimelow, 'Ministers target GPs over hours', BBC Online, 4 February 2008.)

alternative providers where appropriate, is necessary. No doubt government has made mistakes along the way – governments always will – but the GP service has already significantly improved over the past decade, not just for patients, but also for GPs and their staff because of, not in spite of, the government's efforts. No one faced with the facts can dispute this, but it does not solve the problem that critics of *Instruction to Deliver* put to me. Many public service professionals are still deeply frustrated. (The last time I went to the GP for a routine check-up, I tested this by saying 'This must be the best time there's ever been to be a GP' and regretted it immediately!) I suddenly understood Harry Truman's famous quip: 'I never give them [the public] hell. I just tell the truth and they think it is hell.'

So, for all the improvements and the investment, there is clearly a serious problem with the relationship here. It is a problem for government because the credibility of a GP or a teacher will always be much higher than that of a minister or a civil servant. If the professions complain that reform isn't working, people are likely to believe them. It is a problem for the professionals themselves because they are clearly finding their careers less satisfying than they might otherwise, and by persuading people that reform isn't working they undermine the long-term prospects of fully tax-funded services. Above all, it is a problem for citizens because even if it does not affect the quality of their services – which in some cases it might – they must often feel a sense of confusion about what is happening and where the services for which they pay their taxes are headed. What are the roots of this problem?

*

Part of the answer lies with globalisation and technology, which are transforming services of all kinds everywhere. Those who work in media and communications or financial services, for example, have seen their working lives and organisations transformed in the past fifteen or twenty years. This is true too for the professions in the private sector – architects, accountants and bankers for example – whose working methods have been changed utterly. Globalisation and technology influence services such as health, education and policing, which are in the public sector, just as much as they shape those in the private sector. The difference is that in the public services the changes that result are inevitably – precisely because the services are public – mediated through government. When governments urge educators to be 'world class', they are giving voice to what the global market demands in other services. When doctors struggle with the impact of technology on medicine, they are facing what the market drives in other sectors. When police try to keep pace with organised crime, they are competing directly with an endlessly innovating – albeit in this case illegal and immoral – global business. The same is true for the security services.

Charles Clarke, the former Home Secretary, makes a similar case in his chapter in *Public Matters*,[11] arguing that inter alia technological and scientific innovation, empowered and assertive consumers and growing concern about professional standards – in the wake of the horrifying deeds of Harold Shipman and Ian Huntley, for example – have dramatically changed the rules of the game and contributed to a mutual lack of confidence between government and the professions. So when public service professionals complain that government has driven too much change, often the drivers (hidden though they might be) are these wider forces. This does not excuse government coming up with too many initiatives or making mistakes, but it does help to explain why, regardless of the party in power, it generally wants more change while simultaneously public service professionals complain about overload. Yet, while it is true that there has been immense change in the public services over two decades, it is not true that there has been more than in other sectors; indeed there may overall have been less. Take an example. One of the most glaring gaps between the public and business sectors is in the attitude to customers. Public service professionals still too often take them for granted and expect them to be grateful; very few professionals in the business sector can afford to take this attitude.

Take another. In relation to the widespread availability of information, many people are now able to be their own lawyer or doctor or teacher up to a point, thanks to the Internet. It is easy, for the professional, once revered specifically for expertise, to feel threatened or defensive in these circumstances – but in fact the existence of many better-informed citizens or customers is potentially a major gain. I came across a case recently where, having doubted a vet's diagnosis of a dog's condition, the owner searched the Internet, came to a different conclusion and insisted the vet do the appropriate test. When the vet called with the results, his opening remark was far from defensive:

'Congratulations, your diagnosis was right,' followed by a description of the cure. He was consciously building a constructive partnership with his customer, rather than feeling threatened. To reinforce this point, evidence is emerging that appropriately programmed computers can sometimes be better at diagnosis than doctors.[12] This trend will surely intensify. This too might be perceived as a threat, but the better alternative is to see it as an opportunity not just to improve diagnosis, but also to allow more time for doctors to provide cures and enable patients to manage their conditions better, and in these aspects of their work, doctors are incomparably better than technology.

Then take performance data. Most teachers and headteachers I know hate league tables, but this is the era of global media and freedom of information. University vice-chancellors don't like league tables either and the government doesn't publish them for higher education, but the *Times* does, student websites do and so do several outlets on a global basis. When I was in Berlin recently, the front-page headline on the city's main paper related to a website where schoolchildren were able to rank their teachers across the city. Similarly, in France the economist Jacques Attali in an influential, official report has proposed that pupils should grade their teachers. Comparative data will out. Moreover, citizens and customers love it and will not give it up. The only question, therefore, for headteachers in this country is whether they would prefer reliable comparative performance information to be organised and provided by government – in which case there can be an ongoing dialogue with them about what is included and how it is presented – or by a major media organisation, in which case there will be no such dialogue.

I emphasise this point because I believe that the main drivers of public service professionals' frustration are the pressures of accountability and the pace of change, yet both these are ultimately driven not just by government, but by globalisation and technology. When government makes mistakes or suffers 'initiative-itis', it compounds these problems and of course government hugely influences how these forces play out – in deciding the nature of inspection, for example, or who is chief inspector – so of course it bears huge responsibility, but unless this bigger picture is understood, we will never unravel the complexities of the relationship between government and professions.

Does the author of the Christmas circular letter really think any foreseeable government would just give her the money and get out of the way? Surely not. The central issue, therefore, over and above the competence of government, which is a key theme of this book, is how to construct a more effective relationship between government and public service professionals, one in which they develop a deeper understanding not just of each other's views of the world, but also of the profound forces which are reshaping everyone's world and their implications for public services. It was in this respect that the first edition of *Instruction to Deliver* was inadequate. What might a different relationship look like?

*

In that first bold, broadly successful phase of education reform between 1997 and 1999 recounted in Chapter 1, in relation to the teaching profession, we made one of the classic errors listed by Harvard management guru John Kotter (see p. 78), namely 'undercommunicating the vision by a factor of 10 (or 100 or even 1000)'. To be sure, we wrote what was widely recognised to be an ambitious White Paper and promoted it. We consulted widely in its formation too. We sent out thousands of pages of regulations and guidance on everything from the far-flung corners of school governance (unimportant) to the sequence of teaching phonics (vital). In what was widely seen, remarkably, as an innovation, ministers, officials and I visited schools all the time. Less innovatively, ministers delivered speeches all the time. I did many myself. We couldn't be faulted for effort.

Alongside these efforts to communicate directly with the school workforce, we also ran a largely successful media strategy aimed, of course, at parents and taxpayers rather than teachers. The message here was that performance in the education system wasn't good enough, failure would be tackled vigorously, poor schools would be closed and Chris Woodhead, the controversial chief inspector, was right (mostly). Parents and taxpayers heard and generally warmed to the message. Our error was a simple and obvious one – teachers read the *Daily Mail* or the *Guardian* and heard our message to parents loud and clear; they (understandably) didn't read the pages of guidance and White Papers we sent them, so they hardly understood our strategy. The result? They were confused and sometimes offended. It was hardly surprising, then, that when I visited schools the most common response was, 'You might think there's a strategy, Michael; we just think there's one damn thing after another . . . oh, and by the way, we don't like bureaucracy and league tables.'

We understood this challenge soon enough and began to respond. We dramatically cut the amount of paper going into schools, but obviously this did not convey the vision in the way Kotter says you must. We realised that in order to do this we needed intermediaries. The government couldn't communicate directly with more than 400,000 teachers, so we focused on headteachers. Primary heads generally liked the literacy and numeracy events they attended; we introduced a spectacular annual conference from 1998 onwards, aimed at all the newly appointed heads in the country. Benjamin Zander, the inspirational conductor of the Boston Philharmonic Orchestra, regaled them with inspiring stories of musicians transformed – they surprised themselves (they were British after all) not just by singing Beethoven's *Ode to Joy* at the top of their voices, but also by enjoying it. Then, in September 2000 we took a roadshow around the country: five cities in five days, 500 heads in each venue, like a band on tour. We explained the vision and the strategy and debated them vigorously with the very engaged participants. Using interactive technology we asked them to tell us what the worst aspects of our approach were (teacher recruitment and bureaucracy, incidentally) and where we might go next with the strategy. These events were a great step forward, valued greatly by those who attended, but now go back to Kotter's point. This was the boldest direct communication exercise ever attempted by the Department for Education, yet that week just 10 per cent of heads in the country participated in our events. The others were still depending on the *Daily Mail* and the *Guardian*.

We were making progress, but it was not enough. In primary schools at least they knew that literacy and numeracy were the priorities but even here we didn't sufficiently convey the moral purpose. Many primary heads thought it was all about meeting government targets; we thought it was about a better and more equitable society. Meanwhile, a single blunder, trivial in its own way, could drown out all these efforts in the media. For example, one December I had the idea that we should design a poster for every classroom and staff room in primary schools listing the ten most important things to focus on between January and

May to ensure success in the Key Stage 2 English and maths tests. I cleared drafts of the posters before I left for my break and when I returned in early January I found a truly memorable note had been left on my chair. 'Good news, Michael,' it read, 'the posters have gone out. Less good news; they included a couple of typos [and then the immortal conclusion] but it's OK, we don't think anyone will notice.' I was thinking, 19,000 primary schools, 190,000 primary teachers, not to mention 3½ million eagle-eyed children who are better at spelling than ever . . . you don't think anyone will notice! On the contrary, it will be on the front page of a tabloid within three days.

My prediction turned out to be true, but by then we had reissued the poster, typos corrected, and I – having survived a tight-lipped ten minutes with my good friend David Blunkett – had written every primary head in the country a grovelling apology. On reflection, we took a positive perspective. At least as a result of the controversy lots of people read the posters! The serious point here, though, is that in this rough and tumble of communication our efforts, though they went far beyond what any government had attempted in the past, were insufficient.

We needed briefer, clearer, more memorable messages that resonated; we needed to spend even more time than we did on the road; we needed to integrate our media and direct communications approaches; we needed to sustain the same messages for longer; we needed fewer distractions; we needed constant, genuine interaction; and we needed more intermediaries. In addition to headteachers, what about local authority chief executives, chief education officers (now called directors of children's services) and heads of university schools of education? Not all of these would have agreed with us by any means, but we should at least have made sure that they understood. Meanwhile Nigel Crisp, permanent secretary at Health between 2000 and 2005, did meet monthly with the top 200 managers in the NHS and quarterly with the top 600 precisely to achieve clarity.

*

I have spent some time recounting the story of our communication efforts in education reform to make a more general point about the need to invest in much greater, deeper communication between professions and the government. Moreover, it needs to be two-way, interactive (like our roadshow in 2000) and sustained. As I write this, I have a question in my mind which I should come clean about. Much of policy from 1997 to 2000 was of the shock therapy variety. We had set out to jolt a system out of its comfort zone and deliver some results. We were largely successful, but could we have achieved what we did with a different approach, investing more deeply (and inevitably more slowly) in two-way communication early on? Wouldn't we have lost momentum and found the cutting edges bevelled off our policies?

Put the other way around, having applied shock therapy, why should we have been surprised by a degree of resentment? This takes us back to the 'guiding coalition'. It is all well and good to have a small group at the centre of a change who know what they want to do and how they plan to go about it, but over time this must widen out. This is why Michael Fullan and I talk about 'ever-widening circles of leadership': the guiding coalition can stay at the centre, but it needs consciously and constantly to build leadership capacity out through the service for which it is responsible. In Ontario's education reform, on which Fullan is an adviser, this has so far been done well.

In the second Blair term, Estelle Morris began, and then Charles Clarke and David Miliband completed, a process of building a social partnership with teachers' leaders. In return for active involvement in the policy process, the unions (all but one of them) agreed to greater flexibility in working practices. There is the foundation of something here which could be much more radical: imagine a joint declaration that, for example, the teaching profession and government would strive to achieve world-class performance – defined and specified – with both accepting their share of responsibility for achieving it. Imagine if, in the negotiation between the British Medical Association and the government over the GPs' contract in 2002–3, the starting point had been an analysis of the changes necessary to make primary care in England world class; imagine an evidence base shared by both parties informing the negotiation; and imagine both sides really putting the citizen first rather than simply cutting a deal. This points the way to the next phase of my argument. What is needed is not just better communication, but a shared understanding across all public services of what is required to achieve world-class public services and a shared commitment, given the huge investment over the past decade (and still flowing, albeit more slowly, in the next decade), that that is what the country needs to see delivered. To bring this about will require courageous leadership not just in government, but also in the professions. Whether it will emerge remains to be seen, but given that the alternative, over a generation, could be frustration, conflict, disappointing performance, the flight from the public realm of those who can afford the private alternative and thus a residual set of poor public services for poor people (see pp. 125–9), it must be worth a try.

*

In this final section, I want to set out a conceptual framework which might provide an underpinning for this long-term, shared understanding between government and the professions. The basis of it is that the nature of reform and therefore the nature of the relationship between professions and government needs to change and adapt as services improve.

The starting point is the cheese-shaped wedge which appears on page 238 and is reprinted here for convenience.

This crude scale establishes four states – awful, adequate, good and

**THE PUBLIC IS UNIMPRESSED BY 'ADEQUATE'
...THEY WANT 'GOOD' AND ASPIRE TO 'GREAT' ...**

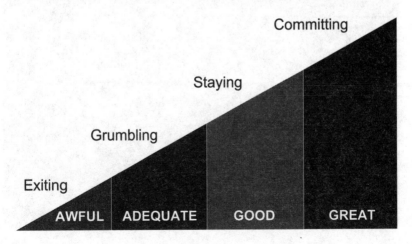

Committing

Staying

Grumbling

Exiting

| AWFUL | ADEQUATE | GOOD | GREAT |

great. In terms of reform it establishes three phases or transitions, namely:

- awful to adequate;
- adequate to good; and
- good to great.

My argument, based not just on the experiences recounted in the earlier chapters of this book, is that as systems pass through these three transitions the nature of the relationship between government and the professions needs to adapt accordingly. The changing nature of the system will be influenced by the models of reform set out in the fan-shaped diagram on page 336, again reprinted here for convenience.

Note that the three responsibilities at the base of the fan remain firmly with government; more importantly from the perspective of the argument here, note too that in the first edition of this book there was insufficient analysis of what it all meant for the relationship between government and the professions. The critics were right to point to this weakness in my argument, and I want to attend to it now.

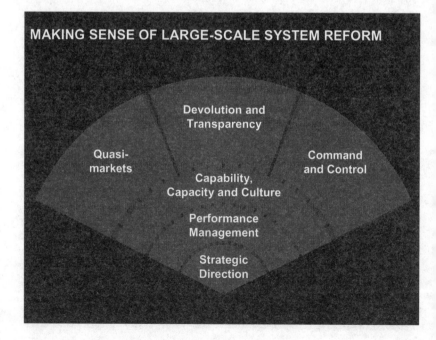

MAKING SENSE OF LARGE-SCALE SYSTEM REFORM

Devolution and Transparency

Quasi-markets

Command and Control

Capability, Capacity and Culture

Performance Management

Strategic Direction

To take a large system such as health or education through these three transitions is a major task by any standards. To take them all the way from awful to great is surely at least a decade's work. Any government, along with its allies in the professions, needs to be committed for the long haul. Indeed, given the vagaries of democracy, it is always possible that governments of different parties will be involved, as in the 1990s in education reforms in England, Texas and North Carolina. Given the long timescales, the key is for those leading the reforms to have two timetables in mind – one leading to short-term results, the other leading ultimately to world-class performance. Both are essential: the former because without short-term results neither those within the system nor those using it will have any confidence that progress is being made; the latter because world class is the ultimate goal. Thus, in the awful-to-adequate phase it is right to emphasise reducing outright failure and achieving a jump in next year's test results, just as the management of a failing company must first stop leaking cash and build some confidence among investors. The key, though, is to take these sometimes drastic actions in a way that does not undermine progress towards the long-term goal. For example, Michael Fullan and I emphasise in our conversations the importance of building the underlying capability and capacity of a workforce and a system through *every* policy. To put the same point in reverse, asset-stripping to achieve short-term results is not a sensible option in the public services. Drawing on Fullan's advice, the government of Ontario has since 2003 consciously modelled its strategy for improving literacy and numeracy in schools on our experience in England between 1997 and 2001, but it has also consciously varied the strategy, with greater emphasis on partnership, less prescription, fewer distractors, as they call them (for example, in England the government pressed for performance-related pay, in Ontario it didn't), and a language about capacity-building and sustainability. They still have targets, but the government doesn't publish league tables (it leaves that to the newspapers), which has downsides but does mean it can deflect criticism. Interestingly, the results so far are very similar – really substantial progress beginning to plateau, and an ambitious target so far remaining unmet. The test will be whether in the next phase they can avoid the long plateau we saw here. I believe they have a strong chance, partly because performance in Canada was already better than in England when they began, and partly because they have done better than we did in bearing the long term in mind throughout the first phase. Much will depend on whether they can sustain their partnership as the strategy becomes more precise and specific. Certainly their dialogue throughout with the teacher unions, principals and school boards was focused on building partnership and has developed and sustained a shared sense of moral purpose.

This is just one interesting contrast. On the basis of education reforms such as these in other countries and our own experience here in health and policing as well as education, it is possible to set out a framework for the changing nature of the dialogue that moves the conversation on as the system goes through the transitions towards world class. The basic premise is that awful-to-adequate does involve shock therapy and therefore a top-down approach, but the further you move towards world class, the less a government's role is prescriptive and the more it becomes enabling. Meanwhile, the professions need to move in the other direction, from being on the receiving end of the shock therapy to, at the world-class end, leading or driving the reform.

At the outset, though, we need some understanding of what it takes to be world class. In education, we have this knowledge from a series of international benchmarking studies. What marks out the best systems in the world is that they recruit great people into teaching, and invest in their skills effectively both at the start of their careers and throughout them so that they teach lessons of consistently high quality. Consistency is the key word from our point of view, for these same international benchmarking exercises reveal that England's education system has many of the qualities of great systems, but far too much variation from classroom to classroom and school to school. In fact, Andreas Schleicher, who organises the OECD's benchmarking of school systems, says, 'Few if any systems are doing more of the right things in policy terms than England's, but this has yet to translate into consistent quality at classroom level.'

This conclusion about education in England is mirrored in other fields. We see the same unacceptable variations in police forces, hospitals and GPs' surgeries. (And indeed in business.) It might have something to do with British culture, its individualism and its scepticism about reliable processes and systems perhaps. This may be why the Australians keep beating us at cricket and we need an Italian to manage our football team. It is also clear that the British businesses which become world class do so by adopting highly reliable processes and managing them consistently. If we want world-class healthcare and education, building this reliability will be crucial, and it begins in GPs' consultations, surgeons' operating theatres, teachers' classrooms and on police officers' beats. In other words, it can only be brought about in the end by frontline professionals who share the mission, benefit from excellent management and are given the tools and incentives to deliver consistent high quality by an enabling government.

With this background, then, the framework shown in Table P1 can be developed as the starting point for dialogue.

Table P1: How the relationship between government and professions could transform public services

Phase of development	Awful → Adequate	Adequate → Good	Good → Great
Chief focus of system	Tackling underperformance	Transparency Spreading best practice	World-class performance Continuous learning and innovation
Role of government	Prescribing Justifying	Regulating Building capacity	Enabling Incentivising
Role of professions	Implementing Accepting evidence Adopting minimum standards	Accommodating Evidence-based Adopting best practice	Leading Evidence-driven Achieving high reliability and innovation
Nature of relationship between government and professions	Top-down Antagonistic	Negotiated Pragmatic	Principled Strategic partnership
Time horizon	Immediate	Short- and medium-term	Continuous
Chief outcome	Improvement in outcomes Reduced public anxiety	Growing public satisfaction	Consistent quality Public engagement and co-production
What the public think	'You should have done that years ago'	'Maybe . . . we'll believe it when we see it'	'That's what we wanted all along'

The table maps the changing relationship between government and the professions through the three phases discussed above. It is part analysis, part history and part aspiration. The first phase coincides with my time in the Department for Education and much of my time at the Delivery Unit. The second phase coincides with the later part of Tony Blair's premiership as the five-year strategies he drove through in 2004 became the dominant influence. The third phase is a first rough sketch of where I believe this crucial relationship should go next. It answers some questions but raises more; not least, is the necessary discipline apparent among leaders either of professions or in government?

At the very least, a framework such as this could provide a common language for a renewed and more productive dialogue between government and the professions. That alone would be a major improvement on talking past each other, as has seemed so common in the past couple of decades. Two factors should enable it. One is that even when a system is awful there are plenty of professionals (headteachers, GPs and so on) who are doing an outstanding job and whom Charles Clarke describes as 'the advocates of change'.[13] Right from the outset, government needs to foster a strong relationship with those in any service who are out in front. If they can express impatience with the pace of change, it helps to counterbalance the drag effect of the many who want to slow things down. Indeed, this alliance with successful leaders is a key part of that process of building ever-widening circles of leadership, mentioned above. The second enabling factor is the vastly improved information available about the performance of public services. This data – everything from the published performance figures to the growing range of international benchmarks – provides (and in future will provide even better) the evidence base on which to have this conversation. Twenty years ago, when I was working for a teacher union (see pp. 18–22) we had no such information base, so building the kind of relationship implied here would have been much more difficult. Clarke argues that part of the new relationship would need to be long-term pay settlements which are both more flexible and more explicit about professionals' responsibilities to develop their skills continuously, with government accepting responsibility for making this possible.[14] The three-year pay settlement for teachers announced in January 2008 may point the way.

These conditions will surely be part of what is required. It is certainly in everyone's interest to make the attempt to create a principled relationship between government and the public service professions. The demand for public services of real quality and universal availability is overwhelming; those who work in the public services would surely prefer to be more motivated rather than less and more successful rather than less, while governments of whatever hue in the next decade will find they need to sign up to this vision too if they are to succeed in meeting bold aspirations. As argued in Chapter 8 (pp. 273–4), a key part of the Blair–Brown legacy already is that no party is willing to countenance the minimalist state option, in which public services are a mere safety net for those who can't afford anything better; in other words, there is no alternative to ambition. By contrast, in the absence of the kind of principled partnership suggested here we would be likely to see the public systems collectively – government and the public workforces – fail to combine and implement reform successfully, fail to communicate to the users of (and payers for) the services where they are heading and, as a consequence, induce a spiral of decline.

Combination is the key word. In a recent book on 21st-century global businesses, Lowell Bryan and Claudia Joyce argue:

> The issue is not whether hierarchy is better than collaboration or vice versa but how we can use both hierarchy and collaboration more effectively, enabling the liberation of talented people from dysfunctional organizations . . . the issue isn't centralization versus decentralization but rather what should be centralized and what should be decentralized?[15]

This puts the challenge very clearly. Moreover, if governments and professions aim their messages only at each other and appear to be at loggerheads, then the public will inevitably be both sceptical and confused. If instead they combine in both implementation and communication, they could be unstoppable. Now this is easy to say, but very hard to do in practice; it will require major culture change all round. It will require professions that embrace transparency, recognise the value of consistently high-quality, reliable processes as well as personalisation, and advocate faster pace. It will require governments that engage in constant, informed dialogue, stick to priorities, understand implementation deeply, avoid gimmicks and admit mistakes. The journey to world-class performance certainly won't lack interest and, as the story of *Instruction to Deliver* makes plain, significant strides have already been taken. It will be tough (who would want it otherwise? Certainly no one with a Quaker background; as my mother used to say, 'life isn't meant to be easy'), but it can be achieved if the right relationships are built at every level.

The penultimate line of Chapter 9 bears repetition: 'The alchemy of good relationships . . . can turn base metal into gold.'

Delivery
manual

Contents

Document 1

Rough guides to deliverology

Rough guide to delivery reports

What is a delivery report?

A delivery report is the six-monthly report the PMDU (Prime Minister's Delivery Unit) submits to the Prime Minister on each of his priority areas.

Purpose of delivery reports

- Provide the Prime Minister with a succinct update on progress against his key priorities over the previous six months and with a traffic light rating of the likelihood of the department delivering against each priority;
- Outline for the Prime Minister what success looks like for these priorities over the next six months, and what key actions are needed to deliver this success;
- Drive a focused discussion between PMDU and department around progress to date and on the best way forward;
- Identify key actions that a department needs to take, with dates and named responsibilities, including major joint areas of work with PMDU;
- Surface areas of disagreement between PMDU and department;
- Form the basis of a joint action plan for next six months between PMDU and delivery priority leader (DPL, the department official with primary lead on a priority area);
- Act as a reference document against which to chart progress between delivery report cycles.

Main processes

At least 10 weeks before	At least 6 weeks before	At least 4 weeks before	At least 3 weeks before	Up to 1 month after
Set up	Departmental self-assessment	PMDU traffic light moderation	Draft delivery report page	Follow up

Who is involved?

Prime Minister
Receives the final delivery report covering his key priorities.

PMDU
- The head of the Unit provides challenge to the initial PMDU traffic light assessments and to the draft version of the delivery report, discusses any differences between our assessment and the departmental self-assessment with relevant permanent secretaries, and makes final edits to the delivery reports.
- The head of the Unit's office secures slots in the permanent secretaries' diaries, pulls together and makes edits to the final version of the delivery report, and circulates final named copies of the delivery report.
- Teams should hold their own moderation meeting to discuss traffic lights in their areas and to produce a ranked list for the PMDU-wide moderation meeting.
- Team leaders should discuss and sign-off traffic light assessments, consider high-level messages for each priority area and comment on all draft delivery pages.
- The relevant staff members are responsible for the creation of the delivery report covering their own priority area, which includes making a traffic light assessment of the likelihood of the department hitting the target and drafting the text of the delivery report.
- Analysts may wish to play a role in departmental self-assessments . . . Tony O'Connor pulls together past and current PMDU traffic light assessments to facilitate the calibration and moderation processes.

Departments
- Secretary of state receives final version of the delivery report.
- Permanent secretary will discuss differences between PMDU and departmental traffic light assessments with the head of the Unit.
- Relevant officials will lead on departmental self-assessment. PMDU teams should decide their approach to the self-assessment.

Treasury/No. 10/Wider Cabinet Office
Receive the departmental self-assessment of progress and a final version of the delivery report. We should also send them the draft delivery report for comment.

Rough guide to PM monthly notes

What is a PM monthly note?

A PM monthly note is a briefing sent to the PM on a monthly basis, from the head of the Unit, which updates the PM on progress towards targets.

Purpose of PM monthly notes

- Provide the PM with an update on progress against targets;
- Update the PM on key actions required (can be used to update PM on key actions taken);
- Can ask the PM for decisions or make recommendations to the PM;
- To reach stakeholders beyond the PM (as copy recipients), and an important part of our branding and visibility;
- An opportunity to provide PM with an early warning of risks to delivery that can be acted on;
- To raise issues beyond immediate performance on targets which may impact on PMDU's agenda, in particular, progress with system reform (e.g. tracking steps to delivery).

Main processes

At least a week before	A week before	3 days before	2 days before	Friday
Prepare	Check data	Draft brief	Send to Unit head	Submit
• Get data, or draft note on performance, from dept • Make sure the Unit head's office are ware of note timing	• Data from dept will need reviewing • Go back to dept with any queries	• Draft the Unit head's covering note • Agree content of note with other team members	• Annexes & draft covering note usually sent to the Unit head to clear the Weds before the note goes to PM	• Note should go to PM in time for the Friday box (ie before 12 noon Friday)

Clearly, when first setting up a note a longer timetable will be required in order to either agree coverage and data with department or internally in PMDU.

Who are notes sent to?

To the Prime Minister, and copies go to:
• Cabinet Office Ministers;
• Cabinet Secretary;
• Relevant staff in No.10.

What should the notes cover and how should they be formatted?

Each individual note will need to be tailored according to business need, but good practice is to aim for a one-page covering note from the head of the Unit, with more detail in an annexe.

Content of covering note
- Ahead or behind trajectory assessment for targets;
- Main action(s) required over next month (can be PMDU or department or both);
- Make best possible use of PM: ask for decisions if any required (may mean more than one page is needed).

Content of annexe
- One side for each target area;
- Use charts rather than tables where possible;
- Could be an attachment from department or PMDU's own annexe.

Rough guide to stocktakes

What is a stocktake?

A stocktake is a meeting between the Prime Minister, ministers from the relevant departments and key officials.

Purpose of stocktakes

- Provide the Prime Minister with an update on progress against his key priorities;
- Enable the Prime Minister to hold ministers/departments to account for progress on targets;
- Provide focus, clarity and a sense of urgency on issues affecting delivery;
- Make decisions and gain agreement on key actions needed to drive progress;
- Remove barriers to and support cross-departmental working on cross-cutting issues (e.g. drugs and asylum) and centre–department working;
- Motivate departments to act on key delivery issues;
- Celebrate success when key milestones are met;
- Develop policy – by No. 10 and the Prime Minister.

Main processes

At least 4 weeks before	At least 2 weeks before	At least 1 week before	Meeting	Up to 1 week after
Set-up	Preparation	Briefing	Stocktake	Follow-up
• Secure time in PM's diary	• Obtain and analyse data	• Brief Unit head on key challenge issues	• Delivery update presentation to PM	• Write and agree minutes
• Allocate times to departments	• Prepare/agree presentation	• Prepare written brief for PM	• Discussion of key issues affecting delivery and emerging policy areas	• Send minutes to department
• Set and agree agenda	• Negotiate key decisions with department(s)			• Follow up agreed action points from stocktake
• Agree cast list and send invitations				

Who is involved?

Prime Minister
- Chairs the meeting
- Holds department to account for delivery
- Challenges progress
- Agrees policy

PMDU
- The head of the Unit represents the unit at all stocktakes and in some cases will present the delivery update.
- The head of the Unit's office secures slots in the PM's diary, assists with the set-up of the meeting in terms of ensuring room is set up to support the meeting and will help pull together the delivery update presentation if PMDU is doing it.
- PMDU staff play a critical part in all parts of the stocktake process from identifying optimum timings of stocktakes, managing the relationships with No. 10 and departments, setting the agenda, preparing the briefing (as part of joint brief with Policy Directorate), agreeing the minutes and following up actions. In most cases,

relevant staff will attend the stocktake and are sometimes required to write the minutes.

- Analysts provide support to the stocktake process by providing the data for the delivery update when the head of the Unit is presenting and assisting others with any analysis required for the briefing.

Policy Directorate
- Have significant influence and input into the agenda, agreeing the cast list and sending out invitations;
- Brief the Prime Minister on any policy issues to be discussed at the stocktake (as part of joint brief with PMDU);
- May provide the Prime Minister with an oral briefing before the meeting;
- Clear and send out minutes.

Departments
- Secretary of state and relevant junior ministers will attend and in some cases provide delivery update.
- Permanent secretary and lead officials for areas to be discussed may also attend and in some cases delivery update is provided by them.

Rough guide to priority reviews

What is a priority review?

A priority review is a rapid analysis of the state of delivery of a high priority strategy and identification of the action needed to strengthen delivery. The outcome is a short report to the Prime Minister, ministers and the permanent secretary.

Guiding principles of priority reviews

- A partnership between PMDU and the department;
- A strong team approach with the right level of expertise and skill mix on the team;
- External challenge to stress-test departmental strategies;

- Non-bureaucratic; a minimum burden and distraction from delivery;
- Sharply focused on the key delivery issues;
- Generates pace and urgency – a report usually within six weeks;
- Involves intensive fieldwork that engages with the delivery chain and tracks delivery down to the frontline;
- Followed up in a planned manner;
- Firmly rooted in evidence and triangulates existing evaluations, data and evidence from reviews;
- Results in a prioritised action plan for strengthening delivery.

Main processes

Week 1	*Week 2*	*Week 3–4*	*Week 5–6*	*Ongoing*
Set-up	Diagnose and planning	Field visits and interviews	Reporting	Follow-up
• team in place	• issue tree	• interview notes	• draft reports	• agreed departmental action plan
• objectives and scope	• initial hypotheses	• outline findings and storyline	• final report	• short revisit report
• delivery chain	• fieldwork programme	• report structure	• note to PM	
• key issues	• interview guides			
• briefing pack	• refined briefing pack			
• project plan	• refined project plan			

- Keep the scope clear and tight
- Get the team skill mix right
- Generate pace and urgency

- Focus on key people in the delivery
- Generate sharp issues and clear hypotheses
- Build a strong evidence base

- Use issues and hypotheses to guide the analysis
- Keep the interviews focused
- Build in sufficient team meetings

- Build momentum and challenge into the report-writing stage
- Avoid too many general recom-mendations
- Syndicate with departmental officials and ministers

- Establish action plan for implementation and ensure there is no loss of momentum
- Invest time in agreeing the scope of revisits
- Invest time in working with critical stakeholders

Rough guide to trajectories

Why build trajectories?

- To predict, monitor and manage performance (at local and national) rather than react, to know whether you are on track;
- To consider the impact of policies on performance using evidence;
- To understand performance, what works and does not work as well as where it works and where it does not;
- To know when an initiative/policy is working;
- To know early enough when something is not working to have time to do something about it.

How to build a trajectory

The following table outlines the key criteria for producing an ideal trajectory.

Issue	Characteristic of an ideal trajectory
Performance indicator	• What is it you're trying to improve? • Well defined and easy to understand by ministers, officials and the public and will it be clear whether the target has been met? • Should do analysis of 'region', 'category' and 'initiative/policy' (see below) BEFORE setting performance indicator and target
What's the target?	• Should be SMART (Specific, Measurable, Achievable, Realistic and Time-limited) – you need to be clear about timing, i.e. financial, calendar or academic year, beginning or end, rolling average for a year or a snapshot • What is the baseline (value and date), to show relative change? • When will it be known (data lag) – how much time between provisional and final figure? • Agreed standard – essential when collecting data from several separate units • Percentage v. absolute numbers – understand the impact of the denominator (% targets could be met with changes in the denominator) and think carefully about 100% targets, which can be difficult to guarantee and cost prohibitive for last few percentage points • Level of accuracy e.g. 10% or 10.1% or 10,000 or 10,301 extra • National average with average performance increasing but not all units • Minimum performance – ensures a basic standard
Data collection mechanism	• Regular and frequent (although cost an obvious limitation) – to monitor trends • Robust – to be sufficiently accurate for measurement

- Consistent – different questions can disrupt time series
- Survey v. census – cost v. sampling errors
- Independent – to avoid perception of results bias where unit being monitored also collects the data
- Contextual data, regional breakdown – additional information helps data interpretation & cheaper to collect at the same time

Historical data run
- At least as long as projection period – helpful to understand past performance (alternative related indicators might be sufficient)
- Seasonality – end of financial year, holidays, winters?
- Previous peaks and troughs – causes?
- 'Policy-off' performance – what happens if you do nothing?

Future estimates
- Intermediate points (as many as possible) – internal not public
- Expected impact of initiatives/policies and by when – how much will each initiative contribute to improvement and when will this impact (immediate, delayed)?
- When will you know if policy/initiative x is working (is it early enough to do something about it?) – test prediction v. reality and where they differ understand why (don't wait for figures to become available and then defend position)
- Evidence of what works needs to be used to identify actions and assessment of initiatives' impact – is the system working?

Breakdown by 'region' or 'locality'
- Breakdowns should be quantified and be consistent with the national target with available data for performance management – helps understanding of what works
- For example, LEA/school, basic command unit, primary care trust and train-operating company
- Range of performance – understand that it is acceptable to have a wide range of performance but

be clear about what is an unacceptable range
- Characteristics of good (or poor) performance – why do some units outperform others?

Breakdown by 'category'
- For example, exam results by gender, eligibility for free school meals or prior attainment (by school type); different categories of violent crime (age/ethnicity of victim/suspect); waiting time by type of operation (in- or outpatient/length of wait); and train delays by cause (see bullet 1 above on consistency etc.)

Breakdown by policy/initiative
- Which are the key policies/initiatives?
- Which are the low-impact policies/initiatives?
- When will individual policies/initiatives impact – monitor the delivery of the plans (collect data which allows evaluation of individual policies/initiatives)? (NB may overlap with 'category' breakdown)

Figure D1.1: Policy delivery trajectories

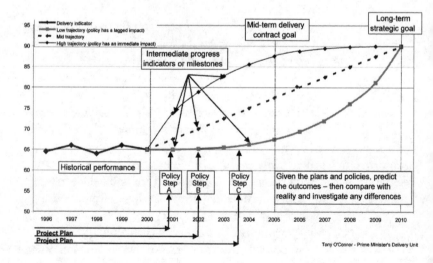

Document 2

Examples of delivery chains

Bus services inside and outside London

Transport for London has direct responsibility for bus services in London, whereas outside London local authorities have direct responsibilities only in relation to the 20 per cent of services they subsidise.

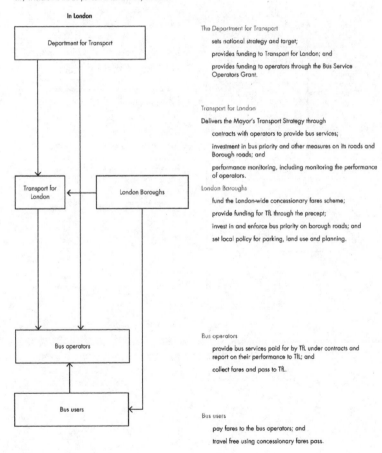

In London

The Department for Transport
- sets national strategy and target;
- provides funding to Transport for London; and
- provides funding to operators through the Bus Service Operators Grant.

Transport for London
Delivers the Mayor's Transport Strategy through
- contracts with operators to provide bus services;
- investment in bus priority and other measures on its roads and Borough roads; and
- performance monitoring, including monitoring the performance of operators.

London Boroughs
- fund the London-wide concessionary fares scheme;
- provide funding for TfL through the precept;
- invest in and enforce bus priority on borough roads; and
- set local policy for parking, land use and planning.

Bus operators
- provide bus services paid for by TfL under contracts and report on their performance to TfL; and
- collect fares and pass to TfL.

Bus users
- pay fares to the bus operators; and
- travel free using concessionary fares pass.

Source: Joint National Audit Office and Audit Commission bus industry workshops

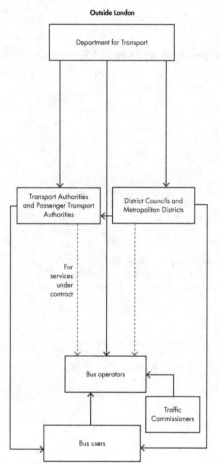

Outside London

The Department for Transport

> sets national strategy and target;
>
> provides capital funding to Transport Authorities;
>
> influences the amount of highways revenue funding provided by ODPM to all local authorities in the Revenue Support Grant; and
>
> provides Bus Service Operators Grant to operators.

Transport Authorities (County Councils and Unitary Authorities)

> set Local Transport Plans in agreement with Districts;
>
> contract for operators to provide socially necessary bus services to complement commercial services; and
>
> invest in bus priority measures.

District Councils

> negotiate and fund concessionary fares schemes;
>
> set local policy for parking, land use and planning;
>
> contract for operators to provide socially necessary bus services to complement commercial services; and
>
> invest in bus infrastructure.

Passenger Transport Authorities

> set Local Transport Plan in agreement with Districts;
>
> negotiate and fund concessionary fares; and
>
> contract for operators to provide socially necessary bus services to complement commercial services.

Metropolitan District Councils

> invest in bus priority measures; and
>
> set local policy on parking, land use and planning.

Bus operators

> provide services commercially (some 80 per cent of routes in 2003-04); and
>
> provide services under contracts with local authorities.

Traffic Commissioners

> licence operators, register routes and monitor operator compliance.

Bus users

> pay fares to the bus operators; and
>
> pay reduced fares while travelling using concessionary fares pass.

Source: *Delivering Efficiently: Strengthening the Links in Public Service Delivery Chains*, Report by the Comptroller and Auditor General, 10 March 2006, HC 940.

Document 3

Assessment framework

ASSESSMENT FRAMEWORK – GUIDANCE FOR DEPARTMENTS

What is the framework for?

(1) The assessment framework is designed to provide a structure to help you to judge the likelihood of delivering your PSA targets. It will also be used by PMDU and the Treasury to develop assessments of your prospects for delivery. It is used in our internal moderation process to ensure that we are consistent in how we make judgements.

(2) The main reason for agreeing the assessment with you is so that jointly we can **identify the areas where you can take action to improve the prospects for delivery.**

Your self-assessment

We will be asking departments to assess their likelihood of delivering each PSA using the high-level summary sheet (p. 2).

The assessment requires four judgements:

* Degree of challenge
* Quality of planning, implementation and performance management
* Capacity to drive progress
* Stage of delivery

We are only expecting three or four bullet points as the rationale for each of the four judgements.

Your Joint Action Leader will be able to provide further support to you in using the framework.

We have provided an overview of the architecture of the framework on page 3.

The framework breaks down each judgement into 'areas to consider' accompanied by some example questions to prompt your thinking.

As every PSA target is different these questions are intended as a guide rather than a strict checklist.

They are **not designed to be a checklist or tick-box, where every issue has to be addressed.** You should judge which are the most relevant for your target and consider whether there are any other questions worth asking.

Recent performance

Recent performance is defined as progress against trajectories over the previous six months. Recent performance is a factor which we take into account throughout our assessment.

Delivery chain

Much of the assessment framework relates to the delivery chain as a whole (e.g. capacity to drive progress). This starts with, and includes, the Government Department, and Departments will need to bear the whole chain in mind when completing self-assessments.

LIKELIHOOD OF DELIVERY

The Prime Minister's
DELIVERY
UNIT

Department: _____

PSA target: _____

Date of assessment: _____

Name(s) of assessors: _____

Judgement	Rating	Rationale Summary
Degree of challenge	L/M/H/VH	
Quality of planning, implementation and performance management		
Understanding the challenge		
Governance, Programme & Project Management		
Managing Performance		
Capacity to drive progress		
Understanding & structure of the Delivery Chain		
Engaging the Delivery Chain		
Leadership and culture		
Stage of delivery	1/2/3/4	

R AR AG G

Recent performance against trajectory and milestones

Likelihood of delivery

Highly problematic - requires urgent and decisive action
Problematic - requires substantial attention, some aspects need urgent attention
Mixed - aspect(s) require substantial attention, some good
Good - requires refinement and systematic implementation

Red
Amber/Red
Amber/Green
Green

3

ARCHITECTURE OF ASSESSMENT FRAMEWORK

The Prime Minister's
DELIVERY
UNIT

Judgement area	*What are we looking for?*
Degree of challenge	Scale of the task, obstacles to be overcome.
Quality of planning, implementation and performance management	
1. Understanding the challenge	Clarity on what success looks like (what we're doing and why), and how much has to be changed to get there, taking account of historical performance.
2. Governance, programme & project management	A strategy which is translated into a usable implementation plan. Clear structures which support accountability for outcomes.
3. Managing performance	Fundamentals of monitoring and reporting performance (measures, trajectories). Proactive responses to reported performance.
Capacity to drive progress	
1. Understanding & structuring the delivery chain	Understanding of the delivery chain; sophistication/comprehensiveness of key elements of the delivery chain, including incentives and prioritisation.
2. Engaging the delivery chain	Winning hearts and minds: mechanisms for influencing; mechanisms for and response to feedback.
3. Leadership and culture	Extent to which the performance ethic of the department and delivery chain supports delivery: leadership; ambition; accountability, working across silos.
Stage of delivery	Current point on the scale between policy development and irreversible progress.

4

Document 4

Speech to Whitehall Delivery Conference, 2002: 'The Five Key Words'

To introduce today's event . . . I've summarised delivery in five words:
- ambition
- focus
- clarity
- urgency
- irreversibility.

The first key word is **ambition.** In Bill Bryson's classic description of this country, *Notes from a Small Island*, he says the British are the only people in the world who, when you ask how they are, reply 'mustn't grumble'. This is a perfect illustration of the fact that ambition isn't necessarily built into the British psyche. We prefer to muddle through. But in this era, with this legacy, and this level of investment, muddling through won't suffice. We need bold ideas boldly executed; we need an expectation of success; and we need success measured by change on the ground, at the frontline.

Often the best delivery comes when people work back from a seemingly impossible outcome:

- 'What would it take to cut crime by 30 per cent in two years?' as police chief Bill Bratton asked in New York City.
- 'How could we ensure that no one waits more than forty-eight hours for a GP appointment?' as GP John Oldham asked in Manchester.
- 'Could we reverse the rising trend in street crime in five months?' as they asked the Home Office in April.
- 'Could the concept of a failing school fade into history like mortarboards and cold baths in the morning?'

In each case, the answer is 'Yes' and the outcome is either delivered or well on the way to being delivered.

We also need ambition in another sense: whether the idea is bold or cautious, our task is to execute it as well as possible rather than as easily as possible. It is quality of execution that decides whether a policy really bites and makes a difference on the ground.

The second key word is **focus**. Delivery requires sustained prioritisation. It demands consistent focus on the targets and the data that show what progress is being made. But the targets, however good, and the data, however clear, are only imperfect representations of something even more important: that is, the real-world outcomes which matter to citizens. The central focus therefore should be

- on the solutions;
- on the real-world changes we're aiming to achieve for the people we serve: our customers.

Whether we're talking about a sustainable rural economy, motorway journeys that are less frustrating, or rapid turnaround of patients in A&E, these are real-world outcomes which people are impatient to see delivered. Achieving these kinds of profound change requires sustained focus.

Focus requires discipline at departmental and other levels. Departments need to ensure the right people are in the right posts with the right support. Delivery can't be driven by people for whom it's a minor part of a much wider role in a bureaucratic hierarchy. It can't be driven by people who have to wait three or four months to get their hands on the staff they need, or who find that the best people in their divisions get promoted just when they are beginning to make a difference. Moreover, follow-through is essential. A White Paper and legislation are the beginning, not the end. Delivery requires focus all the way through to the frontline. Anti-social behaviour orders, for example, have had legal existence for three years now but are only just beginning to make a real impact in places such as Camden and Manchester.

Focus is also required when the going gets tough, as it surely will: compromise too early in pursuit of a quiet life and the focus can be lost. Fail to achieve some quick wins, and momentum can be lost. And when confusion or uncertainty arises, focus is decisive, like the walker with a compass in the mist.

Clarity is the third key word – clarity above all about the diagnosis:

- What is the problem?

- Why have past attempts to solve it failed?
- What do we know about the causal relationships?
- How secure is your knowledge?

The world, for example, is full of urban myths that everyone comes to accept but which turn out not to be true. People say, 'If you focus on street crime, burglary will rise.' Wrong. In the Met and the best street crime BCUs, both are falling. They say, 'A minimum wage will generate unemployment.' Wrong. Its introduction has been followed by the lowest levels of unemployment for over a generation. They say, 'If you teach children to read and write well, science will suffer.' Wrong. Science standards have risen spectacularly alongside improvements in literacy.

You need, as the textbooks say, to confront the brutal facts. But make sure they are facts. And in the search for solutions, where is the best practice

- in your sector?
- in other sectors?
- in other countries?

I hear civil servants talk about how difficult it is to define meaningful measures of success. Yes, it is difficult sometimes, but it has to be done. How else will you or anyone else know what impact you had? Then there's the question of clarity about 'How?' – What are the levers? Who are the key partners?

Quite often in the past year I've heard people complain that they only have 'rubber levers'. Perhaps I should be sympathetic to this thought. But I've come to see it as an excuse – 'I'm powerless,' the metaphor says. It's an interesting example of allowing the human mind to be bound by the choice of metaphor. No one, even in a directly managed service, has pure mechanical levers, like in a steam engine, because people are people, organisations are organisations and structures, incentives and culture are powerful. Even in the NHS (a single organisation managed from Whitehall) you still have to persuade trust chief executives, consultants and over one million employees. In schools, teachers have to unlock imaginations and children have to concentrate. In the police force, chief constables are jealously independent. Leverage is not automatic or mechanical in any service. In each case those responsible have to manage their stakeholders.

So leverage is never simple; but that doesn't mean it's 'rubber'. The

DfT doesn't run the railway, but it does set the regulatory framework, appoint the key people and invest very large sums of money. It also crucially sets the tone.

One civil servant complained that delivery would be difficult because 'government funding is only 20 per cent of the total but the target covers all of it'. Why the 'but' in this sentence? Twenty per cent is a huge proportion! Enough, in another world, to bring in the Competition Commission! There are pension funds which are able to change a company's leadership by buying 3 per cent of the shares and demanding change. If you discount the funding devolved direct to schools with no strings attached, the DfES has far less than 20 per cent to play with. Yet most of you, no doubt, assume it has high leverage.

Next time you hear someone reach for the 'rubber lever' metaphor or tell you their influence is limited, get them to talk about the leverage they do have, rather than its limits. Remind them to manage their stakeholders. Or change the metaphor – tell them to imagine they conduct an orchestra, for example. They don't play a single note, but they shape the entire experience.

One final point about clarity. You need to be clear, at any given moment, what impact your strategy is having. I've learnt to be suspicious in the civil service when you ask someone how their strategy is going and they say, 'It's bedding in.' I follow up and ask, 'How do you know?' I remember my chain-smoking medieval history professor, who asked in response to any assertion, 'Where's the evidence?'

The fourth word is **urgency**. Things have moved on since the then Prime Minister, Lord Salisbury, said at the turn of the previous century, 'All change is for the worse, so it's in our interests that as little should happen as possible.' At the turn of the current century, our Prime Minister has an opposite view. He talks about 'step change' and asks, 'How long have we got?' This is hardly surprising. All the evidence suggests people are impatient for change and are sceptical about our collective capacity to deliver. By contrast, the interest groups we deal with in each policy area want less change, more slowly. In fact, I'm on the brink of patenting a new law of the professions as sound in social science as Newton's three laws of motion are in physics. It goes as follows:

> Members of any given profession are in a hurry to see every profession reformed but their own.

The same is true of league tables. People are in favour of them for everyone else. This creates a tension for civil servants responsible for delivery in any given area: the stakeholders they talk to the most – producers – are urging delay and procrastination, while those they hear from less – customers or citizens – think progress is too slow.

Urgency is not just necessary because it's what customers want; it also helps to ensure effective implementation. It's very British (and very civil service) to think of change as incremental and slow – taking decades, perhaps even centuries. Worse still, deep in the British psyche is a belief that, in the end, whatever we do today, progress is inevitable. This is because (it has dawned on me) we're all closet Whig historians, disciples of Macaulay and Trevelyan. It's no accident that the Trevelyan family, which wrote so much of Whig history, was also responsible for laying the foundations of the modern civil service. But as the Cabinet Secretary has said, he wants to change the metaphor that defines the civil service from 'shock absorber' to 'gearing ratio'. He wants us to ask: for any given change, how can we amplify it or accelerate it rather than dampen it?

This means

- looking for a means of speeding things up;
- knowing fast what's going on;
- identifying and solving problems as they arise or preferably before.

It means, if someone says, 'If it ain't broke don't fix it,' you say to them, 'Look harder.' It means remembering the words of world champion racing driver Mario Andretti (who is still alive, by the way), 'If everything seems under control, you're not going fast enough.' Above all, it means keeping meetings short.

The fifth word is **irreversibility**. In the previous parliament, when we were intervening in failing local authorities, Estelle Morris and I would meet the headteachers of the area on the day the damning inspection report on their LEA was published. We gave them a guarantee: 'We're not going away until the LEA gives you the support you deserve: in other words, until the problem is irreversibly solved.' The key word is irreversibility, and achieving it is a daunting task. To achieve it means that at every level, every stage of implementation, the reform needs cutting edge.

There are many threats to bringing about irreversible progress:

- Being satisfied with the form of implementation, not real change on the ground.
- Giving up because it's simply too difficult.
- Compromising too soon when you run into conflict.
- Negotiating away the central core of the change to buy a quiet life.
- Or the opposite, gaining so much success so soon that you move on to other things before the change is secure. Cultures are often deeply embedded; 'declaring victory too soon', as John Kotter calls it, is tempting to the protagonists of change – they need encouragement after all – but it appeals to the critics of change too, as a means of seeing off a threat before it becomes irreversible.

Irreversibility means

- courage, determination and sometimes bloody-mindedness;
- integrating delivery and communications;
- changing beliefs as well as behaviours;
- staying on the case;
- erring on the side of rigour;
- checking and checking again;
- deepening and broadening the change;
- attending to culture as well as structure;
- and, above all, following through until you deliver results.

Document 5

Previous work locations of Delivery Unit staff 2003–4

Head of Unit	Institute of Education, University of London	
Head of Unit's Office	Cabinet Office	
	Institute of Education, University of London (2)	
Delivery Team 1	Team leader:	Cabinet Office
	Staff:	Major management consultancy
		Audit Commission
		Department for Education and Skills
		HM Treasury
		Office of the Deputy Prime Minister
Delivery Team 2	Team leader:	Audit Commission
	Staff:	Major management consultancy (3)
		Audit Commission (2)
		Home Office
Delivery Team 3	Team leader:	Ofsted
	Staff:	Cabinet Office
		Department for Education and Skills
		Greenwich Borough Council
Delivery Team 4	Team leader:	Major management consultancy
	Staff:	Major management consultancy
		Cabinet Office
		Department of Health
		Guy's and St Thomas' Hospital NHS Trust
		Home Office

Analysts	Team leader:	Government Operational Research Service
	Staff:	Government Operational Research Service
		Government Social Research
		HM Treasury
		National Statistics (2)
Secretariat	Cabinet Office (2)	
Support Team	Cabinet Office (4)	
	Department for Trade and Industry	

Document 6

Delivery in year three: how to make early progress irreversible

Cabinet meeting, Thursday 17 July 2003

Lesson 1: A week may be a long time in politics but five years is unbelievably short

- Is the action you plan by December 2004 and July 2004 sufficient and comprehensive? Or is it just a list of things to do?
- Is anyone in your department anticipating *next* year's major risks and managing them now?

Lesson 2: Sustained focus on a small number of priorities is essential

- Are the priorities set at the start of the parliament still the priorities? If not, is there a really good reason why?
- Do frontline staff really know which two or three things matter most?

Lesson 3: Flogging a system can no longer achieve these goals: reform is the key

- Is your diagnosis of the barriers to delivery sufficiently rigorous?
- Is there a vital reform which has been postponed indefinitely or watered down?
- If so, should it now be brought forward?

Lesson 4: Nothing is inevitable: 'rising tides' can be turned

- Do the people responsible believe it can be done?
- Are you ensuring that for each of the top priorities, however difficult, someone is managing it through to a result?

Lesson 5: The numbers are important but not enough: citizens have to see and feel the difference and expectations need to be managed

- Have you got regular, reliable real-time data so you know what's happening?
- How do you know what frontline staff and service users think?

Lesson 6: The quality of leadership at every level is decisive

- Where the leadership needs changing, have you made the change?
- Are there rewards for those who deliver and consequences for those who don't?

Lesson 7: Good system design and management underpin progress

- For each given service, is there an underlying model of continuous improvement? Does it have clear standards, devolved responsibility, excellent comparative data, effective mechanisms for disseminating best practice, effective accountability, the capacity to intervene, choice where possible and contestability where necessary?

Lesson 8: Getting the second step change is difficult and requires precision in tackling variations and promoting best practice

- Are variations in performance analysed, understood and acted upon?
- Is effort targeted where it will make most difference?
- Is best practice clearly and sharply defined, effectively disseminated and rapidly taken up?

Lesson 9: Extraordinary discipline and persistence are required to defeat the cynics

- Who explodes urban myths?
- Do you consistently advocate with passion and without compromise the controversial measures that will make a difference, such as school tests, hospital star ratings or publication of police performance data?

Lesson 10: Grinding out increments is a noble cause . . . but where progress is slow, it's even more important for people to understand the strategy

- Do you reward the tortoise as well as the hare? Is persistence seen as the quality it is? (If you admire Proust's writing, Mike Atherton's batting, the countryside in Iowa or Liverpool's 0-0 draw in Barcelona in 2001, you will understand.)
- Does the public understand where this will all lead in five years from now?

Michael Barber
Prime Minister's Delivery Unit

Document 7

Letter to permanent secretaries, July 2004

Dear _____

Delivery: Finishing the first thriller, starting the second

This letter has two main purposes.
- The first, as with previous six-monthly delivery reports, is to set this moment in context and draw out some of the common themes from delivery across a number of departments, with the aim of strengthening your capacity to deliver.
- The second is to set out the issues in your five-year strategies which the Prime Minister has asked the delivery unit to work on with you and to describe the initial stages of our collaboration on this new agenda. This follows my consultations with you in April about what the agenda might be and how jointly we might pursue it.

(I also attach a draft of your delivery report.)

The first thriller: delivering by 2005

To understand the stage we're at, it helps (me at least) to use a metaphor. We collectively were asked in 2001 by the Prime Minister to write a thriller on the theme of the public services. Could we, within one parliament, drive through a set of programmes which delivered results of such substance that taxpayers felt the investment they were making was justified? And could we together design a system that would enable government to know at any given point how we were getting on?

Our thriller has had its twists and turns. We've had moments of writer's block and once or twice, like Dostoevsky with *Crime and Punishment*, we have felt like throwing the whole script on the fire and starting again but, especially over the past six months, we've discovered that our text is coming out rather well. The plotlines are sharp, the characters have developed well, the dialogue is rich and the moral of the tale is becoming clear.

Now, three-quarters of the way through this, our first book, an insight of stunning importance has occurred to us. With a thriller, however good the beginning and the middle are, it's the end, that final sequence, which decides whether we have a bestseller or a remainder on our hands. All that work and now everything depends on a few months! That is what this July's delivery reports are about: how to ensure that over the next six months we reap just reward for the huge investment of time, skill, energy and emotion we've all made over the past three years.

The good news

The good news is that we've learnt so much that now we know what to do. Until six months ago, collectively we had a process which was generally found to be valuable, plenty of movement in the right direction and a few stories of how, with the application of the disciplines of delivery, we could change outcomes positively within a relatively short space of time. Now we have progress across such a wide range of areas – the criminal justice system, the railways, secondary schools, accident & emergency, to take just four examples – that we can be increasingly confident that between us we've developed a proven methodology.

PMDU analysis of delivery successes and failures demonstrates that the decisive elements in the methodology are:

- **Prioritisation** – is it sufficiently rigorous?
- **Leadership** – is it in place in Whitehall and beyond?
- **Delivery chain** – is it clear, aligned and capable of doing the job? All the way out to the frontline and back?
- **Performance management** – is it clear at every level who is accountable for what and to whom?
- **Data and analysis** – is good, regular, timely data available so people know how well they are doing? Are the key drivers of

improved results sufficiently understood? Are the messages from the data acted upon?

- **Incentives** – do people and organisations have incentives to succeed? Are there consequences when they don't?

. . . Increasingly, departments drawing on both their own experience and ours are applying these disciplines and, where they are, it is working. In short, to use a different metaphor, we've passed a tipping point . . .

The challenging news

The less good news is that we've learnt that applying these lessons is very tough, requiring great discipline and focus and, if we are to meet our deadlines, a further stepping-up of the urgency in this final phase. Then again, no one ever said this was going to be easy.

Your personal leadership will, in these circumstances, be critical. In this summer's delivery reports we have sought as sharply as possible to set out for each priority what we think 'success looks like' in December 2004 and what the necessary steps are to achieve that success. In the vast majority of cases, what we set out is a shared understanding between the relevant colleagues in your department and ourselves. By integrating the outcomes and actions we specify into your performance management process, I hope you will be able to use this delivery report to strengthen your personal capacity to drive delivery . . .

In addition to taking the actions specified for each priority, it is also important, especially now there is so much green and amber-green, to take urgent and decisive action to tackle the substantial problems indicated by the remaining amber-red or red markings. If the actions specified in our reports are taken and the success criteria achieved, the amount of red or amber-red can be reduced dramatically once again by Christmas.

In short, there is every chance of ensuring that we finish our first thriller with style and panache and leave our commissioning editor and above all our readers both satisfied and expectant.

The second thriller: delivering the five-year strategies

In the meantime, the Prime Minister has developed sufficient confidence in the likely success of our first novel that he has commissioned the second. This too will be on the theme of public services, but now the question is whether, through a combination of bold reform aimed at choice and personalisation as well as high standards, we can achieve a further step change in the quality of public services and thus ensure they are among the world's best.

Against this background, your department has recently published a strategy which sets the agenda for the next five years, and the spending review which underpins it is settled. Following consultation with you, I discussed with the Prime Minister which themes within your five-year strategy he would like us to focus on from 2005 onwards. In most cases the themes are continuations of our existing agenda, but there are some additions and subtractions too.

On these priorities, as on the rest of your five-year strategy, you will no doubt already be gearing up to plan implementation. Following my discussion with you, we don't want to repeat the process of exchanging numerous drafts of delivery plans as we did in 2001. We would rather build on our collective learning over the past few years and on the quality of our working relationship and agree with you a programme for delivery of each of these priorities, which will include a joint action plan setting out how we will contribute. Delivery plans will, of course, still be necessary and our process will involve examining them to ensure they are sound, but importantly it will also ensure our approach is tailored according to your circumstances and the nature of the challenge.

We anticipate in any case that priorities which are a continuation of an existing priority will need to be treated differently from those which are entirely new to the PMDU.

For continuation targets we anticipate undertaking jointly with you a 'healthcheck' of the programme some time in the autumn or early in 2005. We are currently designing (in collaboration with colleagues in departments) the methodology for a healthcheck. The intention is that it should be light-touch, comprehensive and rapid. It will look not just at plans, milestones and trajectories, but also the capacity to deliver them. If this process identifies any major barriers to delivery, a deeper review of that area might follow, along priority review lines.

Following consultation with you, we will tailor the timing and character of the healthcheck for each priority. The feedback you gave us when we met suggests that you find the external challenge we provide valuable; we hope the healthcheck will offer you this effective challenge while at the same time being much less bureaucratic than the original round of delivery planning.

For new priorities in our portfolio we anticipate adopting a different approach which will enable us with you to get fully up to speed on the challenge of delivery. We are currently developing, again in collaboration with colleagues from departments, a 'starter pack' which will set out the key steps necessary to gear up to deliver a new priority. These steps fall under three broad headings which derive from our joint learning about how to move rapidly and effectively from strategy to delivery:

- Analysis → Strategy
- Strategy → Design
- Design → Plan

. . . Our overall objective is that the December delivery reports should give the Prime Minister confidence not only that we are delivering his priorities for this parliament, but also that we have laid the foundations for delivery in the next.

It's been a pleasure working with you on the first thriller, and I look forward to working with you on the second. We might be surprised to discover before too long that we have both an enthusiastic commissioning editor and a satisfied mass readership out there in the country.

Best wishes . . .

Document 8

Introducing choice and contestability

CHOICE AND CONTESTABILITY REFORMS: DESIGN/DELIVERY ASSESSMENT LEVEL 1 DETAIL

	Assessment elements	Red-amber-green assessment
1. Design: Is the design of the reformed system robust and appropriate for meeting system goals?	**1.1 Coherent strategic direction:** Is there a coherent strategic direction which is consistent with system objectives and available funding?	
	1.2 Users/consumers: Does the design enable users (e.g. patients, parents) to play an active role, to exercise choice and to navigate the system effectively?	
	1.3 Commissioners/purchasers: Does the design enable commissioners/purchasers to purchase services efficiently, effectively and in line with system objectives?	
	1.4 Providers: Does the design enable contestability, and enable providers to provide services efficiently, effectively and in line with system objectives?	
2. Delivery infrastructure: Are the right elements in place to ensure successful implementation of reforms, operation of the reformed system and realisation of benefits?	**2.1 Leadership and engagement:** Is there strong leadership of, and organisational engagement in, delivery of the reforms? Is there sufficient public engagement in delivery of the reforms?	
	2.2 Definition of workstreams, milestones and owners: Is there clear definition of the workstreams required to implement the reforms, including owners of each workstream, milestones, and sequencing of streams?	
	2.3 Effective performance management: Are there mechanisms to track the progress and impact of the reforms, to allow appropriate intervention if implementation goes off track, and to operate the reformed system?	
	2.4 Development of required skills, capabilities and practices: Are there plans to develop the skills and capabilities required to implement and operate the reformed system? Are there mechanisms to capture learning and spread best practice?	
3. Delivery progress	**3.1 Delivery progress:** Is appropriate progress being made in implementing reforms and meeting milestones?	

DETAILED ASSESSMENT: ELEMENT 1.3 – COMMISSIONERS/PURCHASERS

Assessment elements	Detailed questions	Red-amber-green assessment
1.3 Commissioners/ purchasers: Does the design enable commissioners/ purchasers to purchase services efficiently, effectively and in line with system objectives?	**A. Commissioner/purchaser objectives and accountabilities** • Is there clarity on who will be purchasers in the new system? • Are the objectives and accountabilities of purchasers clearly defined? • Are conflicts within objectives avoided?	
	B. Commissioner/purchaser decision rights • What decision rights will purchasers have (e.g., pricing, quantity, service level, which providers to use, local staffing/pay agreements)? • Are decision rights appropriate to allow purchasers to meet their objectives?	
	C. Commissioner/purchaser incentives • What incentives will purchasers have to seek out the most efficient and effective services for their populations? • Will the incentives be sufficient to drive appropriate behaviour? • What perverse incentives exist for purchasers? How will these be managed to avoid perverse outcomes?	
	D. Commissioner/purchaser governance and regulation • Are governance arrangements for purchasers clearly defined? • What mechanisms are in place to ensure that purchasers act in the best interests of their populations? • What mechanisms are in place to address performance of failing purchasers?	
	E. Information for commissioners/purchasers • What information will purchasers need to purchase effectively? • How will they get that information?	
	F. Capabilities of commissioners/purchasers • What capabilities will purchasers require? • Do purchasers have those capabilities today?	

Document 9

Extract from delivery update for media, July 2004

DELIVERY UPDATE 2004

Michael Barber

Prime Minister's Press Conference
22 July 2004

PROGRESS ON HEALTH

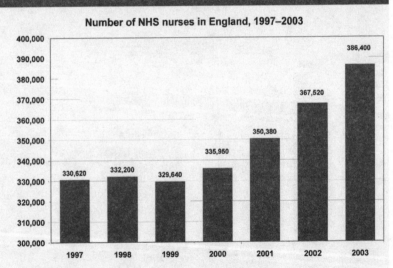

The build-up of capacity is reflected in nurse numbers ...

Number of NHS nurses in England, 1997–2003

Source : Department of Health

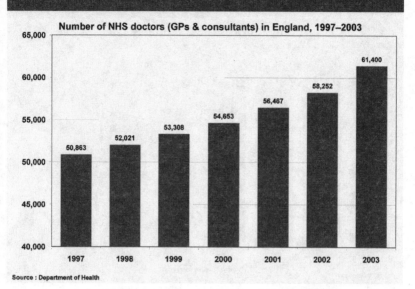

... and in doctor numbers

Number of NHS doctors (GPs & consultants) in England, 1997–2003

Source : Department of Health

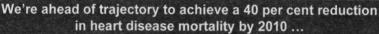

We're ahead of trajectory to achieve a 40 per cent reduction in heart disease mortality by 2010 ...

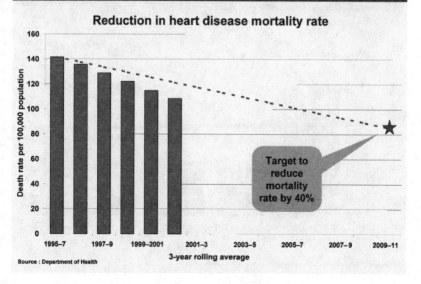

Reduction in heart disease mortality rate

Death rate per 100,000 population

Target to reduce mortality rate by 40%

3-year rolling average

Source : Department of Health

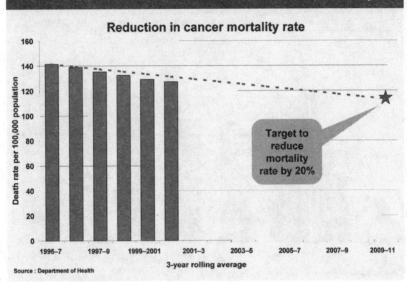

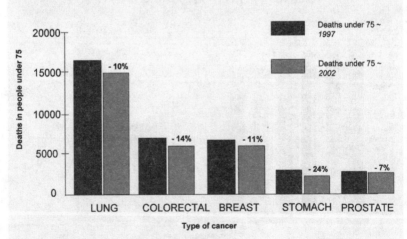

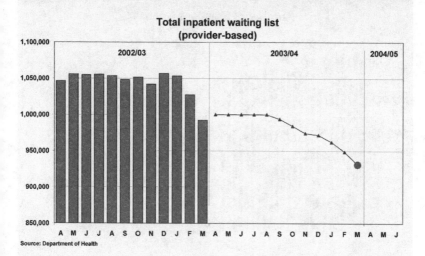

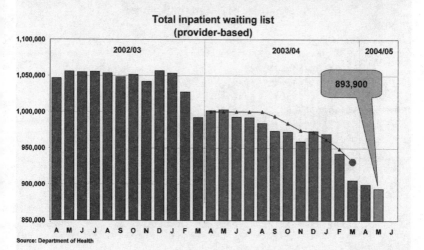

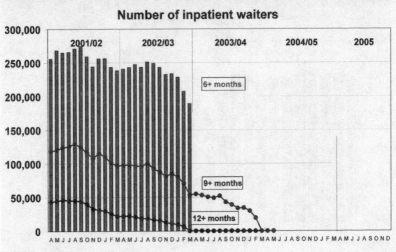

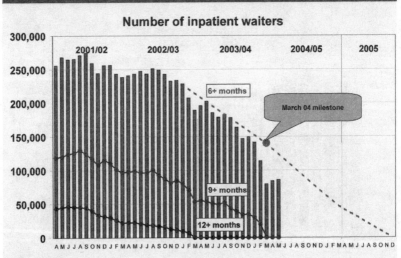

Choice, competition, capacity and three-year funding of PCTs are key drivers of this progress

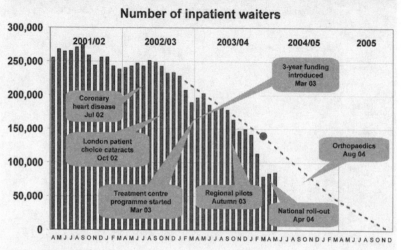

Number of inpatient waiters

Source : Department of Health

The data has been independently verified

'Spot checks indicate that the overall level of accuracy is sufficiently robust to enable reasonable judgements to be made about national trends in the number of people waiting and the length of time for which they have been on this list.'

Information and data quality in the NHS
Audit Commission, 2004

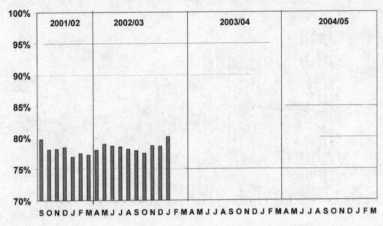

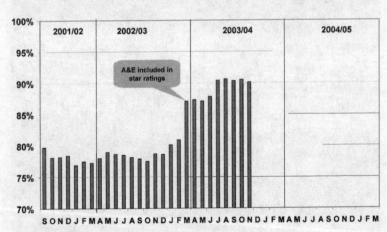

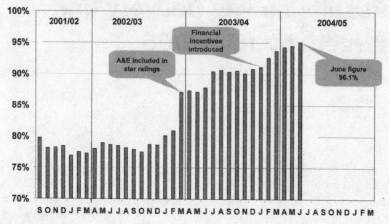

... since January 04 incentives have brought another

A&E attenders spending no more than than 4 hours in A&E, England

Source : Department of Health

OVERALL CONCLUSION

Last year (July 2003)

• Demonstrable progress in most areas but not yet irreversible

This year (July 2004)

• Widespread and significant progress across the public services, becoming irreversible

• Foundations laid for further radical reform: the task is far from complete

Document 10

Results on key Delivery Unit targets by July 2005

Health

Priority	Better than 1997?	Better than 2001?	Heading in the right direction?	Target hit or on target to be hit?
Heart disease mortality	YES	YES	YES	ON TRACK
Cancer mortality	YES	YES	YES	ON TRACK
Waiting list	YES	YES	YES	NO TARGET
Maximum waiting time for non-emergency surgery	YES	YES	YES	ON TRACK
A&E	YES	YES	YES	HIT
GP appointments	YES	YES	YES	HIT
Also				
Nurse numbers	YES	YES	YES	NO TARGET
Doctor numbers	YES	YES	YES	NO TARGET

Education

Priority	Better than 1997?	Better than 2001?	Heading in the right direction?	Target hit or on target to be hit?
11-year-old literacy	YES	YES	YES	MISSED
11-year-old numeracy	YES	YES	YES	MISSED
14-year-old English	YES	YES	YES	MISSED
14-year-old maths	YES	YES	YES	MISSED
5 or more A*–C grades at GCSE	YES	YES	YES	NOT CLEAR
Attendance	NO CHANGE	NO CHANGE	JUST BEGINNING	NOT CLEAR
Also				
Teacher numbers	YES	YES	YES	NO TARGET

Home Office/criminal justice system

Priority	Better than 1997?	Better than 2001?	Heading in the right direction?	Target hit or on target to be hit?
Overall crime	YES	YES	YES	NOT CLEAR
Street crime	NO	YES	YES	MISSED
Burglary	YES	YES	YES	ON TRACK
Car crime	YES	YES	YES	ON TRACK
Likelihood of being a victim of crime	YES	YES	YES	NO TARGET
Asylum applications	YES	YES	YES	BLAIR ASPIRATION HIT*
Offences brought to justice	NO DATA	YES	YES	LIKELY TO BE HIT
Drug-related crime	NO	YES	YES	NO TARGET
Police numbers	YES	YES	YES	NO TARGET

Transport

Priority	Better than 1997?	Better than 2001?	Heading in the right direction?	Target hit or on target to be hit?
Road congestion	NO	NO	BETTER MANAGED BUT NO	NO TARGET†
Rail punctuality	NO	YES	YES	HIT

Notes:

This table is highly simplified to make the information easily accessible for a general reader. Those who want more detail should look at the Treasury website (www.hmt.gov.uk).

* There was no target but Blair set an aspiration in early 2003 which was met six months later (see Chapter 5).

† Original target dropped 2002.

Notes

Chapter 1

1. A. J. P. Taylor, *A Personal History* (London: Hamish Hamilton, 1983), p. 63.
2. Michael Barber, The Learning Game: Arguments for an Education Revolution (London: Victor Gollancz, 1996), p. 65.
3. Quoted in the *Times Educational Supplement*, 12 May 1995.
4. Greg Brooks, A. K. Pugh and Ian Schagen, *Reading Performance at Nine* (Slough: National Foundation for Educational Research, 1996).
5. David Blunkett, *The Blunkett Tapes: My Life in the Bear Pit* (London: Bloomsbury, 2006), p. 8.
6. Ibid., pp. 15–16.
7. Ibid., p. 30.
8. Ibid., p. 61.
9. Ibid., p. 241.
10. Blair letter in possession of the author, June 2001.

Chapter 2

1. Peter Riddell, *The Unfulfilled Prime Minister: Tony Blair's Quest for a Legacy*, rev. ed. (London: Politico's, 2006), p. 39.
2. Ibid., p. 55.
3. Ibid., p. 103.
4. Robert B. Reich, *Locked in the Cabinet* (New York: Alfred A. Knopf, 1997), p. 181.

Chapter 3

1. Nicholas Timmins, *The Five Giants: A Biography of the Welfare State* (London: HarperCollins, 1995), p. 398.
2. Richard Olivier, *Inspirational Leadership: Henry V and the Muse of Fire – Timeless Insights from Shakespeare's Greatest Leader* (London: Industrial Society, 2001), p. 82. The full quote here is from Roosevelt's address at the Sorbonne on 23 April 1910.
3. Theodore Marmor, *Understanding Health Care Reform* (New Haven

and London: Yale University Press, 1994).

4. John Kotter, *Leading Change* (Boston: Harvard Business School Press, 1996), p. 4.
5. Timmins, *Five Giants*, p. 147.
6. Ibid., p. 182.
7. Ibid., p. 370.
8. Ronald A. Heifetz, *Leadership without Easy Answers* (Cambridge, MA: Belknap Press, 1994).
9. Anthony Seldon, *Blair* (London: Free Press, 2004), p. 432.

Chapter 4

1. Andrew Rawnsley, *Servants of the People: The Inside Story of New Labour* (London: Hamish Hamilton, 2000).
2. 'Whitehall's demon Barber', Observer, *Financial Times*, 1 November 2001.
3. Roy Jenkins, *Churchill* (London: Macmillan, 2001), p. 193.
4. Quoted in Robert Peston, *Brown's Britain* (London: Short, 2005), p. 265.
5. Ibid., p. 274.
6. David Blunkett, *The Blunkett Tapes: My Life in the Bear Pit* (London: Bloomsbury, 2006), p. 343.

Chapter 5

1. Quoted in Thomas Friedman, *The World Is Flat: A Brief History of the Globalized World in the Twenty-First Century* (London: Allen Lane, 2005), p. 359.
2. The quote is from a personal email to me. The reference for the academic article that followed is: Steven Kelman, 'Improving Service Delivery Performance in the United Kingdom: Organization Theory Perspectives on Central Intervention Strategies', *Journal of Comparative Policy Analysis* (2006), vol. 8, 393–419.
3. Lincoln's second inaugural address, 4 March 1865.
4. Public Administration Select Committee, minutes of evidence, 27 February 2003, HC 482-i.
5. Michael Barber, 'Courage and the Lost Art of Bicycle Maintenance', Primary Strategy Conference, 2004.

Chapter 6

1. The full text of this is available from the No. 10 website, www.number10.gov.uk.
2. Norman Dixon, *On the Psychology of Military Incompetence* (London: Jonathan Cape, 1976), pp. 152–3.

3. Prime Minister's press conference, 22 July 2004. The full text of this is available from the No. 10 website, www.number10.gov.uk.

Chapter 7

1. Lord Butler, *The Art of the Possible: The Memoirs of Lord Butler, KG, CH* (London: Jonathan Cape, 1971), pp. 118–19.
2. Hebrews 11, v. 1.

Chapter 8

1. Peter Riddell, *The Unfulfilled Prime Minister: Tony Blair's Quest for a Legacy* (London: Politico's, 2005), p. 196.
2. Polly Toynbee and David Walker, *Better or Worse?: Has Labour Delivered?* (London: Bloomsbury, 2005), p. 328.
3. Anthony Seldon, *Blair* (London: Free Press, 2004), p. 691.
4. Simon Jenkins, *Thatcher and Sons: A Revolution in Three Acts* (London: Allen Lane, 2006), p. 300.
5. As measured on the McCarthy Scales of Children's Abilities.
6. Toynbee and Walker, *Better or Worse?*, p. 320.
7. Anatole Kaletsky, *Times*, 24 March 2005.
8. Peter Riddell, *Times*, 9 September 2006.
9. Bagehot, *Economist*, 16 September 2006.
10. Riddell, *Unfulfilled Prime Minister*, p. 197.
11. Bagehot, *Economist*, 21 May 2005.
12. Matthew Parris, *Times*, 23 December 2006.
13. Quoted in the *Daily Telegraph*, 30 August 2006.
14. John Rentoul, *Independent on Sunday*, 26 November 2006.
15. Robert Peston, *Brown's Britain* (London: Short, 2005), pp. 285–6.
16. Ibid., p. 285.
17. 'Breaking the circle', *Economist*, 14 September 2006.

Chapter 9

1. Richard Sykes, *Sunday Telegraph*, 3 September 2006.
2. Anatole Kaletsky, 'The beginning of the end for new Labour', *Times*, 11 October 2007.
3. Quoted in Peter Hennessy, *The Prime Minister: The Office and Its Holders since 1945* (London: Allen Lane, 2000), p. 55.
4. Quoted ibid.
5. Quoted ibid., p. 56.
6. Quoted ibid., p. 54.
7. Quoted ibid., p. 56.

8. Tony Benn, *Arguments for Democracy* (London: Jonathan Cape, 1981), p. 18.
9. Quoted in William Hague, *William Pitt the Younger* (London: HarperCollins, 2004), p. 341.
10. Quoted in Roy Jenkins, *Gladstone* (London: Macmillan, 1995), p. 298.
11. John Colville, *The Fringes of Power: Downing Street Diaries 1939–1955* (London: Hodder and Stoughton, 1985), p. 122.
12. Hennessy, *Prime Minister*, p. 161.
13. Quoted ibid., p. 96.
14. Interview with the author (unpublished), September 1996.
15. Hennessy, *Prime Minister*, p. 95.
16. Quoted ibid., p. 170.
17. Quoted ibid., p. 12.
18. James Naughtie, *The Rivals: The Intimate Story of a Political Marriage* (London: Fourth Estate, 2001), p. xiii.
19. Richard Holt, *Second among Equals: Chancellors of the Exchequer and the British Economy* (London: Profile, 2001), p. 254.
20. Peter Hyman, *1 out of 10: From Downing Street Vision to School Reality* (London: Vintage, 2005), Ch. 1.
21. Quoted in Hennessy, *Prime Minister*, p. 159.
22. Ibid., p. 161.
23. Anthony Howard, 'Introduction', in R. H. S. Crossman, *The Crossman Diaries: Selections from the Diaries of a Cabinet Minister 1964–1970*, ed. Anthony Howard (London: Jonathan Cape/Hamish Hamilton, 1979), p. 9.
24. Jim Collins, *Good to Great: Why Some Companies Make the Leap – and Others Don't* (New York: HarperBusiness, 2001), pp. 41ff.
25. Quoted in Hennessy, *Prime Minister*, p. 175.
26. Quoted ibid., p. 21.
27. Quoted ibid., p. 3.
28. Denis Healey, *The Time of My Life* (London: Michael Joseph, 1989), p. 448.
29. Ibid., p. 458.
30. John Major, *John Major: The Autobiography* (London: HarperCollins, 1999), p. 684.
31. Robert Peston, *Brown's Britain* (London: Short, 2005), p. 80.
32. Mark H. Moore, *Creating Public Value: Strategic Management in Government* (Cambridge, MA: Harvard University Press), p. 10.
33. Hennessy, *Prime Minister*, p. 156.
34. Philip Bobbitt, *The Shield of Achilles: War, Peace, and the Course of History* (New York: Alfred A. Knopf, 2002), p. 229.
35. Ibid., p. 236.
36. Tony Blair, 'Foreword by the Prime Minister', in *Capability Reviews:*

The Findings of the First Four Reviews (Prime Minister's Delivery Unit, 2006).

37. Julian Le Grand, *Motivation, Agency, and Public Policy: Of Knights and Knaves, Pawns and Queens* (Oxford: Oxford University Press, 2003), p. 81.
38. Quoted in Hennessy, *Prime Minister*, p. 54.

Postscript

1. Alexis de Tocqueville, *Democracy in America*, tr. Henry Reeve (New York: Bantam, [1835] 2000), p. 316.
2. The phrase was used by Henry Kissinger in a note to President Nixon on how to respond to tensions in the Indian subcontinent (Robert Dallek, *Nixon and Kissinger: Partners in Power* (London: Allen Lane, 2007), p. 336).
3. Michael Bichard, 'Effective Governance and the Civil Service: The Role of Ministers and Managers', in Patrick Diamond (ed.), *Public Matters: The Renewal of the Public Realm* (London: Politico's, 2007), pp.125–7.
4. Gerald Kaufman, *How to be a Minister*, rev. ed. (London: Faber & Faber, 1997).
5. Guy Lodge and Ben Rogers, *Whitehall's Black Box: Accountability and Performance in the Senior Civil Service* (London: Institute for Public Policy Research, 2006).
6. Bichard, 'Effective Governance and the Civil Service', pp. 127–9.
7. See, for example, Tristram Hunt's outstanding *Building Jerusalem: The Rise and Fall of the Victorian City* (London: Weidenfeld & Nicolson, 2004).
8. *National Improvement and Efficiency Strategy* (Department for Communities and Local Government, 2008), p. 2.
9. See Dermot Finch, 'Governance of Place: Shaping a New Localism', in Patrick Diamond (ed.), *Public Matters: The Renewal of the Public Realm* (London: Politico's, 2007), pp. 208–9.
10. Ibid., p. 210.
11. Charles Clarke, 'Effective Governance and the Role of Public Service Professionals', in Patrick Diamond (ed.), *Public Matters: The Renewal of the Public Realm* (London: Politico's, 2007).
12. See Malcolm Gladwell, *Blink: The Power of Thinking without Thinking* (London: Allen Lane, 2005).
13. Clarke, 'Effective Governance and the Role of Public Service Professionals', p. 135.
14. Ibid., p. 142.
15. Lowell L. Bryan and Claudia I. Joyce, *Mobilizing Minds: Creating Wealth from Talent in the 21st-Century Organization* (New York, McGraw-Hill, 2007), p. ix.

Bibliography

Michael Barber, '"A Heaven-Sent Opportunity": James Callaghan and the Ruskin Speech', *Times Educational Supplement*, September 1996.

Michael Barber, *The Learning Game: Arguments for an Education Revolution* (London: Victor Gollancz, 1996).

Michael Barber, 'Courage and the Lost Art of Bicycle Maintenance', Primary Strategy Conference, Birmingham, February 2004.

Michael Barber and Mona Mourshed, *How the World's Best-Performing Education Systems Come Out on Top* (London: McKinsey, 2007).

Tony Benn, *Arguments for Democracy* (London: Jonathan Cape, 1981).

David Blunkett, *The Blunkett Tapes: My Life in the Bear Pit* (London: Bloomsbury, 2006)

Philip Bobbitt, *The Shield of Achilles: War, Peace, and the Course of History* (New York: Alfred A. Knopf, 2002)

Derek Bok, *The Trouble with Government* (Cambridge, MA: Harvard University Press, 2001).

James Boswell, *The Life of Samuel Johnson* (London: Everyman, [1791] 1992).

Peter Botsman and Mark Latham, *The Enabling State: People before Bureaucracy* (Annandale, NSW: Pluto Press, 2001).

William Bratton and Peter Knobler, *Turnaround: How America's Top Cop Reversed the Crime Epidemic* (New York: Random House, 1998).

Greg Brooks, A. K. Pugh and Ian Schagen, *Reading Performance at Nine* (Slough: National Foundation for Educational Research, 1996).

Lowell L. Bryan and Claudia I. Joyce, *Mobilizing Minds: Creating Wealth from Talent in the 21st-Century Organization* (New York, McGraw-Hill, 2007).

Lord Butler, *The Art of the Possible: The Memoirs of Lord Butler, KG, CH* (London: Jonathan Cape, 1971).

Alastair Campbell, *The Blair Years* (London: Hutchinson, 2007).

James C. Collins and Jerry I. Porras, *Built to Last: Successful Habits of Visionary Companies* (New York: HarperBusiness, 1994).

Jim Collins, *Good to Great: Why Some Companies Make the Leap – and Others Don't* (New York: HarperBusiness, 2001)

John Colville, *The Fringes of Power: Downing Street Diaries 1939–1955* (London: Hodder and Stoughton, 1985).

R. H. S. Crossman, *The Crossman Diaries: Selections from the Diaries of a Cabinet Minister 1964–1970*, ed. Anthony Howard (London: Jonathan Cape/Hamish Hamilton, 1979).

Robert Dallek, *Nixon and Kissinger: Partners in Power* (London: Allen Lane, 2007).

Jon Davis, *Prime Ministers and Whitehall 1960–74* (London: Hambledon Continuum, 2007).

Patrick Diamond (ed.), *Public Matters: The Renewal of the Public Realm* (London: Politico's, 2007).

Norman Dixon, *On the Psychology of Military Incompetence* (London: Jonathan Cape, 1976).

Benjamin M. Friedman, *The Moral Consequences of Economic Growth* (New York: Alfred A. Knopf, 2005).

Mark Friedman, *Trying Hard Is Not Good Enough* (Victoria, BC: Trafford, 2005).

Thomas Friedman, *The World Is Flat: A Brief History of the Globalized World in the Twenty-First Century* (London: Allen Lane, 2005).

Rudolph W. Giuliani, *Leadership* (New York: Hyperion, 2002).

Growing Victoria Together: A Vision for Victoria to 2010 and Beyond (Melbourne: State of Victoria, 2005).

William Hague, *William Pitt the Younger* (London: HarperCollins, 2004).

Denis Healey, *The Time of My Life* (London: Michael Joseph, 1989).

Ronald A. Heifetz, *Leadership without Easy Answers* (Cambridge, MA: Belknap Press, 1994).

Peter Hennessy, *Having It So Good: Britain in the Fifties* (London: Allen Lane, 2006).

Peter Hennessy, *The Prime Minister: The Office and Its Holders since 1945* (London: Allen Lane, 2000).

Richard Holt, *Second among Equals: Chancellors of the Exchequer and the British Economy* (London: Profile, 2001).

Jeremy Hope and Robin Fraser, *Beyond Budgeting: How Managers Can Break Free from the Annual Performance Trap* (Boston: Harvard University Press, 2003).

Tristram Hunt, *Building Jerusalem: The Rise and Fall of the Victorian City* (London: Weidenfeld & Nicolson, 2004).

Peter Hyman, *1 out of 10: From Downing Street Vision to School Reality* (London: Vintage, 2005).

Roy Jenkins, *Churchill* (London: Macmillan, 2001).

Roy Jenkins, *Gladstone* (London: Macmillan, 1995).

Simon Jenkins, *Thatcher and Sons: A Revolution in Three Acts* (London: Allen Lane, 2006).

Gerald Kaufman, *How to be a Minister*, rev. ed. (London: Faber & Faber, 1997).

Steven Kelman, 'Improving Service Delivery Performance in the United Kingdom: Organization Theory Perspectives on Central Intervention Strategies', *Journal of Comparative Policy Analysis* (2006), vol. 8, 393–419.

Charles Taylor Kerchner and Douglas E. Mitchell, *The Changing Idea of a*

Teachers' Union (London: Falmer Press, 1988).

John Kotter, *Leading Change* (Boston: Harvard Business School Press, 1996).

Jan-Erik Lane, *The Public Sector: Concepts, Models & Approaches*, 3rd ed. (London: Sage, 2000).

Julian Le Grand, *Motivation, Agency, and Public Policy: Of Knights and Knaves, Pawns and Queens* (Oxford: Oxford University Press, 2003).

Julian Le Grand, *The Other Invisible Hand: Delivering Public Services through Choice and Competition* (Princeton and Woodstock: Princeton University Press, 2007).

Guy Lodge and Ben Rogers, *Whitehall's Black Box: Accountability and Performance in the Senior Civil Service* (London: Institution for Public Policy Research, 2006).

Isabel de Madariaga, *Russia in the Age of Catherine the Great* (London: Weidenfeld and Nicolson, 1981).

John Major, *John Major: The Autobiography* (London: HarperCollins, 1999).

Peter Mandelson, *The Blair Revolution Revisited* (London: Politico's, 2002).

Mark H. Moore, *Creating Public Value: Strategic Management in Government* (Cambridge, MA: Harvard University Press).

Edmund Morris, *Theodore Rex* (New York: Random House, 2001).

James Naughtie, *The Rivals: The Intimate Story of a Political Marriage* (London: Fourth Estate, 2001).

Richard Olivier, *Inspirational Leadership: Henry V and the Muse of Fire – Timeless Insights from Shakespeare's Greatest Leader* (London: Industrial Society, 2001).

David Osborne and Ted Gaebler, *Reinventing Government: How the Entrepreneurial Spirit is Transforming the Public Sector* (Reading, MA: Addison-Wesley, 1993).

David Osborne and Peter Hutchinson, *The Price of Government: Getting the Results We Need in an Age of Permanent Fiscal Crisis* (New York: Basic, 2004).

Edward C. Page and Bill Jenkins, *Policy Bureaucracy: Government with a Cast of Thousands* (Oxford: Oxford University Press, 2005).

Robert Peston, *Brown's Britain* (London: Short, 2005).

Michael Power, *The Audit Society: Rituals of Verification* (Oxford: Oxford University Press, 1997).

Andrew Rawnsley, *Servants of the People: The Inside Story of New Labour* (London: Hamish Hamilton, 2000).

Robert B. Reich, *Locked in the Cabinet* (New York: Alfred A. Knopf, 1997).

Peter Riddell, *The Unfulfilled Prime Minister: Tony Blair's Quest for a Legacy* (London: Politico's, 2005).

Anthony Seldon, *Blair* (London: Free Press, 2004).

Anthony Seldon, Peter Snowdon and Daniel Collings, *Blair Unbound* (London: Simon & Schuster, 2007).

W. C. Sellar and R. J. Yeatman, *1066 and All That* (London: Methuen, [1930] 2005).

A. J. P. Taylor, *A Personal History* (London: Hamish Hamilton, 1983).

Nicholas Timmins, *The Five Giants: A Biography of the Welfare State* (London: HarperCollins, 1995).

Polly Toynbee and David Walker, *Better or Worse?: Has Labour Delivered?* (London: Bloomsbury, 2005).

Jonathan Williams and Ann Rossiter, *Choice: The Evidence: The Operation of Choice Systems in Practice – National and International Evidence* (London: Social Market Foundation, 2004).

Harold Wilson, *A Prime Minister on Prime Ministers* (London: Weidenfeld and Nicolson, 1977).

James Q. Wilson, *Bureaucracy: What Government Agencies Do and Why They Do It* (New York: Basic, 1989).

Index